THE ECONOMIC AND COMPLIANCE CONSEQUENCES OF TAXATION

THE ECONOMIC AND COMPLIANCE CONSEQUENCES OF TAXATION

A Report on the Health of the Tax System in New Zealand

by

PATRICK JAMES CARAGATA
McCallum Petterson Financial Diagnostics Ltd.,
Wellington, New Zealand

SPRINGER SCIENCE+BUSINESS, MEDIA, B.V.

A C.I.P. Catalogue record for this book is available from the Library of Congress.

ISBN 978-0-7923-8185-3 ISBN 978-1-4615-5695-4 (eBook)
DOI 10.1007/978-1-4615-5695-4

Printed on acid-free paper

DEDICATIONS

To Richard Bird, a truly inspirational teacher, an open-minder thinker, one of world's leading authorities on tax and a relentless challenger.

To David Giles, a world-class econometrician and a pioneer in modelling the hidden economy.

To Gerald Scully, the pioneer in the *growth and tax literature* who gave my project critical mass.

To Knox Lovell, a pioneer in micro-economic efficiency analysis who helped inspire my views on measuring the health of the tax system.

To Jack Mintz, a clear-sighted expert on the consequences of tax who wisely insisted that I not ignore the expenditure side even though it was outside my mandate.

CONTENTS

6. THE MACRO EFFICIENCY EFFECTS OF TAXATION

7. REVIEW AND ASSESSMENT OF THE HEALTH OF NEW ZEALAND'S TAX SYSTEM

Appendices

LIST OF FIGURES

LIST OF TABLES

Preface

This assessment of the *Economic and Compliance Consequences of Taxation: A Report on the Health of the Tax System* examines the effects of tax on individuals, companies and the economy in both the short and long run. The Report arose from the Richardson Committee (1994) recommendation to New Zealand's Inland Revenue Department to provide ongoing estimates of: (1) theoretical or potential tax revenue as compared to actual revenue collected; (2) tax gap factors, measures, and trends; (3) deadweight losses of tax; and (4) taxpayer compliance costs. It also reflects Inland Revenue's responsibility, under *the Generic Tax Policy Process* (under which Treasury and Inland Revenue share responsibility for tax policy development), to review the effects of the tax legislation approved by Government.

This *Report on the Health of the Tax System* also meets the requirements of the *Fiscal Responsibility Act of 1994* which imposes obligations on government for more "responsible fiscal management", notably with respect to "pursuing policies that are consistent with a reasonable degree of predictability about the level and stability of tax rates for future years". To achieve these objectives the Government needs to ensure that all new tax policy proposals are subject to rigorous cost benefit analysis and risk assessment. *The Report* identifies a series of methods for undertaking such analysis and assessments.

Key questions addressed by this *Report* include how much changes in the tax level and mix affect: (1) the level of tax evasion among different taxpayers; (2) the tax gap between current and potential tax revenue; and (3) macroeconomic indicators (the level of economic output, the rate of economic growth, and the rates of unemployment, employment generation and labour force participation).

Given existing tax system trends, including the current level of taxes and the tax mix (personal, indirect, corporate and other taxes), the specific objectives of this *Report* are to determine whether: (1) tax evasion is rising or falling, (2) the tax gap is shrinking or widening, and (3) the prospects for economic growth and employment creation are improving or deteriorating. These objectives can be encapsulated in a summary question: *is the tax system, by virtue of its consequences on the behaviour of individuals, firms and the economy, becoming healthier or not?* Thus, are the consequences of the current tax system moving towards a best practice regime? (Current work has not had time to assess the compliance and administration cost consequences of tax).

We all started this project with an open mind, preferring to let the data and the models speak for themselves. I implemented a multiple methods approach which ensured that no single model was relied on for results. All results had to be cross-checked with other models or approaches. In effect, we went through a 6 tier peer review process that included:

(1) An internal team (including Professors Giles, Lovell, and Scully and Dr. Small) which critiqued models and papers.
(2) A multiple methods approach which ensured that at least two models were used for each key area.
(3) External expert vetting of the papers prior to the workshops. Ultimately we produced 37 working papers which underpin the conclusions in this book.
(4) Full review and assessment of the working papers at 4 technical workshops, held in December 1994, June and December 1995, and May 1997.
(5) The first draft of this technical *Report* was critiqued in October-November 1996 by Professor Alan Auerbach (University of California, Berkeley), Professor Richard Bird (University of Toronto), Professor Erwin Diewert (University of British Columbia) and Professor Jack Mintz (University of Toronto); subsequently, revisions were made over a period of 6 months.
(6) At last count, 7 papers, developed by Professor David Giles and Gerald Scully have been published in internationally respected journals, and an edited book of 17 of the working papers is nearing completion and several more articles have been submitted to international journals.

This book has undergone an additional anonymous peer review by five tax experts for Kluwer Academic Publishers. I am grateful for their support. Finally, I am very impressed with the professional way in which Allard Winterink of *Kluwer Academic Publishers* has managed the process of publishing and introducing this book to readers around the world.

The *Report on the Health of the Tax System* is based on four years' work (1994-1997) by a team which I led when I was first Chief Tax Policy Adviser and then Special Adviser, Taxation Economics in the Policy Advice Division of Inland Revenue. The team included at various times 35 economists, lawyers, accountants and assistants from New Zealand and abroad. I am particularly grateful for the excellent research advice and support of Richard Bird, Johannah Branson, Erwin Diewert, Paul Dunmore, David Giles, Shee Boon Law, Knox Lovell, Jack Mintz, David Petterson, Gerald Scully, John Small and Adolf Stroombergen, as well as the support of Daniel Aldersley, Cherie Ansell, Peter Barrand, Keith Burton, Jan Carr, John Clark, Rosemary Cook, Paul Cooper, Johannah Dods, Michael Dunn, Chris Gillion, Graham Holland, Alan Jenkins, Queenie Masoe, Emily Johnstone, Thomas Mayer, David Mayes, Ewen McCann, Michael O'Connor, Robin Oliver, Dick Poland, Peter Phillips, Alan Rogers, Bob Stephens, Ken White, Judith Wright and Jo Zweng.

I would also like to single out my assistant, Anna Heiler, for special mention. Her technical brilliance, competence, enthusiasm and loyalty in the face of the stiff winds and challenges we faced were fine contributions to the success of this project. I would also like to pay a special tribute to David Henry, former Commissioner of Inland Revenue in New Zealand for his unwavering support and his far-sighted vision in supporting the original proposal. Finally, I would like to thank Bill Birch, New Zealand's Minister of Finance, for his interest in and support of my work and Rodney Hide, Finance Spokesperson for ACT New Zealand who made a mission out of popularising our working papers on the Health of the Tax System. Any errors and omissions are mine alone. This book does not represent the views of the Government of New Zealand or the Inland Revenue Department of New Zealand which I left in September 1997.

Dr. Patrick Caragata, Managing Director, McCallum Petterson Financial Diagnostics Ltd,
Wellington, New Zealand (DPC @mpforensic.co.nz) 30 March 1998

Foreword

All OECD countries have been climbing a tax mountain over the last 50 years and experienced lower growth and employment and higher tax evasion as a result. There is a growing consensus that the welfare state has come unstuck, not because of an ideological attack, but because of its own appetite for spending. By the early 1990s, the principal obstacles to the flourishing of the welfare state were high government deficits and very high government debts.

Taxes have risen more or less steadily for decades, yet why have deficits persisted? Usually the rationale was that higher taxes were needed to reduce the deficit. In fact, higher taxes only encouraged more spending. The welfare state in New Zealand had such a huge base in the benefits pyramid that, despite (some might erroneously say because of) over a decade of economic reform, by 1998 one in three families was receiving some form of benefit. Is this how we reaffirm the pioneering spirit of our early settlers?

There was little constitutional constraint in any developed country that created legal obstacles to further state spending and higher taxes. In effect, it was the credit markets that helped to warn developed country governments of the danger of overspending, just as they do with governments in the developing world. There was a limit to credit for government and spending appetites needed to be restrained.

Our principal conclusion is that we have lost sight of the ancient Greeks' concept of the "golden mean" with respect to tax. We have imposed extreme burdens when in fact, as our models clearly demonstrate, more moderate tax burdens will provide more economic growth and employment and less tax evasion. Less tax evasion will help to improve the ethical standards of the country. This latter point is a very serious matter. We cannot allow the laws of the country, which we ourselves vote for, to turn so many people into criminals because of a high tax burden. This reduces the credibility of the law and government.

This *Report on the Health of the Tax System in New Zealand* offers a technical, but readable approach to the multi-dimensional issues needed to assess the vitality of a tax system. The tax system in any country is an organic whole adapted year after year without any strategic direction. No single individual can understand the complexity of the tax system, and no single individual should have to. We need a revolution in simplicity to ensure that tax systems are not only more user-friendly but less damaging to individuals, business and the economy.

We need to find more simple methods to communicate the problems generated by tax burdens. Here is one useful image. The tax to GDP ratio is a difficult concept for some to grasp. It is the level of total tax relative to the value of goods and services produced each year in a country. An equivalent image would the weight that a mountain hiker carries on his or her back.

Picture three hikers climbing on a mountain. In their backpacks, each carries food and water. Thus, the burden is both a benefit and a cost. One carries 15% of his body weight, another 25% of his bodyweight, and the third hiker 36% of his bodyweight. These backpack burdens represent, respectively, the tax burden in New Zealand during World War I, World War II and in 1991, the peak for the century.

If all three hikers were in a race to get to the top of the mountain at the same time, which one would reach the summit first (assuming they are in similar physical shape)? The obvious answer is the one carrying the least weight. Carrying a heavier burden will reduce the hiker's speed (economic growth) and probably shorten his distance (output of goods and services, and wealth creation).

Less speed and less distance means less achievement, and given rewards for achievement, they imply less money for distribution to those who need it. You cannot distribute what you cannot create.

The concept of a report on the *Health of the Tax System* seems such a natural idea. The development of the concept arose out of an amalgam of factors and circumstances which I would like to relate to you.

- The reorganisation of Inland Revenue and its development of a leading role in tax policy.

- My assessment of the empirical consequences of tax from 1991-1993 with the help of David Giles and John Small, two Bayesian econometricians.

- My puzzlement that tax policy officials in New Zealand and overseas were so wedded to an ex-ante, optimal tax design approach to tax policy that too often ignored the consequences of tax. This was a concern to me given the risks for individuals and corporate taxpayers engendered by getting policy wrong. The tax department is usually larger than any company in its jurisdiction and thus extracts an enormous amount of tax revenue which surely affects the incentive structure of people and businesses. The alternative was Martin Feldstein's optimal tax reform approach which he spelled out in his 1976 paper, *On Tax Reform*, and which I think is one of the best papers ever written on tax policy.

- My experience in risk analysis at the Toronto-Dominion Bank in Canada during the early part of the Latin American debt crisis in 1983-86. From that experience I learned the value of refining information to the point where it was valuable for multi-million dollar decisions.

- The influence of Professors Lennart Hjalmarsson of Sweden and Knox Lovell and Gerald Scully of the United States who provided me with many insights about the dimensions of efficiency analysis. From there, it was an easy step to compare the current versus potential effects of tax on individuals, business and the economy. The gap between the two is the health gap, or the performance gap, or the efficiency gap, depending on what you have in mind.

- My reading of the early microeconomic efficiency work by Melvin Reder in the 1940s and Michael Farrell in the 1950s

- Arnold Harberger's concept of economic "diagnostics", presented in his 1993 Richard T. Ely lecture, along with Richard Bird's guidance of a similar nature, which confirmed my own views and gave me confidence that what I was attempting was possible, even though Richard continually cautioned me that the whole project was very ambitious.

- My determination to provide Cabinet Ministers with better quality information with which they could make better decisions.

Taxes are a double-edged sword, conferring both benefits and costs. Unfortunately, often only the benefits are recognised and the costs are ignored. There is enough evidence now to convince us that there are diminishing returns to rising tax burdens and increasing government expenditure. Our work provides a multi-faceted approach to the search for optimality in tax burdens and the size of the state.

This book, the working papers and the academic publications that have flowed out of our four year journey into the much under-explored territory of the consequences of tax systems should be seen as a point of departure for assessing a new paradigm for tax policy based on the concept of the 'optimal size of government'. We do not present definitive answers. Rather, I present a range of probability (a tax burden between 15% and 25% of GDP) where two objectives, growth maximisation and tax evasion minimisation, can likely be simultaneously realised. Additional objectives make the equations more complicated and require more research. I wish our successors luck and hope that you are stimulated to explore new horizons on tax policy.

Options for dealing with high taxes are covered in my book, *Why Are Your Taxes So High?* which also is a lay-person's guide to the causes and consequences of high taxes. The potential remedies include: (1) holding a referendum to decide the merits of tax increases, using a two-thirds majority rule; (2) requiring a constitutional amendment for tax changes, as is the case at the federal level in Switzerland; (3) putting a sunset clause on any tax increase that requires politicians to demonstrate after 2 or 3 years that tax increases have created net benefits for the country, otherwise the tax increase will be rescinded; (4) putting all government spending under a microscope in order to cut waste in government; (5) targeting the elimination of benefit fraud in order to raise revenue so that taxes can be reduced (roughly 10-12% of all benefits in OECD countries is subject to fraud); (6) targeting tax evasion, especially among criminals (using auditing and asset seizures); and (7) ending universality and applying means tests to all benefits for those who are not incapacitated.

Climbing down from the top of the tax mountain can be very complicated given all of the varieties of dependence created by government as it climbed the tax mountain. A clear vision and a steady policy hand are needed to ensure fairness and efficiency as governments shrink in size toward their optimal level.

EXECUTIVE SUMMARY

Overview

- Overall, New Zealand's tax system is in a moderate state of health with room for improvement in all areas in part because taxes are still too high. Lower taxes would, among other things, generate faster economic growth, higher employment and lower tax evasion.

- A better health report is not possible at this time because, at about 35% of GDP, the total tax burden is close to its highest level in 100 years (the peak was 36.2%, excluding local taxes in 1991).[1] Despite valuable spending in various areas, including health, education, security and infrastructure development, higher taxes have a high opportunity cost or deadweight loss. Each time government raises an additional dollar of tax it diverts that money from productive use in the private sector. Further, because higher taxes reduce disposable income for individuals, people may respond by evading taxes or by aggressively pursuing tax minimisation.

- High levels of tax have powerful negative effects on the incentive structures and behaviour of individuals and firms. High tax burdens weaken the incentives to work, invent, invest, produce and save, thus generating reduced economic output, employment and growth.

- The good news is that the size of our underground economy is smaller than in most OECD countries, and our tax evasion problem in the hidden economy has been growing more slowly than elsewhere in the OECD. Unfortunately, much of the problem is due to high taxes.

- The tax system needs to be examined, assessed and designed as a system. It has systemic impacts on individuals, companies and the economy. Examining only marginal changes for new policy proposals (e.g. affecting pensions or fringe benefits) means we continually risk losing sight of the forest for the trees.

Compliance Effects of Tax:

- Tax evasion and organised and petty criminal activity (including most theft and fraud) are excluded from measured economic activity. They are part of the *hidden, underground, subterranean, unmeasured, shadow, black, or informal economy*, as it is variously called. In 1995, New Zealand's hidden economy was about 11% of measured GDP ($9.6 billion), having grown from about 7.5% of GDP in the late 1960s. Tax evasion is about 3.5% of GDP ($3.2 bn), up from about 2% of GDP in the late 1960s. The tax gap, which is the amount of tax due but not paid on transactions and incomes in the hidden economy, grew until 1995 when, given slower economic growth, it declined modestly. These macro estimates have been confirmed using tax-audit data for taxpayers who evade and those who comply.

- While the hidden economy and tax evasion have grown over the last 30 years, largely in response to higher taxes, inflation and government regulation, New Zealand's record is better than most OECD countries. The underground economy in Britain and Canada is about 12% of GDP, while in the US it is about 15% and in Scandinavia, where tax rates are much higher, closer to 20%. But this good *relative* record should not promote complacency. The hidden economy and tax evasion are much higher than they used to be. They can be significantly reduced only by lower taxes, especially on income, and new funding for scientific (risk based) audit selection to help improve audit targeting and to reduce or eliminate compliance costs for law-abiders.

- Our rising tax burden over the last 25 years is estimated to be the most important factor contributing to a larger hidden economy over the period.[2] These modelled findings are consistent with overseas analysis.

---

[1] About 6 percentage points (which equals the full increase) have been added since the economic reforms in 1984, with 73% of this increase arising from the introduction of GST and 27% from increased corporate tax payments. Since 1970, NZ's tax burden has risen by 35%, 5 percentage points more than the OECD average increase for the period.

[2] In order of importance, rising taxes, inflation, regulation and unemployment interact with changes in real disposable income to increase tax evasion. Factors motivating the growth of organised and petty criminal activity are outside the scope of this inquiry.

- Inland Revenue prosecutions have a counteractive effect on tax evasion in the hidden economy. However, based on modelling, a tax/GDP ratio around 20-25% would likely reduce the level of tax evasion. Greater weight than at present in the tax mix for indirect, versus direct, taxes would also help to reduce tax evasion. The corporate tax system is generating revenue near historically high levels because of improvements since 1987 in tax policy and IRD auditing, combined with higher growth. The main problem of *tax evasion* lies with individuals, the self employed and small not big firms.

Efficiency Effects of Tax:

- Five separate models of New Zealand's taxes and growth relationship over 30-70 years developed for this Report suggest that the growth-maximising tax/GDP ratio lies between 15-25% (avg. of 20%). One model suggests that reducing taxes to 22.5% of GDP would lead to a once-off *long run* output increase of 17% by boosting purchasing power in the rest of the economy by 30%. Another model suggests that a reduction of the tax burden to 20% of GDP would raise *long run* growth by about 2 percentage points. Three others place the growth-maximising tax range between 13.5% and 15.5% of GDP. *This is not a policy advocacy for a tax/GDP ratio of 15%-25%, but it is certainly a strong argument for where the tax frontier is located.* Maximising growth and minimising tax evasion are two of many government objectives, others being reduced taxpayer compliance costs and government administration costs, and enhanced social equity. Given these multiple objectives, the political process may very well prefer a tax rate above 25% of GDP. (It should be kept in mind that non-tax revenue (fees etc) raises the revenue burden on the public even higher). It is up to the public to decide what roles its wants government to play.

- Nonetheless, knowing the optimal tax frontier, from a growth maximisation and tax evasion minimisation perspective, provides Ministers with the basis for a risk assessment of the consequences of their tax policy decisions. A recent IMF assessment of expenditure performance for OECD countries over the last century suggests that there are only small improvements in long run economic performance and social indicators (longevity, literacy etc) after the expenditure to GDP ratio rises above an average of 30-35% of GDP. Obviously, country-specific circumstances need to be taken into consideration. The gap between this optimal expenditure level (the ceiling) and the optimal tax rates (the floor) noted above need to be examined and debated thoroughly.

- Model results for NZ indicate that reducing the level of tax is roughly 6 times more important than changing the mix of direct and indirect taxes in enhancing economic growth, and that reductions to personal and corporate income tax are about 15 times more important in promoting economic growth than reductions in GST.

- The cumulative deadweight loss[3] associated with not having kept the tax burden at about 20% of GDP (a growth maximising tax rate estimated in one study) after WW II is around $2.69 per dollar of tax revenue in 1994. This estimate includes *sunk or irrecoverable costs* from 1946-1993. In another study, introducing a growth maximising tax rate of 22.5% of GDP on 1 January 1995, by year-end, would have led to savings of 47c per dollar of tax. Thus, the $2.69 is an estimate of the *long term cost* per dollar of tax of keeping taxes at sub-optimal levels throughout the period, rather than at 20% of GDP, while the 47c is *the estimated average annual gain* per dollar of tax.

- It should not be assumed that raising taxes promotes long term equity; the opposite may be the case if higher taxes promote lower growth and greater unemployment. Our studies show that the historically high tax/GDP ratio has a negative effect on labour markets, reducing labour force participation, employment generation and raising unemployment rates as well as economic growth.

---

[3] Deadweight loss is the gap between actual and potential performance arising from taxes. That gap represents th opportunity cost of taxes.

1. BACKGROUND AND MANDATE

"Taxation involves compulsion. The taxpayer is required to pay regardless of whether he wants to do so or not. Accordingly, taxation alters the amount of income or wealth at the disposal of private individuals and business enterprises, so dictating the level of their expenditure. This mean that, because all the individual elements of wealth and expenditure in a modern economy are so closely interrelated, taxation today not only directly affects the welfare of every citizen but also has important effects on the progress of the economy as a whole. Taxation policy has therefore come to play an increasingly significant role in shaping the economic growth and development of a nation; and so bears ever more closely upon the life and future of its people" *Ross Report, 1967, Taxation in New Zealand: Report of the Taxation Review Committee, Wellington: Government Printer, p.7.*

"Taxation and its impact continues to grow in complexity. Its effects are far reaching, partly as a result of Government policies but, even more as a consequence of economic changes, which are taking, place quite independently of Government actions. The need for constant and comprehensive review of all aspects of taxation can be easily demonstrated.... If one section of our community is to be asked to shoulder a greater share of the taxation burden, it is entitled to clear evidence of the cause and justification...Unless this information is available, together with evidence that any unsatisfactory features thereby disclosed are being properly dealt with, the willingness of taxpayers to meet their share of taxes will be steadily undermined. The serious effects that such a trend would have upon our traditional social structure cannot be over-estimated" *McCaw Report, 1982, Report of the Task Force on Tax Reform, April, Wellington.*

1.1 Introduction

Taxes have very important effects on income, wealth, economic growth and development as was recognised by New Zealand's Ross Report on Tax Reform in 1967. Likewise, taxes create a more complex economic and social environment that bears close watching, particularly where one section of the population is being asked to bear a larger share of taxes for the benefit of others. In such a case, there is the potential for inducing higher tax evasion and tax minimisation that needs to be managed with the production of better information (among other things), as was recognised by the McCaw Report on Tax Reform in 1982. These two themes from two different reports on tax reform to the New Zealand government set the stage for some of the key questions addressed by this first *Report on the Health of the Tax System* in New Zealand.

The *Report on the Health of the Tax System* examines the economic and compliance consequences of taxation. Because this is the first such report the reader should exercise caution in drawing firm conclusions in light of the fact that the research is on-going and re-estimations of the models employed and revised data from Statistics New Zealand could change some of the results. Thus, all findings reported herein should be considered preliminary rather than definitive. Key questions addressed by the report include the extent to which changes in the tax level and mix affect:

- the level of tax evasion (the illegal non-payment of tax) by individuals, the self-employed and small firms;
- the tax gap between current and potential tax revenue; and
- the level of economic output and the rate of economic growth, the rate of unemployment, employment generation and labour force participation.

The specific objectives of the Report are to determine whether avoidance and evasion are rising or falling, whether the tax gap is shrinking or widening, and whether the prospects for economic growth and employment creation are improving or deteriorating as a result of the trends in the tax system, including the current level of taxes and the tax mix (personal, indirect, corporate and other taxes). In summary, is the tax system, by virtue of its consequences on the behaviour of individuals, firms and the economy, becoming healthier or not?

1.2 The Consequences of Taxation

Taxes provide governments with the principal basis for funding the delivery of important economic and social programs. The issues of the level of, and cost effectiveness in, government spending programs, which are now receiving much attention[1] throughout the OECD[2], are outside the scope of this report. Rather, this report focuses on the economic and compliance (tax evasion) consequences of taxation and attempts to determine, on balance and across time, whether the tax system is generating net positive or negative effects. This is an area of economic analysis where there is considerable scope for improvement:

"Certainly less is known about the economic consequences of taxation than we might feel entitled to expect. The distributional effects of taxation have been much studied, but in spite of that there is no clear verdict on how that has changed over time, nor are there well-founded comparisons across countries. Empirical analysis of labour supply is now extensive, and that of savings behaviour increasingly so, but most other incentive effects are still the subject of conjecture rather than empirical evidence. Questions such as the effects on entrepreneurship...has been very little studied" (Kay, 1990:69).

"There is an enormous – and surprising – amount that we simply do not know about how individuals and firms react to taxes". (Alm, 1996).

Little is also known about the incentives of tax on avoidance and evasion behaviour and the incentives to hire and lay-off. While both taxes and government expenditures are an enduring link between citizens and government, many taxpayers seem to reflect more on the (tax) cost of government than on the benefits. In part this may arise because individual taxpayers are affected by each amount of tax they pay, but are not a recipient of each benefit conveyed by government. As well, they may not take a holistic view and recognise that government has diverse rather than uniform obligations across taxpayer classes. This helps to motivate varying levels of tax minimisation or tax evasion, and suggests the need to develop a better understanding of the impact of taxes on firms and individuals.

When governments tax, there are short term and long term consequences on the economy and taxpayer behaviour. Because each successive government has a different philosophy of taxation and different objectives, the tax system itself becomes a non-strategic, ad hoc amalgamation of intended and unintended

---

[1] The utility of the concept of getting *value for money* in government expenditure is now widely accepted in the public service, just as it was in the 1980s in the private sector.

[2] Especially in Europe in anticipation of the introduction of a common currency.

consequences.[3] Each new tax *change* adds new costs (including transition costs) and/or benefits to corporate and/or individual taxpayers, in particular, and the economy in general. The key thing to remember is that the impact of tax is cumulative.

Each successive generation of tax changes and their effects are added to those of previous generations, unless earlier legislation is abolished. Thus, the tax system creates a cumulative series of incentive effects that shapes behaviour and the evolution of the structural features of the economy. To understand the dynamic relationship between tax stimuli and their effects one needs to have perspective. That perspective can be aided by looking at the evolution of the behaviour and structure of an economy across a long time series of observations.

Taxation's principal consequences fall on revenue, efficiency and equity. The revenue effects encompass the dollar value of taxes collected as well as variations in taxpayer compliance, including potentially preventable tax avoidance and evasion. A combination of the Government's revenue requirement, new tax policy development and variations in taxpayer compliance lead to the need for, and changes in, the administration costs of the tax authority. [4]Administration costs are a function of both managerial efficiency and policy choices such as the elimination of certain taxpayers from the rolls or the introduction of complex tax regimes (e.g. international tax; or an accruals regime).

1.3 The Mandate for the Report on the Health of the Tax System

The Richardson Committee reported in 1994 on the future roles and structure of the Inland Revenue Department with respect to tax policy development and the analysis of both the tax system and the tax administration. The existing tax policy problems that needed to be addressed were (Richardson Report, 1994:78):

- "the tax policy process was not clear, neither were accountabilities [among Treasury and IRD] for the stages of the process";
- "there has been insufficient consultation";
- "New Zealand's tax legislation needs radical updating" and "the rewrite should reflect the separate roles of adjudication and management";
- "the current approach to drafting tax legislation is unsatisfactory"; and

---

[3] "Whether one regards the result as a forest, a jungle or a partly cultivated terrain is less important than the recognition that tax structures that have been evolving for centuries are not quickly changed, let alone transformed" (Rose, 1985:317).

[4] The annual data used in this Report for Total Tax Revenue and the components of total tax revenue are employed on a Budget basis, and are obtained through the New Zealand Institute of Economic Research (NZIER) from Colgate (1991), with post-1990 data from Treasury and NZIER. The nominal GDP variable includes an allowance for stock valuation adjustment, and the data were also taken from Colgate (1990). Matching data for 1991-1994 have been obtained directly from the Budget documents.

- "IRD's policy advice should be more prominent and strengthened".

The Report on the Health of the Tax System, along with its counterpart Report on the Health of the Tax Administration, stems from a number of important considerations raised by the Richardson Committee.

First, the Committee sought to ensure that Inland Revenue had "clear accountabilities and responsibilities" (Richardson Report, 1994:133; 81). Among those many responsibilities is a post-implementation review of the legislative changes to the tax system, as part of the process of strengthening Inland Revenue's policy advice function, in the Generic Tax Policy Process. The overall objective for Inland Revenue is to:

"identify, develop and recommend specific tax policies that will raise tax revenue in the most economically efficient and equitable manner" (Richardson Report, 1994:48; 114).

As part of that process, IRD is required to:

"research, consult, analyse, identify and evaluate options, formulate recommendations, [and] report to Government on the development and implementation of policy i.e., revenue/economic impact and customer compliance and administration costs" Richardson Report, 1994: Appendix B p.10).

The determination of what is economically efficient and equitable requires extensive use of a series of databases and economic models, which provide the basis for a more systematic and comprehensive cost-benefit analysis framework for tax policy development. The Richardson Committee placed great emphasis on the application of cost benefit analysis to tax policy decisions, as indicated below:

- "... ensure that new tax policy initiatives are fully costed and considered to allow Government to make appropriate trade-offs between taxpayer, administrative and economic costs. Costings should also include the best practicable estimates of compliance costs[5]." (Richardson Report, 1994:74);

- "The policy development process should specify trade-offs[7] relevant to the policy (such as revenue impact, compliance and administration costs, economic objectives, social objectives and implementation);" (ibid:80);

- "...this policy unit should identify and develop specific tax policies that will raise tax revenue in the most economically efficient and equitable manner, and provide tax policy advice that meets performance measures specified by Government" (ibid:83);

- "specific and detailed cost-benefit analysis...should be conducted at this (operational) phase" (ibid: Appendix G p. 70); "research, consult, analyse, identify and evaluate options" (ibid: Appendix B p.10); "evaluation of alternatives should occur during detailed development and include more specific, detailed (and accurate) cost benefit analysis" (ibid: Appendix B p.70); and,

- cost benefit analysis is also required during the review phase (ibid: Appendix B p.71).

---

[5] This Report has not had the time to analyse the administration and compliance cost effects on taxpayers. Those issues are an important priority for future research.

[7] The Exploration of the basis for trade-offs is a key focus of this report.

Second, the Committee believed that it was important to strengthen the linkages between the tax system and the tax administration in order to improve Inland Revenue's tax policy advice:

"the tax system and tax administration have pervasive effects on all aspects of economic life in New Zealand. Improvements in tax policy formulation and reductions in taxpayer compliance costs and improved efficiency and effectiveness on the part of IRD provide a basis for improving the economic well-being of all taxpayers, greater revenue flows to the Government...and better economic performance for New Zealand." (ibid:133; 5; Appendix G p.72)

Finally, as part of the development of a more systematic and comprehensive approach to cost benefit analysis, the Richardson Committee assigned IRD responsibility for the development of a series of indicators that would measure the health of the tax system and the tax administration:

"*IRD should develop and maintain* a set of macro information, or indicators, for the purpose of assisting Government and IRD management in making strategic decisions for tax matters, and in particular, as input for the 'health report'. The information may also be useful for high level performance management, but such use should be secondary." (ibid:53; 3; Appendix C p.16; and page 12 of the main report) emphasis added.

The objectives (ibid: Appendix C. p.16) proposed for those indicators are to ensure that:

- "all macro indicators should have the aim of assisting the Minister and/or IRD management make strategic decisions in relation to tax"; and
- "the macro indicators should enable an overall assessment to be made of how well IRD is meeting its overall objective, and contribute to the proposed health report."

The list of those macro indicators that IRD should assemble and employ include:

- best estimate of theoretical revenue
- actual revenue collected
- tax gap: factors, measures, trends
- deadweight losses: identify and assess those elements that are most relevant to tax administration, (and) in particular to policy advice
- taxpayer compliance costs
- total administration costs
- net revenue collected
- taxpayer perceptions as a measure of voluntary compliance
- tax disputes assessment
- return on taxpayer audit, and
- macro benchmarks (e.g. customer service, debt management, and international comparisons) regarding the above list of macro indicators.

The Report on the Health of the Tax System should also be seen as fulfilling the requirements of the *Fiscal Responsibility Act* of 1994. That Act imposes obligations on government for more "responsible fiscal management". The principles of responsible fiscal management involve (1) "reducing total Crown debt to prudent levels", (2) "ensuring that, on average, over a reasonable period of time, the total operating expenses of the Crown do not exceed its total operating revenue"; (3) "achieving and maintaining" adequate levels of net worth as "a buffer" against future risks; (4) prudent management of fiscal risks; and "pursuing policies that are consistent with a reasonable degree of predictability about the level and stability of tax rates for future years".

In order to achieve these objectives, Government will need to undertake on-going cost benefit analysis and risk research and analysis to examine the consequences of taxes on the economic behaviour of individuals and firms. If taxes are too high, they will undermine potential revenue generation because of greater tax evasion and reduced growth and employment. If the right tax rules and regulations and the right tax mix or balance between direct and indirect taxes (and their sub-components) are not chosen, there will be negative effects on economic performance and tax collection.

It is clear that inadequate tax policy will create fiscal risks that need to be anticipated and managed. The best way to anticipate those risks is to subject each new tax policy proposal to rigorous cost benefit analysis and risk analysis and to produce an regular report on the health of the tax system every two or three years so that there is greater transparency for taxpayers about their tax system and its consequences.

The purpose of this Report is to estimate and describe as accurately as possible the economic and compliance consequences of taxation. The research on equity and compliance costs has yet to be undertaken. Until that work is completed, no definitive conclusions can be reached. Thus, this in an initial, partial view of the consequences of taxation. It is neither prescriptive nor does it pretend to be a policy document.

Thirty-seven completed technical working papers have been produced as background inputs to the *Report on the Health of the Tax System* and have been professionally vetted at three workshops in NZ in December 1994, July 1995 and December 1995 and May 1997. In addition, many of the papers have been critiqued overseas by one or more economists in Canada, the United States and Australia. Four papers have been published as of September 1997 in reputable international journals, two others are currently being reviewed by a leading journal, and others are being prepared for publication. A list of the working papers is found in Appendix 1.

2. THEORETICAL AND METHODOLOGICAL FRAMEWORK

2.1 The Scope of the Research Project on the Health of the Tax System

The basic approach developed for estimating the health of the tax system is a multiple methods approach comparing current with potential performance. Building a single model for estimating accurately all of the diverse and related impacts of taxation was considered to be unwise. Multiple perspectives and multiple methods were required if one is to have confidence in the results. Insofar as possible, every key conclusion has been based on weighing the results of alternative approaches.

The emphasis is not on predicting the path of events or relationships. Rather the aim is to estimate relationships, for example, between the level of taxes and the level of economic output, or the rate of economic growth, and between the level of taxes and the size of the hidden economy and the level of tax evasion. This is accomplished by examining long time series data using a variety of different models that were developed specifically for New Zealand's Inland Revenue Department. The results of each model were used to critique the results of the other models. Once the estimation stage had been completed simulation models were developed, where appropriate, in order to test policy shocks.

Support for this multi-tiered methodological approach comes from Harberger (1993) as will be discussed shortly, as well as from a critical assessment of Karl Popper's highly constrained deductive approach to science and his proposed use of 'falsification' in the evaluation of scientific theory (Redman, 1994). The approach taken is not to determine whether or not a particular theory is correct or incorrect. Falsification[6], as a methodological tool, "fails" for a number of reasons: (1) "the complex web of assumptions, laws and various restrictive conditions" that underlie theories, as compared to the simplicity of Popper's single universal statement, 'All swans are white', imply that a theory "can never be falsified conclusively" because one can't be sure of which assumption is false (the Duhem problem); (2) a series of severe tests can, through induction (to which Popper was hostile), lead to a valid inference that a theory is reliable; (3) deductive approaches are inevitably ahistorical and require reference to past experience and empirical observation; and (4) the empirical basis of observations is not absolute (Redman, 1994:70-71).

Rather, the approach is probabilistic, with the aim of determining the degree to which a relationship between variables will hold across time, and across countries. It was expected that many relationships would exhibit some variation, albeit sometimes within a narrow range. Thus, the theories we are exploring and developing in this paper are being subjected to "criticism, revision [and] further criticism" (Redman, 1994:87).

---

[6] "Popper's critical rationalism does not always call for rules. His philosophy is frustratingly inconsistent. Like most of Popper's other concepts, falsification conflated too many ideas - testability, empirical refutation, intellectual honesty, logic, and the Socratic method, inter alia - some of which are incompatible with rules" (Redman, 1994:94).

Figure 2.1 illustrates the configuration of approaches used in managing the research process for this report. There are eight separate project areas, represented by the wedges. (See Appendix 1 for the Working Papers produced in each of these project areas). In each area, either simple or more complex models have been built to provide estimations. The more one learns about taxation and its impact in each area, the deeper the wedges are driven into the circle. In each area, then, there are generally two or more ways of looking at a problem. As the wedges are driven into the circle, they begin to over-lap, with the result that one project cross-fertilises the other.

Project No. 1, the deadweight loss project area examined the deadweight loss (or efficiency or welfare losses) of taxation in terms of the loss of output and employment over time, as well as the deadweight loss stemming from tax evasion. Some of this work has been accepted for publication overseas. This analysis complements the results of Diewert & Lawrence (1994).

Project No. 2, the effective tax rates area, examines effective tax rates using profits, revenue, cost and asset bases. Earlier work concentrated on the macro-estimation of a single effective tax rate for all firms per annum. After careful consideration, this top-down approach was considered to be biased because it failed to take into consideration the broad variation of types of taxpaying behaviour (See Appendix 1 for the different ways in which effective tax rates are measured).

Such behaviour includes: firms that are long term residents of the zero-zone[7] (both profits and tax payments), migration by many firms back and forth between zero and positive taxpaying, and variations in behaviour by scale, sector, residency, country of origin, and perhaps most importantly, the revenue and profit generating efficiency performance of firms. The effective tax rate problem is now considered an index number problem which requires careful sorting and weighting of one pocket of homogeneity from another in the skewed distribution of taxpaying behaviour. This work will lead to the development of comprehensive risk profiling of low-risk and high-risk taxpayers (both firms and individuals).

Project No. 3 looks at the impact of the revenue and profit generating efficiency performance on tax payment behaviour and on the consequences for efficiency performance of tax as a cost of doing business. Typically, economics has looked at the latter rather than the former, but the former is quite important in terms of estimating starting points, distinguishing between normal commercial behaviour (commercially driven tax paying behaviour) and strategic behaviour (potentially preventable avoidance and evasion), and developing probability profiles of high versus low-risk taxpayers. Future research needs to look at the investment and production consequences of differential tax burdens across sectors, variations in compliance costs across sectors, and the impact of tax changes on international competitiveness.

[7] The zero taxpaying zone is composed of firms that do not pay taxes for whatever reasons.

Figure 2.1
Monitoring The Tax System And Its Impacts: Pieces Of The Puzzle

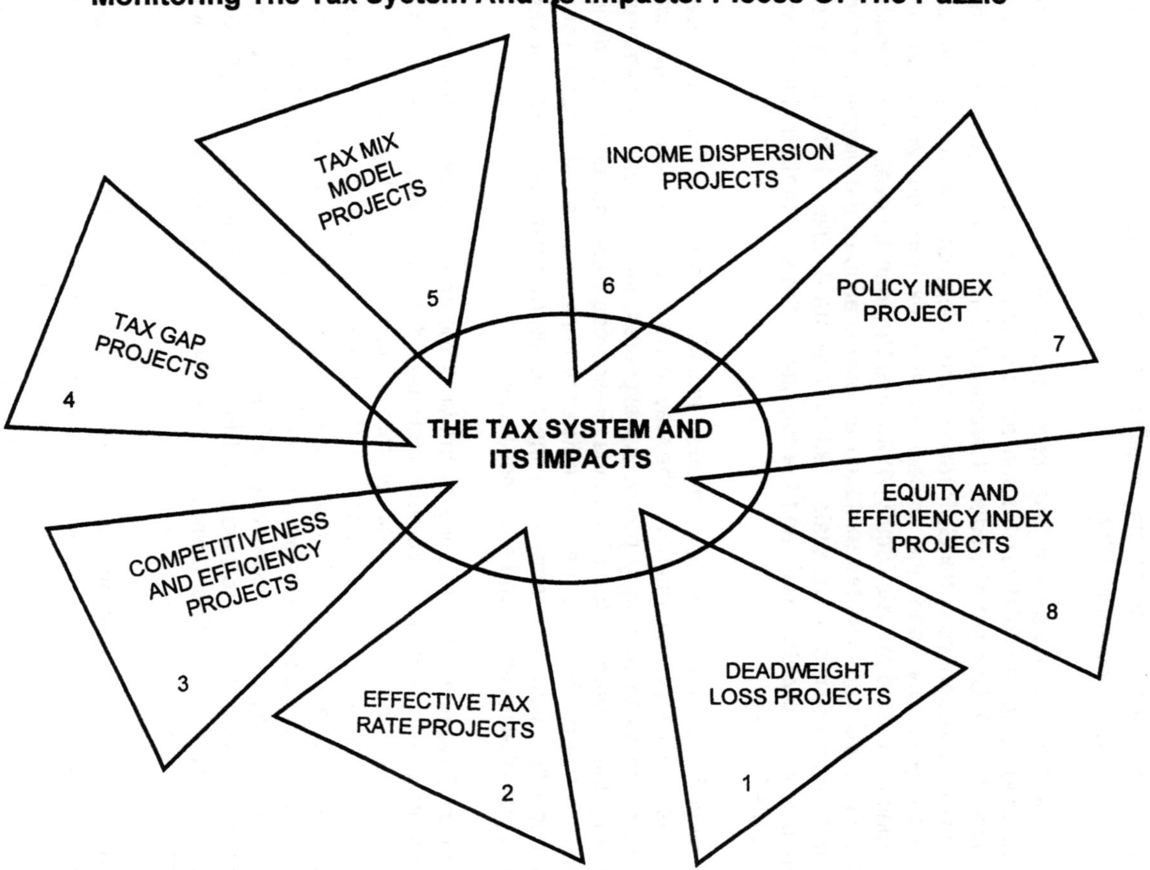

Source: Inland Revenue, New Zealand, June 1995

The tax gap project, project No.4, developed models to estimate the size of the hidden economy and the tax gap over the last quarter of a century. The macro-estimates are finished and some of the work has been published. Most recent work has concentrated on developing profiles of high versus low-risk corporate taxpayers and differentiating between evasion and potentially preventable tax avoidance. Work on developing profiles of high-risk versus low-risk individuals commenced in December 1996.

In project No. 5, there were four separate estimates of the economic effects of adjustments to the total tax burden and the tax mix (personal, corporate and indirect taxes). One set of models (Caragata & Small, 1996, 1996a) concentrates on the consequences of tax/GDP ratio changes for real economic growth and the hidden economy, and the impact of the tax mix on economic growth, respectively. Two models (Scully, 1996; and Brandon & Lovell, 1997) focused on the same tax variables but excluded an examination of the hidden economy. A fourth model (Giles & Caragata, 1996; Caragata & Giles, 1996) examined the impact of the tax/GDP ratio and the tax mix on the size of the hidden economy and the tax gap.

Project 6 focuses on the link between taxation and equity. Project 7 develops models for better understanding the way in which the taxation system interacts with changes to monetary policy. As expected, interest rate adjustments can modify the consequences of tax cuts. Resources were inadequate to do justice both to the equity, revenue, and efficiency consequences simultaneously, and hence effort was concentrated on the revenue (the evasion effects of taxation and potential revenue) and efficiency issues.

Project 8 was intended to bring all the work together in a comprehensive set of weighted (using data envelopment analysis) indices that will provide the basis for a thorough assessment of the welfare trade-offs of taxation between equity, efficiency (including compliance costs), revenue (avoidance and evasion) and tax administration costs across time. Kaplow (1996:147) has developed a descriptive conceptual framework covering these issues, but stated that "it is of little use without empirical evidence". As the cost benefit and risk analysis foundations for this Report were laid in 1993, a dynamic, cost benefit analysis framework evolved. This framework is in the spirit of Alm (1996) and Kaplow (1996).

The conclusions based on the revenue and efficiency consequences of taxation in NZ need to be viewed cautiously and should be qualified once the work on equity and administration and compliance cost impacts has been completed. It also needs to be kept in mind that the voters and politicians may agree, during elections, that certain expenditures are required, regardless of the consequences. The Report on the Health of the Tax System will provide some objective insights into the trade-offs or sacrifices required in such decisions, and *should not be construed as a document that dictates* solutions. The intent is to provide an objective, cost benefit analysis framework for improving the decision-making process in government by arming decision-makers with the facts (sometimes a scare commodity given the time pressures of the political process).

As described in **Figure 2.2**, there are 15 major economic and social impacts of taxation which are matters of concern. There are four major *revenue* impacts. These concern: (1) the tax gap (and related potential revenue), (2) the general components of the tax gap (the avoidance and evasion mix, and the personal and firm mix), (3) the probability profile distribution of high and low-risk corporate and individual taxpayers, and (4) the development of probability analysis concerning the relative balance of policy and audit options for dealing with high-risk taxpayers.

The efficiency effects of taxation arise from the failure of current economic performance to equal potential performance with respect to allocative efficiency issues (the pattern of consumption and the pattern of investment), and technical efficiency issues (cost minimisation and output maximisation). These efficiency effects may be looked at either from a static perspective (which unfortunately tends to be the most common approach), or a dynamic perspective (favoured in this report). Dynamic efficiency analysis emphasises the evolving effects of tax on allocative and, more importantly, technical efficiency performance. This latter approach would incorporate the impact of taxes on international competitiveness, market competition and employment. Equity effects of taxation are divided into intra-generational and inter-generational consequences. Finally, tax changes affect the administrative costs of the tax authority.

What is the optimal balance of the revenue, efficiency, equity and administrative cost effects? What tax/GDP ratio and tax mix (personal, indirect, corporate and other taxes) most closely delivers the optimal result? Are the consequences of taxation in NZ getting better or worse? To answer these questions, one needs to measure the *health of the tax system* over a long time period.

Full tax system health is defined as reaching the evolving best practice frontier, or closing the gap between the current and potential consequences of taxation. Health is always a matter of degree. If no further adjustments need to, or can, be made to modify the revenue, evasion, efficiency, equity, compliance cost and administration cost effects, then the tax system is at a best practice or healthy frontier (given constraints) for that period of time. Of course, best practice changes and frontiers move.

For example, if the tax gap between current and potential revenue collection is $2.5 billion and a combination of tax policy, audit and information service changes can only reduce the tax gap to $2 billion, then that point establishes the best practice or healthy frontier. Obviously, it is very important to establish the constraints[8] which prevent further progress beyond the best practice frontier, or which impede progress to the frontier.

[8] Some key obstacles will be the required trade-offs between equity, efficiency, revenue and administration costs, given important constraints such as government policy preferences, imperfect information, real and financial resource limits, and changes in the general economic environment at home and abroad.

Figure 2.2
An Integrated Macro-Micro Framework for Tax System Health: Revenue Generation and Conservation Objectives

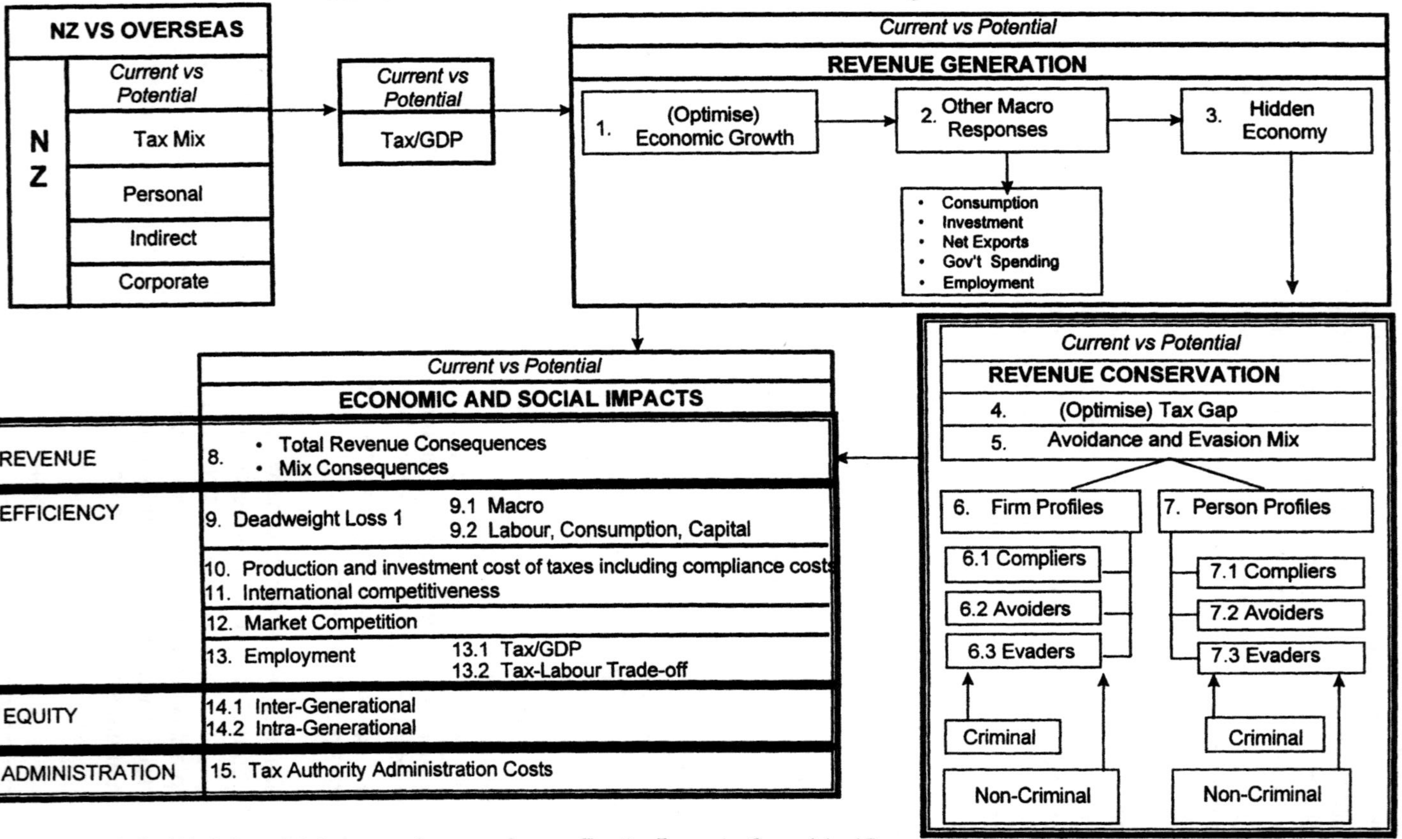

1 Could include capital stock per worker

Source: Taxation Economics Group, Inland Revenue NZ June 1996

The Report on the Health of the Tax System presents the results and analysis to assist in measuring the gap between current and best practice and to measure the trade-offs that constrain progress towards the frontier. The ultimate aim of the Report is to provide better information for:

- enhancing the general process of tax reform by highlighting key strengths and weaknesses of the tax system, and identifying better strategic guidelines for policymaking;
- improving the cost-benefit analysis of case-by-case tax policy development; and,
- improving the quality of decision-making in government and the Inland Revenue, including improved auditing and joint audit and policy approaches to high - risk taxpayers.

2.2 Defining and Measuring the "Health" Consequences of Taxation

To measure the "health" of a tax system one should compare "actual" performance with "potential" best practice[9] performance, given constraints, as is the standard practice in the efficiency literature[10]. Reder (1947a:453) defined the efficiency index as follows:

"Corresponding to a given set of factor inputs, we take the ratio of the actual output... to the maximum output that is technically possible with that set of inputs. The ratio will be the 'efficiency index'; maximum efficiency will correspond to a ratio of one".

The efficiency index, which can also be called an efficiency ratio or a performance ratio, divides actual output by potential output. Typically, although not always (it depends on the nature of the indicator involved), actual

---

[9] Forsund and Hjalmarsson (1987:6) tracked down the development of the concept of best practice as compared to average productivity to Akerman's 1931 analysis of Swedish saw mills covering the period 1923-26 and Wesley Mitchell's (1937) use of the term in his analysis of a survey of 28 engineers' suggestions for enhancing industrial output across sectors in the United States. Grosse (1953:364; 402-3), in her work with Leontief (1953), employed the notion of "best practice" based on a definition of the latest "vintage" of technology. Grosse's inspiration appears to have come from an industrial consultant for the cotton industry, Barnes Textile Associates (undated), *Survey of Technological Improvements and Developments in the Cotton Textile Industry, 1910-36*. This stress on the importance of the vintage of technology and best practice was later adopted by Salter (1960), and is consistent with a European tradition going back at least to Heckscher (1918). The original source for the "sorted average cost diagrams" identified by Heckscher (1918) and revived by Salter (1960) and Forsund and Hjalmarsson (1987) is to be found in the work of Marshall (1890; Appendix H, "the particular expense curve"), and Wright (1917) and Taussig (1919), with the latter two providing and summarising, respectively, the basis for the "bulk-line cost curve" analysis that was undertaken by price-fixing tribunals in the U.S. during World War I. Farrell's (1957) contribution was to broaden the notion of "best practice" to include managerial or technical efficiency.

[10] The origin of the concept of maximum efficiency in real world terms apparently comes from Watkins (1915:753; 767). He defined the "capacity factor" as: "the ratio of average output of a given period, usually a year, to the theoretical potential output, supposing continuous use of rated capacity". The original empirical work on the capacity factor appears to have been done in the manufacturing sector in 1911 by New Jersey's Bureau of Statistics of Labour and Industry.

performance will be less than potential performance. Hence, the efficiency or *performance ratio* will be less than one, although for some variables, such as costs, actual costs will be greater per unit than potential costs and thus the efficiency ratio will be greater than one.

The gap between actual performance and potential performance is the performance gap and is measured in decimal places or as a percentage of potential performance. The gap reveals the percentage distance required to travel before 'best practice' performance is achieved in any particular area of analysis.

It appears that the earliest study where this concept of a performance gap arose was in Grosse's (1953:407) productivity analysis of the American cotton textile industry. She compared the current productivity standard of output per hour with a 'best practice' standard of output per hour, and hence measured (in percentage terms) a productivity performance gap.

A Wider Scope for Applications

The gap between actual and potential performance is a deadweight loss or a welfare loss. This insight suggests that a welfare loss is a performance cost based on certain constraints on behaviour (a commitment or a decision, resource inadequacy, information deficiency, managerial inefficiency, time deficiency etc). Thus, under-performance with respect to consumption, investment, output, quality of product are examples of deadweight loss.

In **Figure 2.3**, firm B produces more output with the same amount of inputs as firm A. The gap between B and A is A's output, or efficiency loss, owing to the latter's inefficient use of its resources. Thus, A will need to undergo some change in management strategy and its vintage of technology, among other factors, if it expects to close the gap and aspire to the best practice frontier.

Under-performance not only occurs at the micro level but also at the macro level. In contrast to the problematic (Pack, 1994:68) neo-classical assumption[11] that "all economies are on the same international production frontier", the under-performance of economies is a widespread problem:

"The sums lost because the poor countries obtain only a fraction of - and because even the richest countries do not reach - their economic potentials are measured in the trillions of dollars" (Olson, 1996:22).

What are the principal factors that have a significant impact on the under-performance of economies? What creates the performance gap across countries? In the last decade, as international data sets have become available, this has become a more answerable question and the answers are becoming more consistent. The countries which are the most efficient and hence grow the

---

[11] "Delusions... arise from the habit of treating the organisation of an economy as an optimum when it does not form a familiar type" (Hicks, 1939:122)

Figure 2.3
Production Frontiers and Inefficiency:
Measuring the Performance Gap

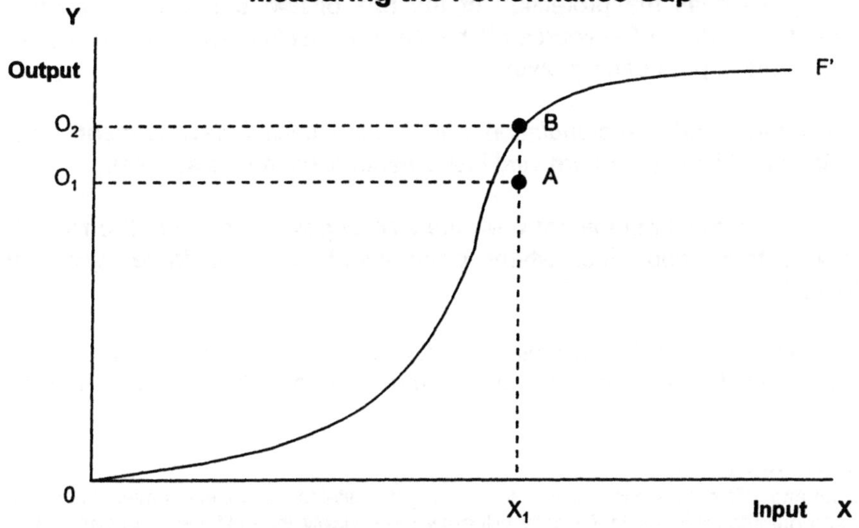

Source: Reder, M.W. 1947, "*A Reconsideration of Marginal Productivity Theory*", Journal of Political Economy, Vol. 55, No. 5, 451 (adapted).

Figure 2.4
A Unit Cost and Cumulative Production Learning Curve with an Illustrated Static and Dynamic Best Practice Frontier
(the airframe industry)

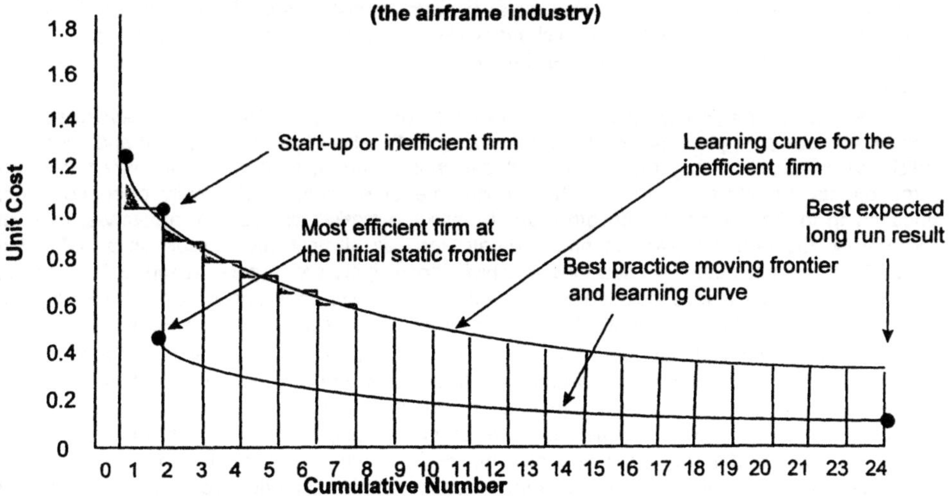

Source: Asher, H., 1956, "*Cost Quantity Relationships in the Airframe Industry*", Santa Monica : The RAND Corporation p.37, based on the Boeing Aeroplane study "*The Experience Curve*"(adapted by Patrick Caragata)

fastest[12] are those which have created the most favourable structure of incentives for the development of individuals and firms (Olson, 1996:6; 22). The optimal incentive structure minimises risks for investors (an idea which has been around for a long time[13]) and promotes economic growth. The optimal incentive structure

- best guarantees the protection of the rule of law, property rights and the market allocation of resources;[14] hence, the *institutional framework* plays a critical role in promoting growth;

- maximises *capital accumulation and human capital development*;[15] hence savings and investment are vital instruments of economic success;

- finds an optimal balance between the *size of government* and the role of the market; thus, countries, where governments are too large, grow more slowly;[16]

- ensures *good quality monetary policy* (by ensuring low inflation[17]), *good quality fiscal policy* (this is the essential argument of this Report and the

---

[12] "Growth and efficiency are linked. For equal rates of capital formation, economies that transform inputs into outputs relatively inefficiently will grow more slowly than efficient economies. But the order of magnitude of this effect is unknown" (Scully, 1988:659).

[13] Haynes (1895:415) was among the first modern economists to conclude that "risk is a deterrent to production, not only as acting upon the production of consumption goods, but it is a hindrance to the savings of capital". Woodall (1995), citing Frankel (1993) observes that "If capital was fully mobile, then, in theory, it would flow from countries to those with high real interest rates until the two had evened out. Why has this not happened? ...(E)ven in a global capital market with no capital barriers to mobility, currency risk will cause real interest rates to differ across countries. Investors view assets in different currencies as imperfect substitutes for each other and demand a risk premium to compensate for the exchange-rate uncertainty. To this extent, therefore, even if capital is perfectly free to move, exchange rate variability remains a source of market segmentation".

[14] These conclusions (Scully, 1988; 1992) are based on a study of 115 countries across several decades. In comparing measures of freedom with growth rates of per capita output and economic efficiency measures, Scully (1992:12) concluded that: "...the rights structure has significant and large effects on efficiency and on the growth rate of economies. Politically open societies, subscribing to the rule of law, private property, and the market allocation of resources, grow at three times the rate and are two and one-half times as efficient economically in transforming inputs into national output as societies in which these rights are largely proscribed". Likewise, Olson (1996:7) has also concluded that "...variations in institutions and policies are surely the main determinants of international differences in per capita incomes". Compare Pack (1994:60).

[15] In an econometric study covering 124 countries over the period 1950-90, Scully (1996d) argues that deficiencies in the institutional framework (the rule space of a country which promotes or undermines economic freedom) are almost as important as deficiencies in investment and human capital in explaining the under-performance of economies; the next most important factor explaining under-performance is policy deficiencies. In another multi-country, multi-period study, Bass and Scully, (1995:11) conclude that "nations ...have different levels of skills, rates of technical change and efficiency [capital stock per worker]. These differences prevent convergence of per capita incomes to the same level".

[16] Quite a few studies have indicated that there is a "negative relationship between relative government spending and economic growth" (Scully, 1992:44). "The empirical evidence is that nations with large public sectors grow more slowly" (Scully, 1992:12).

working papers that have contributed to it; the health of the tax system plays a critical role in promoting long term economic welfare), and *good quality trade policy*;[18] thus the quality of advice by public servants must be continually subjected to cost benefit analysis and risk assessment, and

- ensures timely market adaptability and flexible market responses.[19]

In summary, an optimal incentive structure will best promote economic growth if it: (1) minimises risks for investors, provides an efficient institutional framework; (2) maximises capital accumulation and human capital development; (3) finds the right balance between the size of government and the role of the market; and (4) ensures good quality monetary, fiscal and trade policy. The structure of incentives plays a direct and enduring role in shaping the opportunities and constraints of agents and hence the performance and wealth potential of each nation. A performance gap arises with departures from the optimal incentive structure.

The *performance gap approach* can be applied to the consequences flowing from the decision-making process for any organisation, including government policy making, if data are available.[20] This methodology can be applied to the revenue, efficiency, and administration cost consequences of taxation given the equity constraints[21] that arise from the political arena:

"As is now known...income distribution remains a normative issue, attempts to introduce an objective criteria in this area having persistently failed" (Burgenmeier,1994:347).

Generally, equity directions are based on popular demand in the political arena. The types of intra-generational vertical equity measures that currently prevail concern the following types of ratios, including, for example:

- the ratio of the top 20 percentile of taxpayers to the bottom 20 percentile;
- the Gini coefficient (concerning the concentration of income by household); and,
- the ratio of income earners above and below the average weekly wage.

---

[17] "Although the adverse influence of inflation on growth looks small, the long-term effects on standards of living are substantial. For example, a shift in monetary policy that raises the long-term average inflation rate by ten percentage points is estimated to lower the level of real GDP after 30 years by 4%-7%, more than enough to justify a strong interest in price stability" (Barro, 1995:166).

[18] What are the sources of international productivity differences? "Among many reasons are imperfections in the market for knowledge, the requirements for local technology absorption, and protectionist policies that decrease the need for cost-reducing labour" (Pack, 1994:67).

[19] "A prerequisite for high productivity growth in small open economies is the ability to rapidly adjust to changing international market conditions" (Forsund and Hjalmarsson, 1987:1).

[20] Hence, efficiency analysis involves both a widely generalisable method of analysis, as well as an examination of the efficiency (and other) consequences of some action or decision.

[21] For example, *if* society desires that the top 20% of earners have no more after-tax income than two times that of the bottom 20%, then that is the normative equity constraint. The actual top 20/ bottom 20 ratio can be compared to the normative ratio.

Also important are measures of *horizontal equity* which require an examination of the extent to which individual taxpayers in the same class are taxed the same amount for a given level of income. Beyond this, there is a need to consider *inter-generational* equity which measures the extent to which the benefit of expenditures and the cost of tax burdens are shared equally across decades for different generations of taxpayers.

Thus, the estimation of the health of the tax system is ultimately (when all the work is completed) based on these four key consequences of taxation. Any comprehensive estimate of the health of the tax system must take into consideration all of the revenue (including evasion), economic efficiency, equity and administrative cost impacts of taxation. The issue of taxpayer compliance costs is incorporated into the efficiency effects of taxation.[22]

Performance can be looked at from a static and a dynamic perspective. When the dimension of time is introduced, a series of empirical observations (e.g. per annum) for actual performance describe the learning curve performance of an entity, organisation or a system.

A learning curve[23] is a performance curve[24] which exhibits progress or deterioration based on some standard of measurement such as unit cost. Critical learning takes place by decision-makers either in managing a firm, an organisation, government institutions, or the economy (the collective responsibility of Cabinet and the central bank). A useful interpretation is that progress along a learning curve exhibits some degree of cost savings, revenue gain, or efficiency gain.[25] Retrogression along a learning curve means a

---

[22] Future versions of the report on the health of the tax system should deal with the equity effects, the administrative cost effects and the compliance cost effects of taxation. Current resource constraints prevent this work from being undertaken.

[23] The original sources in this important field are (1) Asher, H., 1956, *Cost-Quantity Relationships in the Airframe Industry*, R-291, Santa Monica California: The RAND Corporation. (2) Crawford, J.R., 1944, *Estimating, Budgeting and Scheduling*, Burbank California: Lockheed Aircraft Corporation. (3) Crawford, J.R., (n.d.) *Learning Curve, Ship Curve, Ratios, Related Data*, Burbank California: Lockheed Aircraft Corporation. (4) Wright, T.P. 1936, "Factors Affecting the Cost of Airplanes," *Journal of Aeronautical Engineering Sciences*, 3, 122-128.

[24] Other names developed in the aircraft industry for the learning curve are the "expansibility" curve, the "acceleration" curve, the "progress" curve, and the "experience" curve. The Stanford Research Institute (SRI) in Menlo Park, California has a comprehensive archive of this important pioneering work. The initial research on the learning curve was undertaken by German psychologists in the 1880s, and was subsequently pursued by American psychologists. Performance curves were thoroughly examined beginning with Vincent (1912), Melton (1936) and Hull (1943). In general, the incremental theory of learning specifies that "learning increases gradually as a result of reinforced practice" (Houston, 1976:131). This approach is substantiated by research in brain physiology among babies which demonstrates that there is a positive, permanent evolutionary neuron response to repeated performance. The notion in psychology of 'negatively accelerated learning curves' where there is continuing gain from performance but with eventually diminishing returns (until the next innovation), is just another way of looking at Wright's (1936) progress curve. What is unknown is what were the non-aviation industry influences on the development of Wright's statistical and conceptual tool kit.

[25] By contrast Arrow (1962) did not model learning at all. He modelled the stock of knowledge embedded in technology. The learning curve literature models learning as a flow not a stock. Of interest is that Arrow was exposed to these air-frame industry papers on learning curves through his association with the RAND Corporation after World War II.

deterioration in the cost or gain position. An example of the learning curve is presented in **Figure 2.4**. As learning takes place, some best practice performance level may be kept in mind. Unit cost (or some measure of savings or benefit), by and large, improves with the accumulation of experience and the increase in output. But there are different starting points in terms of efficiency and learning performance and different rates of progress, hence there are different frontiers.[26]

A *best practice* performance frontier curve in a static context exhibits one point of potential convergence where best practice performance is to be discovered. When the element of time is introduced, it is obvious that best practice will change. Hence the best practice performance frontier is a moving frontier, an insight first developed by two Scandinavian economists, Forsund and Hjalmarsson (1974) (see **Figure 2.5**). As the firm follows its optimal path across time, it is producing the same level of output with progressively less inputs. This is just a different way of looking at one type of learning curve where output is constant.

A useful generalisation is that a change in best practice is reflected in a change in cost savings, a revenue gain, an efficiency gain, or an equity gain. Thus, in a static context, one can divide actual performance by potential best practice performance to obtain a static performance ratio and a performance gap. Likewise, *in a dynamic context, one can also divide the learning curve (which represents point estimates of actual performance at different times) by the best practice performance frontier curve (which represents point estimates of potential performance at different times)*. The result is a widely applicable dynamic tool of economic analysis that measures dynamic performance on the learning curve and the performance gap.

In summary, a healthy tax system would have tax levels, tax rates and a tax mix that optimise economic efficiency (including economic growth, compliance costs and employment), and minimise tax evasion and potentially preventable tax avoidance and tax administration costs given an inter-generational and intra-generational, politically-determined equity constraint. As constraints (including equity preferences, technology, motivations, information, financial resources, and learning behaviour) change across time, these best practice frontier tax levels, rates and mix will also change, albeit perhaps slowly.

More work on the equity-efficiency trade-off, compliance costs, risk profiles of taxpayers, and the effect of tax on employment and competition is needed. This Report should be construed as a descriptive and analytical exercise rather than a policy advisory and normative exercise. The purpose of the Report is to lay the foundation for applying a rigorous cost benefit analysis and risk management framework for the assessment of the consequences of taxation on the behaviour of taxpayers, and the structure and performance of the economy.

---

[26] The notion of a *relative (across agents)* frontier is common in the learning curve literature, but is surprisingly not illustrated in the diagrams from earlier in the century. We added the moving frontier for illustrative purposes. See Figure 2.4 for the first development of a moving frontier in dynamic efficiency analysis.

Figure 2.5
Dynamic Efficiency Frontiers for an Industry with Two Inputs and Fixed Output

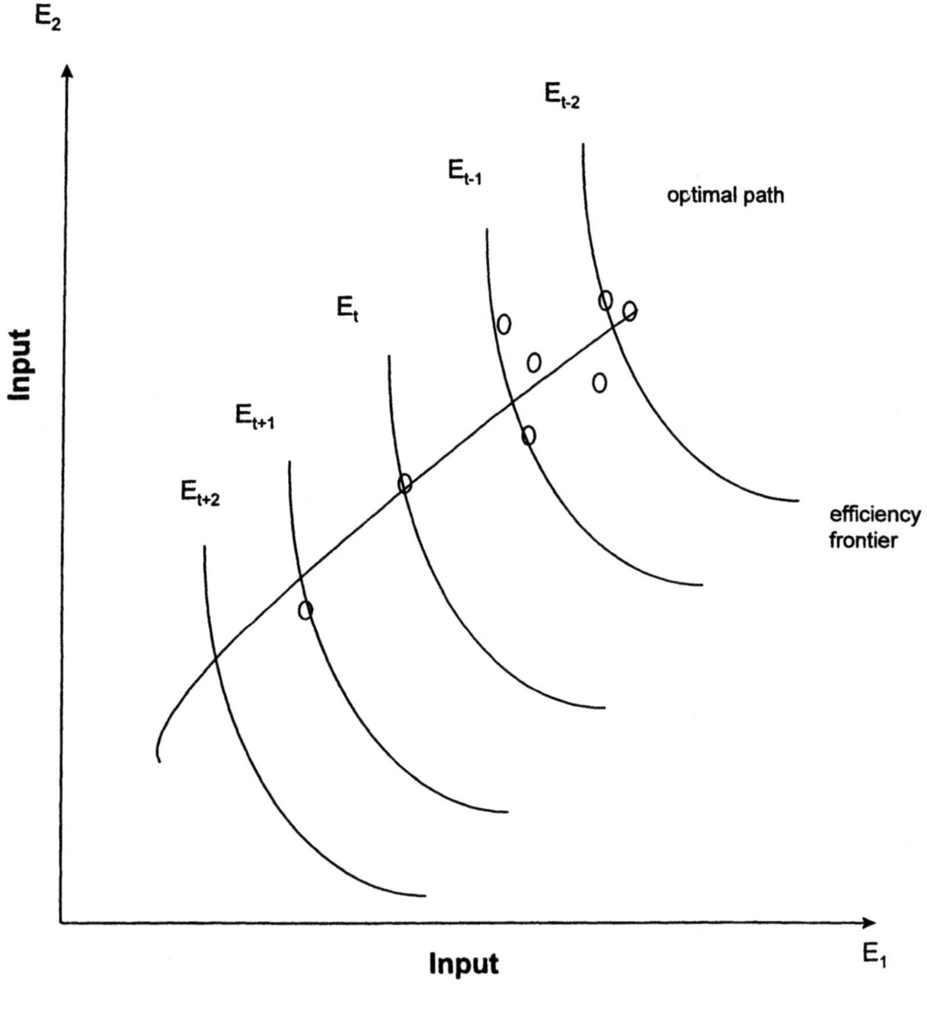

Source: Forsund, F., and Hjalmarsson, L., 1974, "*On the Measurement of Productive Efficiency*", Swedish Journal of Economics, p.140 (adapted)

The prospect in the offing is a better understanding of the state of voluntary compliance and the factors which shape it. Also achievable is a better understanding of how the balance of weight between government and the market in the economy shape the future wealth generating potential of the economy. With some additional research it may be possible to construct an index of the overall health of the tax system, but much more work is necessary on issues related to equity, compliance costs and administration costs.

Deadweight Loss Analysis: The Tradition

While Adam Smith did not identify the need to compare actual with potential performance, he did have a concept of welfare loss arising from imperfections in product markets. For him, competition had superior welfare effects to monopoly because of both the output and employment losses as well as price distortions:[27]

"By a perpetual monopoly, all the subjects of the state are taxed very absurdly in two different ways; first by the high price of goods [allocative inefficiency] which in the case of a free trade, they could buy much cheaper; and secondly by their exclusion from a branch of business, which it might be both convenient and profitable for them to carry on" [technical inefficiency] (Smith, 1786:vol.III p.143).

Even though the focus of his concern was the problem of monopoly behaviour, the conclusions are generalisable to taxation. Thus, first there is a wedge between pre-tax and post-tax prices. This price difference distorts the choice of the mix of inputs for producers and the mix of items in the consumer's basket. These distortions in the choices of both consumers and producers represent the *allocative inefficiency* effects of taxation.

Second, there is also a direct output under-performance or a cost over-performance both of which constitute a technical inefficiency loss that is just as, if not more, important. This is an empirical matter. This direct production loss has a long term macroeconomic effect on the standard of living because less resources are available for consumption. A combination of the technical and allocative efficiency losses equals the total static efficiency loss at any point in time, and over time, they equal the dynamic efficiency loss.[28] Smith paid particular attention to the output or technical efficiency loss issue because he

---

[27] This perspective had a tradition in English jurisprudence 200 years before Adam Smith. In 1588, there was an important "Case of Monopolies" wherein the High Court decided against a monopoly on 'playing cards' assigned by the Crown to Ralph Bowes and Co. Three basic distortions created by monopoly were identified: (1) price increases; (2) deterioration in product quality and (3) the loss of output and employment for those who would have otherwise been producers. All three factors led to the reduction of the 'commonwealth'.

[28] The terms "allocative efficiency", "technical efficiency" and "productive efficiency" are used as they have become established in the production frontier literature, stemming largely, although not completely, from Farrell's (1957) work 40 years ago: "In a path breaking and belatedly influential paper Farrell investigated the structure of production efficiency. He showed that productive (or overall) efficiency could be decomposed into the product of technical efficiency and allocative efficiency. He also showed how to measure production efficiency and allocative efficiency, and its two components, and provided a cost interpretation for each" (Fare, Grosskopf and Lovell, 1983:181).

realised it had a permanent effect on a country's "power of accumulation". Monopoly

"...renders the quantity of productive labour annually maintained [and] the whole annual produce of the land and labour of that country less than they otherwise would be. It keeps down the revenue of the inhabitants of that country below what it would naturally rise to, and thereby diminishes their power of accumulation" (Smith, 1786: vol.II p.430-1).

In modern terminology, the total productive (both allocative and technical) efficiency loss of monopoly and taxation create a long term reduction in the country's ability to generate growth, employment and related wages and salaries, and thus moves the economy to an inefficient point below the production frontier. Just as monopoly limits the scale and scope of a country's wealth generation, so too do taxes.

Jules Dupuit (1844), the father of cost benefit analysis and opportunity cost analysis[29], placed emphasis on both the technical and allocative efficiency consequences of taxation at the micro level. In the former case, he observed that a tax affecting a canal operator would increase "production costs" and lead to a permanent reduction in "traffic" (Dupuit, 1844, 1952:92). In the latter case, as the creator of the producer surplus and consumer surplus, he provided the foundation for later work by Hotelling and Harberger on allocative efficiency. He captured both notions as follows:

"the tax affects not only those who pay it, but also those who would have been consumers but for the tax" (Dupuit, 1844, 1952:92).

Hotelling (1938) was apparently the first to employ the term "dead loss" in the analysis of taxation. Dead loss is a precursor to the term deadweight loss. He attributed two dimensions to "dead loss": a technical efficiency loss arising because the tax reduces total production ("with this diminution is associated an approximately measurable net social loss") and an allocative efficiency loss because of a reduction of the consumer and producer surpluses. He devoted considerable attention to this latter issue and was an important influence on Harberger.

Hicks (1947) provided a combined assessment of the deadweight loss of government intervention and taxation in his review of post-war Britain. His key points were that both heavy-handed intervention and taxation undermine productivity, reduce output and result in a lower standard of living (Hicks, 1947:3; 7). With respect to taxes in particular, Hicks (1947:8) stated that:

"...it is easy to put the case for a reduction in taxation on grounds which sound economically impressive, by referring to the adverse effects on incentive of high taxes, especially high income taxes...It is true that a given amount of taxation will have less adverse effects on incentive if it is raised by taxes which are more proportional to income, or less progressive".

---

[29] Among many other contributions.

Earlier, Hicks had examined the issue of the dynamic income, or "capital effects", of a price change in a dynamic context.[30] This dynamic income effect needs to take into consideration "the whole expenditure plan" and not just static expenditure in a static snapshot. The focus is still on the extent to which individuals are made better or worse off, but, in a dynamic context where price and various conditions change, there are important consequences for both income and asset values:

"an individual will be made worse off if he is unable to expect, under new conditions, to be able to purchase the same quantities as before of all goods at all dates, but must retrench somewhere; he will be better off if he has something left over, after planning the same purchases as before. The effect in question therefore depends on the relative movements in the capital values of his previously planned stream of expenditures and of his expected stream of receipts. Looking at it this way, it appears that it would be more logical to call it a 'capital effect', or something of that sort, rather than an 'income effect'. However... I do not think that ... is necessary... if we remember the precise meaning which has been given to it from now on" (Hicks, 1941:231).

In speaking about retrenchment of consumption, income streams and changing capital values, it is clear that Hicks had in mind variations in the standard of living of consumers. After World War II, Corlett and Hague (1953:22), whose analysis focused on commodity taxation and not income taxation, employed the concept of the "excess burden"[31] of taxation in their analysis of the micro-economic effects of a choice between direct and indirect taxation. They emphasised both the income as well as substitution effects of taxation:

"when a tax change occurs there will be an income effect and a substitution effect. The income effect will cause the consumer's real income to rise or fall... The income and substitution effects combined will determine whether the consumer will hold more or less of the [different] goods with indirect tax than with the income tax".

Musgrave (1959) continued this tradition of examining both technical and allocative efficiency consequences of taxation in emphasising both the utility of "differential incidence" as compared to "balanced budget incidence" experiments:

"All taxes have an income effect, but they may or may not have a substitution effect. As a result of the income effect, all taxes tend to reduce consumption, saving for future consumption, and saving for accumulation... While the direction of the substitution effect is clear in most cases, its

---

[30] Nonetheless, for the purposes of his own detailed technical analysis Hicks (1941, 1941a) specified that "income effects are to be neglected", but of course not forgotten. Real income can still change when utility is kept constant. In his development of the term "compensating variations", Hicks (1941:41) placed his analytical focus clearly on the distortion of relative prices. When this model is applied to tax analysis, users often have a tendency to focus exclusively on the allocative efficiency effects of tax, and to ignore the static and dynamic technical efficiency effects (See Lipsey & Lancaster, 1956).

[31] They state that "...a direct tax system will nearly always impose an 'excess burden' as compared with some system of indirect taxes" (Corlett and Hague, 1953:30). Note that in this usage 'excess burden' is not a synonym for deadweight loss, rather it describes the additional deadweight loss created by the choice of a less efficient tax system, direct taxes, (in deadweight loss terms) as compared to a more efficient system of taxation (indirect taxes). Ballard (1990:264) notes that there is some confusion in the use of the term 'marginal excess burden'. He notes that the term generally refers to deadweight loss arising from the substitution effects of taxation rather than from the income effects. He prefers the term "marginal welfare cost" for the deadweight loss arising from balanced budget calculations.

magnitude is not easily assessed. It would seem to be of minor importance if we compare a flat-rate tax on income with a flat-rate tax on consumption, and it may well remain of modest importance, even if progression in the income tax is allowed for" (Musgrave, 1959:268; 272).

Bergson (1973:854; 856), who examined the welfare effects of monopoly, noted that the value of using Hicks' compensated variations approach lies in measuring welfare losses or gains, if income is actually constant. In such a case, the principal concern is with the misallocation of resources. Where income is not held constant, the emphasis in welfare analysis shifts to an examination of the welfare effects in terms of employment and output losses.

Bergson's (1973:860; 862) theoretical analysis also suggested that the income effects of monopoly welfare losses can "often be rather large", and criticised Leibenstein for understating the complexity and magnitude of the income effects, while he also supported the use of uncompensated demand schedules in applied welfare analysis. As well, he foresaw the need to explore the welfare effects of monopoly on the development of inventions and the introduction of new technology (ibid:868). In the academic community, for theoretical and paradigm reasons, currently, there is no widespread support for the use of uncompensated demand in welfare analysis.

Differential incidence experiments are used in examining the deadweight loss of taxes, importantly, under conditions of constant revenue and constant government expenditure, through the assessment of the substitution effects of a shift in the tax regime from lump-sum taxes to some type of distortionary tax. On the other hand, balanced budget experiments must be used when examining the deadweight loss of taxes under conditions of changing tax revenue and government expenditure:

"since the balanced-budget analyses involve changes in the overall amount of resources taken from the private sector, income effects can no longer be ignored. Harberger formulas, which are appropriate for differential calculations, will not generally be appropriate for these balanced budget calculations. (Harberger formulas will be approximately correct for small balanced budget changes in tax rates if the exhaustive government expenditures are perfect substitutes for cash...[which is generally not the case])" (Ballard, 1990:264; 266).

Are transfers perfect substitutes for cash? Not for the taxpayers who have to reduce investment to pay for transfers. Perhaps for beneficiaries but the deadweight loss effect on taxpayers of transfers is real (Alesina and Perotti 1994; and Frantz 1985).

Given all these assessments, is Harberger's (1954; 1964) original approach to deadweight loss narrow because it had no dynamic dimension? Despite drawing on Hotelling and Dupuit, Harberger concentrated on the allocative efficiency effects of monopoly (1954:77)[32] and the allocative efficiency or "substitution

[32] Harberger did not use a best practice frontier analysis. Instead he used a simple average. Harberger's normal rate of return was established by the average return for all industries. Therefore, he concluded that all profits above average were excessive. This conclusion ignores risk premia across sectors, the supply side efficiency of firms and the degree of competition in each market. In other words many firms in Harberger's sample were probably earning efficiency-based rather than monopoly based profits.

effects" of taxation (1964:61), and deviation from taxation neutrality, rather than examining the impact of a change in the level of total taxes on the output of the economy or of taxpayers. Part of the problem may stem from the fact that, from its inception modern, welfare economics has emphasised allocative efficiency issues:

"all propositions of welfare economics concerned with the degree of utilisation of resources can be treated as allocational propositions" (Lange, 1942:226).[33]

In microeconomics, starting in the 1950s and 1960s, concern was expressed by some prominent efficiency pioneers about the dominant role played by allocative efficiency as compared to technical efficiency in economic analysis:

"microeconomic theory focuses on allocative efficiency to the exclusion of other types of efficiencies that, in fact, are more significant in many instances. Furthermore, improvement in 'non-allocative efficiency' is an important aspect of the process of growth" (Leibenstein, 1966:392; see also Farrell, 1957).

Leibenstein's X-efficiency analysis, which is consistent with Farrell's concept of technical efficiency, argued that the Harberger welfare triangle understates the welfare loss from monopoly (power) because the latter assumes that firms with market power are all cost minimisers, which is inconsistent with reality. Thus, the welfare loss is greater than predicted by a narrow approach based solely on "the misallocation of scarce resources by the market" because there is also an additional cost[34] resulting from a *transfer of resources* from an efficient competitor to a less efficient monopolist"(Franz, 1985:39). Frantz (1985:43), describes Leibenstein's concept of "pure X-inefficiency... [as] a deadweight loss". Tullock's (1967) analysis also supported the view that the welfare triangle underestimates the cost of monopoly or taxation. Where a tariff is levied, there is also a shifting of resources to less efficient producers (those protected by the tariff).

One of the important points that comes up in deadweight loss analysis is the value to be placed on what the government does with the tax revenue in assessing the cost-benefit ratio for taxation. As Frisch (1939a:150) first pointed out, in critiquing Hotelling's original interpretation of 'dead loss':

"the nature of this 'net social loss' should be clearly understood. It emerges only because the money taken away from the consumers and producers is valued according to a 'utility' principle - the producers and consumers surpluses... while the same money in the hands of the government is only valued according to its number of monetary units. The relevant question, of course, is what the government *does* with the money, and this must in all fairness be valued by applying the same sort of 'utility' principle to the good which the money in question enables the government to produce and distribute to the consumers free of charge (or at reduced cost). If this is done, there will not be any 'net social loss', but possibly a great gain, the size of the gain depending on the nature of the demand curve for the good produced by the government".

---

[33] Some issues in welfare economics are examined in the next section.
[34] "Production efficiency and production costs are...seen as influenced by 'pressures' or motivators such as degree of market competition, size of firm, type of ownership (owner-managed, public, regulated, or private), as well as the ('vertical' and 'horizontal' norms, relations, and sanctions that govern behaviour in particular production units" (Frantz, 1985:39).

This is as strong a set of conditions as Pareto Optimality for it requires that for every economic unit (firms, households, factors) marginal cost must be equal to marginal benefit. This condition is unlikely to hold and no tax system in the world has such a pretence. Further, it assumes that every taxpayer gets value for money in government spending, and that there is no waste. As Hotelling (1939a:154) pointed out in his rejoinder, the calculation of dead loss

"...for the whole of the economy, represent(s) the social loss from a system of excise taxes in contrast to more efficient types, regardless of what the government does with the money. Whether the government spends the money wisely or badly, and the total amount to be spent by the government, are of course matters of grave public concern. But for a given total of taxation, these measures of the inefficiency of excise taxes, and other additions to marginal costs, are accurate so far as terms of the second order can go".

Over some range of tax (expenditure) benefits exceed costs (when the government is using the money for roads, harbours, police, fire, etc). Beyond some level of transfer payment cost exceeds benefit. As in Diewert & Lawrence (1994), this Report begins by assuming that each dollar of tax revenue has one dollar of expenditure value. But, this choice needs to be qualified from two different perspectives.

First, for some government expenditure, such as much (but not all) spending on education, health and economic infrastructure, the long run benefits per dollar of tax revenue would certainly exceed one dollar. This is quite an important point that suggests the need to go deeply into the expenditure accounts of government to examine the short and long run growth benefits of government spending.

Second, in other cases, the benefit is less than a dollar because there is considerable waste in government spending in some other areas as well as mistakes, inefficiency, fraud and corruption which reduce the value of government spending. For example, the wave of restructuring and privatisation of state-owned enterprises, SOEs, combined with the indebtedness and price distortions of these firms occurring throughout the world in the 1990s, suggests that the public may not have received sufficient benefit for each dollar of tax used in the billions of dollars invested in SOEs in these countries.

What is the right course to steer through this complex information problem? One option is to estimate the welfare costs per dollar of tax, and then specify that, for each project, the benefits per dollar of tax should try to match the costs. What orders of magnitude might one find? The reader should keep in mind that there are two different approaches to welfare loss, one based on allocative efficiency analysis and the other based on technical efficiency analysis.

Within the last 20 years there have been a number of studies that challenged the Harberger triangle, both from within the Harberger triangle perspective and from outside. Those studies, which focused on a number of adjustments or interpretations to *the existing paradigm*, challenged Harberger's original conceptualisation of deadweight loss. These critics raise four general points:

- First, the original Harberger triangle is insufficient to capture the full effects of taxation. It is necessary to broaden the range of areas of impact that are affected by taxes. In the allocative efficiency tradition, Lindbeck (1986), for example, has stipulated the necessity of examining the loss or distortionary effects of taxes on (a) leisure, (b) work intensity (shirking), (c) do-it-yourself work, (d) barter, (e) legal tax avoidance, (f) investment in human capital, (g) labour mobility within and across countries, (h) savings, and (i) asset selection. Also in the same tradition, Feldstein and Feenberg (1995:16-17) note the necessity of going beyond the traditional approach that "assumes that taxes distort only the supply of labour". They underline the necessity of examining "the effects of changes in the tax rate on the taxpayers' use of deductions and on the shift of compensation to excludable forms (fringe benefits, work environment, etc)". Further, Feldstein (1995) refers to the value of examining deadweight loss as a "trapezoid" rather than a "triangle".

- Second, the results of these extensions and adaptations is that the deadweight loss estimates are found to be much larger than originally anticipated.

- Third, there is a need to look beyond the allocative efficiency effects of tax to the dynamic analysis that focuses, among other things on, output and income losses. For example, Feldstein (1996:10) in his examination of "How Big Should Government Be?" specified five areas where deadweight loss estimates could be extended and thus made more robust. Three of those areas involved a dynamic focus:

  (1) "reliable estimates of income effects need to be developed". This can be interpreted in short term sense as a current income effect and in a long term Hicksian sense as "capital effects".
  (2) "Additional work needs to be done on the long run effects of tax changes. Over time, the magnitude of the response may increase as individuals have more opportunity to adjust the kinds of work that they do, their specific jobs, etc., but also decrease to the extent that some of the observed short-run response reflects timing of receipts and expenditures"; and,
  (3) "Evidence is needed on the extent to which corporate income tax liabilities are affected by the observed changes in personal tax liabilities".

- Fourth, allocative efficiency effects of distortions are probably smaller than the technical efficiency effects (in other words, the effects of the misallocation of resources is smaller than the loss of output)(Farrell, 1957; Liebenstein, 1966).

In summarising Usher's (1991) contribution to the analysis of the hidden costs of government expenditure, Bird (1991:8) has observed that

"...the real economic cost of raising a dollar in taxation and transferring it to someone else (or even to the same person) may be as much as two or three times the recorded amount of the tax burden as usually measured. Usher's careful analysis serves to put us on notice that an additional dollar of public expenditure must be similarly 'profitable' - that is, produce two or three dollars of 'excess benefits' - if expansion of the public sector is to make sense".

Feldstein (1996a: 27) developed a similar perspective:

"Past experience suggests that financing additional government spending by across-the-board tax rate changes would involve a total cost of more than two dollars for every additional dollar of government spending. More research on the deadweight loss of tax rate changes and other ways of increasing revenue deserves high priority. This type of understanding and information would also provide the ingredients for assessing alternative tax reforms".

Analysis presented later in this Report based on Scully (1996) and Caragata & Small (1996) confirms that this order of magnitude of the welfare loss from taxation is found in New Zealand: $2.69 per dollar of tax revenue over the long run. This suggests that the government should consider trying to obtain about $2.70 in long run economic and social benefits for each dollar of tax collected. This welfare loss, or opportunity cost, approach to analysis might provide some incentive for more rigorous analysis of the value of government expenditure. The evaluation of the long run benefits of government spending is due for reconsideration in order to differentiate between valuable and wasteful expenditures.

Scully (1996) was careful in his analysis not to claim that his deadweight loss numbers were directly comparable with those of Feldstein (1995, 1996). He was aware of how small the Diewert & Lawrence (1994) estimates were for the welfare loss in New Zealand with respect to the taxation of labour (18c per dollar of tax), and consumption (14c per dollar of tax). His principal purpose was to point out that the Harberger paradigm was under challenge and that the estimates of deadweight loss were much bigger than originally anticipated, as has already been noted by several authors above.

Figure 2.6 takes an integrated approach to the examination of static and dynamic deadweight loss, combining the technical efficiency effects with the allocative efficiency effects of a tax change. E is the equilibrium in the absence of taxes (Phase 1). A static approach to deadweight loss tends to examine only the losses due to allocative inefficiency (distortions in the patterns of consumption and investment) and usually ignores total output loss due to technical inefficiency, including the impact of taxes on capital. A dynamic approach to deadweight loss takes into consideration both the technical and allocative efficiency losses across time as well as the value of government spending. Finally, further recent support for this dynamic approach comes from Koop, Osiewalski and Steel (1997) who note that:

"countries can be thought of as operating either on or within the frontier; and the distance from the frontier as reflecting inefficiency. Over time, a country can become less efficient and 'catch up' to the frontier or the frontier itself can shift over time, indicating technical progress. In addition, a country can move along the frontier by changing inputs. Hence output growth can be thought of in terms of three different components: efficiency change, technical change and input change".

Figure 2.6
Integrated Approach to the Deadweight Loss of Taxation

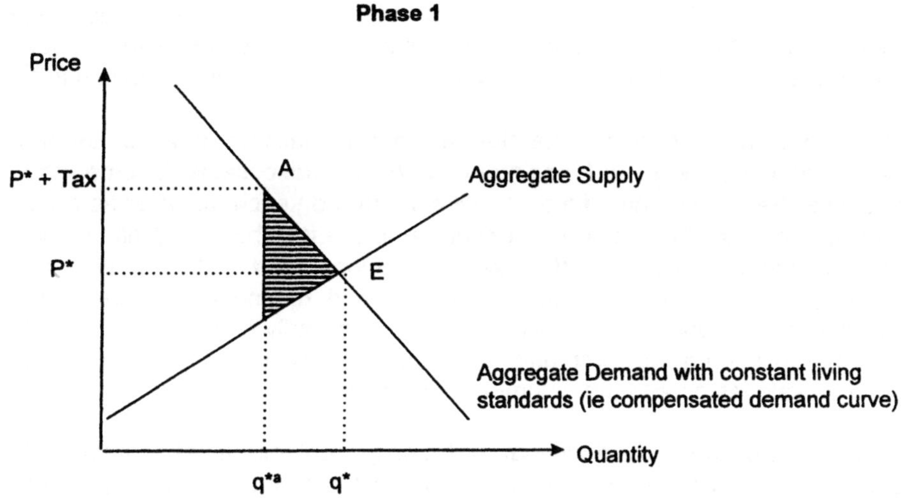

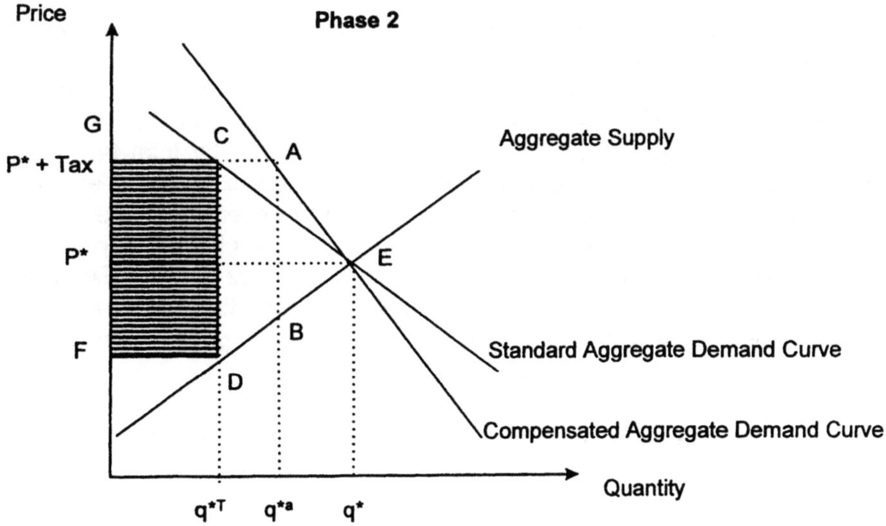

F = Producer Price

Source: Dr John Small - University of Auckland

Taxes change the relative prices of goods and services so that, even with no change in their standard of living[35], consumers choose to buy and sell different combinations of goods and services, and investors change their pattern of investment (e.g. as between portfolio and direct investment). Thus, even if one were to restore consumers' and investors' standard of living after imposing a tax, the original equilibrium point E would not be reached.

Instead, the economy would move to a point like A. The value of the triangle ABE is a measure of the deadweight loss attributable to this *misallocation* of resources as a result of taxation. This is one of the measures used by Diewert & Lawrence (1994) in their examination of the deadweight loss of taxation in NZ.

In the real world, of course, the standard of living falls when taxes rise because individual consumers and investors have less disposable income after tax because there is no immediate benefit conferred on each taxpayer as a result of having paid tax. Government expenditure is not distributed equally to all firms and individuals that pay tax (for example, regional road development or transfer payments in the form of welfare benefits and unemployment benefits).[36] In addition, the full value of the benefits is not necessarily realised until well into the future (education or research and development funding) even if current expenses such as salaries go into the community immediately.

As a result of these distributional and timing problems, most taxpayers do not experience compensated demand with respect to taxes. Rather they experience an uncompensated, or partly compensated, cost. This is one of the principal triggers for tax evasion and avoidance. If taxpayers believed they were fully compensated for the taxes they pay, they would be less likely to avoid or evade.

One way of dealing with the different perspectives on the value of government expenditure is to measure deadweight loss in dynamic terms, comparing current versus potential economic growth or output, as Scully (1996) has done. This approach takes into consideration the effects of current (in each year) government spending.[37] The output gap value is divided by total tax revenue. Thus, this approach encompasses both the tax-related expenditure effects and the beneficial consequences for economic growth of government spending. It is not possible, however, in these diagrams to depict the full benefit of government spending; instead government revenue from this particular tax (FGCD) of Phase 2 is depicted. If a dollar of tax leads to a dollar of expenditure, then the shaded rectangle also represents the short-term benefits of government spending derived from this tax.

In Phase 2, the assumption that the standard of living is unchanged by taxation is relaxed. A higher tax burden leads to reduced output. As output falls, demand

---

[35] Some may wish to interpret 'standard of living' to mean 'utility'.

[36] As Kaplow (1994:3) has noted: "when there are millions of tax units, it is inconceivable that any reform, no matter how wonderful, would literally improve everyone's lot".

[37] Both the compliance costs effects and the administrative costs effects of taxation are incorporated in Scully's dynamic deadweight loss analysis because they both affect economic growth.

for goods and services must fall below $q*^a$. This is represented in Phase 2 by using a standard demand curve which does not include the assumption of constant living standards. The total effect of the tax is now evident. Actual output has fallen to $q*^T$ and the total value of output lost as a result of taxation is the area of the triangle CDE, which is necessarily larger than ABE, assuming normal as distinct from inferior goods.

The area CDE encompasses all output losses as well as losses due to the misallocation of resources arising from the substitution effects of taxation on consumption and investment. The difference between the areas of CDE and ABE is the measure of the static output loss effect of taxation. Alternatively, one can regard ABE as measuring the loss due to allocative inefficiency and CDE as measuring the loss due to *both* technical and allocative inefficiency. These measures are only valid for one time period, however, because their effects in terms of lost investment potential accumulate over time and give rise to dynamic inefficiency.

Notice that in phase 2 the area of CDE does not include government expenditures in the economy as a result of government spending. As discussed, a measure of these expenditures (but not necessarily value of the resulting outputs) is the area of the shaded rectangle in Phase 2.

Small's (1995) critique of the Diewert & Lawrence paper (1994) helps to put our approach into perspective:

"If the amount of tax paid by each agent remains unchanged by the experiment, all that has happened is that the *form* of taxation has altered on the marginal unit. This is known as a *differential* experiment and is the approach used by Harberger (1964). One attractive feature of this method is that there are no income effects to consider (because income remains constant), so that behavioural effects are purely due to substitution responses. Given that the optimal tax design literature provides a strong endorsement for lump-sum taxes, the differential experiment seems a natural way to analyse movement towards this form of taxation. A criticism of this method is raised by Ballard (1990, p275):

"Methodologically, it is incorrect to calculate marginal welfare costs on the basis of the Harberger formula, unless one believes that the relevant government expenditures are a very close substitute for cash".

Of course, transfers might be considered a close substitute for cash. But on what terms? Certainly not in terms of their long run effects on investors who fund the transfers through taxes and on economic performance. Transfers also carry welfare losses (Tanzi & Schuknecht, 1995). Small's (1995) analysis continues:

"One further consideration is that it is simply impossible for marginal welfare costs to be negative using this method, unless non-normal goods are taxed. This is because the substitution effects of price rises for normal goods are always negative, and these are the only effects considered.

"If we were interested in the effects of a tax financed increase in government spending on a given project, the differential experiment would not be appropriate (unless the project was a perfect substitute for handing out cash, which seems unrealistic). Since this project will be fully funded by taxation we refer to this as balanced budget experiment. Income effects will play an important role in the determination of the efficiency costs. Accordingly, welfare costs arising from balanced budget experiments are based upon *uncompensated* elasticities rather than the compensated elasticities used in differential analysis. Although the differences between the differential and balanced budget methods may appear subtle, the effects on the final figures can be very large. The reasons lies in the familiar difference between income and substitution effects".

Finally, Ballard & Fullerton (1992) examined the two main alternative approaches to deadweight loss in economic literature: (1) the Pigou-Harberger-Browning (PHB) approach that uses compensated labour supply elasticities and that ignores the income effects of taxation; versus (2) the Stiglitz-Dasgupta-Atkinson-Stern (SDAS) approach which uses uncompensated labour supply elasticities and incorporates the income effects of tax changes, and supports the use of the SDAS approach.[38] Diewert & Lawrence (1994) reference both but actually calculate only the PBH approach. This underpins the points made by Small (1996).

In their approach to deadweight loss analysis, or the marginal cost of funds, Ballard & Fullerton (1992:119; 124) note that they are concerned with the level of taxation and its efficiency effects, rather than the composition of the tax mix and its efficiency effects. With respect to the *PHB approach* they conclude that it "seems poorly suited to the cost-benefit problem of whether the level of government spending should increase, given that spending must be financed with additional distortionary taxes". They note that it is a "strong" assumption to assume that the income effects are washed out by government spending. The same analysis holds with respect to a tax cut; that is to say, the income effects of tax cuts are important for cost benefit analysis. Ballard & Fullerton (1996:118-19) note that all deadweight loss analysis has typically ignored the effects of administration costs and compliance costs. In contrast, the work of Scully (1996), Caragata & Small (1996) and Branson & Lovell (1997) pick up these effects in their analysis of dynamic deadweight loss.

A dynamic approach to deadweight loss thus needs to take into consideration three elements: technical efficiency, allocative efficiency and government spending. The effects of the change in these variables are reflected over time in the level of economic output and rate of change of economic growth. This integrated approach to deadweight loss has been pioneered by Scully (1996) and confirmed by Caragata & Small (1996) and Branson & Lovell (1997).

Conclusions

At its inception, the implicit (monopolies court case, Smith, Dupuit) and explicit (Hotelling, Corlett & Hague, Musgrave) deadweight loss analysis focused on both output and allocative efficiency losses. This balanced approach was partly diminished at mid-twentieth century because of formal welfare economics' emphasis on resource allocation problems.

A current focus (beginning with Farrell (1957) and Leibenstein (1966) and continuing with Feldstein (1996) and Scully (1996)) places strong emphasis on

[38] This same distinction was used by Dahlby (1996) who critiqued Diewert & Lawrence's recent paper "The Marginal Cost of Taxation in Canada" published in the *Canadian Journal of Economics*.

the technical as compared to the allocative efficiency consequences of taxation and, more recently, the dynamic efficiency losses of tax and suggests that they are more important than the static allocative efficiency losses. In general, in order to develop a comprehensive picture of deadweight loss, it is preferable to integrate the analysis of allocative, technical and dynamic efficiency losses due to taxation, including the effects of changes in government spending. This approach is usefully developed by comparing current versus potential levels of output and rates of change of economic growth given current versus optimal tax rates and mixes.

2.3 Welfare Economics and the Efficiency, or Performance, Ratio

The efficiency, or performance, ratio divides actual output by potential output. Thus, risk analysis and cost benefit analysis begin with the "actual" consequences of taxation. This means that one starts with an accurate *description* of economic reality and, therefore, of the current revenue, efficiency, and administrative cost consequences of taxation, given an equity constraint. Thus, the numerator of the efficiency ratio must be an empirical estimate. It cannot be anything else.

Pareto optimality is an imaginative conceptualisation based on conditions that are unlikely to hold in the real world. As Harberger (1964:58) pointed out: "we do not live on the Pareto frontier, and we are not going to do so in the future. Yet policy discussions are constantly being made which can move us either toward or away from that frontier".[39] Viner (1931; 1953:206) noted that "the ordinary economic situation is one of disequilibrium moving in the direction of equilibrium rather than of realised equilibrium." Finally, as Fisher (1983:11) has observed "it is a mistake to ground disequilibrium theory in the *equilibrium* behaviour of agents".

In addition, there are also serious problems for comparative static equilibrium analysis if "the stability and uniqueness of the equilibria" are provided by the assumption of a *representative individual* (Kirman, 1992:120) and/or a *representative firm* approach (Caragata, 1996).[40] Hence, efficiency analysis cannot begin at the theoretical frontier, it must begin with empirical reality. One cannot start with modern "welfare economics" because it does not accurately describe reality:

---

[39] This is also true with respect to equity. As Kaplow (1994:3) has observed, "when there are millions of tax units, it is inconceivable that any reform, no matter how wonderful, would literally improve everyone's lot. Moreover, tax policy often is concerned with the appropriate distribution of income, which is not a question the Pareto principle purports to address".

[40] Hahn (1973:12) affirmed that "...there are logical difficulties in accounting for the existence of agents called firms at all unless we allow there to be increasing returns of some sort. But when there are increasing returns it may not be possible to show that there are any logically possible economic states which qualify as either Arrow-Debreu equilibrium or as members of the Core". General equilibrium can only cope with increasing returns when "increasing returns to scale are small" (ibid:p.13) and when there is no learning ("it will be a condition of the agent being in equilibrium that he is not learning" - ibid:19). Of course, learning-generated cost savings are a crucial component of increasing returns, hence continual learning implies continuing efficiency-motivated disturbances to equilibrium.

"Neither the assumptions nor the concepts of normative and deductive welfare economics are necessarily useful for descriptive purposes[41]. But this is no excuse at all for neglecting or despising welfare economics. On the contrary, resource allocation is a legitimate and very important problem, though not of course, as has been alleged, the only economic problem." (Wiles, 1956:3-4)

To be more precise, the first order (*marginal*, *stability* and *total)* conditions of welfare economics (Hicks, 1939:704)[42], and the assumptions[43] which underpin them, by and large, may very well not hold in reality because of risk, uncertainty, information deficiency, real world imperfect competition (Frisch, 1939b:157), inherent differences[44] across firms, "if convergence[45] takes place slowly" (Fisher,

---

[41] Perhaps the best example stems from Hotelling's (1938:242) rule that welfare is maximised when the "sale of everything [is] at marginal cost". It is quite incorrect to argue that *price equals marginal cost* is typical of economic reality. On the contrary, pricing is typically at a fixed or variable mark-up above average cost. For an excellent cross country survey of this reality see Martins, Scarpetta, and Pilat (1996); see also OECD (1996). But even Hotelling (1938:264) recognised that the actual ability to price at "marginal cost depends on [the] extent of unused capacity" and the absence of overhead costs (ibid, 1938:267) and unused capacity and the presence of overhead costs are as common as air. How did this state of affairs come about, so that normative assertion dominated the description of reality? A useful insight has been provided by Burgenmeier (1994:344) in his re-examination of Walras. In the last half of the 19th century, "moral philosophy and law still overshadowed economic research which, as a consequence, was strongly biased by value judgements expressed in endless rhetoric about the virtues of competition, imperilled by socialist views .....". In effect, the conflicts extant at the early stages of development have long term consequences. A related problem is the dependence of the neo-classical model on a deductive approach and its neglect of "empirical testing and hence falsification" (Burgenmeier, 1994:342) as compared to combining induction with deduction. Note Fair's (1993:287) comment that "macroeconomics has not been well served by the real-business cycle approach, which is not interested in testing models in a serious way, and by new Keynesian economics, which has moved macroeconomics away from its econometric base". Similar problems confront endogenous growth theory: "Endogenous growth theory has led to little tested empirical knowledge" (Pack, 1994:69; 63).

[42] The optimum allocation of products; the optimum degree of specialization; the optimum factor-product relationship; the optimum allocation of factors; the optimum direction of production; the optimum allocation of a factor-unit's time; and inter-temporal conditions of maximum welfare (Reder, 1947).

[43] Each individual has one utility function (including his preferences between work and leisure) and owns definite quantities (which may be zero) of each product and each factor; each firm has a given transformation function determined by the "state of the arts" (each firm is at the production frontier and operating at full capacity); each firm and individual has perfect information (no risk and uncertainty) about available resources and the implications of each option; each firm and individual is perfectly rational; and markets are perfectly competitive; there are no fundamental differences across firms in terms of cost, efficiency and profitability (Hicks, 1939; Reder, 1946); thus the representative firm is accepted as a fundamental assumption, as compared to the *differentiated features approach* (Caragata, 1996) which is more typical of reality [see Heckscher, 1919; Taussig, 1919; Secrist, 1924; Rustow (various); Clark, 1961; Salter, 1960; Forsund and Hjalmarsson, 1987] and there is a closed economy with no new products that enter the market and no new firms; there is no learning and innovation, no producer surplus and no consumer surplus, no labour mobility, no unemployment, no capital mobility, no increasing returns only diminishing returns, and no economic reform (Hicks, 1939:704-710; Lange, 1942:226). This implies that taxpayers not only do not learn to adapt to tax shocks, but also have no behavioural responses stemming from that learning (See Feldstein and Feenberg, 1995:4). The conditions and assumptions which characterise a perfectly static world are perfectly unrealistic (Reder, 1946:15).

[44] See for example Taussig, 1919; Gibrat, 1931; Simon and Bonini, 1958, Ijiri and Simon, 1974.

[45] To equilibrium where differences across firms' performance disappear.

1983:217) as is common [if convergence occurs at all], and, perhaps most importantly, because not all relationships and cost-benefit changes and outcomes are mediated through the price system[46] (Hicks, 1939:707-9).[47]

More serious concerns were raised by Little (1957:1), a modern father of cost benefit analysis, who critiqued the formal, non-empirical, non-scientific, mathematical basis of welfare economics:[48]

"economists have used no methods of scientific research in arriving at their conclusions about economic welfare; and since there are no methods of scientific research involved there can be no methodology... Any further extension of welfare theory is unlikely to be at all valuable, except as a mathematical exercise".[49]

Wiles and Little were perhaps the first[50] of many noted economists who have expressed concerns about the application of *formal* economics to real world problems (for example, compare Hahn, 1970:1; Leontief,[51] 1971:1-3; Zeeman, 1979:vii; Baumol, 1991:2; Harberger, et al. 1992:1; and Coase 1992:714). In reviewing this issue, Mayer (1993:7) concluded that:

"...we should draw a much sharper distinction than is usually done between two types of economic theory. One, formalist theory, is abstract theory that is concerned with high-level generalisations, and looks towards axiomisation. The other, empirical science theory, focuses on explaining past observations and predicting future ones. While both are perfectly legitimate, applying the criteria appropriate to one to evaluate the other generates confusion and misunderstanding. Such confusion is common because the great prestige of formalist theory has allowed it to invade the territory that rightfully belongs to empirical science theory, and to impose on it unrealistic criteria of rigour and precision. In trying to meet these unrealistic criteria empirical science economists have been tempted either to dress up formalist theory as empirical science theory, or to focus attention on the strongest link in the chain of their argument, and to pretend that their whole argument is rigorous because this one link is. This I will refer to as the principle of the strongest link".

---

[46] Hicks (1939:707) noted that "the ultimate implications of this exception are indeed very large. Hidden under this heading are some of the grave philosophical issues about the relationship between the individual and society".

[47] Hotelling (1938:260; 258) also cautioned economists about the need to make a "distinction of optimum from competitive conditions" and to be careful about using "a theorem" whose "premises do not apply" in real world cases.

[48] See also Nelson & Winter's (1982:405) concerns about the inflexibility of formal "commitments to unbounded rationality and optimization".

[49] Almost 40 years later Coase (1992:714) stated that: "What is studied is a system which lives in the minds of economists but not on earth. I have called the result 'blackboard economics'. The firm and the market appear by name but they lack any substance. The firm in mainstream theory has often been described as a 'black box'. And so it is. This is very extraordinary..."

[50] Marshall (1907:417), however, in his critique of Ricardo had earlier raised a similar concern: "There is, however, no scope in economics for long chains of deductive reasoning; that is chains in which each link is supported, wholly or mainly, by that which went before, and without further support and guidance from observation and the direct study of real life".

[51] For example, Leontief (1971:1-3) wrote that: "uncritical enthusiasm for mathematical formulation tends to conceal the ephemeral substantive content of the argument behind the formidable font of algebraic signs...In the presentation of a new model, attention nowadays is usually centred on a step-by-step derivation of its formal properties... By the time it comes to interpretation of the substantive conclusions, the assumptions on which the model rests are easily forgotten...Continued preoccupation with the imagery, hypothetical, rather than observable reality has gradually led to a distortion of the informal valuation scale used in our academic community to assess and to rank the scientific performance of its members".

Reder (1947:176-77) raised two additional considerations. First, welfare economics "tends to ignore all but 'long-run' phases of economic problems", and thus transitional matters. The welfare gain promised under equilibrium circumstances must be compared with the welfare loss incurred during the transition. Hence, and second, welfare economics policy recommendations are "subject to challenge on welfare grounds". He concluded that

"a consideration of dynamic factors merely serves to make us cautious concerning the application of static welfare criteria to a dynamic world" (Reder, 1947:177).

An examination of the dynamic behaviour of economies in transition reveals two important facts which underline the value of using long time series and econometric analysis in understanding evolutionary behaviour. First, "in a real economy ...trading as well as production and consumption goes on out of equilibrium". Secondly, the performance of economies "...is path dependent...[and thus] depends not merely on the initial state but on the dynamic adjustment process" (Fisher, 1983:14; 216-217).

Our approach follows Wiles' and Mayer's view and accepts Fisher's conclusion that the foundations of analysis *in the market* are disequilibrium foundations. Our research suggests that *it is the order in which welfare economics makes its appearance that is important*. It must come after the empirical research has been completed. In any type of efficiency analysis, including an examination of the health of a tax system, actual performance is always compared to potential performance. This is called the efficiency ratio. Since the measure must be accurate, if the analysis is to have any utility, an empirical estimate of actual performance (the numerator) is required. But, potential performance (the denominator) must also be based on observed 'best-practice', not on theoretically perfect performance, otherwise the efficiency ratio will be meaningless. Thus, the efficiency ratio must be an empirical estimate for actual performance divided by an empirical estimate for potential performance.

An accurate assessment of the *starting point* (Haavelmo, 1956)[52] is crucial both for determining performance destinations as well as progress on the learning curve (e.g. dynamic unit cost performance in the case of the firm, or dynamic cost minimisation in the case of government). In essence, a well-estimated efficiency ratio per annum, using time series data, combines learning curve information with production frontier information.

---

[52] Haavelmo's *theory of evolutionary dissimilarities* utilized "comparative dynamics" and emphasized the importance of "initial conditions" and the "environment" in shaping the future "path" of economic change. Moreover, that path is characterised by "irreversibility" and "a process of trial and error" (Haavelmo, 1956:111; 56-9). He noted that in using "rigid dynamic models", and restrictive assumptions: "...the resulting paths of development tend to be too rigid for us to have much confidence in the idea that our model framework could adequately describe the shifting picture - even in the broadest macro terms - of actual economic developments. It is therefore, *desirable to look for other theoretical frameworks* that could be more satisfactory in this respect". (Haavelmo, 1956:63) (emphasis added).

Thus, even when first estimating and measuring the potential "best" practice (as compared to "perfect" practice in *formal* welfare economics) performance of individuals, firms and the economy with respect to taxation, we need to delay using a normative approach so as to avoid colouring the data:

"the main point to notice is that the endeavour to merge questions of what ought to be with questions of what is tends to confuse, not only economic discussions themselves, but also discussions about economic method" (Collander, 1992:193).[53]

It is only after one has estimated the gap between current and best practice that the normative contributions of welfare economics must come into play. At that point, welfare economics can play a role by designing how best to achieve objectives[54] with respect to closing the gap, but even then it operates under the restriction that "constraints rule"[55]. It is the existence of constraints that help to explain why the gap between current and potential performance is not simply a matter of improving learning. In addition, normative practice may not achieve *perfect* practice, rather it may reach *second best* (Lipsey and Lancaster, 1956) or *third best* practice, depending on constraints. Perhaps, just as important, insisting on 'first best' may have negative consequences for the acceptability of the final choice:

"...economic policy is not made in a political vacuum. What might be optimal policy recommendations in the abstract may therefore not be the policy recommendation that is feasible and appropriate given other constraints.... You have to remember that the worst enemy of the second best policy may be the first best, and that if you persist in rigidly pressing for the first best, even when it is not feasible, you may end up with third or fourth best outcomes" (Frenkel, 1993:5).

The approach taken here is similar to Harberger's (1993:4-12) concept of "*applied welfare economics"* which emphasises the critical value of *empirical observation, "diagnostics",* multiple methods in the analytical process, and making improvements in both the 'decision-making process' and 'overall economic efficiency'. His *diagnostics*[56] apply the art and science of economics to real world problems.

His diagnostics recognise the overwhelming importance of constraints and stress starting with non-optimal, real world situations to which dynamic analysis is applied. His dynamic analysis is based on applied cost benefit analysis and includes observing real world starting points, the adjustment path, being familiar with "normal behaviour", as distinct from "outliers" or extreme cases, using best

---

[53] See also John Neville Keynes' (1891) distinction between positive economics, normative economics and the art of economics.

[54] Hicks (1939:706) noted that there were certain limits on the normative role of welfare economics: "welfare economics ...cannot lay down what is the optimum method of raising a given revenue - the 'least sacrifice' method, as taxation theorists would call it. That is impossible without inter-personal comparisons. It can, however, distinguish between those methods of raising revenue which are consistent with optimum production and those which are not."

[55] This aphorism is from Richard Bird in a private communication. See also Harberger (1993).

[56] "The analogy I like best [for economics] is with medicine. Law and accounting do not fit because they are not inferential; in that sense they have no scientific component. Physics, chemistry, and biology are at the opposite extreme: much more science than prescription. None of these fits as nicely with economics as medicine - a profession with one foot planted in medical science, the other in what we know as the practice of medicine" (Harberger, 1993:1).

practice benchmarks, and looking for overshooting or undershooting of expected performance targets in the market.

These are the new frontiers and directions in cost benefit analysis that Harberger (1993:12) believes need to be incorporated in applied welfare economics:

"As one who has written and taught in the field of applied welfare economics for more than four decades, and on the subject of cost benefit analysis of investment projects for more than three decades, I feel quite safe in stating that we do not have, in the United States, either the amount or the kind of training that is needed for our profession to make its appropriate contribution to our society's decision-making process...We need to take cost benefit analysis more seriously...[and] we need a significant volume of academic work to extend the frontiers of cost benefit analysis to new areas".

The *Report on the Health of the Tax System* places a strong emphasis on this vision of applied welfare economics. Through the application of the efficiency or performance ratio, the Report offers some new directions for applying cost benefit analysis to an assessment of the diverse and cumulative impacts of the tax system on individuals, firms and the economy. The result should permit some contribution toward the development of an applied theory of tax reform, a field in which there is considerable scope for new ideas. For example, Kay (1990:39) noted that "the theory of income tax reform has yet to be far developed".

A firm advocate of *applied* welfare economics, Feldstein (1976:77; 90; 93) critiqued both the practicality of the comprehensive income tax (Haig-Simons) because it is distortionary and hence inefficient, as well as the practicality of the formal optimal tax theory literature.[57] Instead, echoing Haavelmo's stress on starting points, Feldstein proposed starting with the tax system as it is, in its historical context (optimal tax reform), rather than assuming that one can start with a clean slate (optimal tax design, or optimal tax theory) and impose a perfect system in one fell swoop. Like Lipsey & Lancaster (1956), he cautioned against assuming that first best conditions do, or will ever, prevail in the real world, and promoted the use of dynamic analysis examining "the life-time path of consumption and labour supply" (Feldstein, 1976:88). Finally, he warned that an optimal tax reform approach will lead to a different "tax structure" (level, mix and rules) than optimal tax design. Alm (1996) has a similar view.

Bird (1992:x) was critical of the practical value of both the assumptions and conclusions that arise from formal optimal tax theory, with its normative emphasis and its reliance on formal welfare economics tools of analysis:

"Much fiscal analysis of developing countries is on the following pattern: the academic literature is drawn on to construct a model fiscal system; the existing situation in a particular country is examined to determine how it diverges from the model; and a fiscal reform is then proposed to transform what *is* into what *ought to be*. This approach is deficient because it does not require sufficiently detailed examination of existing reality to ensure that the assumptions postulated in the model are congruent with reality, that the recommended changes can in fact be implemented, or that, if implemented, they will in fact produce the desired result".

---

[57] For a similar view see Guesnerie (1977) and Buchanan (1975).

"In contrast, my approach is first to study in detail exactly *how* the existing system works, and *why* it works that way, in order to have a firm basis for understanding what changes may both be desirable and feasible. My emphasis has thus always been more on what *can* be done than on what *should* be done - if only it could be! This approach is both time-consuming and tends to induce caution with respect to drastic change. Nonetheless, experience shows that many administrative (and political) constraints must be accepted as immutable in the near term if one is to design a useful tax proposal for any country".

One of the principal deficiencies of the optimal tax theory literature is the difficulty of integrating the assumptions that drive the static models with the development of dynamic models:

"The reasons dynamic theory is less developed include problems with the analytical tractability of even those dynamic models which attempt to retain the basic structure of the static model. Furthermore, difficult and interesting issues arise in a dynamic context which are either not present or are much less severe in the static theory" (Stern, 1992:273).[58]

The key issues which arise in a dynamic context are "...(i) incorrect expectations, (ii) the generation of knowledge; (iii) dynamic inconsistency; (iv) the absence of [future] consumers from markets; and (v) modelling inter-temporal behaviour. Whilst some aspects of these have analogues in the static theory, crucial elements of each of them are not only essentially dynamic in nature but can take us substantially beyond the Arrow-Debreu framework" (Stern, 1992:289).[59]

Stern's summary of the difficulty in making the transition from the restrictive assumptions of static optimal tax theory to dynamic optimal tax theory suggests the need for an empirically based approach to taxation that reflects the behavioural responses of firms and individuals to taxation[60]. In particular, he observed that "we cannot... settle the issue between expenditure and income taxation on theoretical grounds" (Stern, 1992:286).

Slemrod (1990, 1991) has also called for a more empirically-based optimal tax theory because of the growing importance of the changing "technology of collecting taxes". But he goes further than that. He has called for the development of a "multidimensional measure of the success of a tax system"(Slemrod, 1991:74-5). His criteria were preliminary steps in the direction taken in this report. He posited several characteristics of a successful tax system:

- low rates and low allowances;
- a small number of tax rates, with minimal dispersion between the rates;

[58] Serious concerns about the value of applying the standard static assumptions from optimal tax theory to real world dynamic models have also been raised by Tanzi (1992), Buchanan (1993) and Griffith (1996). Taxation economics is not the only area where there is increasing discontent with the use of static assumptions and models. Rogerson (1997:75) notes that "modern theories of unemployment stress dynamic and stochastic elements... (M)uch language that once may have been viewed as useful is now either empty of meaning or dominated by clear precise terms that are standard in dynamic stochastic economic theory".
[59] Much earlier, Diewert (1981:1242) noted that the "fundamental problem is that it is difficult to define optimality in an economy with incomplete markets, a situation which characterises all real life economies".
[60] See the non-linear dynamic theoretical framework developed in Caragata & Small, 1996.

- equal priority between tax policy and tax administration;
- ensure that the *marginal cost of enforcement* never rise to the level of a marginal dollar of enforced revenue because of the deadweight loss considerations of enforcement; and
- emphasis on *rules* rather than *discretion* in order to avoid corruption.

More recently, Alm (1996) has underlined the growing frustration with formal optimal tax theory. There is;

"...a schism, if not animosity, between those who work on the rarefied heights of optimal tax theory and those who toil in the trenches of practical tax design...Optimal taxation ... is in fact largely irrelevant to practical tax design, because it typically ignores a range of considerations reflecting fiscal and societal institutions...In particular, [it] ignores the equity and efficiency effects that arise because taxes must be collected, at some cost both to the tax agency and the taxpayer, and this collection must be enforced, again at some cost to the agency and the individual. Given that most analyses in the optimal tax tradition ignore these features, their basic policy prescriptions are unlikely to lead to an improvement in welfare, when compared to those policies derived from a less formal but more realistic perspective; in fact, they are even unlikely to be implemented or to be taken as serious guides to policy."

The shift toward a more empirically-oriented optimal tax theory began in the 1980s and can be traced, as Blundell (1995:107) has noted, to two key factors:

"...the important questions growing out of applied theory research for which theory alone could not provide complete answers and ...from the dramatic increase in the accessibility of large micro-data-sets. The subsequent move toward the careful use of cross-section survey data provided considerable insight into distributional questions and gave life to theories based on individual behavioural responses to tax policy reform. However, gaining a reliable picture of behavioural responses has been a more difficult nut to crack".

Econometrics is a principal tool in the development of an empirical approach to optimal tax theory. The debate that is beginning to emerge in economics between the old, formal optimal tax theory approaches and the new applied, empirical science approach to tax policy is reminiscent of an earlier debate. That debate was over the explanation of business cycles in the 1920s and 1930s between Hayek, Robertson, Keynes, Myrdal and Lindahl, as the standard bearers of traditional theory, and Mitchell, Frisch, Tinbergen, and Schumpeter, representing the application of dynamic, empirical and econometric methods in economics to problem solving (Andvig, 1981). [61]

2.4 Taxation and Incentive Structures

The approach to tax evasion in the economic literature, generally, is to examine the causes of compliance for individuals. The literature on compliance motivation has been reviewed by Alm, McCelland and Schulze (1992) who summarise the motivations as follows: (1) the threat of detection and punishment create a deterrent effect; (2) some taxpayers miscalculate the odds of detection and over-estimate the chance of being caught; (3) some individuals believe that evasion is

[61] "The development of empirical business cycle research in the 1920s was a rather dramatic episode in the historical development of modern economics. Seldom has a research field increased so fast and apparently become so like a mature science" (Andvig, 1981:699).

morally wrong, and (4) some individuals pay tax because they place a high value on the services government provides.

An additional factor is the demonstration effect. Individuals will comply with tax system rules (insofar as they are understandable) as long as they see most other people doing the same thing. But, if confidence in the credibility of the tax system and government, and respect for the law in general, begins to break down and evasion begins to mount, those that were previously compliant taxpayers will begin to consider evasion as justified because more people are doing it. The same logic can be used to help explain mass looting during riots.

In general, however, economic theory has said relatively little about both tax avoidance and tax evasion (Kay, 1990:58). More fundamentally, Kaldor (1980:18) observed that "the existence of widespread tax avoidance is evidence that the system, not the taxpayer, stands in need of radical reform". Likewise, one could make the same case with respect to the presence of 'widespread' tax evasion.

Lindbeck (1986:36), who chaired the Committee of the Royal Swedish Academy of Science for the Prize in Economic Science in memory of Alfred Nobel, suggests that 'honesty' should be treated as a collective or public good and the government should "be careful not to construct economic and political systems that 'tax away' honesty". When taxes become too high, regulation too onerous and benefits too accessible, there are "increased temptations both to cheat the authorities over taxes and benefits" and engage in legal tax avoidance. In response,

"...the authorities in some of the most advanced welfare states have recently started to strengthen their efforts against such activities by increased control over the activities of individuals. Indeed, in Sweden, the development of a strong 'control state' is pronounced, with increased reporting, inquiry and control of the lives of citizens [i.e. the diminution of individual responsibility coupled with increased state monitoring and stiffer penalties e.g. for tax evasion], and with the burden of proof of innocence more and more shifted to the individual himself. This means the growth and interventionism of the public bureaucracy in a welfare state will be even more pronounced. There is also a tendency to reallocate resources within the legal system to fight economic crimes against the state, at the expense of resources devoted to the protection of, and the prosecution and punishment of crimes against, individuals" (Lindbeck, 1986:36).

Lindbeck's analysis suggests that at the micro level, there may be an optimal rate of taxation which would minimise the negative effect of tax on ethical conduct and thus honesty. That issue will be explored later.

Our particular concern here is to examine incentive effects of tax on companies rather than individuals. The approach is to assess the nature of the incentive structure of firms to avoid or evade taxes, rather than to examine the incentive structure of taxpayers to comply.

Incentive structures are shaped by both policy and institutional parameters (Olson, 1996) as well as the rewards for effort and the availability of opportunities to capture rewards. Thus both opportunities and constraints shape incentive structures. There are two types of opportunities: structural and cyclical.

Of course, in the finance and accounting literature, taxes are also generally recognised as a business cost because corporate taxes affect cash flow in the short-medium term and thus induce, along with other factors, efforts at tax minimisation (Scholes and Wolfson, 1992:2-3). This suggests that taxes can be a variable cost by choice, but it also suggests that the total amount of tax is capable of being strategically determined for some firms. Therefore, in the short term, taxes may be treated by some firms, depending on their ability, as a fixed cost rather than a variable cost of doing business[62]. The extent to which firms' effective tax payments (relative to a base such as sales, net assets, costs or gross profits) are fixed in the short term and variable in the long term, or variable across sectors, or variable across efficiency performance (Caragata, 1996), are empirical matters that require further investigation.

One tax minimisation strategy is to employ higher leverage in order to take advantage of interest deductibility. This can be a risky strategy because high leverage mandates high fixed interest costs that can tip the balance against corporate survival during recessions.

Empirical work previously undertaken across 10 countries suggests that for firms which pay tax, taxes range (quartal[63] medians) between 0.25% and 8.0% of total costs. Thus, the reward for the minimisation of the tax burden can be significant. These percentages represent a large share of the gross margin (Caragata, 1996) and help to put in perspective the attractions of tax avoidance and evasion.

Taxes and the Incentive Structures of Firms: The Direct and Indirect Effects of Company Taxation

Because taxes have a current and potential impact on a firm's cash flow they affect the immediate choices that firms make. In particular, those choices concern the decisions to purchase inputs, to avoid or evade taxes, produce outputs, and make investments. Compliance costs also have an immediate effect on cash flow because they are current and possibly permanent (depending on the success of future minimisation efforts) costs. Thus, compliance costs are direct effects of taxation and affect the productive and dynamic efficiency performance of the firm just like taxes.

Regardless of how long these effects persist, they are the direct consequences of taxation. In other words, the direct effects should not be considered the short-term effects, and the indirect effects should not be considered the long-term effects. A better distinction is that the direct effects of taxation are the micro effects that affect the choices and behaviour (and hence the incentive structure) of taxpayers. The relative effects of taxation across firms and the macro consequences of taxation should be considered the indirect effects.

---

[62] For the first treatment of taxes as a fixed cost of doing business, see Ripley's (1921) work on *Railroads: Rates and Regulations* (chapter ii) as reported in Clark (1923:11).

[63] The term 'quartals' (quadrisections of a skewed distribution) was noted in Gibrat, 1931, 1957:67). The original source is Dudley Baxter, 1868, *National Income*.

For example, a firm may eventually shift production to another jurisdiction. That decision is still a direct effect of taxation, regardless of how long the lag is between the imposition of the tax or tax change, and the decision to shift investment. The observable effects of tax on choice and behaviour are the direct effects of taxes. Indirect effects would include the impact of taxes on the relative or cumulative development of (1) competition across firms within one sector or across sectors; (2) the pattern of investment, which is one aspect of macro allocative efficiency effects; (3) international competitiveness; (3) the growth of the hidden economy and the tax gap; (4) the loss of output or production across all firms; (5) the pattern of resource use - another aspect of the macro allocative efficiency effects; (6) employment; and (7) investment.

In this framework, the deadweight loss at the macro level is an indirect effect of taxes. At the micro level, it is a direct cost to the firm because the firm suffers a direct reduction in cash flow and this has a direct effect on the purchasing, avoidance, production and investment behaviour of the firm.

The following discussion briefly elaborates on the direct effects of taxation. The spending behaviour of firms largely concerns the choices to purchase one input as compared to another (supply-side substitution effects) as compared to purchasing one input along with another (supply-side complementarity effects). The choice between labour and capital, or between labour and taxes that a firm makes because of taxation is a direct effect of taxes. The potentially preventable tax avoidance behaviour of firms largely concerns the choices among the levels at which tax can be minimised within the framework of the law. Expenditures on avoidance advice would be considered a direct cost.

The production behaviour of firms largely concerns the choices to continue or not to continue producing various outputs in current locations. Changes to the price of products as a result of a tax change would be considered a direct effect. The investment behaviour of firms largely concerns the choices among maintaining, diminishing or increasing the scale and scope of production facilities. Changes to the cost of the next unit of investment would be considered a dynamic direct effect of taxes.

Summary

Applied welfare economics and efficiency theory require that both actual performance and potential performance be based on empirical estimates. After these estimations have been made, normative assessments about the best ways to close the gap between actual and potential performance can be introduced. The gap between actual and potential performance is deadweight loss.

The under-performance of economies is a widespread problem. Countries do not operate on the efficiency frontier. As a result, the output reduction for many countries can be "measured in the trillions of dollars" (Olson, 1996:22). Taxes are one factor that shape this under-performance. An optimal incentive structure will promote economic growth if it minimises risks for investors, provides an efficient institutional framework, maximises capital accumulation and human capital development, finds the right balance between the size of government and the role of the market and ensures good quality monetary, fiscal and trade policy. A performance or "health" gap arises where there are departures from the optimal incentive structure.

3. NEW ZEALAND TAX BURDEN, TAX MIX AND EXPENDITURE TRENDS IN THE TWENTIETH CENTURY

3.1 Tax Burden Trends: 1890-1994

The total tax burden and the tax mix have very important revenue (including compliance), efficiency and equity consequences. The total tax burden is defined as total tax revenue divided by GDP, while the tax mix is composed of personal taxes, indirect taxes, corporate taxes and other taxes relative to GDP. Both the total tax burden and the tax mix are constantly changing across time for policy, structural and cyclical reasons. These long and short-term trends need to be understood thoroughly before the health of the tax system is analysed in order to provide an appropriate perspective.

As is the case in many OECD countries in the post-war period, New Zealand's tax system became progressively more complex and burdensome for individuals, business and the economy. The tax system was characterised by large loopholes in the tax base created by tax favouritism for specialist interest groups. This ultimately led to tax reform, beginning in the mid-1980s, which was characterised by the reduction of statutory tax rates, the reduction of the number of personal tax rates, broadening of the tax base, simplification, and greater attention to compliance costs. The complexity of the previous tax has been captured by Brash (1996:16):

"Prior to its reform, the New Zealand tax system was an awful mess judged by almost any standard. Personal income tax rates were ostensibly steeply progressive, reaching a top marginal rate of 66 percent, but that rate of tax was reached at such a relatively low level of income (NZ$38,000 per annum) that avoidance and evasion were widespread – with resultant loss of revenue and considerable misallocation of investment (to tax advantage of tax shelters). Whole sales taxes were widely used, but varied from very low rates to 50 percent, with the higher tax rates sometimes applying to items for no better reason than that they did not form part of the CPI regimen, and so would not adversely affect the measured inflation rate".

Tax reform included the elimination of the wholesale sales taxes, the introduction of a comprehensive Goods and Services Tax (GST), excluding only financial transactions, elimination of tax subsidies and most industry-specific concessions, and the closing of many loopholes with respect to financing, intra-company transactions and overseas investments. The principal problem with the reform was that it raised the overall tax burden by about 6 percentage points of GDP by the early 1990s. This higher tax burden had important negative implications for tax evasion and, it appears, has placed a constraint on improving economic growth and employment.

3.2 The Ratios of Tax Revenue Streams to GDP: Total Tax/GDP Ratio

Figure 3.1 illustrates data on the tax/GDP ratio for NZ over the period 1918-1995, roughly three-quarters of a century of experience, and includes a step-wise presentation of the decade averages for the ratio. Unfortunately, GDP data for earlier years are not available. **Table 3.1** summarises the tax/GDP averages

Figure 3.1
Total Tax Revenue as a Percentage of GDP in New Zealand (with Decade Averages): 1918-95

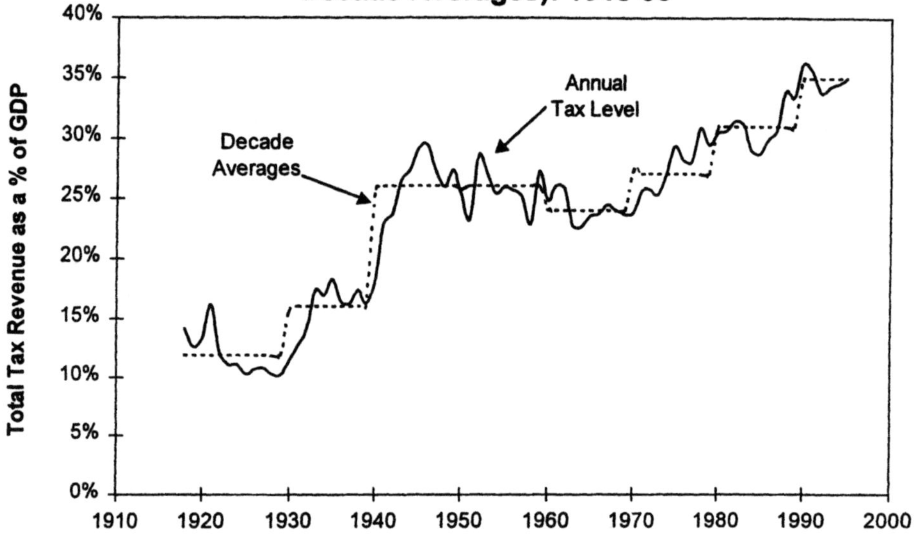

Source: NZ Institute of Economic Research, Inland Revenue, Treasury

Table 3.1
The Evolution of the Tax Burden and Tax Mix in New Zealand: 1918-1995

Period	Direct Tax/ GDP Ratio	% of Total	Indirect Tax/ GDP Ratio	% of Total	Tax/GDP Ratio	Direct/ Indirect Tax Ratio	Personal/ Corporate Tax Ratio
1890-99	n/a	n/a	n/a	n/a	n/a	0.20	n/a
1900-09	n/a	n/a	n/a	n/a	n/a	0.32	n/a
1910-19	8.5*	63.0	5.0*	27.0	13.5*	0.78	0.51*
1920-29	5.1	44.4	6.4	55.6	11.9	0.78	0.51
1930-39	6.9	43.7	8.9	56.3	15.8	0.77	1.72
1940-49	16.8	65.4	8.9	34.6	25.7	1.85	2.33
1950-59	16.8	65.9	8.7	34.1	25.5	1.93	2.52
1960-69	16.3	67.4	7.9	32.6	24.2	2.08	3.83
1970-79	20.0	73.0	7.4	27.0	27.4	2.68	4.27
1980-89	22.1	71.8	8.7	28.2	30.9	2.64	6.78
1990-95	22.3	64.1	12.5	35.9	34.8	1.77	4.36

* 1918 and 1919 only
Source: Inland Revenue, 1996

per decade as well as the direct and indirect tax/GDP ratios and their respective shares of total tax.

In the 1920s, the average tax/GDP ratio was 11.9%. This represented a decline of 2 percentage points over the last two years of the previous decade, reflecting a drop in government expenditure after World War I, similar to what happened after World War II. In the 1930s, the average ratio rose to 15.8% of GDP, a 33% increase. This jump of 4 percentage points of GDP over the previous decade partly reflects the decline of GDP, rising indirect taxes, and the new social security tax.

In the 1940s, the average tax/GDP ratio jumped again, this time to 25.7%, representing an increase of 63%. This dramatic increase of 10 percentage points of GDP could be one measure of the cost to NZ of its participation in World War II. This suggests that NZ's initial down-payment on the welfare state was about 40% of the cost of World War II, in terms of tax dollars raised to pay the bills. The increase in the tax/GDP ratio at the beginning of World War II was the largest increase this century. WW II marked the real watershed in the development of the country's tax system. After the war, the tax take did not drop back down for very long, suggesting that unless there is deliberate policy intent, major tax increases, even if only identified as temporary, may very well become permanent because decision-makers, advisers and voters develop new ideas on how to spend existing revenue. After the WW II, expenditures that had previously been applied to the war effort were shifted to building the welfare state and the education system.

Over the 1950s and 1960s, the tax/GDP ratio was relatively stable, remaining around 25%. In the 1970s, there was yet again another rise in the average ratio, this time to 27.4%, an increase of 13% over the 1960s' average. The probable causes of this 3.2 percentage point jump include the cost of government intervention in the aftermath of the oil crisis of 1973-74, the related jump in inflation which affected taxes paid on incomes, and the increase in transfers as a share of total expenditure which are explained in detail in Section 3.5. **Figure 3.2** presents actual and projected government expenditure relative to GDP for the period 1950-2000.

In the 1980s, with respect to the tax/GDP ratio, there was a slightly larger jump of 3.4 percentage points to 30.9% of GDP. This increase may be attributed to bracket creep arising from inflation, the introduction of GST in 1987, and the gradual tightening up of loopholes as a result of sustained tax reform that began under the new Labour government in 1984. In the first half of the 1990s, the tax/GDP ratio has experienced a dramatic jump to 34.8% (through to the end of 1995 and prior to the 1996 tax cuts). The probable causes of the 13% increase in the average ratio are the continuation of tax reform under the National government beginning in 1990 and the economic recovery beginning in 1992.

Figure 3.2
Government Expenditure as a Percentage of GDP in New Zealand: 1950-2000

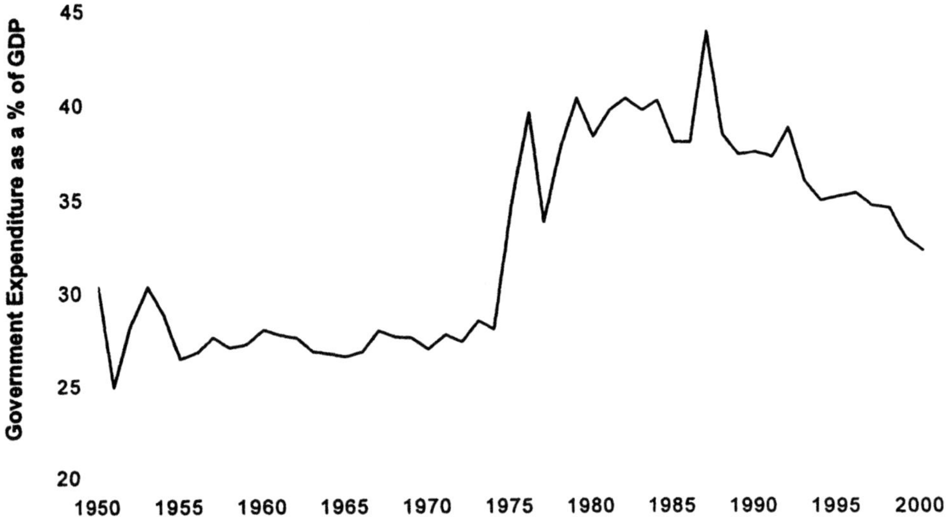

Source: New Zealand Planning Council, Treasury

Table 3.2
Thresholds in New Zealand's Tax Burden and Tax Mix: 1918-1995

Tax/GDP Ratio	
1921	rises above 15% for the first time
1941	rises above 20% for the first time
1943	rises above 25% for the first time
1980	rises above 30% for the first time
1990	rises above 35% for the first time
Direct Tax/GDP Ratio	
1940	hits 10% for the first time and surpasses indirect taxes permanently
1941	hits 15% for the first time
1945	hits 20% for the first time
1978	hits peak at 24%
Indirect Tax/GDP Ratio	
1935	hits 10% for the first time.
1948	hits 11% for the first time.
1988	hits 12% for the first time.

Source: Inland Revenue, 1996

As summarised in **Table 3.2**, the principal turning points for the tax/GDP ratio occurred in 1921 (breaches 15% for the first time), 1941 (breaches 20%), 1943 (breaches 25%), 1980 (breaches 30%), and 1990 (breaches 35%). The tax/GDP ratio in 1996 remains close to 35%.

Why is the actual aggregate tax burden at an historic high?

What factors explain why the total tax to GDP ratio is at an historic high in NZ? Rose (1985) has developed an empirical based theory that provides a beginning. During World War II most Western governments raised taxes to meet the financial requirements of the emergency. With a few exceptions, why did these higher tax levels persist and increase after the war? Rose's theory of *the law of inverse tax reform* offers some insights. The more important the revenue source, the harder it is to make all but small changes.

"*The amount of change that can purposefully be introduced into a national tax structure varies inversely with its effect on total tax revenue.* The more money that a tax raises, the greater its inertia force, whether in motion (a force against repeal) or stationary (a force against adoption). Conversely, the less money raised by a tax, the easier it is to alter because it will have virtually nil effect on total revenue. From a revenue perspective, tax reform is about fringe tuning; it must leave the core of revenue secure" (Rose, 1985: 316).

Rose[64] also observed that new types of taxes are generally not large revenue producers. In New Zealand, an exception to this rule occurred with the introduction of GST, because taxpayers were promised and received a simultaneous cut in high marginal tax rates on personal income.

Rose's theory examines the preference politicians have for "minimising political costs through taxation by inertia". This is just a complicated way of saying that the status quo is like a security blanket for many politicians and they become dependant on existing revenue sources that solve current problems. It is easy to justify current spending patterns because of economic and political constraints, and hard to depart from. Among the factors that concerned him were: inherited obligations, the ratchet effect (up is easier than down), politicians' risk aversion, consistency in revenue policy, and tax revenue buoyancy (inflation raises total revenue). These factors provide some insights into the inertia that helps to protect high tax regimes, but there are other equally important factors as well.

A complementary approach is to explain why expenditures rise and remain high. Lindbeck (1995) links the disconnection between paying tax and receiving benefits combined with an habituation to benefits by a growing *majority* on the demand side, and the iterative (reflecting inherited obligations) nature of expenditure systems:

---

[64] "Successful proposals for new taxes usually contribute little to public revenue; the motive for their adoption is not to increase revenue but to promote economic activity, simplify the administration of taxation, or occasionally advance what is perceived as greater horizontal or vertical equity. Very occasionally, a new tax may balloon up, producing large revenues after it has been in effect for decades or, in the case of income tax, a century." (Rose, 1985:305) op cit.

"...in the same way that the combination of specific benefits and general financing, strengthened by the recursiveness [sequential nature] of the spending process, all help to explain the expansion of the welfare state, the same factors all help to explain why it is politically difficult to reverse the process. An unwinding of welfare-state spending could be expected to be particularly difficult in societies where a large share of the electorate is financed by the public sector (i.e. tax financed rather than market financed)" (Lindbeck, 1995:14).

The disconnection between tax and expenditure may be based on taxpayer ignorance that higher taxes are needed to pay for higher expenditures, and that lower taxes cannot be paired with frozen or higher expenditures. This is a combined taxpayer perception, motivation and information problem. But the problem also arises because taxes are not targeted, or that expenditure is not generalised instead of being targeted.

One way around this latter problem is to have taxpayers vote on how they want their money to be spent. But the probability of that idea catching on is not necessarily high. The alternative is to provide taxpayers with more information about the impacts of taxes raised and expenditures allocated, and the related costs and benefits. The problem of reducing habituation to tax-financed income is a matter of relative incentives to work and a deeper understanding of the relative efficiency of government as compared to private sector operations.

To do proper justice to the analysis we need to differentiate between the factors that give rise to high taxes in the first place and those that sustain taxes at high levels, for they may not necessarily be the same. Very briefly, the factors promoting higher spending and taxes are: (1) external and domestic crises (crises have been important in New Zealand); (2) political and bureaucratic ambitions to create new benefits for voters as the need arises; (3) the short time horizon of politicians and bureaucrats; (4) tax revenue buoyancy; (5) pressure group activity for *specific benefits*; and (6) demographic trends and future commitments.

In addition, there at least six factors that help to ensure that taxes remain high: (1) inherited obligations; (2) the ratchet effect; (3) risk aversion by politicians and bureaucrats; (4) taxpayer information deficiency; (5) tax reform fatigue; and (6) the de-motivation of taxpayers who are distracted, alienated, tired of major tax reform, or evading tax because they are fed-up, opportunistic, or both. These points are briefly outlined below.

Factors Promoting Higher Taxes

(1) Crisis Management:

The development of domestic and international constraints can force governments into a financial crisis cycle, where first they borrow to raise spending to resolve a problem, and then need to raise taxes to pay for on-going debt service costs. The domestic constraints in New Zealand have included: (1) paying down the debt incurred during World War II; (2) rewarding soldiers for military service; (3) pursuing more comprehensive social and education policies;

and (4) coping with the rising indebtedness stemming from the Think Big energy projects and other government waste.

The international constraints that affected government expenditure included: World War II, the Korean War, the Vietnam War, the Cold War, the loss of preferential access to the UK market, and the two energy crises. When government is successful in managing such crises the public, perhaps unwisely, develops confidence that government can do even more things successfully.

In New Zealand, the government's handling of new social welfare legislation in the late 1930s and its successful conduct of New Zealand's war effort imbued the public with strong confidence in the efficacy of government. This created momentum for the development of the post-war welfare state.

(2) Ambitions of Politicians and Bureaucrats:

Ambitions are stirred during crises, serious challenges to the existing order, and when new visions of reality are given birth. Once politicians get a taste for raising taxes and the new spending implications, it is very hard to give up the appetite. That taste seems to arise most strongly in response to crises, such as war, depression, or oil shocks, and in response to the threat that most western politicians perceived arose from communism and socialism. When faced with crisis and threats politicians are most bold in promoting new ideas and competing for voter support.

But there have also been new theoretical visions about the role of the state. Bold new visions (e.g. the new role conceptualised for government in the 1930s, 1940s and 1950s by Keynes, Musgrave and others, that the state has an important role in providing allocative, stabilisation and redistributive functions) provided incentives for politicians and bureaucrats to advance new proposals for widening the scope of governmental responsibility (Tanzi & Schuknecht, 1995:5). Welfare economics also has played a very important role in enhancing the role of government because of its strong *normative* overtones. Thus, politicians over the last 50 years have increasingly embraced advice about what they *should* do based on normative views of reality that, in many cases, were founded on very unrealistic assumptions.

Many bureaucrats identify success with larger budgets, rather than delivering "more with less", and providing taxpayers with value for money. Buchanan (1974:161) has summarised this aspect of the incentives for bureaucrats:

"There is little or no potential reward to the government employee who proposes to reduce or limit his own agency or bureau. Institutionally, the individual bureaucrat is motivated toward aggrandisement of his own agency. And, since the effective [employment] alternatives for most governmental employees are other agencies and projects, this motivation for expansion will extend to government generally".

Bureaucrats have also become much more sophisticated and better educated over the course of the century. This professionalisation of the bureaucracy enhances its ability to deliver what politicians want, and of course, to develop their own ideas on how the state should be run. Each department of government is a lobby group for government action. In fact, departments have the inside track, as compared to external lobby groups, because they have better information, a contractual obligation to deliver outputs for Cabinet, and they have a right to offer 'free and frank advice" without prejudice.

(3) Short time horizon:

The incentive structure is improperly developed for both politicians and bureaucrats to control expenditures and emphasise efficiency because the time horizons of both is short, perhaps 1-2 years at most, and typically less, coinciding with the current work program and the development of the next budget. Both of these incentives can thwart fiscal responsibility. Since the implementation of the Fiscal Responsibility Act (1992) in New Zealand that is harder, but the new Act would certainly not impede a determined government from raising taxes.

It is important that much longer term horizons are embraced by both politicians and bureaucrats because all policy decisions have long term consequences. New Zealand is still paying off the debt that arose because of the failed Think Big energy projects, the early retirement scheme of 1978 and other government expenditure in the 1970s-1980s.

(1) *Pressure group activity*:

As the state gets bigger, more lobby groups arise to bid for special benefits from government. This rent-seeking behaviour, when it succeeds, which can be quite often, leads to a greater level of government expenditure. As Buchanan and Tullock (1971:286-87) noted;

"the activities and the importance of special-interest groups in the political process are not independent of either the over-all size or the composition of the government budget...The organised pressure group ...arises because differential advantages are expected to be secured through the political process, and, in turn, differential advantages for particular groups are produced because of the existence of organised activity".

Tanzi & Schuknecht (1995:5), in examining the powerful leap in the size of the state for most OECD countries over the period 1960-1980 attributed the leap in part to "the tyranny of past commitments" and "the power of interest groups".

(5) Tax revenue buoyancy[65]:

Tax buoyancy arises where the level of taxes increases faster than real GDP owing to the combined effect of growth and inflation's on statutory tax rates which bring many people into higher tax brackets. "Buoyancy" is a major reason

[65] "The buoyancy of a tax's contributions to total national revenue, i.e. its propensity to rise faster than the increase in national product due to the conjoint effect of economic growth and inflation, can be indicated by dividing the percentage increase in the current-money revenue yield of a given tax by the percentage increase in the current-money value of the gross domestic product during the same period" (Rose, 1985:309)

for the emphasis on personal income tax, social security taxes, VAT, and sales taxes (Rose, 1985: 309-10).

(6) Demographic trends and future commitments:

In the future, three factors may lead to higher tax/GDP ratio for many OECD countries: (1) social security and health expenditure obligations as the baby boom generation retires after the turn of the century; (2) equity considerations; and (3) the greater risk absorption role played by government as economies become more open.[66] Of these three, the most important are future commitments to superannuation and health driven by demographic trends. The constraints that superannuation obligations will place on the budget will be examined later.

Factors Sustaining Higher Taxes

***(1) Inherited obligations*:**

There is a need for consistency and reliability of tax revenue to finance "inherited obligations" (including various social programs, defence spending contracts and interest payments on government debt) or new programs. In many OECD countries rising interest payments now account for larger share of national expenditure than defence spending (Rose, 1985:304; 312; 316).

(2) *Ratchet effect*:

Recall that taxes in NZ, especially on personal income, jumped considerably because of World War II and never came down for long afterwards. This *ratchet effect* occurred because it was easier for politicians to retain and make marginal adjustments to past new tax revenue generating measures, regardless of a change in purpose, owing to various new demands from interest groups for new services, than it was to give up that revenue and revert to a lower level of taxation in the economy. (Rose, 1985:305; 314).

Raising taxes can be addictive because of the positive response of those benefiting. Many new social programs are very valuable for their reduction of pain, suffering, ignorance, discrimination etc. Thus, lowering taxes is seen to cause more pain than raising taxes. This means that when taxes go up they seldom come down, or at least it is very difficult to bring them down. As a recent Nobel Prize winner noted:

"When the list or menu for political choice is not predetermined [e.g. by commitments to voters]...the directional bias towards expanded budgets again arises. The politician who secures his utility only because he chooses for and thereby pleases the largest number of constituents will

---

[66] Experience suggests that "public spending is a risk-reducing instrument on which there is greater reliance in more open economies" (Rodik, D., "Why Do More Open Economies Have Bigger Governments?", *NBER Working Paper Series*, Working Paper 5537, December, Cambridge, MA: National Bureau of Economic Research p3). The quality of that spending, of course, is another matter, but it is clear that interest groups apply pressure to secure regulatory intervention to minimise the risks of external shocks. The recent policy changes in NZ appear to have reduced the need for such shock absorption, but only time will tell.

find that favourable action on differentially beneficial projects offers more reward than favourable action reducing general tax costs" (Buchanan, 1974:157-8).

(3) Risk aversion:

Politicians and bureaucrats tend to be risk averse and generally prefer "keeping out of trouble" by avoiding the blame and controversy for new taxes, or the blame for cutting programs. (Rose, 1985:306-7).

(4) Information deficiency:

If people are ill-informed, they may not focus properly on the risks. This reinforces the status quo with respect to the level of taxation. The absence of information about the cumulative efficiency consequences of taxation and the increase in tax evasion and avoidance arising from higher total taxes can also have an important influence in preserving the status quo with respect to the level of taxation. In essence, taxpayers need much more public information about the consequences of higher taxes, and about the impacts of proposed new taxes. This important factor can also be considered as a contributor to the rising level of taxes.

(5) Tax reform fatigue:

Tax reform fatigue can set in after years of important changes to tax legislation. The multiplicity of small changes and the growing complexity of the tax system can overwhelm taxpayers, tax professionals, bureaucrats and politicians, with the result that there is less enthusiasm for more big changes. As a result, there is less interest in re-appraising the consequences of the existing tax system.

(6) De-motivation of the taxpayer:

Finally, there is *the de-motivation of the taxpayer*. Some taxpayers become jaded and disillusioned about the tax system. Many do not understand what *voluntary compliance* means. Many complain about paying tax and getting nothing in return. They feel alienated and powerless to change their burden. Many taxpayers become distracted because of past or future personal concerns. They may even engage in some tax evasion, for whatever reason, and therefore stop thinking about the amount of tax they *should* pay. Most would not think about what an effective tax rate is, in terms of the total tax burden they pay (including local tax). Sometimes that alienation and frustration with the tax system, however, bubbles to the surface and is capitalised on by political parties and has some important consequences.

The California tax property tax revolt of 1978 (Proposition 13)[67], the election of Margaret Thatcher's Conservative Party in 1979 in Britain and Ronald Reagan's Republican presidential election victory in 1980 in the US signalled that political

[67] In June 1978 California voters approved Proposition 13 by a 2 to 1 majority in a state-wide referendum. As a result, a constitutional restriction was placed on taxes on real property, with a ceiling of 1 percent of market value being imposed.

movements or parties could turn tax frustration into votes. The tax reform that was initiated in NZ in the mid-1980s was similar, although more far-reaching than in other OECD countries, and was triggered by factors similar to those in other countries. John Kay (1990:18), a prominent British economist, has summarised these developments as a "revolt" against higher levels of tax and the multiplicity of rates, leading to general support in the OECD member countries for "lower direct tax rates on a broader base". But, quite frequently the taxpayer is too alienated and distracted to become deeply involved in tax policy issues.

Direct Tax/GDP Ratio

In the period 1918-1919 (**Table 3.1**) the ratio of direct taxes to GDP was 8.5%, dropping to 5.1% in the 1920s. Roughly two percentage points were added during the course of the next decade. The most dramatic jump this century occurred in the 1940s when the ratio climbed to 16.8%, an increase over the previous decade of 143%.

The path of the *direct tax/GDP ratio* is illustrated in **Figure 3.3** while the major trends are presented in **Table 3.2**. The principal turning points for the ratio occurred in 1921 (hits 10% for the first time), 1941 (hits 15%), 1945 (hits 20%), and 1978 (peaks at 24% of GDP). It is evident that the government requirement for revenue during World War II was largely responsible for tipping the balance of the tax mix in favour of personal income, and for raising the tax/GDP ratio to a new, long-term plateau.

Indirect Tax/GDP Ratio

The evolution of the *indirect tax/GDP ratio* is illustrated in **Figure 3.3**, while the major trends are provided in **Table 3.2**. The principal turning points for the indirect tax/GDP ratio occurred in 1934 (hits 10% for the first time), after which it dipped slightly for a decade. In 1948, the ratio hit 11%, and again dipped to high single digit numbers until 1988 when it reached 12%. It has remained at the 12% level ever since. Indirect taxes were given their first big boost during the Great Depression in order to help finance the welfare state. Probably the next most important step was the introduction of GST in 1987.

At the end of 1930 in NZ, indirect taxes rose to a post World War I high of $25.4 million, or 65.2% of total revenue, while personal tax was only $2.4 million or 6.2% of total tax revenue, a drop of over 50% from WW I when the income tax was first introduced, and company tax was $4.6 million, or 11.8% of the total. By 1936, as the development of the welfare state was underway, indirect tax revenue had risen to $29.8 million or 58.5% of total tax. This was the peak of the contribution of indirect taxes to the tax mix during the period 1932-1995.

Social security taxes, which had commenced in 1931 at $600,000 had risen to $7.8 million by 1936, and together with personal income tax accounted for $11.1 million, or 21.8% of total tax in 1936. Meanwhile, corporate tax reached $5.8 million, or 11.4% of total tax. Other taxes accounted for about 8% of the total.

Figure 3.3
Direct and Indirect Components of the Tax Mix as Percentages of GDP in New Zealand: 1918-95

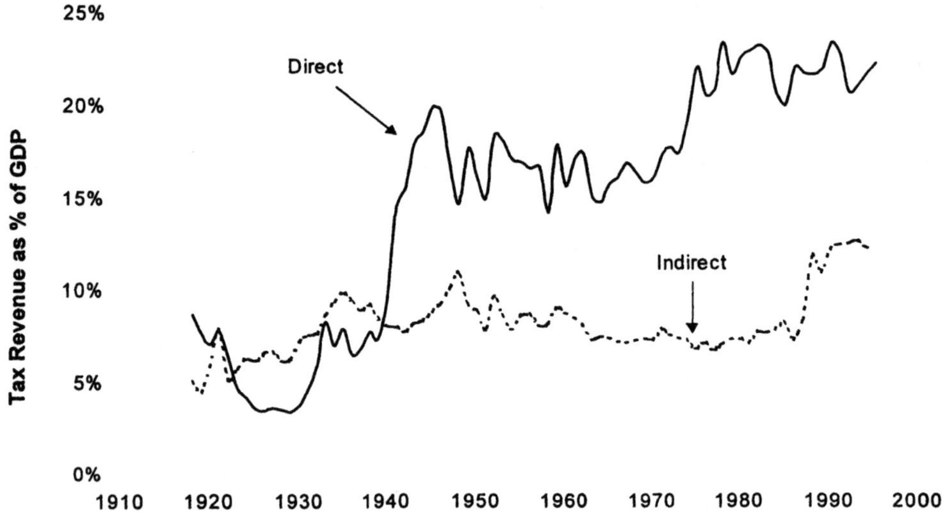

Source: NZ Institute of Economic Research, Inland Revenue, Treasury 1996

Figure 3.4
The Ratio of Direct to Indirect Tax Revenue in New Zealand: 1890-1995

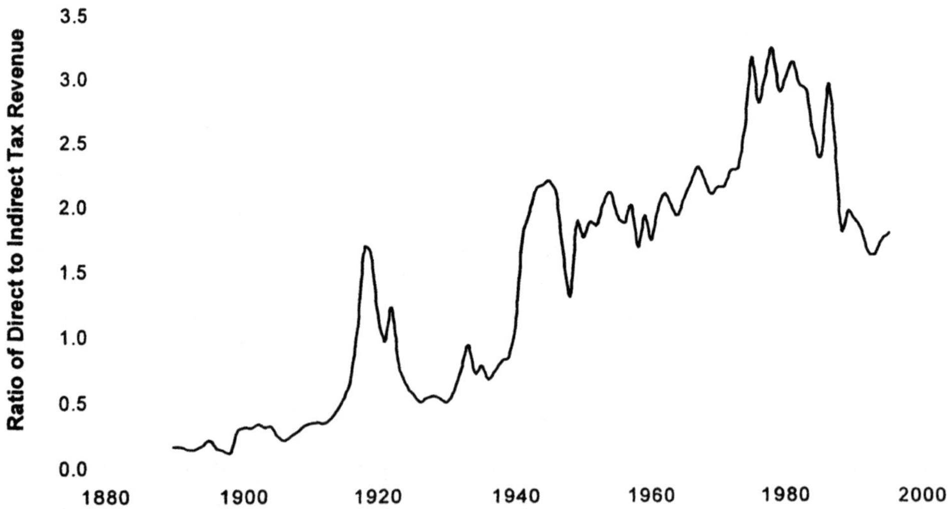

Source: NZ Institute of Economic Research, Inland Revenue, Treasury 1996

Thus, at that time, the easiest way to extract tax from the economy was through indirect taxes that formed the largest portion of the fiscal base for funding the development of the welfare state.

Given that indirect taxes are considered by some to be less equitable than direct taxes, in retrospect, it is ironic that the origin of the modern welfare state, which was intended to enhance equity, was financed more by the use of indirect rather than direct tax revenue. Perhaps this funding pattern in the 1930s reflected the increase in tariffs under the protectionist state. It may also have been a reflection of the high level of unemployment, and the immaturity of the income tax system, as much as it was a search for the most efficient means of revenue collection. On the other hand, a higher level of indirect taxes can be used to increase spending to the disadvantaged, so indirect taxes should not be seen as necessarily regressive.

3.3 The Evolution of the Tax Mix

The Balance Between Direct and Indirect Taxes

Figure 3.3 clearly demonstrates that World War II was a watershed in the development of the tax mix in NZ. During the war, the tax mix shifted dramatically in favour of direct taxes. To better illustrate this shift we have constructed a direct/indirect tax ratio (**Figure 3.4**). As indicated in **Table 3.1** in the 1890s, the aggregate amount of direct taxes was only about 20% of the value of indirect taxes. That is to say, for each dollar of taxes raised through indirect taxes, 20 cents was raised by direct taxes.

Over the course of the next 30 years, the ratio of direct to indirect taxes rose and then stabilised at about 0.78. Hence, for the first 50 years of the last 100 years, indirect taxes were the dominant form of taxation by quite a margin, while for the next 50 years direct taxes have been dominant.

All the Allies in World War I introduced some form of personal income tax withholding. This created the first major shift in the tax mix. In 1918 the direct/indirect tax ratio climbed to 1.7 as compared, for example, to only 0.73 in 1916. The ratio remained above, or at, 1.0 until 1923, when it dropped to 0.83 and then declined more or less progressively to a nadir of 0.53 in 1930. Here was the first indication that during a war-time economy direct taxes were a preferred instrument for revenue extraction from the economy.

As observed earlier, World War II played a crucial role in catapulting direct taxes into a permanent, pre-eminent position. During the 1940s, the ratio of direct to indirect taxes rose to 1.85, and then climbed steadily to 1.93 in the 1950s, to 2.08 in the 1960s and peaked in the 1970s at 2.68. The revenue impact of GST, beginning in 1987, forced the ratio down to 2.64, and that change, combined with the economic recovery[68] beginning in 1992, led the average ratio to dip to 1.77

[68] New Zealand has undergone major economic reforms in the last decade designed to rebalance the relationship between the state and the market (e.g. removal of agricultural subsidies, strict control of inflation, removal of foreign exchange controls, freer international trade, fiscal discipline and

for the first half of the decade, approximating the ratio 50 years earlier in the 1940s. The most recent data for 1995 indicate that the ratio was 1.8. Thus, currently, $1.80 of direct taxes is collected per dollar of indirect tax.

It would appear that the generic tax mix, direct versus indirect, has historically been chosen largely with an emphasis on revenue collection efficiency as a first priority, and the balance between the two has adjusted as opinion has changed about the revenue collection efficiency of each. Equity considerations, reflecting the development of the welfare state after World War II, would appear to have been the next most important factor in influencing the choice of the mix, and helped to sustain the increase in the level and number of rates over the next few decades.

The principal benefits of the 1980s tax reforms were: (1) the reduction of distortions in the pattern of investment as a result of the removal of accelerated depreciation and export incentives, (2) the reduction in the tax favouritism toward debt through the introduction of the imputation regime that removed the double taxation of dividends, and (3) the reduction of tax avoidance by the closure of loopholes (fringe benefit tax; the CFC and FIF regimes; and in 1991, the elimination of tax favouritism for redeemable preference shares). The tax cuts beginning in 1996 and for 1998 are targeted at improving the incentives for individuals to work, save, invent and invest, by raising after-tax disposable income. In brief, the 1980s tax reforms have improved the allocative efficiency of New Zealand, while the 1990s tax cuts are likely to improve the technical or output efficiency of the economy.

The Balance Between Personal and Corporate Taxes

Figure 3.5 presents the evolution of the balance of the components of direct tax over the period 1918-1995. **Figure 3.6** examines the ratio of personal tax to corporate tax over the same period. Decade averages for the ratio are presented in **Table 3.1. Table 3.2** examines the key thresholds.

In the aftermath of World War I and during the 1920s, the ratio of the personal to corporate tax mix was about 0.5. By 1931 the weight of the two came into balance and has never reverted back since. The principal thresholds for the ratio were reached in 1933 (rises above 2.0 for the first time), 1978 (rises above 5.0), 1979 (rises above 7.0), 1982 (rises above 8.0) and 1984 (almost reached 9.0). Since then there has been a very rapid decline. The decade averages reached a high of 6.8 in the 1980s, and then dipped to 4.4 in the first half of the 1990s.

Early in the century, for each dollar of tax raised by corporate taxes, 50 cents was raised through personal taxes, as compared to $4.40 on average in the 1990s. This represents another dramatic shift in the tax mix, and raises questions about the appropriate level for direct tax. Given that the tax/GDP ratio

---

reductions of public debt, privatization of state-owned enterprise, labour market reforms, and so on). The move to a less interventionist and more market-oriented set of policies has resuscitated economic progress.

Figure 3.5
Components of Total Tax Revenue from Direct Taxation as Percentages of GDP in New Zealand: 1918-95

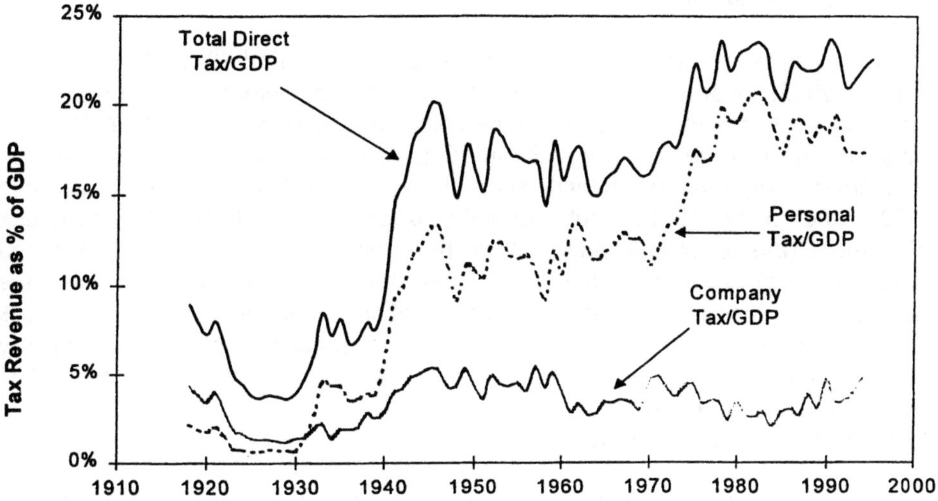

Source: NZ Institute of Economic Research, Inland Revenue, Treasury 1996

Figure 3.6
The Ratio of Personal to Corporate Tax Revenue in New Zealand (with Decade Averages): 1918-95

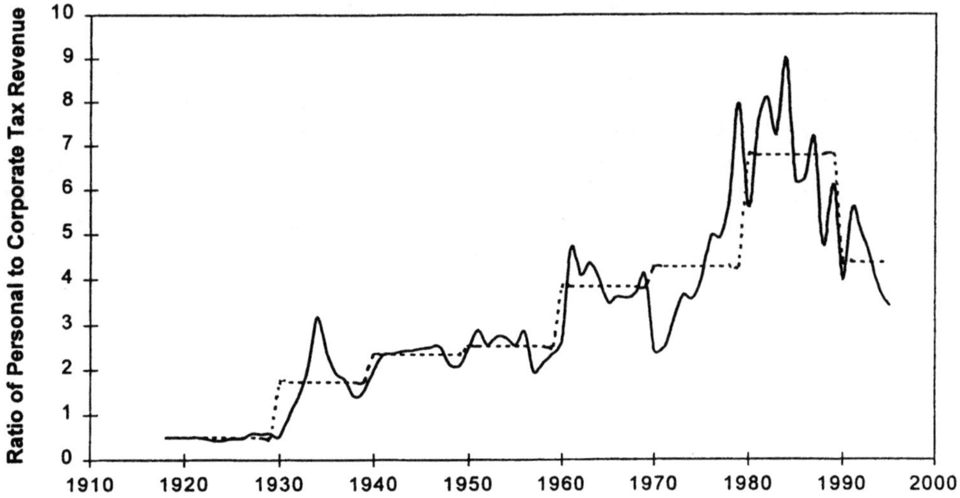

Source: NZ Institute of Economic Research, Inland Revenue, Treasury

is now close to an historic high and, as indicated later see below, that corporate tax revenues have staged a remarkable recovery, the high personal/corporate ratio does not suggest that corporate taxes are too low. The principal problems with corporate taxes concern evasion and loopholes that permit potentially preventable tax avoidance. Of course, more information is required about the revenue, efficiency, equity and administrative consequences of taxation before any firm conclusion is reached.

Figure 3.7 presents trends in company tax over the period 1965-1995. The key factors which explain the long term structural downturn in corporate tax performance from 1965 to 1991 are the collapse in wool prices in 1967, Britain's entry into the European Community in 1970, the 1973-74 and 1979 oil shocks, government emphasis on subsidisation, heavy use of tax incentives in the late 1970s and early 1980s, subsequently, beginning in 1984, the structural adjustment (that *inter alia*, deregulated the economy and significantly reduced import barriers) program beginning in 1984, the rise of tax avoidance as firms reacted to the loss of tax incentives, higher inflation and higher taxes, the stock market collapse in 1987, and the severe 18 month recession in 1990-91. The key factors promoting higher aggregate effective tax rates for all firms since 1991 include the corporate tax reform and improved tax auditing in the 1980s and 1990s and strong economic recovery in 1993-1995.

The total tax burden on all firms, at 5.1% of GDP in 1995, was near its highest point since corporate tax was introduced in 1918 (**Table 3.3**). From 1980-92 NZ either matched or under-performed on corporate tax revenue collection relative to the OECD average. Before and since then NZ's performance has been well-above the OECD average (**Figure 3.8**), suggesting NZ now has a relatively tough corporate tax regime, despite having lower statutory rates than many OECD countries. But, there is a puzzling trend among publicly listed firms and non-resident controlled firms that bears much closer examination.

A relative decline in corporate tax versus indirect tax and personal tax over the last 100 years occurred in most OECD countries. Factors which have influenced this trend are: (1) lower transport costs; (2) lower trade barriers, and (3) faster dissemination of technological knowledge. These factors will tend to reduce monopoly profits that in turn will lead to lower corporate income tax payments. In other words, increased global competition has eroded monopoly profits and corporate tax revenue over the century.[69]

[69] I wish to thank Erwin Diewert, Professor of Economics at the University of British Columbia for this insight.

Figure 3.7
Trends in Company Tax in New Zealand: 1965-95

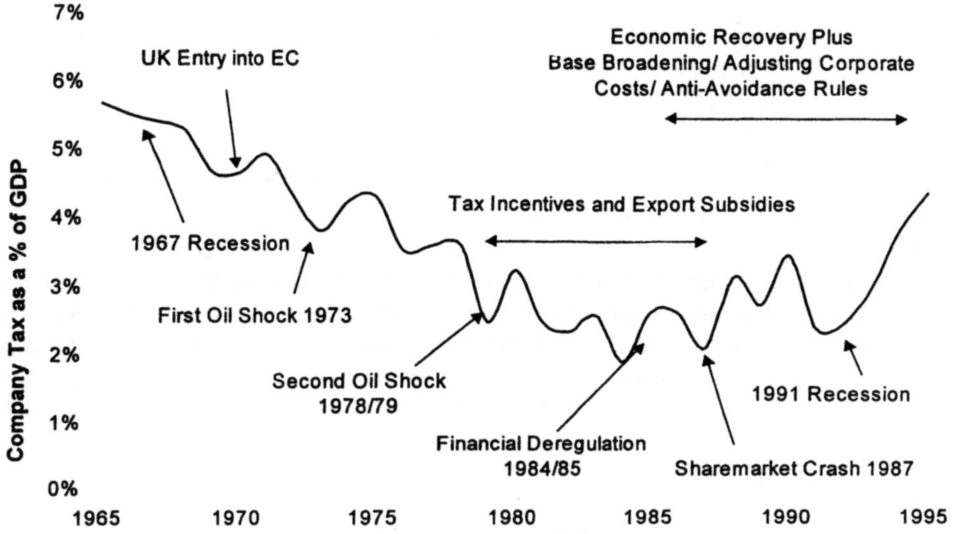

Source: NZ Institute of Economic Research, Inland Revenue, Treasury 1996

Figure 3.8
Taxes on Corporate Income as a Percentage of GDP - New Zealand and the OECD Average: 1965-94

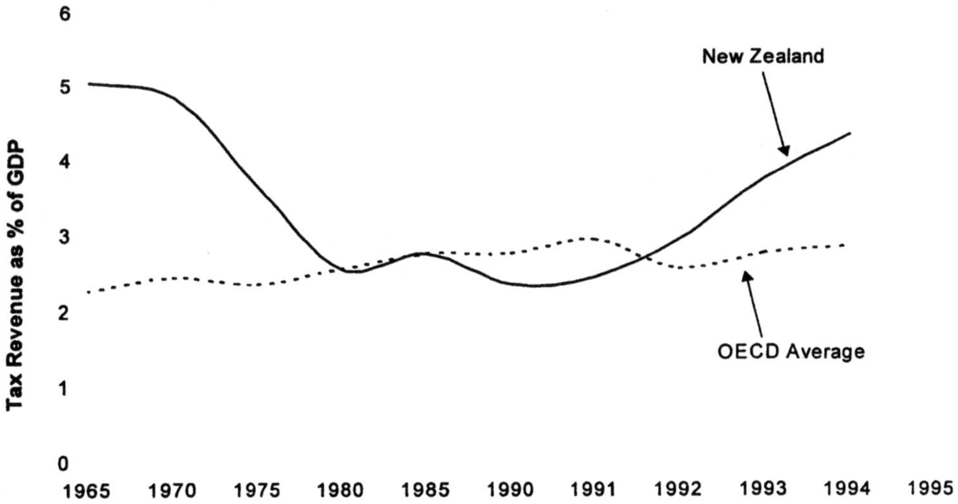

Source: Revenue Statistics 1965-95, OECD, 1996

Table 3.3
Trends in Company Tax

Period	% of GDP	Period	% of GDP
1940-44	4.2	1965-69	5.2
1945-49	4.9	1970-74	4.5
1945	5.33	1975-79	3.6
1950-54	4.3	1980-84	2.8
1955-59	4.7	1985-89	3.3
1957	5.38	1990-94	4.1
1960-64	4.5	1995	5.1

Source: Inland Revenue, New Zealand, 1996

There is now serious discussion about the long-term survival prospects of the corporate income tax, in light of the erosion of that tax base by a combination of tax relief by governments and transfer pricing manipulation by foreign controlled firms.[70] But, the evidence (Tanzi, 1996) suggests that international tax competition for investment is having only a modest effect on the total tax/GDP ratio in individual countries, but a much stronger impact on the tax mix. Owing in part to tax competition for investment across countries, it appears that governments are increasing taxes on consumption and labour in order to compensate for reduced taxes on firms and to maintain current levels of government spending. Thus, if governments were to reduce their spending, international tax competition would then have an effect on the total level of taxes.

The Balance Between Zero and Positive Tax Payers[71]

It appears that many medium and large sized firms in New Zealand go for years without paying much tax. Inefficiency and looming bankruptcy explain many of the cases, but more research is required to determine the status of the other long term residents in the zero taxpaying zone.

In 1982 in NZ (**Figure 3.9**) 29% of publicly listed and non-resident controlled corporate taxpayers (*larger firms*) in a sample of 500 firms were zero-taxpayers (ZTPs).[72] By 1991, the depth of the worst recession since 1945, about 43.5% of these companies paid no tax. But, about 1/3 of the 43.5% can be explained by structural adjustment, the stock market crash of 1987 and the recession in 1990-91, since these factors entered after 1982 when the ratio of ZTPs to TTPs was

[70] For example, Tanzi (1996:18) comments that: "some authors have raised the possibility that over the long run the taxes on corporate income may be driven towards zero. It is more likely that they will be reduced towards lower statutory rates. The country-specific reasons for investing in particular countries will still play an important role. It is an open question whether the current determination of tax liabilities, which attempts to allocate profits to the various parts of a multinational enterprise on the basis of cost accounting will survive. It is conceivable that taxes based either on the value of assets or on other criteria will replace the taxes now determined. In this sense the taxes on corporate income, as we know them, may in fact be driven to zero".

[71] Material in this section is based on an assessment of roughly 291 firms for which data are available each year in our public domain commercial database for the period 1982-1992.

[72] This data is in a public domain data base created by Inland Revenue from publicly listed firms and firms required to file annual reports in the Companies Office.

already at 29%. Why are so many companies in the ZTP zone? There are two approaches for examining this question.

First, the *larger NZ firms* with similar firms overseas listed on Standard and Poor's Compustat Global Vantage Database in 18 OECD countries. The results (**Figure 3.9**) reveal that during recessions (1982, 1992) the ratio of ZTPs to total corporate taxpayers in the sample is about 14%-17%. Over the entire period, OECD average is about 13%. In New Zealand, the long run average is about 35%, or 2.5 times the OECD average. More research is needed.

Second, *larger firm* data were compared with all corporate taxpayers (*ACTs*) for the period 1991-95 (**Figure 3.10**). In 1991, the ZTP rate for *larger firms* was 1.7 times greater than *ACTs*. This gap continuously narrowed so that by 1995 the results for the two databases were exactly the same: 27% of all firms on each data base were zero taxpayers in that year. The gap between the two data sets in earlier years needs to be explored further, so caution is advised.

The remaining explanations lie in legitimate commercial reasons such as reduced demand, financial mismanagement and tax avoidance. It is unlikely that the firms captured in this sample of incorporated firms are engaged in evasion to any significant degree. Past experience in NZ and overseas indicates that smaller firms and the self-employed tend to evade, with inevitable exceptions. Additional research is needed.

3.4 A Comparison of New Zealand and OECD Tax Trends

The comparisons in this section should be treated with some caution. First, the OECD's data, which is the source of the information in this section includes local government taxes. They are excluded from the rest of this study because they do not represent national policy instruments. Future cross-country comparisons of the total national tax burden would usefully include local taxes, but for our purposes, this Report is only concerned with how taxpayers and the economy respond to national policy choices. This does not mean that local taxes should be ignored or that they are unimportant; it is just that they are outside the mandate of the Report. Second, an OECD average is far from being a 'best-practice' frontier. The data here merely represent trends in policy-making, regardless of the quality of policy.

Kay (1990:23) has captured the general recent trends in OECD taxation that suggest the dominance of the hybrid system of personal income tax and consumption tax:

"in the modern state...we tax income, consumption, rents and wealth and that is broadly the order of their importance. Increasingly, we raise revenue from labour income and from consumption".

But, as indicated, current practice is not best practice, and the best practice mix and tax level for each country remains to be discovered.

Figure 3.9
The Proportion of Corporate Taxpayers Paying No Tax: a comparison of companies in New Zealand (1982-95) with the average for companies in 18 OECD countries (1982-92; 1993-95 estimated)

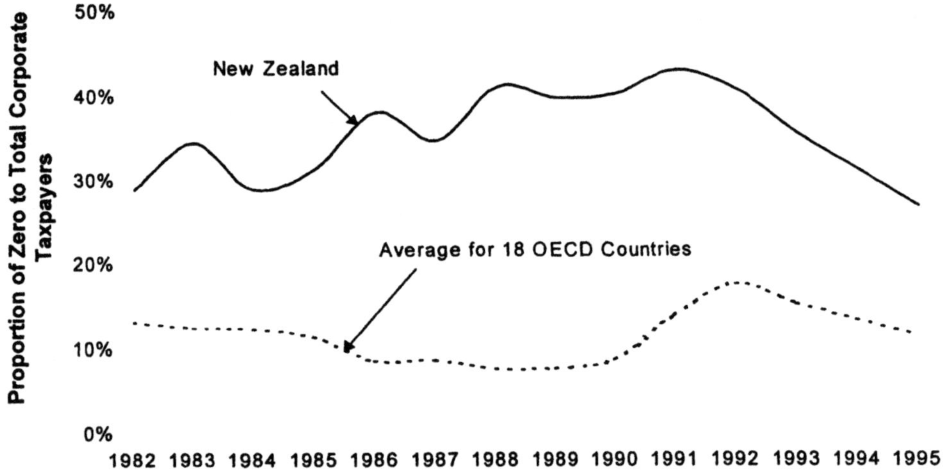

Source: New Zealand Corporate Database, Compustat's Global Vantage Database, Inland Revenue, 1997

Figure 3.10
The Ratio of Zero to Total Corporate Taxpayers by Frequency: FIRST* database, 1991-95, 671 companies; NZCDB**, 1982-95, 507 (average p.a.) companies

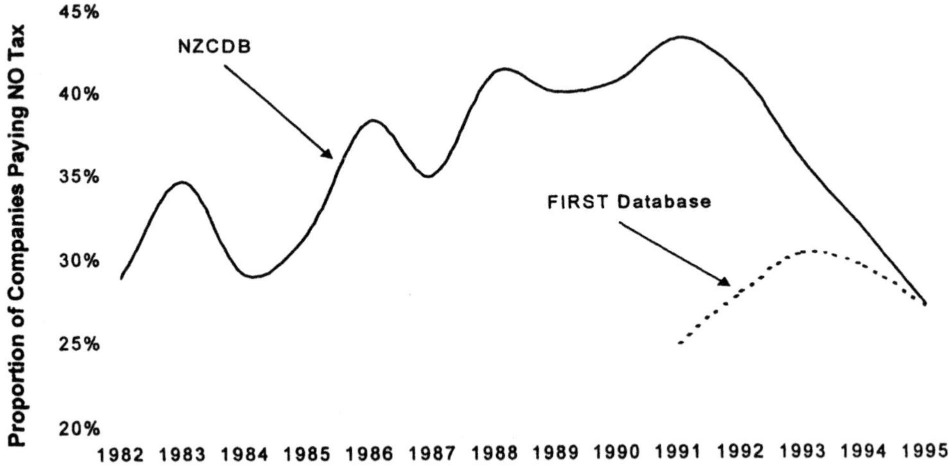

Source: * FIRST - Inland Revenue's taxpayer database of all taxpayers in New Zealand; **NZCDB - New Zealand Corporate database of all public and foreign-owned companies in New Zealand, 1997

Personal and Indirect Taxes

Table 3.4 presents trends in the tax mix for all OECD countries as well as NZ for selected years: 1965, 1975, 1985 and 1992. Across all OECD countries, the ratio of personal taxes to GDP (including social security taxes) has exhibited a steady upward trend for the last three decades, with the ratio climbing from 12.0% in 1965 to 21.1% in 1994 (the latest year in which data for all countries is available). This represents a 76% increase, and indicates that personal tax revenue has stayed well ahead of the growth in real GDP. By comparison, in our snapshot years, the NZ personal tax/GDP ratio has been consistently below the OECD average, except for 1985, when the two were approximately equal.

The OECD average ratio of indirect taxes to GDP has exhibited a very modest upward shift over the last three decades. The ratio rose from 9.9% in 1965 to 12.1% in 1992. This represents an increase of 22%, and indicates that indirect tax revenue has stayed ahead of the growth in real GDP by a small margin. By comparison, for the same years, the NZ indirect tax/GDP ratio was consistently below the OECD average, except for 1994 when, because of the earlier introduction of GST, NZ (12.5%) rose above the OECD average (12.1%).

Corporate and Other Taxes

Over the period 1965-1992 the average corporate tax/GDP ratio in the OECD was very stable, moving from 2.3% in 1965 to 2.9% in 1994. This represents an increase of 26%, and indicates that corporate tax revenues in the OECD have also stayed ahead of the growth in real GDP. By comparison, in our snapshot years, the NZ corporate tax/GDP ratio has been consistently *above* the OECD average, except in 1985 when the two were approximately equal. Across all OECD countries, the ratio of *other* taxes (including local government taxes) to GDP has been very stable until recently in 1994 when they have evidenced an increase of 20% over the 1965 level. By comparison, in our snapshot years, the NZ *other* tax/GDP ratio has been consistently *above* the OECD average.

Summary and Conclusions

As indicated in **Table 3.1**, in the early part of the 20th century, New Zealand's tax/GDP ratio was small and generally under 15%. At the same time, the tax mix was dominated by indirect taxes, with direct taxes only being 20-30% of indirect taxes just before and after the turn of the century, and personal taxes being about 50% of corporate taxes close to the same time. World War 1 evidenced a sharp increase in the total tax take from direct taxes, causing a shrinkage in the direct to indirect tax ratio to 0.78. The ratio remained at that level for the next 30 years.

World War II witnessed the doubling of the tax/GDP ratio to 26% compared to only 12% in the 1920s. The War led to a reversal in the tax mix, with the ratio of direct to indirect flipping from 0.77 in the 1930s to 1.85 in the 1940s, while the ratio of personal to corporate tax also flipped from 0.51 to 1.72. This dramatic

Table 3.4
OECD and New Zealand Tax Mix Comparison

	Personal Tax/GDP*				Indirect Tax/GDP				Corporate Tax/GDP				Other Tax /GDP			
	1965	**1975**	**1985**	**1994**	**1965**	**1975**	**1985**	**1994**	**1965**	**1975**	**1985**	**1994**	**1965**	**1975**	**1985**	**1994**
Australia	8.0	9.3	13.6	12.0	8.1	8.1	9.9	8.9	3.9	4.4	2.7	4.2	3.2	5.7	3.8	4.8
Austria	15.5	19.1	23.6	23.1	13.0	13.3	14.0	13.2	1.9	1.7	1.5	1.3	4.3	4.5	4.5	4.9
Belgium	16.2	26.6	32.1	30.0	11.6	11.0	11.7	12.5	1.9	3.0	2.6	2.8	1.5	1.2	1.3	1.3
Canada	7.3	13.9	16.1	19.5	10.5	10.4	10.5	9.5	3.9	4.4	2.7	2.4	4.2	3.7	3.8	4.7
Denmark	14.0	23.6	26.5	29.3	12.1	13.9	16.8	16.5	1.4	1.3	2.4	1.9	2.4	2.6	3.3	3.9
Finland	12.2	22.4	24.1	29.6	12.9	12.2	13.9	14.5	2.4	1.5	1.4	1.9	2.8	1.6	1.4	1.3
France	15.5	19.5	25.0	25.3	13.2	12.3	13.2	12.0	1.8	1.9	2.0	1.6	4.0	3.2	4.3	5.2
Germany	16.7	23.0	24.8	25.8	10.4	9.7	9.8	11.3	2.5	1.6	2.3	1.1	2.0	1.7	1.2	1.1
Greece	8.4	9.8	17.4	19.2	10.7	11.9	15.0	17.4	0.4	0.9	1.0	2.4	2.5	2.9	1.7	3.5
Iceland	7.2	6.8	6.3	12.0	16.4	18.6	17.4	15.2	0.5	0.8	0.9	0.8	2.1	3.4	3.8	2.9
Ireland	6.0	12.2	16.8	17.2	13.6	14.6	16.2	14.7	2.3	1.5	1.2	3.3	4.0	3.0	2.2	2.3
Italy	11.5	16.0	21.2	23.6	10.1	7.7	8.8	11.8	1.8	1.7	3.2	3.7	2.1	0.8	1.3	2.6
Japan	8.0	11.1	15.2	16.2	4.8	3.6	3.9	4.3	4.1	4.3	5.8	4.1	1.4	1.9	2.7	3.2
Luxembourg	17.5	24.5	24.3	21.7	7.6	8.9	11.4	12.3	3.4	6.7	8.3	7.6	2.1	2.7	2.7	3.4
Netherlands	19.2	28.1	28.1	28.6	9.4	10.4	11.3	11.9	2.6	3.3	3.1	3.3	1.5	1.1	1.6	2.1
New Zealand	**9.7**	**16.9**	**19.9**	**16.6**	**6.9**	**7.5**	**7.7**	**12.5**	**5.1**	**3.7**	**2.8**	**4.4**	**3.0**	**3.0**	**2.9**	**3.5**
Norway	17.2	25.2	20.4	20.7	13.7	16.9	17.8	15.8	1.3	1.3	8.1	3.5	1.1	1.5	1.3	1.0
Portugal	-	-	-	14.9	7.2	8.9	11.9	14.7	-	-	-	2.3	-	-	-	1.1
Spain	6.3	12.1	17.6	21.9	6.0	4.7	8.3	10.0	1.4	1.3	1.5	1.7	1.0	1.4	1.4	2.2
Sweden	21.3	28.5	31.9	32.6	10.9	10.6	13.3	13.2	2.1	1.9	1.7	2.8	0.7	2.4	3.1	2.4
Switzerland	11.2	19.3	21.5	23.9	6.3	5.9	6.1	5.5	1.5	2.3	1.9	2.0	1.7	2.1	2.5	2.5
Turkey	3.2	6.8	6.5	8.8	5.7	6.6	5.6	8.3	0.5	0.8	1.5	1.3	1.2	1.8	1.8	3.8
United Kingdom	13.8	19.7	17.1	15.5	10.0	9.0	11.7	12.0	2.2	2.4	4.7	2.7	4.4	4.4	4.4	3.9
United States	10.9	14.8	16.5	16.8	5.5	5.2	4.9	5.0	4.0	3.0	2.0	2.5	3.9	3.7	2.6	3.3
OECD Average	**12.0**	**17.0**	**20.2**	**21.1**	**9.9**	**10.1**	**11.3**	**12.1**	**2.3**	**2.4**	**2.8**	**2.9**	**2.5**	**2.6**	**2.6**	**3.0**

* Includes all social security payments
Source: New Zealand Planning Council, Treasury

change has charted a course that has been retained for the last 50 years. As the tax/GDP ratio has risen, there has been a marginal preference for direct over indirect taxes through the end of the 1980s, and a larger preference for personal tax revenue over corporate tax revenue. Only in the 1990s did these trends witness a turnaround. Even though the tax/GDP ratio continued to climb, the direct/indirect tax ratio has dropped to 1.8 and the personal to corporate ratio has dropped from 6.8 in the 1980s to 4.4 in the 1990s.

The introduction of GST and the recovery of the NZ economy have muted the previously strong upward trends in the direct/indirect and personal/corporate ratios, but the path established for the tax/GDP ratio and the tax mix during World War II is still very much in place. On average OECD countries tend to favour personal tax revenue more than NZ, while NZ tends to favour securing tax revenue through indirect, corporate and other taxes more than the OECD.

3.5 Total Government Expenditure Trends: 1950-2000[73]

For the 25 year period from 1951-1974, the ratio of New Zealand government expenditures to GDP was very stable, remaining between 26% and 29% for 23 years. This is a remarkable level of stability. The importance of stability in the share of government in the economy will be discussed in detail later. There were three exceptions to this stability within a narrow range of expenditure. In 2 years (1949-50 and 1952-53), largely due to the effects of the Korean War on economic growth - the wool boom - the ratio jumped to just above 30% of GDP, while in the one year (1950-51) it fell to 25%, the lowest level in the last half of the twentieth century.

Beginning in 1974-75, the expenditure to GDP ratio rose to 34.9%, an increase of 23%. New Zealand's loss of preferential access to the UK market along with the first energy crisis in 1973-74, the onset of a new Labour government with strong social policy ambitions, combined with other exigencies, led to an average annual increase of 2 percentage points of GDP in government expenditures over the period 1971-75 compared to the previous five years. Thereafter, except for a brief respite in 1976-77 (34%), the ratio jumped to between 38% and 40%, until 1986-87 when it peaked at 44.2%. This level of government spending was 16 percentage points higher than in 1973-74. In other words, at its peak, government spending was 56% higher than 12 years earlier.

For the remainder of the Labour regime, government spending dropped to about 38% of GDP, still 10 percentage points above the 1973-74 level. Thus, even under the reformist Labour Government of the 1980s, expenditures were not cut, rather they were reallocated as government corporatised and privatised parts of the public sector, and liberalised and de-regulated the private sector. The ratio also remained at 38% for the first 2 years of the National government in 1991 and 1992.

---

[73] The sources for the data on government expenditure since 1950 are NZPC, 1980, *Public Expenditure and Its Financing: 1950-1979*, Wellington, The Treasury, 1996, Historical Fiscal Updates and Peters, W., 1997, *The Budget Economic & Fiscal Update, 1997*, Wellington: The Treasury, 26 June.

Table 3.5 presents actual and projected average total government expenditure relative to GDP, in five year intervals, covering the period 1950-2000. In brief, in the 1950s, the ratio averaged about 27.8%, in the 1960s about 27.5%, in the 1970s about 34%, in the 1980s about 39.5%, and 36.7% in the first half of the 1990s. For the last half of the decade, the figure is expected to be 34% of GDP. This huge increase in the role of government from 28% to a peak of 44% of GDP, was strategically unplanned and not managed in a scientific fashion. That is to say, there was no proper cost benefit analysis and risk assessment of the potential consequences of this major increase in government intrusion in the economy.

As a result, this enhanced role of the state from 1975-1992 appears to have led to massive waste that eliminated much of the gains of the previous 25 years, sharply reduced the per capita income of New Zealanders, and brought the country perilously close to debt crisis, given the response of creditors after 1984.

Double-digit inflation became the order of the day. Regulation of the economy intensified dramatically. Economic growth stagnated. The new enhanced role of government was clearly unsustainable precisely because the consequences of the new role were unproductive in protecting the wealth of the nation. On the contrary, the enhanced role of the state appears to have been undermining the wealth of the nation by reducing the annual rate of economic growth, adding to the national debt and increasing interest payments required to pay for the mistakes of the past.

The last half of the 1980s are included in the interventionist period because expenditures remained so high even though government was intent on reducing the role of the state in the economy. The years 1990-93 are included because they represent the final effects of the interventionist policies.

How do trends in New Zealand government expenditures relative to GDP compare with other OECD governments. Over the period 1913 to 1994, for 11 OECD governments, for which data are available, there has been a significant jump in the level of government participation in the economy (Tanzi & Schuknecht, 1997:165). The countries are France, Germany, Italy, Japan, Netherlands, Norway, Spain, Sweden, Switzerland, the UK and the US. In 1913 the average expenditure to GDP ratio for these countries was 9.1%. By 1920 it had risen to 15.4%, by 1937, to 21.2%, by 1960 to 27.7%, by 1980 41.9% and by 1994, 48.4% of GDP (Tanzi & Schuknecht, 1995:4).

After World War I, the expenditure to GDP ratio did not drop for any of the 11 countries. After World War II, the ratio did not drop for 9 of the 11 countries, in comparing the ratios for 1960 versus 1937. Only Germany (-23.6%) and Japan (-31%) experienced declines in the ratio over this 23 year period. Their expenditure to GDP ratios had been quite high prior to World War II because of rearmament and military adventurism (e.g. Germany in Spain and Czechoslovakia and Japan in China) (Tanzi & Schuknecht, 1995:4).

Table 3.5
Total New Zealand Government Expenditure, percentage of GDP: 1950-2000, 5-year averages

	1950-55 Actual	1956-60 Actual	1961-65 Actual	1966-70 Actual	1971-75 Actual	1976-80 Actual	1981-85 Actual	1986-90 Actual	1991-95 Actual	1996-2000 Projected
Social Security and Welfare	8.4	8.1	8.2	6.9	6.9	10.0	11.3	12.8	13.8	13.2
Health	3.0	3.3	3.7	4.0	4.5	5.5	5.4	5.3	5.3	6.0
Education	2.5	2.9	3.3	3.9	5.0	5.4	5.1	5.0	5.8	5.7
Interest Paid on Public Debt	2.3	2.3	2.4	2.8	2.4	3.2	5.0	7.2	5.1	2.9
Core Government Services	1.5	1.3	1.3	1.3	2.3	2.8	2.0	2.2	2.2	1.6
Law and Order	0.2	0.3	0.3	0.3	0.4	0.6	0.8	1.1	1.5	1.3
Defense	2.6	2.3	1.9	2.1	1.8	1.7	2.0	1.9	1.5	1.0
Transport & Communications	1.9	1.9	1.7	1.5	2.0	1.8	1.5	1.4	1.0	0.9
Other*	5.6	5.2	4.5	4.8	4.0	7.2	6.7	2.4	0.4	1.6
Total Expenditure	**28.0**	**27.6**	**27.3**	**27.6**	**29.3**	**38.2**	**39.9**	**39.3**	**36.7**	**34.2**

Source: (1) Peters, Hon. W., 1997, The Budget Economic & Fiscal Update, Wellington, The Treasury; (2) New Zealand Planning Council,1980, Public Expenditure and Its Financing: 1950-1979; (3) The Treasury, 1996, Historical Fiscal Data, 14 May

There appear to be five great leaps in expenditure among the 11 countries over the period 1913-1994. On average, the cost of World War I in terms of an annual increase in the expenditure to GDP ratio was 6.5 percentage point of GDP by 1920, as compared to 1913. The average cost of setting up the welfare state in the 1930s and re-arming was 5.6 percentage points of GDP by 1937. The average cost of World War II and the post-war reconstruction and welfare programs by 1960 was a government expenditure to GDP ratio that was 6.5 percentage points higher than in 1937. The average cost of the modern welfare state, largely the increase in subsidies and transfers, but also taking into consideration current and capital expenditures in the budgets of the 11 countries was an additional 14.2 percentage points by 1980, as compared to 1960. Finally, the additional average cost of state intervention over the period 1980-1994 was 6.5 percentage points of GDP by 1994.

Of interest is the fact that, again in average terms across 11 countries, the annual cost of increase in government intervention from 1960-1980 was more than equal to the costs of both World War I and World War II, as well as part of the cost of funding the initial welfare state and re-arming in the 1930s. This is a staggering comparison and it indicates how deeply the government has entered the pocket books of taxpayers. Tanzi & Schuknecht (1995:17) concluded that:

"the growth of government in today's industrialised countries reflects largely the growth in the provision of goods and services over two World Wars, and, more importantly, the rapid growth of the welfare state since 1960".

In 1960, the average expenditure to GDP ratio for these countries was 27.9%, but by 1990 this had risen to 44.9%, an increase of 61%. By comparison, New Zealand climbed from 26.9% to 41.3%, for an increase of 53.5%. Thus, the size of government, during this 30 years period was advancing at a slightly lower rate than the OECD average. Nonetheless, New Zealand still advanced from 13th in 1960 to 11th place among these countries.

Should transfers be treated as neutral with respect to the efficiency performance of the economy? The traditional argument is that if a dollar paid in tax by an individual or a firm is transferred to a beneficiary via the tax system, it has no dampening effect on economic performance. But, there is mounting empirical evidence that this is not the case. Alesina & Perroti (1994:abstract) have provided both theoretical and empirical support for the view that redistributive fiscal policies have a negative effect on the efficient performance of open economies. How do transfers affect the productive side of the economy? Their conclusion is that

"in all modern industrial societies, redistributive expenditures are a larger component of the government budget than consumption of goods and services.... (A)n increase in transfers to, say, retirees financed by distortionary taxation, can generate a loss of competitiveness (defined as an increase in relative unit labour costs for tradeable goods), an appreciation of the relative price of non-tradeables, and a decrease in employment in all sectors of the economy. The same qualitative effects would also obtain in the case of an increase in transfers towards the unemployed even if financed by non-distortionary taxation. Moreover, all these effects of labour taxation depend in a non-linear way on the degree of centralisation of the wage setting process in the labour market. We then estimate the effects of labour taxation on unit labour costs and the relative price of non-tradeables in a sample of 14 OECD countries. We find considerable support for the model".

Consumption to GDP Ratio

Over the period 1960-1994, government consumption to GDP ratios for 17 OECD countries rose on average by 5.2 percentage points from 12.3% of GDP to 17.5% of GDP. Countries which experienced the increases well above the average OECD results were Sweden (11.3 percentage points), Spain (8.7 percentage points), Norway (7.9 percentage points), Australia (6.0 percentage points), and Austria (6.0 percentage points). New Zealand's increase in the consumption to GDP ratio (4.9 percentage points) was just below average (Tanzi & Schuknecht, 1995:9).

Transfers and Subsidies to GDP Ratio

Over the period 1970-1992, government expenditures on subsidies and transfers for 17 OECD countries increased by an average of 7.8 percentage points of GDP. Countries whose performance was well above average include: Sweden (18.2 percentage points), Spain (14.3 percentage points), Italy (11.2 percentage points), Norway (10.9 percentage points), and Netherlands (9.0 percentage points). New Zealand's increase (5.0 percentage points) was below average (Tanzi & Schuknecht, 1995:11).

Interest Payments on Public Debt to GDP

Over the period 1970-1992 government spending for interest on the public debt for 17 OECD countries increased by an average of 2.9 percentage points. Countries above the average increase included Italy (9.6 percentage points), Belgium (7.3 percentage points), Ireland (4.0 percentage points), Canada (3.4 percentage points), Austria (3.1 percentage points), and New Zealand (3.1 percentage points) (Tanzi & Schuknecht, 1995:15).

Patterns of New Zealand Government Expenditure: 1950-2000

Over the last half century, the pattern of government expenditures (**Figure 3.11**) has varied quite considerably, reflecting changing domestic and international constraints, and the objectives of each new government. The domestic constraints included: (1) paying down the debt incurred during World War II; (2) rewarding soldiers for military service; (3) developing natural infrastructure; (4) pursuing more enlightened social and education policies; and (5) coping with the rising indebtedness stemming from the Think Big energy projects and other government waste. The international constraints that affected government expenditure included: World War II, the Korean War, the Vietnam War, the Cold War, the loss of preferential access to the UK market, and the two energy crises.

Figure 3.11
Composition of Government Expenditure in New Zealand as Percentages of GDP: 1950-2000

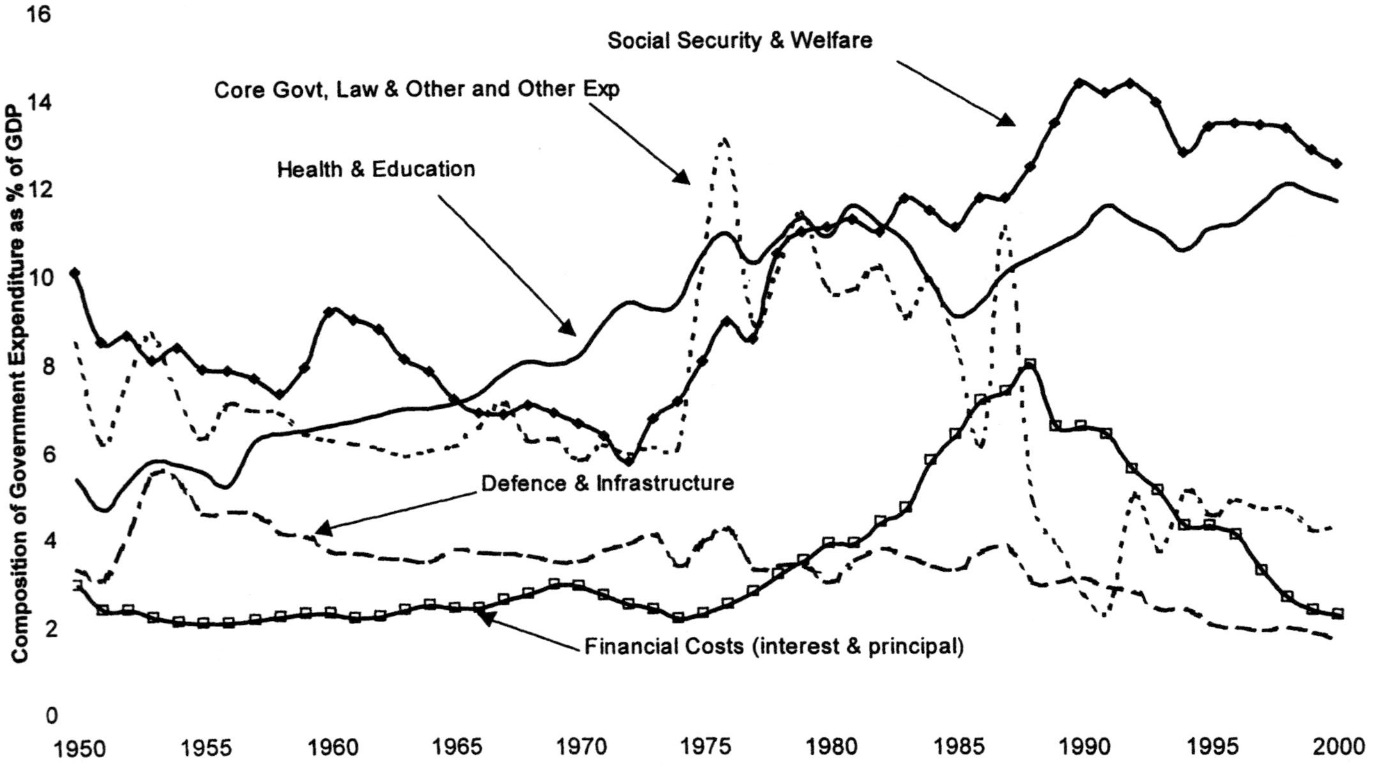

Source: New Zealand Planning Council, Treasury

Social Security & Welfare Spending

The Social Security Act of 1938 created by the first Labour government was introduced in response to the hardships of the Great Depression.[74] This Act laid the political foundations for future government intervention and the expansion of the modern role of the government in the New Zealand economy, and strengthened the influence of *egalitarianism* in New Zealand politics.

Throughout the period since mid-century social security and welfare payments have dominated government spending as its first priority (**Tables 3.5** and **3.6** and **Figure 3.11**). Moreover, this priority has become progressively more important over the last 45 years, except for the last half of the 1960s and the first half of the 1970s, when New Zealand was enjoying the fruits of economic growth.

Spending on social security peaked in the first half of the 1990s and is expected to fall slightly in the last half of the decade. Nonetheless, as **Table 3.6** indicates, social security and welfare spending is at its highest level in the last 50 years. The number of New Zealanders receiving some form of social benefit remains very high. For example, in 1997 it is estimated that one in every three families receives some form of benefit, and that for every two people employed, one person receives some form of benefit.

Health and Education Spending

Expenditure on health has doubled in real terms in the last 45 years and has sustained its position as the second most important priority for government attention in each decade, except in the first half of the 1970s and the 1990s when education took priority. Given the ageing of the New Zealand population and prominence of health issues on the political agenda, health expenditures can be expected to remain the second priority for government spending for the remainder of the century.

Spending on Defence, Transportation, Communications and Energy

As might be expected in the aftermath of World War II, the early 1950s were characterised by high expenditure on defence and the costs of rehabilitating the returned servicemen and women. In line with this focus, housing construction expenditures as percentage of GDP also peaked in the 1950s. This decade also witnessed the peak in government expenditures on railways and telecommunications, relative to GDP. These new infrastructure developments were to be expected of a country that was only 100 years old. They helped to underpin the view that the government could be relied on to deliver valuable

---

[74] The focus of the Social Security Act of 1938 emphasized universality in health services and social security. The state would both provide and fund the health system. With respect to social security, the state would provide a means-tested pension for those over 60, to be replaced by universal superannuation for those reaching 65. Earlier legislation provided for the introduction of old age pensions (1898), special benefits to widows (1911), and family allowances (1926).

Table 3.6
Changes in the Pattern of Government Expenditure: 1950-2000
% Higher or Lower for 1990s Spending as compared to:

Expenditure		1980s	1970s	1960s	1950s
Social Security/Welfare	1990-94	14.5	62.4	82.8	67.3
	1995-2000	9.5	55.3	74.8	60.0
Health	1990-94	-1.0	6.0	37.7	68.3
	1995-2000	12.2	20.0	55.8	90.5
Education	1990-94	14.9	11.5	61.0	114.8
	1995-2000	12.9	9.6	58.0	111.1
Financial Costs	1990-94	-16.4	82.0	96.2	121.7
	1995-2000	-52.5	3.6	11.5	26.1
Core Government Services	1990-94	4.8	-13.7	69.2	57.1
	1995-2000	-23.8	-37.3	23.1	14.3
Law & Order	1990-94	57.9	200	400	500
	1995-2000	36.8	160	333	420
Defence	1990-94	-23.1	-14.3	-25.0	-38.8
	1995-2000	-48.7	-42.9	-50.0	-59.2
Transport & Communications	1990-94	-31.0	-47.4	-37.5	-47.4
	1995-2000	-37.9	-52.6	-43.8	-52.6

Source: New Zealand Planning Council, 1979

Table 3.7
New Zealand Government Expenditure, percentage of GDP: 1974, 1979

	1974		1979		% Increase	
	Rank	% of GDP	Rank	% of GDP	1979/1974	Rank
Current Expenditure		14.1		18.5	31.7	
General Administration	7	1.48	6	1.90	28.4	10
Interest on Domestic Debt	14	0.39	10	1.19	205	1
Law & Order	13	0.44	12	0.70	59.1	5
Develop of Industry	9	1.12	9	1.65	47.3	8
Health	3	4.08	2	5.25	28.7	9
Education	2	4.17	3	4.86	16.6	14
Other Social Services	17	0.28	15	0.55	96.4	2
Defence	5	1.59	7	1.80	13.2	15
Maintain Public Works	12	0.50	13	0.60	20	13
Capital Expenditure		4.5		5.19	15.1	
Housing Construction	19	0.21	18	0.33	57	7
Electricity	8	1.16	5	2.05	76.7	3
Railways	18	0.27	17	0.34	25.9	12
Post & Telecommunications	15	0.37	19	0.28	-24.3	
Roading	13	0.44	18	0.33	-25.0	
Forestry	20	0.09	20	0.09	0	
Education (Schools)	11	0.78	11	0.76	-2.5	
Health (Hospitals)	16	0.34	14	0.56	64.7	4
Transfers		9.47		13.94	47.2	
Social Security	1	6.74	1	10.70	58.8	6
Interest	4	1.89	4	2.42	28.0	11
Subsidies	6	1.52	8	1.74	14.5	15

Source: New Zealand Planning Council, 1980, Public Expenditure and Its Financing, 1950-79

services efficiently. This view had been fostered by the government's successful management of social security since 1938 and its centralising and successful management of the war effort.

But, unfortunately, these expansions were accompanied by the growing economic isolationist views embedded in the *Fortress New Zealand* policies of the Holland National government that sprang from the disruptions of the balance of payments crises in the early 1950s. As a result, New Zealand strengthened its trade protectionism and its regulatory[75] approach to the economy. A by-product of this intervention was a redistribution of income in the form of a new wealthy class of entrepreneurs whose prospects flourished under government intervention, sheltering from the winds of international competition. In particular, import licensing provided monopoly rights for product marketing.

In 1973 when New Zealand was hit by the energy shock and the loss of preferential access to the UK market after it joined the European Community, it reached back to its *Fortress New Zealand* policy responses for protection. The loss of preferential access to New Zealand's largest overseas export market for its agricultural products was a difficult hurdle for a country dependent on agriculture. Increasing government's commercial and social role in the economy, accompanied by rising taxes and regulations was the response deemed to be appropriate at the time. The *Think Big* energy projects, and especially rising social welfare spending pushed up the national debt significantly.

Interest Payments on the National Debt

Interest payments on the public debt began to play a much more important role as government spending increased after the mid-1970s. Over the period 1950-1975 interest payments on the national public debt averaged 2.4% of GDP. This jumped to 3.2% in the last half of the 1970s, 5% in the first half of the 1980s and 7.2% in the last half of the 1980s. The peak year was in 1987-88, when interest on the public debt reached 8% of GDP.

Another way of examining their prominence is relative to total expenditures. In 1986-87 interest payments reached 16.7% of all government spending. This figure peaked at 20.7% in 1987-88. This level was comparable to the early years of World War II (1940-42), when the average ratio reached 22.4% of total expenditures. The peak came after the war in 1947 when interest service reached 29.6% of total spending.

We can draw several lessons from this analysis. First, the level of debt during the interventionist period, 1975-1993, was reaching crisis proportions, having attained a debt service level comparable to the early years of World War II.

[75] The New Zealand regulatory approach is captured in Evans et al. (1996:1860): "Although government expenditure ratios, in relation to gross domestic product ("GDP"), were similar to those of many smaller OECD countries, government regulation was more pervasive – encompassing wages, imports, foreign currency, some commodity prices, and the methods and manner in which primary products were sold abroad. Government ownership was also widespread in banking, insurance, health, education, transport, energy, and utilities".

Secondly, the peak of a financial crisis where government significantly extends its role should be seen as the peak of the debt service payments. Third, the debt service level may peak a number of years after the spending peak (in real terms), depending on interest rates. Fourth, interest rates may remain high after a spending binge by government as markets raise the premium that the government pays for being prolifigate.

The Acceleration of Government Spending

Significant acceleration in New Zealand Government spending began in the last half of the 1970s. Hence, that five year period bears close examination to determine the areas which led the major increase in spending.

Table 3.7 provides an initial set of insights. Over the period 1974-75 through 1978-79, social security transfers relative to GDP recorded the largest rise among the three major categories of expenditure, increasing by 47% over the period. Current expenditures jumped by 32% and capital expenditures by only 15%.

In 1974, the top ranking expenditures, as a percentage of GDP were social security transfers (6.7%), education (4.2%), health (4.1%), interest on overseas debt (1.9%), defence (1.6%), subsidies (1.5%), general administration (1.5%), electricity (1.2%), and the development of primary and secondary industry (1.1%).

Over the period 1974-75 to 1978-79, the fast rates of expenditure (relative to GDP) growth were recorded by spending on interest on domestic debt (205%), other social services (96%), electricity (77%), health (65%), law and order (59%), social security transfer (59%), housing construction (57%), and the development of primary and secondary industry (29%).

Five years later in 1979, the ranks were slightly altered. In 1979, the top ranking expenditures, as a percentage of GDP, were social security transfers (10.7%), health (5.3%), education (4.9%), interest on overseas debt (2.4%), electricity (2.1%), general administration (1.9%), defence (1.8%), subsidies (1.7%), and the development of primary and secondary industry (1.7%).

This picture tells us a lot. If 1970s' rates of expenditure were maintained, debt service payments were destined to become a major obstacle to discretionary spending. This in fact happened, and persists as a problem into the late 1990s. The government was pouring a significant amount of money into the electricity industry and into other industries, as part of the Think Big projects. If these projects did not yield an adequate rate of return, as in fact often happened, then the total debt would mount even more and so would debt service.

But something even more troubling was happening. Social security transfers were not only maintaining their reign as the dominant expenditure category but were also experiencing a high rate of growth.

In the 5 years before the beginning of the massive increase in government intervention in the economy in 1974, total social security transfers accounted for an average of 6.2% of GDP. By 1979, they reached 10.5% of GDP, an increase of 69%. Between 1974 and 1979, transfers to the aged rose from 3.5% of GDP to 7.1%, an increase of 105%, as a result of the lowering of the retirement age from 65 to 60, at an annualised cost of $2.5 billion. Meanwhile transfers to widows and especially solo parents jumped from 0.5% of GDP in 1974 to 1.2% in 1979. Finally, transfers to invalids, and those on the sickness and unemployment benefit rose from 0.39% to 0.76% of GDP. This represented an increase of 95%.

It is clear from this that payments to the unemployed did not dominate the growing emphasis on transfer payments. The new commitments by political parties that were competing for votes on social issues (old age early retirement, the domestic purposes benefit etc) created a new series of horizons. Politicians were racing to outperform the current paradigm.[76]

Finally, subsidies continued to experience growth. Thus, New Zealand was running deficits and borrowing (increasingly abroad) in order to finance a growing level of consumption, and not just the *Think Big* energy projects. This was disastrous fiscal policy, the kind of foolishness that characterised Latin American government spending prior to the debt crisis in August 1982. For example, Argentina borrowed abroad to subsidise domestic petrol prices, among other things. Each of these developments, in retrospect, was a warning sign that New Zealand expenditure policy was going out of control.

The employment implications of this growing government role in the economy were quite spectacular. Total core public service employment in central government departments rose from about 52,290 in 1949 to about 83,242 in 1978 and about 88,000 in 1986. On top of this there were tens of thousands of employees in state-owned operations or enterprises. For example, there were 16,000 teachers in 1949 and about 45,000 in 1978. Hospital service staff jumped from about 15,000 in 1949 to just under 49,000 by the end of the 1970s.

Employment in the railways shrank from about 26,500 in 1949 to 22,000 in 1978, but post office and telephone workers rose from about 18,000 in 1949 to around 39,000 at the end of the 1970s. Thus, as the state sector grew, employment largely expanded in the areas of education and health workers, core government administration, and in the Post Office. Hidden unemployment was largely confined to the latter two (NZPC, 1980:64; Britton, LeHeron & Pawson, 1992:164).

A Preliminary Calculation of the Cost of the Interventionist Period

The power to tax is a sacred trust that forms the basis of the social consensus governing every country. The power to tax lies in the consent of the people. It is sometimes difficult in the short term to determine when that trust is being

[76] The analysis excludes ACC payments and health benefits.

abused. But this preliminary examination suggests that the key indicators that one should look at are the impact of rising government expenditures on:

- the level of government debt (relative to GDP);
- the annual level of interest payments (relative to GDP) on the public debt; and
- the rate of economic growth (and business confidence) over the long term.

What is the probable cost of the interventionist period? For purposes of this brief, preliminary analysis, the interventionist period includes the 15 years from 1975-1990, plus the period of weak performance as the economy struggled to improve in 1991-1993.

Government expenditure peaked in 1986-87 at 44.2% of GDP, after having risen from 28.3% in 1973-74. This represents an increase of 56% in less than 15 years, or an increase of about 3.7% per annum.

The Opportunity Cost of Lost Economic Growth

Table 3.8 indicates that, in the 20 years (1955-74) before government intervened heavily in the economy, the average annual rate of economic growth was 4.4% while the government expenditure to GDP ratio was 27.6%. During the 19 year period of increased intervention (1975-90), including the subsequent three years of recovery (1991-93), the average annual real rate of growth was 1%, while the government expenditure to GDP ratio was 36.5%. Since this great Intervention, the rate of growth has averaged 3.9% during 1994-1997, and is expected by the New Zealand Treasury to average 3.4% during the final three years of the century[77]. For the period 1994-97 the government expenditure to GDP ratio was 35.3%. This suggests, but does not prove, that if government expenditure were reduced below 30% that the growth rate could be improved. **Figure 3.12** helps to put this potential relationship into context. More research on this issue is needed.

Thus, during the 7 years following New Zealand's interventionist period the average annual real rate of economic growth is expected to be about 3.5%. If we subtract the average growth rate (1.1%) during the period of heavy intervention from the average for 1955-74, the difference is 3.3 percentage points. If we subtract the intervention period average growth rate from the rate expected after 1993 we obtain the estimate of 2.1%. Thus, even a conservative estimate would suggest that this great intervention may have reduced economic growth by as much as 2 percentage points per annum over the period of increased government intervention.

This would represent the opportunity cost of the Great Intervention period. A rough calculation suggests that the economy would have been 45% percent larger in 1993, at the end of the intervention period if government expenditure

[77] Peters, W., 1997, *The Budget Economic & Fiscal Update,1997*, Wellington: The Treasury, 26 June.

Table 3.8
Economic Growth Before, During and After the Major Government Intervention

Real Economic Growth (5 year period averages)					
1955-59	3.0	1975-79	0.2	1994-97	3.9%
1960-64	5.9	1980-84	2.4	1998-2000	3.2%
1965-69	2.1	1985-89	2.2		
1970-74	6.5	1990-93	-1.0		

Table 3.9
Growth and Expenditure Before, During and After the Major Intervention and its Effects

	1955-74	1975-1993	1994-1997
Average Real Growth Per Annum	4.4%	1.0%	3.9%
Average Expenditure to GDP Ratio Per Annum	27.6%*	36.5%	35.3%

* For the period 1950-1974, the expenditure to GDP ratio is 27.8%.

Source: NZ Institute of Economic Research, Treasury, Reserve Bank, 1997

Figure 3.12
Government Expenditure and Real Economic Growth in New Zealand, 5-year averages: 1950-99

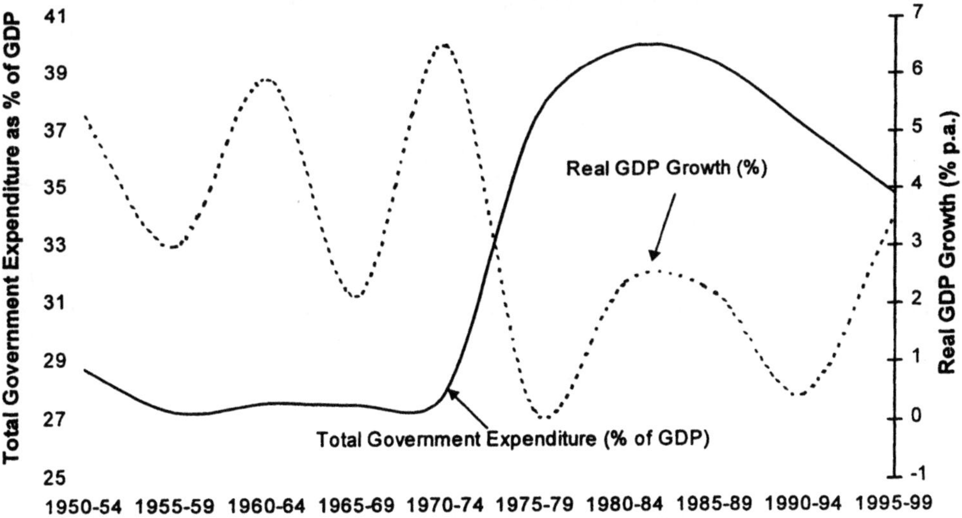

Source: New Zealand Planning Council, Treasury, NZ Institute of Economic Research

had been restructured to 1974 levels. Based on a nominal GDP in 1993 of $75.9 billion, this means that perhaps as much as *$34 billion in nominal wealth was foregone and thus lost as a result of the negative effects of the intervention.* But this is a gross estimate and would need to net out the temporary benefits of the increased social benefits stemming from increased government spending. The net amount would still be significant and represents a permanent reduction in the standard of living of all New Zealanders.

This analysis also suggests, but does not prove, that New Zealand's economic growth rate may be significantly improved when the expenditure to GDP ratio is below 30% for several decades. More on this later.

The Public Debt, Debt Servicing, Credit Rating and Exchange Rate Consequences

(1) Public Debt and Debt Service Implications

Not only did New Zealand experience a slower growth rate during the enhanced intervention period, it also witnessed a significant jump in the public debt and in the related debt service payments. Just prior to this interventionist period, in 1973-74, New Zealand had a gross public debt that was 40.5% of GDP. In the same year, the financing costs of this debt was 2.2% of GDP. Within 5 years the public debt had climbed to 52.6% of GDP, an increase of 30 percent. Interest service payments on the public debt rose to 3.9% of GDP, an increase of 77%.

At its peak in 1986-87, the gross public debt reached 77.2% of GDP, a 91% rise over 1973-74. In 1987 this represented *$21 billion in lost assets since 1974, owing to the mistakes of public policy over the previous decade.* In 1993 dollars the amount would have been $28.9 billion.[78] In 1988, interest on the public debt also peaked at a high of 8% of GDP, more than two and half times the figure in 1973-74.

By 1994 after the end of the great intervention period and its slow growth aftermath, the gross public debt had dropped to about 57% of GDP, still 17 percentage points above the level 20 years earlier. At the same time, debt service payments were still almost double the pre-intervention period.

The cumulative effect of these additional debt service payments is quite staggering. The pre-interventionist average level of debt service over 1950-74 was about 2.45% of GDP. If we subtract that amount from each subsequent year, over the next 19 years, that is until the end of fiscal year 1992-93, in 1993 dollars there was an annual loss of $1.95 billion owing to interest payments to

---

[78] 1993 is used as a terminus year in this analysis because it was the end of the period of sustained government intervention. In 1993 actual public debt was 62.2% of GDP. Thus, from the peak in 1987, the government paid off about 15% of GDP of the public debt, which amounted to $11.4 billion. These were repayments that could have gone to social services or some other government account. In 1993, the total public debt was 21.7 percentage points of GDP higher than in 1974; this was equivalent to $16.5 billion.

pay off the debt increase caused by the interventionist period. The total loss in 1993 dollars was $37 billion.

But this cost is on-going and post-Intervention financing costs on the public debt will not drop back to pre-Intervention levels until the year 2000. If we stop the clock back in 1993 and add up the cost of this great intervention, rounding off, we would add possibly as much as $34 billion in foregone economic wealth as a result of lower growth rates, $29 billion in higher total public debt, and $37 billion in financing costs on the public debt over 19 years. This represents an estimated cost of $100 billion for the mistakes made in government intervention in the 15 years from 1975-1993. This represents a loss of $5.3 billion per year, or $1500 per person in New Zealand per year. Obviously, this is a rough estimate that requires modelling refinements. It should be taken as an order of magnitude rather than a precise figure.

Of course, the clock is still ticking with respect to the interest payments on those still higher public debts.

Table 3.9
Public Debt and Interest Payments on the Public Debt Before, During and After the 1970s and 1980s Intervention

	Public Debt (% of GDP)		Interest Payments on the Public Debt (% of GDP)	Nominal GDP ($ billions)
	Gross	Net		
1973-74	40.5	4.5	2.2	$8.7
1979-80	52.6	16.4	3.9	$19.8
1986-87	77.2	46.2	8.0	$57.0
1992-93	62.2	48.6	5.1	$75.9
1993-94	56.6	43.2	4.3	$81.6

Source: New Zealand Planning Council, The Treasury

(2) Credit Rating Implications

One of the long-term consequences of the wasteful spending by government was a deterioration in the country's external credit rating by Standard & Poor's and Moody's.[79] It is interesting to see when the ratings changes occurred. Over the period 1975-1982 New Zealand enjoyed a "Triple A" credit rating. A "Triple A" credit rating confers a lower risk premium than for higher risk borrowers. This allowed the New Zealand government to borrow as cheaply as the best credit risks in the world.[80] As a result, when New Zealand borrowed abroad it achieved

[79] Todd (1997:168) summarises the changes in New Zealand's international credit ratings over the period 1975-1997.
[80] Another cost is the effect of the government's lower credit rating on the terms on which the business sector can borrow. The credit rating for the sovereign borrower sets the ceiling in international markets on the credit rating and borrowing terms for most private sector borrowers. As New Zealand's credit rating reduces its interest costs rise and so do those of the business sector. This cost has not been factored in to the $100 billion estimates.

comparative savings, relative to higher risk borrowers. This, unfortunately was an inducement to borrow more abroad which, in turn, put upward pressure on the exchange rate and undermined New Zealand's international competitiveness.

Credit rating agencies begin to get concerned about the level of public borrowing when the gross debt to GDP ratio gets close to 60%. In 1983, New Zealand's gross public debt to GDP ratio hit 59.1%. In April 1983 Standard & Poor's (S&P) downgraded New Zealand's credit rating to AA+. Moody's followed suit in October 1983 by reducing its rating of New Zealand to "Aa".

In 1985 and 1986 New Zealand's total public debt reached about 70% of GDP and again the country's credit rating was downgraded by Moody's in August 1986 to "Aa3",and in December 1986 by S&P to AA. Moody's 1986 rating was the lowest for New Zealand during the period, but it represented a reduction of three ranks (from Aa, passing Aa1 and Aa2 to Aa3). During this time, New Zealand's interest payments as a percentage of GDP were skyrocketing. They climbed steadily from 3.9% of GDP in 1980 to 6.4% in 1985, 7.2% in 1986, 7.4% in 1987 and reached a high of 8% of GDP in 1988. Thus, Moody's rating change was anticipating increased debt servicing risk for New Zealand. S&P did not downgrade the country's credit rating again until January 1991, by which time the debt to GDP ratio had fallen to 61.7%, and the debt service to 6.6% of GDP.

In March 1994, Moody's upgraded New Zealand to Aa2, by which time the public debt to GDP ratio had fallen well below 60%, a level similar to that prior to the initial downgrades. By January 1996 S&P raised New Zealand to AA+, the level to which it first downgraded the country in April 1983. By March 1997 Moody's had not yet upgraded New Zealand to its previous 1983 ranking. In 1996, the gross debt/GDP ratio had declined to 45.9% and is expected by Treasury to fall to 29.4% by 2000 (Todd, 1997:206).

This analysis indicates that credit rating agencies generally anticipate deterioration in the debt management of a country, and that the higher borrowing costs associated with reduced credit ratings persist for many years, even after the old risk level (in terms of the basic debt indicators) prior to a crisis has been regained. Of course, those are not the only indicators on which credit rating agencies focus. New Zealand's current account deficits in the balance of payments may be holding up the New Zealand's reacquisition of a Triple A credit rating. In summary, it is clear that there are very serious long term consequences when government spending is not subjected, ex ante, to long term cost benefit analysis and risk assessment.

(3) Exchange Rate Implications

The excessive government spending in the late 1970s and the 1980s also helped to contribute to a decline in the exchange rate. At its peak, the New Zealand dollar was at a considerable premium to the US dollar. At the end of 1973, US$1.4284 was required to buy NZ$1.00. By the end of 1974 the NZ dollar had devalued by almost 8%. A year later the currency had fallen by a further

21% over the end of 1975. By the end of 1976, the currency had fallen by a further 9%. Thus, the currency adjustments came well in advance of the exchange rate adjustments, which should tell the reader something about the relative efficiency of exchange rate markets as compared to credit risk analysis.

By the time the NZ currency had hit bottom (for a year end figure) in 1984 at US$0.4776, the NZ dollar has experienced a devaluation of 67%. By the end of March 1997, the currency had not yet recovered to its 1982 year end level.

The devaluation of the New Zealand dollar led to higher import costs for domestic consumers, higher debt repayment costs for private sectors that borrowed in foreign currency, and higher investment costs for New Zealand firms investing overseas and funding their investment with New Zealand dollars. These costs should also be aggregated and added to the total costs of the intervention. Unfortunately, there was insufficient time to model this additional cost.

Long Term Future Expenditure Requirements and the Tax/GDP Ratio

It would seem obvious that, where non-discretionary spending in the future rises (e.g. superannuation and health costs), the government will have to ensure that the tax level is sufficient to meet those obligations. After 2020, government operating expenditure[81] (including superannuation, health, education, social welfare and other core activities, but excluding debt servicing costs and capital expenditures) is expected to rise gradually to around 39% of GDP by 2050. This projection assumes no expenditure cuts from current levels.

Assuming that the current policy is not changed, gross expenditure on New Zealand Superannuation would peak in the middle of the next century when 20% of New Zealanders are over age 65. This compares with around 11% in 1990. Thus, spending on superannuation:

"...will more than double over the next 50 years, from 5% to 11% of GDP, and net expenditure will grow from 4% to around 9% of GDP [and]... will not exceed the levels of the early 1990s until after 2020. By way of comparison, average expenditure on public pensions as a proportion of GDP is already nearly 10% for OECD countries. In Japan, Germany, France and Italy, government pension expenditures are projected to rise to between 14% to 20% of GDP in the first few decades of the next century" (Todd, 1997:103).

Assuming no change in policy, taxes would have to rise to meet those expenditures, but not until after about 2015-2020. Even though some countries now have tax/GDP ratios over 40% with more expected in the future, the Todd Committee's Interim Report expressed concerns that a tax/GDP ratio close to 40% "would place strains on New Zealand's productive capacity" (Todd, 1997: 110-11) and "such tax increases may not be economically desirable or politically viable" (ibid: 200). Hence it is preferable to find the right mix of tax changes,

[81] These projections are based on Treasury's Long Term Fiscal Model and exclude capital expenditure.

public debt reduction and expenditure cuts that would allow the government to meet future superannuation obligations without having such high debt.

The key policy options examined by the Todd (1997) Committee with respect to future funding of superannuation involved different scenarios. Each of the major scenarios has different implications for the tax/GDP ratio. Under scenario #1, given some adjustments to the age of eligibility and the use of targeting, the expected tax/GDP ratio peak is 36.5%, compared to 38.8% in the central scenario. Under scenario #2, again with adjustments, the expected tax/GDP ratio is 35.9%. Interestingly, scenario #2 offers a tax/GDP ratio that is almost identical to the 20th century peak in the tax/GDP ratio of 36.1% in 1991, (pp119-124).

In general, the tax/GDP ratio, under each scenario, will arise gradually after 2015 when the baby boomers start to retire. In the next 20 years or so, however, there is clearly room for continuing the tax cuts:

"By deferring any change to around 2015, we are foregoing the opportunity to have lower spending (and lower taxes) in the intervening period. Lower taxes could promote higher growth in this period. This should be factored in when deciding on the timing of introduction of policy options..." (Todd, 1997:111).

On the basis of the numerous scenarios run for this project by the New Zealand Institute of Economic Research[82], it seems reasonable to conclude that, given

---

[82] These 54 year projected budget and superannuation policy scenarios are based on modelling undertaken by NZIER (Cook, 1997, 1997a, and Cook and Briggs, 1997). As with any long term projections, they should be treated cautiously. The budget scenarios (Cook & Briggs, 1997) test for the impact on the tax/GDP ratio of various changes in policy approach to net government debt and balancing the budget. Four scenarios were examined: #1 balancing the budget from FY 1997-98 and freezing the net public debt (NPD) at the 1996-97 level. In this scenario the tax/GDP ratio falls to 29.6% of GDP in 2001, but, beginning in 2009 rises gradually to 39.3% in 2051. In scenario #2, the budget gradually moves into balance by 2004, and, in the meantime, net debt is repaid and taxes are cut. In this scenario, the tax/GDP ratio falls to 29.5% in 2004, remains close to that level until about 2015, and below 33% of GDP until about 2025, and then rises to 38.9% in 2051. In scenario #3, net debt is left at 20% of GDP beginning in 2000 and the government is permitted to run small deficits. In this scenario, the tax/GDP ratio falls to 28.5% by 2001 and gradually rises to 39.5% by 2051. In scenario #4, net debt is reduced to zero and the tax/GDP ratio gradually rises to 38.7% in 2051. In summary, all of these scenarios are within a tax/GDP range of 28.5% to 39.5% over the next 50 years, given current expectations of spending. These scenarios can be modified, as they were by the Todd Committee including by examining other options for reducing the amount of government spending on superannuation, the largest item in predicted future budgets. Cook (1997) explores a range of 5 scenarios based on (a) switching indexation of superannuation from prices to wages (tax/GDP ratio peaks at 33.1% in 2041); (b) reducing the indexation of superannuation payouts to 50% of the growth in the real wage (tax/GDP ratio peaks in 2051 at 36.2%); (c) raising the age of eligibility from 65 to 67 (tax/GDP ratio peaks at 36.6% in 2051); (d) means testing eligibility for superannuation (tax/GDP ratio peaks at 37.6% of GDP in 2051); and (e) the central scenario used in examining the extension of current policy into the future, including the reduction of net public debt to zero by 2015 and cutting taxes (the tax/GDP ratio peaks at 38.7% of GDP in 2051). The assumptions behind the Long Term Fiscal Models used by NZIER and Treasury are found in Cook (1997, 1997a) and Todd (1997). All scenarios that project out 50 years should be treated with great caution. These scenarios which played an important part in influencing the Todd Committee conclusions generally confirm that through a combination of tax cuts, debt reduction and adjustments to the superannuation regime, the tax burden for New Zealanders can realistically be expected to be no higher than about 29-33% of GDP until about 2025, peaking at 36%-37% near mid-century. All of these scenarios thus indicate

expected expenditure commitments by government over the next 50 years, there is scope for tax reductions through until about 2005 to a level somewhat below 30% of GDP. There is also a good chance that the tax/GDP ratio can remain in stable narrow range between 30-33% for about 20 years until about 2025. This would have important long run implications for investor confidence and economic growth. Finally, the peak in the tax/GDP ratio can be restrained to about 36-37% by 2051, assuming no expenditure cuts.

The gap between these expenditure driven tax/GDP ratios and the growth–maximising tax rates of 20-23% of GDP identified elsewhere in this report should be considered the basis for an analysis of the opportunity cost (in terms of reduced growth and wealth generation) of remaining at these constrained levels of expenditure (assuming a balanced budget). Ultimately, tax policy must be responsive to expenditure policy, but expenditure policy must be fiscally responsible because of the deleterious effects that rising taxes have on growth, employment, investment, tax avoidance, tax evasion and ethical standards in the country.

In effect, this gap between the optimal level of tax (relative to GDP) and the current and expected level of expenditure (relative to GDP) can also be used to measure the health of the tax system.

3.6 Conclusions

Traditionally, economic theory examines how to *improve* the role of government in its relationship with the market in terms of a range of factors such as: (1) offering an *appropriate range* of services such as national defence, the protection of property rights, social services, income redistribution, the development of infrastructure etc; (2) improving the *efficiency* of the services offered; (3) developing a fair and cost effective tax system and being *fiscally responsible* with respect to debt, tax and expenditures; (4) providing the market with a *stable policy environment*; and (5) *sending the market clear signals* about future policy directions. It would be wise to add to this list the necessity of ensuring that government expenditures as a share of GDP are stable for a long period of time at an appropriate level.

This suggests that if governments offer more services than appropriate, and take on too much new responsibility too fast and without appropriate cost benefit analysis and risk assessment of the consequences of the new roles and related policies, it would be difficult to maintain quality and control the costs and efficiency of existing service delivery. Signals to, and relations with, the market will become distorted, while expenditures, tax revenues and national debt will rise unnecessarily.

---

continuing room for tax cuts from the current level of 34% of GDP through until about 2005, and that a stable tax/GDP ratio around 29-33% of GDP is possible for up to 20 years after that, assuming, of course, there are no major economic disasters, wars overseas that disrupt NZ exports, and no devastating earthquakes or civil disruptions at home.

Of course, this working hypothesis that there is perhaps an equilibrium level of government expenditure relative to GDP, given constraints, needs to be tested formally. If this equilibrium level of expenditure to GDP which maximises growth is higher at any one time than the tax to GDP ratio, that may be because of demographics, changes in international market conditions, the business cycle etc. In such as case, wise policy would try to balance the budget by both reducing expenditures if possible and raising taxes above the optimal level.

4. THE HIDDEN ECONOMY, TAX EVASION AND THE TAX GAP

4.1 Introduction

Static and Dynamic Tax Gaps

How big is the gap between the amount of tax that is currently collected and the amount that is theoretically collectable under existing law? The total tax gap is the estimated value of tax evasion and potentially preventable tax avoidance by firms and individuals. The estimates for the tax gap used in this report include tax evasion only. When the tax gap is calculated based on existing law, it is a static estimate of potentially recoverable tax revenue. A dynamic estimate of the tax gap is obtained where the impact of micro and macro changes in taxpayer behaviour due to current and anticipated tax policy changes are included in the analysis.

In brief the *static tax gap* is the amount of tax that theoretically could be collected from evaders and problem avoiders *under existing law where there is no change in taxpayer behaviour, while the dynamic tax gap* is the amount of tax that theoretically could be collected from evaders and problem avoiders *if taxpayer behaviour changes as a result of changes in the tax law* (that is, if the tax/GDP ratio, the tax mix, tax rules and regulations, and auditing procedures are adjusted). The focus of this analysis is the static tax gap. More sophisticated models would have to be developed to estimate the dynamic tax gap.

This chapter examines the size of the hidden economy in New Zealand and the tax evasion gap that arises from the tax evasion of participants in the unreported economy. This chapter also presents an initial approach to determining the tax evasion minimising macro effective tax rate. What are the values of the tax/GDP ratio and the tax mix at which tax evasion begins to decline significantly? To answer this question, one needs to examine the link between the tax/GDP ratio and the related tax mix and the size of the hidden economy and the tax evasion gap. The closer to the optimal tax level and mix (in terms of the tax/GDP ratio and the components of direct and indirect tax relative to GDP), the healthier is the tax system because of the reduction of tax evasion.

Before exploring these issues it is necessary to review briefly the literature on factors which promote tax compliance and non-compliance.

Motivations for Tax Evasion and Compliance

Three Theoretical Frameworks

Three theories[83] have been developed to help explain tax evasion. The first, the rational maximising model, is based on the assumptions that individuals have perfect information, act rationally and act to minimise penalties and risks, and

[83] For a summary see Wearing & Headey, 1997.

maximise rewards. Unfortunately, this approach assumes that income is positively correlated with the propensity to evade taxes (the rich evade more because they have more to lose), which is not supported by empirical evidence.

The second approach is called the community commitment or identification model. The less that an individual identifies with the community (e.g. in terms of believing that government does not provide value for money when it spends taxpayers money), the greater the level of tax evasion.

The third theory involves a political view about government. It is held that people who believe that government should be smaller than it currently is are more likely to evade. In their survey analysis of would-be Australian tax evaders, Wearing & Headey (1997) find that the community commitment model fits best those with a propensity to evade taxes.

Early Views on Tax Evasion

The incentive to avoid and evade taxes in response to increasing tax rates[84] has been long-recognised, For example, early in the century, Taussig (1911, 1925:528) noted that:

> "not a little depends, to be sure, on the amount of the tax. The higher it becomes, the greater is the danger of evasion, [and] the greater is the difficulty of preventing demoralisation".

When more people cheat on their taxes, tax evasion becomes 'respectable' and hence more cheating takes place. The US property tax system (on the state level) has provided some dramatic examples of this. Cheating also depends on perceived fairness and equity of the tax system, and the general attitude towards the government[85].

But while high taxes promote tax evasion and potentially preventable tax avoidance, and taxpayer revolts,[86] they can also induce additional illegal activity. That is to say, high taxes can be an important factor in encouraging activity in the

---

[84] The statutory tax rate is not a good predictor of the total amount of future tax revenue. Effective tax rates are generally always lower than the statutory tax rate because of deductions, exemptions, losses, credits, and avoidance and evasion. The level of avoidance and evasion is positively correlated with the rise in the level of taxes. Thus, higher rates do not necessarily hold the promise of higher revenue.

[85] I wish to thank Tom Mayer, Professor Emeritus in Economics at the University of California (Davis) for these insights.

[86] The California taxpayer revolt in 1978 and the reaction to the poll tax in Britain in the early 1990s are two examples. More recently, corporate taxpayer protests have become common in Germany and Italy in response to both high rates and persistent raids by tax inspectors searching for evidence of evasion (*Financial Times* of London, 30 May 1996; 2 April 1996). A broader tax base and lower tax rates, as in New Zealand, can alleviate some of these problems, but better information about, and targeting of, high-risk (non-paying) taxpayers and about the economic consequences of an inappropriate tax mix and higher than optimal tax rates would provide a better basis for redesigning the tax system so as to boost tax system credibility and voluntary compliance. That is to say, somewhere below the current rates and tax mix in Italy and Germany there is the potential for reducing preventable avoidance and evasion.

underground or hidden economy. These points were recognised over 200 hundred years ago by Adam Smith (1786:350, vol. III):

" The high duties which have been imposed upon the importation of many different forms of foreign goods, in order to discourage their consumption in Great Britain, have in many cases served only to encourage smuggling; and in all cases have reduced the revenue of the customs below what more moderate duties would have afforded".

"High taxes, sometimes by diminishing the consumption of the taxed commodities, and sometimes by encouraging smuggling, frequently afford a smaller revenue to government than might be drawn from more moderate taxes. When the diminution of revenue is the effect of the diminution of consumption, there can be but one remedy, and that is the lowering of the tax." Smith (1786:354)

That is to say, the level of the tax rate is linked to the security of the tax base. The higher the tax, the greater the risk to the base, if one is an optimist, or, the smaller is the base, if one is a pessimist. In effect, high taxes undermine both public confidence in the tax system and voluntary compliance and make it harder for a tax authority to do its job.

At what rate does the propensity to evade begin to accelerate? Are these rates the same for individuals and firms, and across individuals and firms? These are very important questions. There are revenue gains as well as gains from the reduction of deadweight loss (in general, economic welfare gains), to be had if evasion-minimising tax rates can be discovered. The performance frontier for a healthy tax system would be determined by a weighted average of those rates to which corporate and individual tax evaders accelerate their response.

The incentive to minimise taxes and the ability to take advantage of provisions within the law to minimise tax burdens should not be confused with abusive or potentially preventable tax avoidance and evasion. *Legal* tax minimisation should not be viewed as a social 'bad'.

There is an apparently puzzling set of trends in current research on tax evasion. Macro-estimates of the hidden economy, which shall be presented shortly, indicate that the total tax burden and the tax mix (relative to GDP) both play a very important role in determining the size of the hidden economy and related tax evasion.

On the other hand, micro economic research, while sometimes acknowledging the importance of increases in the marginal effective tax rate (usually for individuals), sometimes tends to downplay the importance of the level of tax and the tax mix. Instead, the micro approach emphasises the deterrent effect on tax evasion by the level of potential penalties and the probability of audit, combined with the influence of sociological and psychological factors such as the behaviour of peers,[87] and perceptions of the fairness[88] of the tax system based on a number of factors:

---

[87] "One of the most consistent findings in survey research about taxpayer attitudes and behaviours is that those who report compliance believe that their friends (and taxpayers in general) comply, whereas those who report cheating believe that others cheat" (Carroll, 1992:47).

- the taxpaying behaviour of others,
- perceptions of whether the government offers value for money in its services,
- the compliance costs of paying tax, and
- how taxpayers are treated by the tax authority.

The position established in this Report is that these macro and micro explanations of tax evasion are related. That is to say, higher taxes, inflation and government regulation create disaffection and cynicism among taxpayers that promote a higher propensity to evade tax obligations. Higher tax evasion leads to stronger compliance laws and higher compliance costs. Higher compliance costs tend to promote more tax evasion.

As well, higher government expenditure and higher taxes lead to more government waste and greater cynicism about the value of government spending. If the tax rate rises too high, this produces a credibility spiral in which government fights a losing battle to convince taxpayers of the value of government spending and to force taxpayers to comply. Picking the threshold for the level of tax/GDP which manages best the level of tax evasion is a new research field that needs much more work.

Who are the evaders? Research by Clotfelter (1983:368) and Slemrod (1985:234; 237) found that married (as compared to unmarried) individuals, and people under 65 (rather than those over 65) have a higher propensity to evade taxes by underreporting income, although Clotfelter (1983:368) found that married evaders tended to be more concentrated in non-business rather than business returns. An Internal Revenue Service report in the United States in 1983 found that the tax evasion gap for wage and salary earners was about 6%, for interest and dividend income, about 14%, and for income derived from partnerships and small business, about 53% (Slemrod, 1985:236).

Thus, it is clear that there is some relationship between the opportunity to hide income (e.g. a wage earner's pay check is part of a PAYE (pay as you earn) return, deducted at source - unless there are under the table payments), and the ability and willingness to evade taxes. Clotfelter (1983:370-71) also found that about half of the value of the evasion problem came from individuals, about one-third from non-farm businesses, and the rest from farms.

In a survey of 393 people in metropolitan Melbourne, Wearing & Headey (1997:9-11) found a consistent pattern among those that indicated they would be sympathetic to tax evasion. The would-be evaders, as compared to compliant

---

[88] "The sense of fairness is very important for maintaining the legitimacy of taxpaying. When people think taxes are unfair, they spend less time reporting carefully and may be motivated to produce what they perceive to be a fair outcome even when this does not conform to the law. Public opinion polls show, during the 1970s, an increasing sense of unfairness and failure to get value from tax dollars. In short, people may be motivated to work hard to report accurately and pay what they owe by their sense that the laws and their application are fair in terms of the distribution of tax payments, the way taxes are spent, the process of tax reporting and paying, and the way they are treated by the IRS" (Carroll, 1992:47).

taxpayers, tended to be younger, and have lower occupational status, lower education, lower income, fewer children, less competence, less economic knowledge and less confidence in the efficacy and fairness of the tax system. They also tended to be self-employed and borrow money from friends and family rather than from financial institutions. These latter two characteristics are common features of the hidden economy.

With respect to the efficacy and fairness of the tax system, these features are measured by whether or not taxpayers feel they get value for money from their taxes through government spending and how satisfied they are with government control of inflation. The important role of taxes and inflation in determining the level of the hidden economy and tax evasion is highlighted later in this chapter in the work of Giles (1996) and Giles & Caragata (1996).

Do higher taxes promote evasion? Gutmann (1977:5) suggests that "higher and higher taxes drive more and more of the economy underground, beyond the reach of the tax collector". Slemrod (1985:237) found that high marginal effective tax rates promote evasion, although there is no evidence that higher income earners engage in tax evasion more than lower income earners.

What proportion of taxpayers are engaged in tax evasion? Much of the research on this issue has been undertaken in the United States. The estimates vary with assumptions and with the sample employed. Clotfelter (1983:366), using 47,000 individual returns from American taxpayers in 1969 estimated that "...from 20% to 58% of taxpayers are evading taxes, if only by small amounts", and assuming that "reporting mistakes are random". Slemrod (1985:236) estimated that the figure was between 1.3% and 3.5%, based on analysis of 23,111 American returns in 1977. In a recent Australian paper, Wearing & Headey (1997:9) report that two surveys undertaken in the 1970s and 1980s in Sweden suggest that the level of tax evasion is about 20-30% of the population of taxpayers. Estimates for New Zealand companies suggest 3% - 7% of all audit firms evade taxes. The percentages may be higher for the full population of companies if there is selection bias in auditing samples. Estimates of the percentage of individuals have not yet been undertaken.

Looking at the problem the other way, what are the factors that promote taxpayer compliance? Key factors include providing evidence that there is a reduction of tax evasion, ensuring that government provides value for money in its expenditures, lower tax burdens, a tough but fair penalties regime, a tough but fair and realistic disclosure requirements regime[89], requiring deductions at source, and using a scientific-based audit selection approach based on econometric risk analysis using the taxpayer databases. The key to compliance is to ensure that the tax burden is set at the right level with the right mix of direct and indirect taxes, as will be discussed in the modelling results below, and to ensure that scientific audit selection is implemented.

[89] Publicly listed firms, by and large, tend to be larger companies, and larger companies tend to be wary of engaging in tax evasion, and, instead, concentrate on legal tax minimisation. Smaller firms which are not widely held are likely to avoid becoming publicly listed, and therefore would not have the same disclosure requirements as publicly listed firms.

Scientific audit selection ranks all taxpayers from lowest to highest risk and permits rational audit selection by profiling taxpayers based on key attributes. This approach offers the prospect of significantly reducing audit compliance costs of firms which are typically compliant (by refocusing audits on higher risk firms), and reducing operation costs by permitting an efficient reallocation of audit resources to higher risk firms.

And how much progress is being made on these points? First, there is evidence that tax evasion has risen significantly over the last ten years, thus no progress here. Second, the government needs to continue its effort to prove to taxpayers that it provides value for money in its expenditures (some progress here). Third, tax burdens are close to an all-time high (36.1% of GDP in 1991), but tax cuts are slowly reducing this (some progress here). Fourth, a tough but fair new penalties regime was just introduced in April 1997 (good progress assuming no bugs in the new legislation), but a tax cut will be much more important in reducing tax evasion than a tough penalties regime (which may drive some tax evasion deeper underground). Fifth, there are no current discussions about improving a public disclosure requirements regime (no progress). Sixth, New Zealand already extensively uses the deduction at source method (good progress), except in some areas such as for homeowner dealings with resident contractors. Seventh, scientific based audit selection has not been tried by New Zealand's Inland Revenue (no progress).

Perhaps one of the reasons why the level of tax is not emphasised too much in analysis of tax evasion lies in the assumption that if the tax burden is cut there will be very little return to the Treasury as a result of the tax cut. For example,

"the marginal tax rate is associated negatively with compliance, although a cut in the marginal tax rate would cost the U.S. Treasury a dollar in revenue for every 5.3 cents it could raise via enhanced compliance" (Rice, 1992:152).

The problem with this conclusion is that it is based on static analysis. It does not take into consideration the positive impact of a reduced tax burden on investment, employment and growth. For New Zealand, Branson & Lovell (1997) have concluded that a reduction in the tax/GDP ratio from its current level of 35% to a growth-maximising rate of 22.5% of GDP would, taking the revenue dynamics into consideration, result in a reduction of tax revenue by only 6% and increase purchasing power in the private sector by 30%. The lesson in this analysis is that the dynamic effects of tax cuts must be factored into the models used to estimate taxpayer responses.

4.2 The Legal Limits of Tax Minimisation

There is a tradition in common law countries that taxpayers have every right to minimise their tax burden. If there is a problem, it is often (but not exclusively) with the law and its interpretation. Taxpayers react to the scope and the scale of tax requirements and related loopholes. Perhaps the most cited legal opinion on this matter comes from the eminent American judge, Learned Hand, in Commissioner v. Newman (159, F.2d 848, CA-2, 1947), who wrote:

"over and over again courts have said that there is nothing sinister in so arranging one's affairs as to keep taxes as low as possible. Everybody does so, rich or poor, and all do right, for nobody owes any public duty to pay more than the law demands: taxes are enforced exactions, not voluntary contributions. To demand more in the name of morals is mere cant."

British jurisprudence has reached a similar conclusion:

"Every man is entitled if he can order his affairs so that the tax attracting under the appropriate Acts is less than it would otherwise be. If he succeeds in ordering them so as to secure this result, then, however, unappreciative the Commissioner of Inland Revenue or fellow taxpayers may be of his ingenuity, he cannot be compelled the increased tax" (IRD vs Duke of Westminster, 1936, AC 1 at 19).

4.3 The Threat of the Hidden Economy

Most overseas studies of the hidden economy took place 15-20 years ago when inflation began to be a serious problem. At that time, the estimated range for the size of the hidden economy in OECD countries was between 7% and 16% of GDP. Higher tax burdens since then, high inflation earlier in the period, and improved economic growth would probably have raised that range to between 10%-20% of GDP by now. Thus, most western economies are probably experiencing a larger hidden economy and higher tax evasion than 20 years ago:

"Unreported enterprise is as old as tax collection itself, but new research suggests that the shadow [economy] is spreading ever wider. Including both illegally earned income and illicit activities, such as drug dealing, it may now account for one-seventh [14 percent] of total output in the world's wealthiest countries. That means that governments face a worrying problem. They may know less than ever about what is really going on in their economies jobless rates, for instance, will over-state the true level of unemployment – and will have an increasingly difficult time taxing it".[90]

Research undertaken by Friedrich Schneider of Lintz University in Austria suggests that the hidden economy in Switzerland and Austria is about 7% of GDP, in Japan, the USA, Britain about 12% of GDP, in Australia and the Netherlands about 13% of GDP, in Germany and France about 14% of GDP, in Canada and Ireland about 15%, in Denmark, Norway and Sweden about 18% of GDP, in Belgium about 22% of GDP, Spain about 23% of GDP, and Italy about 26% of GDP. We have been unable to obtain his models so that we can evaluate the quality of his results.

According to Schneider, the principal factors that contribute to a growing hidden economy and thus higher tax evasion are higher taxes (social security, pay roll taxes, GST), greater regulation of labour and product markets, the strong growth of the service sector, and self-employment.[91] These explanations for the causes of the size of the hidden economy accord with the research undertaken by Giles (1996), Giles & Caragata (1996) and Caragata & Giles (1996) for New Zealand's Inland Revenue Department. The prospect for the hidden economy to grow

[90] *The Economist*, "Light on the Shadows", 3 May 1997 p. 63-64.
[91] *The Economist*, "Light on the Shadows", 3 May 1997 p. 63-64.

because of commercial activity on the internet must also be considered a real threat to tax revenue.

At 11% of GDP in 1995, New Zealand's hidden economy (and thus its tax evasion problems) are near the low-end of the estimated range for the OECD, and similar to both Canada and Britain's level. Another recent estimate for Canada placed the size of the hidden economy between 8-11% of GDP (Spiro, 1994). For the UK, an estimate prepared for the European Commission[92] was 12% of GDP (about $130 billion) with the cost to the Treasury being about $32 billion in lost taxes (about 3% of GDP). Particular concerns in the UK are evasion of GST by companies in the construction industry. Older estimates of the size of the hidden economy for the UK had placed the ratio at about 6-8% of GDP.

Activity in the hidden economy can pose a serious threat to both fiscal and monetary policy, as well as to a respect for law. As the ratio of the hidden economy to the reported economy grows so too does the level of tax evasion and potentially preventable tax avoidance, financial activity beyond the control of the central bank, and the potential for political police and judicial corruption. As tax evasion grows, so too does cynicism about government and about the credibility of the tax system, while public support for the philosophy of 'voluntary compliance', which underpins tax system stability in democratic countries, wanes.[93]

Revenue forecasting and government expenditure are constrained if a rising segment of the population is not paying tax. This will promote larger than necessary fiscal deficits that will have important implications for investor confidence, the balance of payments and the exchange rate. This will ultimately affect the efficacy of monetary policy. At the same time, the control of inflation becomes more problematic when activity in the hidden economy is not immediately responsive to changes in policy by the central bank. A good example in recent times is Albania (Caragata, 1995).

The gravity of this threat has recently raised the hidden economy and the related information and social control problems to the top of the agenda of the International Monetary Fund. New research is highlighting the importance of treating the hidden economy as relevant for policy-making purposes (Rahman, 1992; Caragata, 1995)[94].

An uncontrolled money supply undermines the inflation policies of the central bank and has negative effects on the efficiency performance of the economy. Each additional percentage point rise in inflation can cause a significant long

---

[92] Deloitte & Touche, 1997, Report for the European Commission on Britain's shadow economy (as cited in the Financial Times, 26 May 1997).

[93] Clotfelter (1983:363) observed that tax evasion "...fosters disenchantment over taxes and poses a serious threat to the voluntary compliance on which the American income tax is based".

[94] The author worked on mission to Tirana, Albania in December 1995 dealing with both the growth and threats posed by the informal financial sector. The confidential paper examined the scale and scope of the informal financial sector and the extent to which it was taking away business from the formal banking sector.

term deadweight loss (Feldstein, 1996). Both fiscal and monetary policy deficiencies engendered by a growing hidden economy will have strong negative implications for future economic growth, and both will lead to the erosion of public confidence in government.

It is important, therefore, to learn more about: (1) the incentive structures that affect the behavioural responses that shape the development and evolution of the unreported economy, (2) the profiles of high-risk as compared to low-risk taxpayers, and (3) the limits of tax policy in addressing these problems.

Finally, there is the issue of deadweight loss. High taxes not only have important legal and revenue effects, they also create two forms of deadweight loss even though the evader is not, paying tax on the non-declared income. First, there is a "concealment cost" that the evader incurs while disguising income in order to evade tax (Usher, 1991). Slemrod (1991:68-9) observes that Usher's analysis involves a useful reinterpretation of Harberger's deadweight loss triangle. The social cost of evasion "is an excess amount of resources spent on hiding income and avoiding detection...[and] one way to limit the deadweight cost of evasion is to have a very high penalty on evasion". Thus, this deadweight loss involves the diversion from normal behaviour to illicit behaviour. This is a technical efficiency loss.

The second deadweight loss related to tax evasion is an allocative efficiency loss. This cost arises from the fact that the tax burdens of honest taxpayers are higher than they would otherwise be if all evasion were eliminated, because the total tax burden is less evenly shared owing to evasion. The marginal increase in the tax burden of honest taxpayers leads to a distortion in their relative consumption and investment patterns and to a further misallocation of resources because investment flows to those areas or firms which pay less tax (Harberger, 1964).

This state of affairs also violates the principal of taxation neutrality across firms, and undermines the principal of fairness across all taxpayers by shifting the tax burden to taxpayers who are not exploiting the loopholes or evading. This in turn weakens voluntary compliance, which is the heart of a healthy tax system, because free-riders (abusive avoiders and evaders) are rewarded (tax cost savings). Thus, while the tax minimisers and evaders reduce or eliminate the deadweight loss of paying tax, society as a whole bears the burden in the form of allocative inefficiency.

4.4 Learned Behaviour and The Theory of Incentive Structures

While this analysis about tax evasion and the hidden economy is helpful, it still is not set in a theoretical structure that offers a useful analytical framework. One option is to set tax evasion behaviour in the context of learned behaviour and the theory of incentive structures.

Incentive structures in general are shaped by a combination of economic policy and institutional parameters (Olson, 1996),[95] as well as the rewards for effort and the availability of opportunities to capture rewards. A combination of opportunities and constraints shape incentive structures. There are at least two types of opportunities: structural and cyclical.

Structural opportunities arise from *supportive changes* in institutional parameters determining property rights and in the development and allocation of resources, technology, capital accumulation and human capital development, the size of government and the role of the market, fiscal, monetary and trade policy, and finally, changes in the market's response and adaptability to challenges and crises. Cyclical opportunities arise from an increase in the growth rate of supply and demand for goods and services affecting the country's economic performance.

The constraints are those factors which impose costs and curtail the exploitation of existing and potential opportunities. Hidden within each cost is an incentive to save. That is, there are opportunities within constraints.

Structural constraints arise from *non-supportive changes* in institutional parameters determining property rights and the allocation of resources, technology, capital accumulation and human capital development, the size of government and the role of the market, changes in fiscal, monetary and trade policy, and changes in the market's response and adaptability to challenges and crises. Cyclical constraints arise from a decrease in the rate of growth of supply of, and demand for, goods and services affecting the country's economic performance.

The stimulus-response link shapes the learning curve. That is a combination of incentive structures and constraints affect perceptions and behaviour which in turn shape the learning curve. In general, the incremental theory of learning specifies that "learning increases gradually as a result of reinforced practice" (Houston, 1976:131). Practice is reinforced because of the presence of opportunity, constraints (which contain costs and penalties) and rewards. The learning curve literature has demonstrated for decades that the standard reward in the market place for learning is cost savings (see Asher, 1956; Crawford, 1944, n.d.; Delionback, 1987; Hirsch, 1952, 1956; and Wright, 1936). Learning is measured by performance improvement. Hence, if the tax system's design reaches toward best practice, then one would expect the behavioural response of taxpayers and the economy to be close to the performance frontier.

The learning curve is an evolutionary depiction of the behavioural consequences of the incentive structure operating in a particular jurisdiction or organisation. Learning curve analysis can be applied to all important behavioural adjustments to tax, including the production, investment, evasion and avoidance responses to

[95] "The structure of incentives depends not only on what economic policies are chosen in each period, but also on the long run institutional arrangements: on the legal systems that enforce contracts and private property rights and on the political structures, constitutional provisions, and the extent of special-interest lobbies and cartels" (Olson, 1996:6).

a tax change. Understanding these effects is crucial for understanding the impact of taxes on the economy, in particular the revenue generation, revenue conservation, efficiency (including deadweight loss) and equity features of the economy.

This theory of the formation of incentive structures helps us to understand the stimulus-response link between tax shocks created by government and subsequent behavioural responses by firms and individuals. The interaction between the tax shock stimulus combined with the learned response to opportunities and constraints affect the size of the hidden economy and the tax gap.

Taxes are constraints which impose a current and potential cost of doing business for firms, and a current and potential cost of living for individuals. Just as taxes reduce cash flow for firms, they also reduce disposable income for individuals. As a result, progressively higher taxes progressively affect the incentives structures of firms and individuals.

Tax as a Cost of Doing Business

Because taxes have a current and potential impact on a firm's cash flow they affect the immediate choices that firms make with respect to the purchase of inputs, the avoidance or evasion of taxes, the production of outputs, and undertaking new investments. For individuals, taxes are a cost of living. Their choices concern the decisions to purchase items in the consumption basket, and to avoid or evade taxes by not reporting income or purchases.

Taxes are a current and potential cost of doing business for firms and a current and potential cost of living for individuals. Just as taxes reduce cash flow for firms, they also reduce disposable income for individuals. As a result, taxes affect the incentives structures of firms and individuals. The analysis in this report will concentrate on the impact of taxes on the incentive structures of firms.[96] This theory of the formation and evolution of incentive structures will be particularly relevant to our work on the hidden economy and the tax gap. But it also has more general relevance. As Blundell (1995:124) has pointed out:

"...knowledge of behavioural responses considerably improves our ability to measure the welfare gains (or losses) of [tax] reform)".

The reality that taxes are an endogenous *direct* cost of doing business is a long standing conclusion in various parts of economic literature, notably Dupuit's (1844)[97] work on cost benefit analysis, Senior's (1862:19) analysis of the expenses of mills, Taussig's (1911; 1925:185) assessment of the survival and profitability of firms, J.M. Clark's (1923:189-90; 202) analysis of plant scale and

---

[96] Time and resource constraints prevent an examination of the impact of taxes on the incentive structure of individuals.

[97] "the tax affects not only those who pay it, but also those who would have been consumers but for the tax" (Dupuit, 1844; 1952:90).

overhead costs, Rustow's (1926, 1967, 1978:412; 1991:15; 67)[98] work on the "cost/receipts relationship", "cost structure"[99], unit costs, and related production, investment and employment decisions, Musgrave's (1959:286) discussion of short-run adjustments[100], and Coase's (1937:393) analysis of the existence and structure of firms (by vertically integrating firms avoid taxation).

Of course, in the finance and accounting literature, taxes are also generally recognised as a business cost because corporate taxes affect cash flow in the short-medium term and thus induce, along with other factors, efforts at tax minimisation (Scholes and Wolfson, 1992:2-3). This suggests that taxes can be a variable cost by choice, but it also suggests that the total amount of tax is capable of being strategically determined for some firms.

Therefore, in the short term, taxes *may* be treated by some firms, depending on their ability, as a fixed cost rather than a variable cost of doing business.[101] The extent to which firms' effective tax payments (relative to a base such as sales, net assets, costs or gross profits) are fixed in the short term and variable in the long term, or variable across sectors, or variable across efficiency performance (Caragata, 1996), are empirical matters that require further investigation. Some analysis of the profiles of the migration or non-migration of firms across effective tax rate bands is presented later in this report.

---

[98] These conclusions largely apply to his micro or firm level analysis. At the macro level, Rustow argued that taxes do not affect the "macro-economic cost-revenue ratio" because profitable firms pay taxes that subsidise services (e.g. bridges) for marginally profitable firms and thus create free-riders. This analysis neglects the existence of deadweight loss, assumes full value for money in government expenditures, ignores the large role played by other taxes, and ignores tax avoidance and evasion. Of interest, though, is that Rustow asserted that when statutory tax rates on corporate profits was pushed above 50%, "the dampening effect which it has on entrepreneurial ambitions sooner or later exerts a negative influence on their investment activity" (Rustow, 1991:39-40).

[99] Independent of the work of the German founder of the cost structure approach, a segment of the American cost structure approach to efficiency analysis has also treated tax as a cost of doing business (e.g. Meyer, 1978).

[100] Musgrave (1959:286) distanced himself from the traditional economics approach of not treating taxes as a cost of doing business that affects price and output decisions: "The traditional rule that a profits tax cannot give rise to short-run adjustments in price remains a good point of departure, but hardly more. Without falling back upon the practical argument that businessmen do not act this way, we find a variety of situations where the tax may lead to adjustments in price and output. These include the return to working capital, monopoly pricing under restraint, oligopoly pricing, and situations of collective bargaining where the firm's ability to pay is taken into consideration. Possibilities such as these throw considerable doubt on the conventional position that price policy remains unaffected in the short run. In addition, there are long-run considerations where the tax may act on the supply of capital and entrepreneurship. On balance, the theoretical argument lends more support to the moderate conclusions that short-run adjustments in price (1) play a significant role, and (2) that a part of the tax is passed on, than it lends to the extreme position that no such adjustments occur". As a rule of thumb, but without empirical evidence, Musgrave usually assumed that one-third of the profits tax was passed on. See Mintz (1995) for the continuing lack of empirical evidence on the incidence of the corporate profits tax. But see Auld and Wilton (1988) for evidence that in highly unionised sectors labour has the ability to ensure that firms eat most of a personal tax increase.

[101] For the first treatment of taxes as a *fixed* cost of doing business, see Ripley's (1921) work on *Railroads: Rates and Regulations* (chapter ii) as reported in Clark (1923:11).

One tax minimisation strategy is to employ higher leverage in order to take advantage of interest deductibility. This can be a risky strategy because high leverage mandates high fixed interest costs that can tip the balance against corporate survival during recessions.

Empirical work previously undertaken across 10 countries suggests that for firms which pay tax, taxes range (quartal[102] medians) between 0.25% and 8.0% of total costs. Thus, the reward for the minimisation of the tax burden can be significant. These percentages represent a large share of the gross margin (Caragata, 1996), and help to put in perspective the attractiveness of tax minimisation and tax evasion.

Tax Savings Are High-Powered Money

Minimising taxes is a true cost saving. It is a substitute way of developing cost savings, as compared to reducing labour, materials or equipment purchases. In fact the cost savings from tax minimisation on evasion is "*high-powered money*" (Caragata, 1995a) compared to employing or diverting other sources of savings and revenue for the firm, each of which entails an opportunity cost. Tax savings are 'high-powered' because they have the potential of generating a high multiple of the original amount saved given the potential rate of return compared to other sources of financing.

A loan carries a market interest rate. An equity float has a dividend yield. A reduction of a unit of labour, materials, or equipment, or the postponement of a new unit of investment has an output cost. Ear-marking a proportion of current cash flow (e.g. for R&D) has opportunity costs - e.g. a reduction in current production. But tax savings have none of these opportunity costs, nor are their transaction costs likely to be as high as the transaction costs involved in efficiency savings related to employment (labour shedding), physical capital (refurbishing), credit markets (asset sales to reduce debt), and equity markets (share repurchase).

For the firm, the high powered money value of savings from tax minimisation comes from (1) the value of a dollar of savings from tax minimisation *plus* (2) the rate of return anticipated for that invested dollar, *plus either (3)* the value of the opportunity cost of some substitute source of financing from debt or equity markets, or cash flow diversion, or (4) a weighted average of all of these alternative sources of financing. These insights help to explain the high powered money value of tax minimisation savings and why tax minimisation is so ardently pursued by firms, and why tax lawyers and accountants are so well paid.

Opportunities to disguise income are pro-cyclical (Giles, 1995), gaining strength with each business upturn. They are also dependent, impart, on the use of cash in transactions (Giles, 1995) and the ability to shield information from the tax authority.

---

[102] The term 'quartals" (quadrisections of a skewed distribution) was noted in Gibrat, 1931, 1957:67. The original source is Dudley Baxter, 1868, *National Income*.

Community Commitment and Learned Behaviour

Taxes are also a symbol of government. Taken together with the impact of inflation and the consequences for taxpayers of cumulative government rules and regulations (including regulations that affect employers and employees), existing tax burdens and rising taxes are often resented by individuals. Tax evasion can be seen (but never justified) as a way of getting even or protecting one's territory. There is

"...some survey evidence indicating a positive correlation between committing evasion and a professed sense of dissatisfaction with the tax system, although there is no evidence that the marginal tax rate successfully proxies for such an attitude" (Slemrod, 1985:234).

The degree of compliance by individual taxpayers is also a matter of learned behaviour that responds to a variety of constraints. There is general agreement that compliance rises with the risk of detection such as the:

"...fraction of income subject to information reporting, the audit rate, perceived detection risk, or the difficulty of constructing an audit trail..." (Klepper and Nagin, 1989:1)

But tax evasion is a learned process that is shaped simultaneously by the cost savings in the opportunities to evade and the constraints and related penalties against such illegal activity. Thus, evasion opportunities are continually being shaped at finer levels of detail by the coefficient between perceived reward and probability-adjusted risk. Klepper & Nagin (1989:23) have captured this pursuit of detail in the search for risk-minimising evasion opportunities, in their study of 50,000 taxpayer returns in the United States in 1982:

"our findings suggest that compliance behaviour conforms closely to the incentives and deterrents created by the enforcement environment. We find marked variations in compliance levels across line items which appear to be systematically related to the difficulty of establishing non-compliance and the penalties for detected non-compliance. We also find that the influence of the endogeneity of detection risk and penalties is pervasive. Ex ante, taxpayers appear to allocate their non-compliance across line items to minimise expected penalties. They avoid extreme non-compliance on specific line items and appear to recognise the influence of non-compliance on one line item (or set of line items) or the risk of detection of non-compliance on other line items".

The results of our modelling suggest that any increase in taxes promotes higher avoidance and evasion (Giles, 1996). In addition, with respect to income versus sales taxes, our results suggest that there appear to be more opportunities and less constraints for individuals and firms to minimise income as compared to indirect taxes.

First, income is easier to disguise than a sales transaction because individuals have more control over opportunities to disguise income than over opportunities to disguise purchases because income is generally from a few sources known personally to the taxpayer, while purchases are generally made in stores owned and managed by people with whom the taxpayer has no personal contacts. The transaction costs of organising a network of non-market transactions or organised tax evasion of sales are high as compared to the transaction costs of evading personal income tax (beyond the scope of pay-as-you-earn or income withholding tax at source regimes).

Second, taxpayers are more motivated to protect their income from all incursions such as taxation because income is a personal possession and a tax on such income is a direct threat to a personal possession, whereas a tax on a consumption item is a tax on an item owned by someone else, and only becomes a threat if the taxpayer decides to buy the item (as compared to doing without, bartering or stealing, each of which contains costs and risks). As well, consumption taxes are generally, but not always (Canada is an exception) hidden in the price of the good, so that such taxes are less noticeable than income taxes deducted in individuals' paychecks.

Third, the risks of paying penalties related to evading income taxes are higher than for sales taxes for several reasons. It is difficult and costly for the tax authority to obtain information about persons' income outside the PAYE (pay-as-you-earn) tax collection system, whereas consumption transactions (except in sectors dominated by cash transactions such as some retail trade and homeowners' arrangements with small builders) generally have a paper trail. Related to this, the tax authority has more resources to target business than to target individuals and a firm, faced with GST payments, needs to keep audited records of sales for which "benchmark" or "comparable" firm profiles are available to the tax audit team. Discrepancies, or deviations from normal commerical behaviour, can be spotted more easily for these firms than for individuals.

Fourth, the rewards for evading on personal tax are higher than the rewards for evading consumption tax because income is generally larger than purchases. Related to this is the fact that the tax rate on income is higher than on consumption. Thus, the taxpayer will see that there is more at stake in income tax evasion as compared to consumption tax. As a result of these elements of control, transaction costs, private property perceptions, risks of getting caught, and potential rewards, the opportunities and constraints favour the choice of income tax evasion as compared to consumption tax evasion. Therefore, individuals probably devote more learning time to minimising income as compared to indirect taxes, which reinforces their preference for income tax evasion.

Finally, it should also be recalled that tax evaders who do not declare their income generally do pay GST when they purchase items because it is embedded in the price. As a result, tax revenue is higher than would be the case if only the income tax were used to collect tax revenue.

All of this raises the following question. If taxes are lowered, will the learned evasion behaviour also be reduced, or will evasion behaviour remain at previously high levels because of the benefits identified by evaders. In other words, once learned, does evasion ever diminish?

The answer to this question will require an empirical response, but, while both hypotheses seem viable, it is clear that learning is a dynamic phenomenon that responds to changes in the incentive structure. To maintain that learning will remain fixed at a given level is like trying to ensure that water doesn't leak out of your hands. Recall also that rising taxes are a threat to a property right. As income taxes fall, current evaders may very well revive interest in the credibility of government spending programs because they feel less threatened by government.

In a related vein, it would be a mistake for the tax authority to presume that "once an evader, always an evader" because it implies that many taxpayers will only respond to a stick and not to a carrot. An approach based totally on negative reinforcement would do damage in the long run to government's attempt to have the taxpayer view "voluntary compliance" as the basis for the tax system. These are obviously serious matters that merit further careful analysis.

Analysis of Tax Minimisation by Firms Stemming From Their Economic Success

The tax system provides opportunities for firms to minimise their tax burdens through their use of, for example, interest payments and depreciation. Given that taxes are a cost of doing business, it is rational for firms to minimise their tax burdens. The following very preliminary analysis considers whether the proportion of profits paid in taxes by companies change as their sales increase. Underlying this analysis is a belief that companies that are more successful (in terms of greater turnover) generally have better cashflow, a broader and more flexible asset portfolio and a better credit rating. Thus, these companies have more opportunity to manipulate their portfolio to maximise their use of the tax instruments such as depreciation and interest expenses and thus minimise their tax burdens. This would imply that companies pay tax on their ability to minimise rather than their ability to pay.

(1) Data Issues

The analysis uses taxpayer information for 6,571 companies in total in New Zealand for the period 1993-95. Profile, financial and tax information on each company is from Inland Revenue's FIRST database of New Zealand taxpayers. A random sample of 20% of companies was taken for each year (44,734 companies in total). The randomly selected company data for each year was assumed to be independent, and thus the data for the three years was combined into one cross-sectional dataset.

Removing all companies with missing income statement or tax data reduced the original sample. The sample was further constrained to focus only on companies which paid some tax during the income year (i.e. tax expense > 0). Thus, the analysis considered only those companies that interact with the tax system and thus for which there exists a relationship between sales, profit and taxes.

Some financial variables contained negative values[103]. For variables where this seemed unlikely to reflect reality (i.e. the revenue and expense components), the absolute value of the variables was taken. Net profit was left unchanged. A further constraint was imposed that revenue and sales must be non-zero.

(2) Model Construction

The purpose of this study is to analyse how taxes and net profit varies as sales increase and the cost structure of the company varies. The relationship between these variables is expected to differ across industries. Thus, the sample is separated into nine industries.

Industry[104]	Description	ANZSIC Code
1	agriculture and mining	0-199
2	manufacturing	200-299
3	construction	400-449
4	wholesale trade	450-499
5	retail trade	500-599
6	transport, communication & storage	600-729
7	finance, insurance & property services	730-779
8	business services	780-799
9	community & personal services	820-899

The impact of sales and the cost structure of the company on the proportion of net profit the company pays in taxes is considered. The coefficient on sales will indicate whether companies vary in their ability to minimise their taxes as their sales increase.

A log-linear functional form was used. However, due to the existence of negative and zero values of net profit, and in the cost structure breakdown, the traditional log transformation was replaced by a hyperbolic sine:

$$H(x) = \ln (x + (1 + x^2)^{1/2}) \tag{1}$$

Thus the resulting regression for each industry (i = 1-9) takes the following form:

$$H(np_i) - H(tax_i) = \beta_{0i} + \beta_{1i}H(sales_i) + \beta_{2i}H(lab_i) + \beta_{3i}H(kap_i) + \beta_{4i}H(mat_i) \tag{2}$$

where:
np = net profit after interest and before tax
tax = total tax expense to IRD over the income year

---

[103] The following variables contained negative values: sales (0.2% of the sample), opening stock (0.2%), purchases (0.1%), closing stock (0.4%), total revenue (0.2%), advertising (0.3%), bad debts (0.8%), communications (0.2%), depreciation (0.7%) and net profit (4.4%). Entertainment, FBT, insurance, interest expense, legal expenses, consultant & management fees, rent paid, repairs, research & development, royalty expenses, wages & salaries, sub contractors payments, travel & accommodation, motor vehicle expenses and taxes (by definition) did not contain negative values.

[104] Utilities and government services were excluded from the sample (ANZSIC 300-399 & 800-819).

lab = (consultant & management fees + FBT + wages & salaries + sub contractors payments) / total revenue

kap = (interest expense + depreciation + rent paid + repairs & maintenance + royalty expenses) / total revenue

mat = (opening stock + purchases - closing stock + advertising + bad debts + communications + entertainment + insurance + legal expenses + research & development + travel & accommodation + motor vehicle expenses) / total revenue

(3) Results

The results of this analysis should be treated with caution. They are a first attempt at analysis of this issue and are thus subject to change.

Diagnostic tests revealed heteroskedasticity in some of the regressions. It is possible that the existence of heteroskedasticity reflects a non-linear relationship between the variables, which was not reflected fully in our log-linear functional form. Unfortunately, time constraints meant that the form of the heteroskedasticity and other potential functional forms were not investigated further. Rather, White's (1980) standard heteroskedastic-consistent covariance estimation was used to correct the estimates for an unknown type of heteroskedasticity. Those regressions for which this was done are denoted by an * in the table below. The brackets contain t-ratios.

Regression Results: H(np)-H(tax)

	H(sales)	H(lab)	H(kap)	H(mat)	constant	R^2 adj.
all industries *	0.061	-0.244	0.079	0.037	-0.430	0.0011
6566 df	(1.966)	(-1.823)	(0.410)	(0.611)	(-1.021)	
agric & mining *	0.390	-1.475	1.601	-0.500	-5.016	0.0156
545 df	(2.337)	(-2.191)	(2.004)	(-1.246)	(-2.249)	
manufacturing *	0.145	-0.003	-0.250	0.204	-1.748	0.0059
1179 df	(1.838)	(-0.010)	(-0.605)	(0.963)	(-1.557)	
construction *	-0.084	0.236	-0.309	-0.131	1.713	-0.0029
591 df	(-0.933)	(0.595)	(-0.446)	(-0.559)	(1.409)	
wholesale trade *	-0.055	-0.551	0.313	0.176	1.252	0.0017
999 df	(-0.763)	(-1.960)	(0.889)	(1.306)	(1.284)	
retail trade	0.026	-0.437	0.586	-0.061	0.047	-0.0016
1253 df	(0.395)	(-1.201)	(1.200)	(-0.438)	(0.052)	
trans & comm'n	-0.077	0.248	0.268	-0.350	1.547	0.0002
365 df	(-0.879)	(0.403)	(0.334)	(-1.419)	(1.237)	
fin, insurance etc	0.061	-0.925	-0.030	0.111	-0.615	0.0044
586 df	(0.692)	(-1.474)	(-0.041)	(0.456)	(-0.542)	
business services	0.103	-0.498	0.050	0.043	-0.582	-0.0003
702 df	(1.628)	(-1.235)	(0.087)	(0.197)	(-0.724)	
personal etc	0.220	-1.385	-0.807	0.594	-1.948	0.0186
306 df	(2.088)	(-1.987)	(-0.664)	(1.359)	(-1.372)	

The regression for each industry given above shows the impact on the change in the proportion of profits paid in taxes of changes in sales (and the cost structure).

All this preliminary analysis assumes a linear relationship between the dependent variable and the explanatory variables. Further analysis may show that this relationship is, in fact, non-linear.

The log-linear form of the equation means that the dependent variable, H(np) – H(tax), is interpreted as (np/tax) rather than (np-tax). Thus, a positive coefficient on the sales variable indicates that the proportion of pre-tax profits paid in taxes falls as sales increase[105]. Conversely, if the coefficient is negative.

Using a two-sided t-test, the coefficient of sales with respect to the proportion of profits remaining after taxes are paid is significantly positive above the 95% level (i) for the economy as a whole; and in the (ii) agriculture & mining; and, (ii) personal & community service industries. With 90% confidence, the coefficient on sales in the manufacturing industry is also significantly positive. The coefficient on sales is positive, but not significant for the (i) retail trade, (ii) finance, insurance & property services, and, (iii) business service industries. It is likely that further refinements to the functional form of the equations and more specific adjustments for heteroskedasticity will improve the level of significance of this result across the board.

The results imply that companies in these industries, which are more successful in terms of their turnover, are able to utilise the tax system to a far greater extent than their less successful competitors. This would suggest that companies pay taxes on their ability to minimise rather than their ability to pay. Thus, the tax system tends to favour successful companies in these industries.

The coefficient on sales is negative, but not significant for the (i) construction, (ii) wholesale trade, and, (iii) transport, communication & storage industries. This would suggest (although it is in no way conclusive given the lack of significance) that companies in these industries with smaller turnovers tend to pay proportionately less tax than companies with higher turnovers. It is difficult to explain why this is the case. It is possible that the negative coefficient reflects significant levels of losses for less successful companies brought forward from the preceding years of recession (1991-92) which have been used to offset their tax expense in the more recent years.

It is interesting to note that in most industries, the proportion of profits paid in taxes tends to increase as the proportion of total revenue spent on labour increases. The exceptions to this are in the (i) construction, and, (ii) transport, communication & storage industries. The relationship is significant at the 95% confidence level (i) for the economy as a whole, and in the (ii) agriculture & mining, (ii) wholesale trade, and, (iii) personal & community service industries. This result suggests that labour intensive companies are disadvantaged in terms of utilising the opportunities available in the tax system to minimise their taxes. The relationship between the other components of the cost structure and the proportion of profits paid in taxes is less evident. The only industry in which

---

[105] The dependent variable, H(np)-H(tax) is interpreted as the proportion of profits remaining after taxes are paid.

either of the other components are significant is the agriculture & mining industry. In this industry, companies that spend relatively more on capital costs and relatively less on other costs (materials) tend to pay a smaller proportion of their profits on tax.

Preliminary Profiles of Strategic Tax Minimisers in New Zealand

Who are the corporate strategic tax minimises in New Zealand? One should keep in mind that tax minimisation is within the law. One way forward is to engage in extensive profiling of high relative to low risk taxpayers. This analysis has the potential for:

- more accurate determination of the weaknesses in the tax base in order to improve the tax policy focus;
- the introduction of scientific audit selection, whereby taxpayers which pose a high risk to the tax base are targeted, and taxpayers which pose little risk to the tax base are ignored; in the latter case, there will be a considerable compliance cost saving; and
- improved corporate tax revenue forecasting because of a better understanding of the variance in the taxpaying behaviour of high versus low risk corporate taxpayers (by sector and scale).

The following are some preliminary profiles of corporate taxpayers. The conclusions should be treated as preliminary and not definitive. It is based on work by Law (1997) for New Zealand's Inland Revenue using public domain data. The sample was cross-referenced to the taxpayer database to determine if the publicly listed sample of firms is similar to the profile of firms in the taxpayer database.

Publicly listed firms, and firms registered in the Companies Office tend to be different from unlisted firms. In general, they tend to be larger, more profitable (higher return on assets) and much less likely to evade taxes than are unlisted firms. Preliminary analysis suggests that, *among* publicly listed firms and firms registered in the Companies Office, as distinct from unlisted and unregistered firms:

- New Zealand controlled firms tend to pose a higher risk to the tax base than North American firms, but somewhat less of a risk as compared to firms from Australia, elsewhere in the Pacific Region, Europe and Asia, ranked from lowest to highest risk.

- Firms in the retail, wholesale and service sectors in general, tend to pose a higher risk to the tax base than firms in manufacturing and primary sectors.

- The tax minimising firms which are most risky to the tax base are those that have moderate, as compared to very low or very high effective tax rates. Firms with low effective tax rates are often inefficient and struggling to survive, but this is not always the case.

- Listed firms and firms that are registered in the Companies' Office that are strategic tax minimisers also tend to reduce their tax burdens more during recessions than other firms. This may be because they are more sensitive to tax costs when profits are squeezed.

Risk Profiling Firms in the Taxpayer Data Base (FIRST System)

Heiler (1997) examined financial and tax data for 672 firms from New Zealand's Inland Revenue corporate taxpayer data base in order to develop profiles of companies with respect to the degree of risk they pose to the tax base. She found:

- The probability of being high risk (i.e. paying no tax) is higher during periods of low economic growth;
- Companies with high revenue generating efficiency (sales/net assets) and high profit generating efficiency (profits/assets) are more likely to pay no tax than companies which are less efficient in this regard;
- Companies in the construction and retail trade sectors have higher probability of paying no tax as compared to other sectors;
- Scale is not a significant indicator of taxpaying behaviour; and
- Higher interest expenses, depreciation costs and losses carried forward are closely related with a higher probability of paying no tax.

Risk Profiling Evaders in the Corporate Taxpayer Data Bases (FIRST and ORACLE)

Who are the evaders? These are the firms that reduce their taxes illegally. Giles (1997), in an examination of the ORACLE database for 51,356 cases over the period 1993-95, developed the following preliminary profiles of tax evaders compared to tax compliers:

- Larger firms tend to be significantly more compliant than smaller ones.
- Firms which are relatively efficient (in terms of their "activity ratio") tend to be significantly more compliant than do relatively inefficient firms.
- There is a significant positive relationship between a firm's pre-audit effective tax rate and its propensity to comply with tax legislation.
- Firms which use standard tax-minimisation instruments tend to do so in a legitimate manner, and there is a significant relationship between the active use of such instruments and taxation compliance.
- There is a significant variation in the probabilities of compliance, avoidance and evasion across different industrial sectors of the economy, the details of which require further investigation before definitive judgements can be made.

In summarising the Taxation Economics Group's use of taxpayer data, Giles (1997) observes that, "the Inland Revenue Department's ORACLE database, used in conjunction with information from the FIRST database, provides an extremely powerful foundation for predicting the likely non-compliance risk of New Zealand firms."

4.5 The Hidden Economy Model

The Hidden Economy MIMIC Model[106] (Giles, 1995) uses a *latent variables*[107] approach to estimate the size of the hidden economy and to derive the related tax gap. A modelling approach to estimating the hidden economy is considered to be superior to a survey approach because the latter tends to under-estimate the size of the hidden economy (Aigner et al. 1988). As well, a latent variables approach is considered to have better potential for measuring the size of the hidden economy than other methods. Thomas' (1992) book on *Informal Economic Activity* is a good summary of the state of the art in this field in the early 1990s. He concluded that:

"there are many examples of conventional econometric methods producing unsatisfactory results when applied to misspecified models and/or poor data, but these do not lead to rejection of econometric techniques; they are rather a spur towards higher standards. In the same way, one should see the latent variable approach as offering a promising theoretical solution to the problem of estimating models containing unobserverable variables" (Thomas, 1992:168).

The MIMIC approach uses a modelling technique which recognises the inherent invisibility of the underground economy, but simultaneously recognises that there are many measurable factors which cause agents to operate this way, and many measurable indicators that they may be doing so. Each of these causes and indicators provides only a partial explanation of the extent of unrecorded activity, and so a multiple equation structural model is estimated. This model explicitly allows for the fact that there are no directly observable data on the hidden economy itself.

---

[106] "...our basic stance is to view the (relative) size of the Hidden Economy as an unobservable variable, or 'latent variable'. We then ultimately use the MIMIC ("Multiple Indicators, Multiple Causes") model of Zellner (1970), Goldberger (1972), Joreskog and Goldberger (1975), and others to model and measure this variable. The MIMIC model is in effect a particular variant of the LISREL ("Linear Independent Structural Relationships") family of models, as developed by Joreskog and Sorbom (1993a,b) and others. However, the MIMIC model yields only an (ordinal) index for the time series of the Hidden Economy, and so extraneous information must be used to calibrate the index by providing a bench-mark value at some particular point in time. This, then, permits us to construct a time-path of the actual (or relative) magnitude of the underground economy, rather than just a time-path of the changes in its size. Our calibration is achieved by using a relatively sophisticated and novel currency demand equation, which allows for both measured and hidden economic activity. In this respect our calibration is placed on a much more rigorous footing than that associated with the very few other studies of this problem which have used the MIMIC model. The observed demand for currency is modelled in two parts, with demand for currency from measured activity modelled in the conventional way, and demand arising from hidden activity modelled using a non-linear currency demand equation. Our approach is more sophisticated than others because we introduce different velocities of circulation in the two sectors, provide variables which explain hidden activity, and allow for non-stationarity of the data. We developed two models for New Zealand allowing for these two different approaches and the results were similar, which is reassuring." (Giles, 1995:8-9) The models are structural econometric models, not pure time-series methods of the Box-Jenkins type (i.e. ARIMA modelling). The MIMIC model is a multivariate structural model which was estimated by full maximum likelihood methods. The other model is a non-linear regression model, constructed to "explain" the demand for currency.

[107] Latent Variables modelling has been widely used for years in many of the social sciences - psychology, political science, sociology, and economics. The *Handbook of Econometrics* (now in 4 volumes) - essentially the "Encyclopaedia of Econometrics" - devotes all of Chapter 23 to this topic (Aigner *et al.* 1984). By way of comparison, demand analysis gets one chapter, as do simultaneous equations models.

The modelling approach provides an estimated time-path of the extent of unrecorded, or hidden, economic activity in the form of an index. To calibrate this index, the demand for currency in NZ was modelled. This latter model provided our estimate of the average, long-run (1969-1994) size of the hidden economy of 8.8% of measured GDP. The figure for 1994 is 11.3%. During the period 1990-94 the average size of the hidden economy was 9.5% of GDP (about $7.1 bn). These figures are well within the range reported for the hidden economy for other OECD countries.[108] Differences in the hidden economy estimates within and across countries reflect:

"...differences in such things as the extent of the tax burden, the relative sophistication of the regulatory system, the success of the revenue agencies in prosecuting offenders, and the degree VC of 'tax morality'... Indeed, the extent to which underground economic activity takes place varies over time, even within one jurisdiction. Quantitative measures of the historical time-path of the size of the underground economy are of special interest, as they can the be linked (ex post) to the effects of major policy changes, and to cyclical activity in the economy at large" (Giles, 1995:7).

Most overseas studies of the hidden economy took place 15-20 years ago when inflation first began to be a serious problem. At that time, the estimated range for the size of the hidden economy in OECD countries was between 7% and 16% of GDP (Giles, 1996). Higher tax burdens, higher inflation and more government regulation, combined with improving economic growth, since the late 1970s appear to have raised that range to between 10%-25% of measured GDP by the mid-1990s. This would mean that most western economies are probably experiencing a larger hidden economy and higher tax evasion than 20 years ago.

New Zealand's hidden economy and tax evasion problems are near the low-end of the present estimated range for the OECD. At 11% of GDP in 1995 New Zealand's hidden economy (and thus its tax evasion problems) is near the low-end of the estimated range for the OECD. Relative to GDP, New Zealand's underground economy is larger than estimates for Switzerland and Austria (7%), just below the size of the hidden economy in Canada,[109] Britain, Japan, the USA, Australia, the Netherlands, Germany, France, Canada, Ireland and Denmark (11%-15%), and much lower than Norway and Sweden (about 18% of GDP), and Belgium, Spain and Italy (22- 26% of GDP).[110]

In keeping with the work on the efficiency impacts of taxation, a multiple methods approach was adopted. In the 5 models developed to examine the hidden economy, the 'causal' variables allow for: (1) unemployment and income effects; (2) factors which measure the extent to which the economy is regulated; (3) the

---

108 Many of the estimates are old now. The percentage of GDP is provided in brackets after the country, along with the estimated date. The various sources are provided at the end of the paragraph: Japan (4.1%, 1978); USA (8.3%, 1978; 4%, 1979; 33%, 1982); Sweden (13.2%, 1978). The different results for the U.S. reflect different methodologies, models and data. (Aigner et al 1988; Feige, 1982; Frey and Weck-Hanneman, 1984; Park, 1979; Schneider and Pommerehne, 1985; and Tanzi, 1980).

109 Another recent estimate for Canada placed the size of the hidden economy between 8-11% of GDP (Spiro, 1994).

110 *The Economist*, "Light on the Shadows", 3 May 1997 p. 63-64.

development of taxation legislation; (4) the tax bracket creep effect of inflation; and (5) various measures of the 'tax burden', including allowances for the introduction of, and increase in, the goods and services tax. These models also incorporate up to three 'indicator' variables: real GDP growth; male labour force participation rates, and a 'cash economy' indicator, measured by the proportion of currency to M3.

Testing indicated that the data were non-stationary so, the data were filtered to ensure stationarity. The results indicated that the time series for the measured and hidden economies are cointegrated, so there is no tendency for one to depart from the other as a result of exogenous shocks to the economy. There is also clear evidence of causality running from the measured economy to the hidden economy, and mild evidence of reverse causality.

4.6 The Learning Paths of the Hidden Economy and the Tax Gap

a. Key Model Results

The following are the key results of the model on the hidden economy in NZ based on Giles' (1995:5) research:

- Over the period 1969 to 1994 the hidden economy increased as a ratio to GDP from 7.8% to 11.3%, while the total tax evasion gap jumped from 1.84% of GDP to 3.94% of GDP **(Figure 4.1, Table 4.1)**; the long run average for the period is just below 9%, while the average for the first five years of the 1990s is 9.5%.

- The rate of growth of real GDP, the male labour force participation rate, and currency (relative to the money stock) are important indicators of unrecorded activity.

- The tax burden (tax rates and tax revenues relative to total output) is *positively* related to the size of the hidden economy, as are the inflation and unemployment rates, the degree of regulatory intrusion by government and the level of *per capita* disposable income.

- Changes in measured real GDP have a causal impact on the size of the hidden economy, and possibly vice versa; the hidden economy is pro-cyclical; it expands when the business cycle improves, and declines relatively when there is an economic downturn; this is an important finding because it indicates that acceleration in the size of the hidden economy can sometimes (if there is no change in the tax or regulatory burden) be accounted for solely by an increase in economic opportunities to make and disguise income.

- The major changes in the tax regime in the mid-1980s (the introduction of GST at a rate of 10%, the reduction in the personal income tax rate from 46%

Figure 4.1
The Size of the Hidden Economy as a Percentage of GDP - Annual Estimates and 5-Year Moving Averages: 1968-94

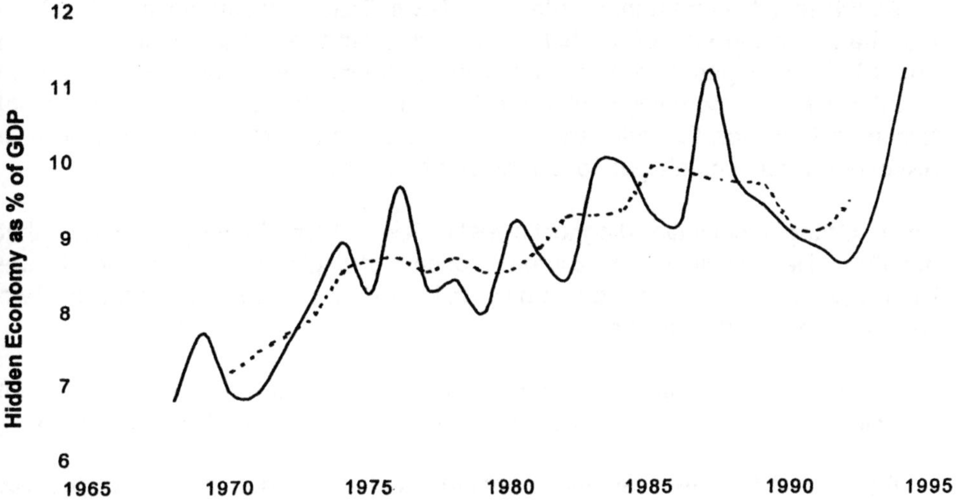

Source: Giles, 1996

Table 4.1
The Evolution of the Tax Burden, the Hidden Economy and the Total Tax Evasion Gap in New Zealand: 1969-94

	A Tax/GDP Ratio	B Hidden Economy/ GDP Ratio	C Total Tax Evasion Gap/ GDP Ratio	D Total Tax Collected ($ Millions)	E Cents Evaded Per $ Of Tax Collected
1969	23.62	7.77	1.84	1,059	7.8
1970	23.83	6.95	1.66	1,181	7.0
1971	25.66	6.95	1.78	1,445	7.0
1972	25.73	7.60	1.96	1,707	7.6
1973	25.30	8.29	2.10	1,927	8.3
1974	27.04	8.98	2.43	2,395	9.0
1975	29.40	8.31	2.44	2,865	8.3
1976	28.28	9.71	2.75	3,185	9.8
1977	28.24	8.36	2.36	3,845	8.4
1978	30.90	8.47	2.62	4,626	8.5
1979	29.42	8.04	2.36	4,990	8.0
1980	30.41	9.24	2.81	6,020	9.2
1981	30.56	8.80	2.69	7,050	8.8
1982	31.40	8.52	2.67	8,798	8.5
1983	31.99	10.03	3.21	10,097	10.0
1984	29.76	10.01	2.98	10,431	10.0
1985	30.03	9.37	2.81	11,914	9.4
1986	31.10	9.23	2.87	14,236	9.2
1987	31.64	11.27	3.57	17,408	11.2
1988	34.43	9.81	3.38	21,528	9.8
1989	34.01	9.47	3.22	22,864	9.5
1990	36.56	9.09	3.32	26,105	9.1
1991	35.53	8.89	3.16	25,979	8.9
1992	34.01	8.73	2.97	24.795	8.7
1993	34.13	9.56	3.26	25,974	9.6
1994	34.86	11.30	3.94	28,187	11.3

Source: New Zealand Planning Council, 1980, Public Expenditure and Its Financing, 1950-79

to 33%) and the late-1980s (the increase in the GST rate to 12.5%), made an important contribution in reducing the size of the hidden economy at that time; this suggests that indirect taxes have an important role to play in reducing the size of the hidden economy and the tax gap.

With respect to the specific causes of the size of the hidden economy, Giles' (1995:54) results can be interpreted as follows. Taxes account for about 57% of the change in the size of the hidden economy (and thus tax evasion), inflation about 24%, changes in real personal disposable income about 7.5%, regulation about 6.5% and unemployment about 5.3%. It is the interaction of these causal factors, rather than the independent effect of any one factor, which is crucial to discovering the dynamic path of the hidden economy.

Using Granger causality diagnostic tests, Giles (1996a:8) has concluded that growth in New Zealand's measured economy strongly promotes growth in the hidden economy, but that there is only "mild evidence" of reverse causality. Two issues arise from this analysis:

- as policy makers are promoting growth in the measured economy they will unintentionally promote growth in the hidden economy and tax evasion; and
- the causal link between the measured and unreported sectors of the NZ economy "is consistent with a situation where individuals and firms engaged in 'underground' economic activity are also part of the 'regular' economy, in general. This is very plausible in the New Zealand context" (Giles, 1996a:8).

As disposable income rises (or as opportunities for earning disposable income grow) in economic upturns current or potential evaders become even more sensitive to the fact their rising potential income is being threatened by taxes and inflation. A key insight is that changes in real personal disposable income are the catalyst for changes in the level of hidden activity that is based largely on tax evasion.

Tax changes occur only periodically, whereas real disposable income is changing continuously. During recessions, even though the tax burden may be high, real disposable income will be stable or shrinking, while the reverse will be true during economic expansions. A small increase in real disposable income makes taxpayers much more sensitive to the amount of tax that they currently pay and the amount that they will pay in the future. Thus, there is a non-linear, positive relationship between real disposable income (as the catalyst), and the level of tax evasion (as the dependent variable) given the current level of taxation, inflation and regulation.

As real disposable income rises, taxpayers become much more sensitive to the fact that they are paying a rising amount (but not necessarily a rising share) of total income in taxes. That sensitivity becomes intensified when the tax rates on both/either income (especially) and/or on consumption are raised. Either way, subject to the risk of prosecution and fines, this may trigger a protective or defensive reaction because taxpayers treat income as a property right and do not believe that tax is paid on the basis of voluntary compliance. For many taxpayers, tax is an enforced reduction of "hard-earned" income, and a therefore a threat to a property right. Inflation and regulations (with their accompanying compliance costs) are usually seen as additional threats to the property right of personal income. This helps to explain why taxpayers when surveyed in the US will deem tax evasion to be less serious than bicycle theft.

There is an important element of crowd psychology concerning "fairness" that plays a role in determining the total value of tax evasion in a country. Taxpayers' perceptions of the integrity and credibility of government policy, politicians and bureaucrats help to shape taxpayers willingness to comply fully with existing tax law. As the tax base weakens because of loophole exploitation by those with the means to exploit tax laws legally, there is a negative spillover, especially for the self-employed, individuals and small businesses. From their perspective, these potential evaders believe, *in all fairness*, that they have the right to the same bargain as those more sophisticated tax minimisers, but do not have the means to enter (i.e. resources to pay tax lawyers and accountants) the game.

As a result, they resort to tax evasion. The more acceptable the game becomes because everyone is doing it (the demonstration effect), the more unhealthy the tax system and the higher the level of expected tax evasion. This same phenomenon can be witnessed during riots in the US when masses of people participate in *looting* from stores, when normally they would not consider *stealing* to be the right thing to do.

In summary, there is a non-linear, catalytic relationship between changes in real disposable income and tax evasion which intensifies when tax rates are increased because individuals perceive that their property right (income) is under threat. This suggests that as economies enter into upturns in the business cycle, they can expect potentially explosive increases in tax evasion, depending on how high tax rates were to begin with, and whether or not, and by how much, tax rates, inflation and regulation increase during the course of the upturn, and of course depending on the existing level of government credibility. Low tax jurisdictions (e.g. below 20% of GDP) in developed countries can probably expect less explosive upward paths for tax evasion as economic growth rises. Developing countries which have large informal markets likely have much higher tax evasion levels than developed countries.

Inflation pushes income-earners into higher tax brackets, so positive inflation has the effect of increasing the marginal tax burden. Thus, at least part of the inflation weight is implicitly an addition to the impact of taxes. In brief, it is the interaction of taxes, inflation and disposable income that trigger the evasion response, and as disposable income rises rapidly so too does the evasion response.

b. The Tax Evasion Gap

The tax evasion gap is composed of an illicit-activity sector and a tax-sensitive sector. Both concepts are new and need to be explained. A simulation model of the hidden economy that we have created (details are presented in section 4.8) reveals that about 30-40% of the size of the hidden economy is not driven by a tax evasion or avoidance motivation.

If taxes are reduced to zero, this portion of the hidden economy would remain. We have called it the *illicit-activity sector* of the hidden economy. It is composed of criminal activity such as theft, fraud, illicit gambling, protection rackets, prostitution, the manufacture and sale of illicit drugs, smuggling of weapons and drugs, money laundering etc. In short, it is, in one form or another, *petty and organised* criminal activity. Such activity may lead to tax evasion, but tax evasion is not the driving force of the activity. The portion of the hidden economy driven by tax considerations is the *tax-sensitive sector* of underground activity. This includes non-declaration, or under-reporting of, income by firms and individuals for whatever reason, as well as barter and home production, the failure to collect GST from those offering services to the home, including child care workers, trades-persons and building contractors.

Another way of looking at it is that the hidden economy is divided into illicit sector and tax-sensitive sector segments. The tax-sensitive sector will modify its tax evasion behaviour if the rules of the game are made more or less punitive, or if enforcement and penalties are made more or less threatening to the evader. In contrast, it is doubtful that the petty and organised criminal element will cease its behaviour because of more punitive tax rules, but it may adjust its behaviour. [111] In this sense, the illicit sector of the hidden economy is difficult to eradicate by tax policy and tax auditing. But such criminal activity can be reduced by judicious risk profiling and auditing.

There are two additional dimensions of difficulty in dealing with both the illicit sector and the tax-sensitive sector of the hidden economy. First, there are serious obstacles in identifying tax evasion in both areas. Second, there are difficulties in obtaining information about the extent of the tax evasion in each area. In comparing the illicit and tax-sensitive sector elements in NZ with respect to each of these three levels of difficulty, we have tentatively concluded the following:

- illicit sector tax evasion is more difficult to eradicate than tax-sensitive sector tax evasion because its motivations are more complex and deeply rooted than tax-sensitive sector tax evasion;

- within the illicit sector of the hidden economy, the ease of identifying tax evasion depends on the sophistication of the criminals; those engaged in sophisticated tax planning such as the use of family trusts are difficult to pin

[111] Any tightening of tax rules and regulations will always need to take into consideration both privacy and human rights issues.

down; moreover, once criminals have "legitimised" their incomes by investing the proceeds of crime in normal commercial activity or various financial investments, it becomes much harder to identify tax evasion;

- on the other hand, those criminal elements that do not file tax returns and have lavish lifestyles without comparable legitimate income are more easily targeted and prosecuted; supporting evidence from the police (in contrast, Inland Revenue does not supply information to the police) can help to target criminal elements that evade taxes.

- by comparison, it is very difficult to identify randomly occurring tax evasion across all firms and individuals. It is difficult for the tax authority to observe the breadth and depth of tax evasion by individuals, the self-employed and small business in the tax-sensitive sector because the transaction costs of dealing with these problems on a case by case basis (where only relatively small amounts of money may be involved) are very high.

- in conclusion, it is harder to eradicate illicit sector tax evasion, but it also very hard to identify tax-sensitive sector tax evasion among a diverse range of individuals and small businesses.

Given that these two elements of the hidden economy have different sources, the tax gap for each of these two cores also needs to be distinguished. We have called the tax gap related to the illicit sector of the hidden economy, *the illicit sector evasion tax gap* and the tax gap related to the tax-sensitive sector of the hidden economy is *the tax-sensitive sector evasion tax gap*.

Preliminary estimates suggest that tax-sensitive sector activity, largely under- or non-reporting income for tax purposes, accounted for about 7% of GDP (about $6 bn) in 1994, and an average of 5.5% of GDP ($4 bn) over the period 1990-94. Illicit sector activity accounted for about 4% of GDP in 1994, and an average of 4% of GDP over the period 1990-94.

The size of the hidden economy and Inland Revenue's prosecutions, which historically have a high conviction rate, have been modelled (Giles, 1996b). The results indicate that IRD takes a pro-active rather than reactive approach to offences against the Inland Revenue Acts, and that these prosecutions shrink the size of the hidden economy and tax evasion. The new penalties regime (1997) will also help in this regard.

c. The Hidden Economy Path in New Zealand

Figure 4.1 illustrates the results of the model's estimation of the size of the hidden economy relative to real GDP across the period 1969-1994 (all data here are for calendar years). **Table 4.1** provides annual estimates of the ratios of total taxes to GDP, the hidden economy to GDP, the total tax gap to GDP, the total nominal value of tax collected each year, and the total value (in cents) of evasion per dollar of tax collected. The latter is also an estimate of the deadweight loss of evasion. **Table 4.2** presents period averages for the same data.

In 1969, 23.6 cents of every dollar of national, measured income was collected in tax, and the hidden economy generated 7.8 cents per dollar of measured economic activity. The figures in 1979 were 29.4 cents and 8 cents, respectively. By 1989, 34 cents were being taxed per dollar of measured national income, while the hidden economy was generating almost 9.5 cents per dollar of national measured income.

In 1994, the tax/GDP ratio rose to 34.9 cents per dollar of economic activity, and hidden economy activity hit 11.3 cents per dollar. From this exercise, it should be clear that the rate of increase of the hidden economy is about the same as the rate of increase in the tax burden. In fact, over the period, the tax/GDP ratio rose by 47.6%, while the hidden economy increased by 45.4%. Thus, it seems that there is a relationship between the two. While any tax rise should expand hidden economic activity, it really depends on the type of tax and other existing circumstances.[112]

Table 4.2 smoothes these changes out by taking pictures of period averages. So, during the first half of the 1970s the tax/GDP ratio was 25.5%, rising to 34.8% in the first 5 years of the 1990s, an increase of 36.5%, while the hidden economy jumped from 7.8% in the early 1970s to 9.5% in the early 1990s, for an increase of about 23%. The reason for the lack of equality in the rates of change lies in the averaging; the early 1990s proved to be the worst recession NZ has faced in the last 30 years.

As Giles (1995) has demonstrated, the hidden economy is pro-cyclical. During recessions the hidden economy grows very slowly, if at all. The jump in the hidden economy to 11.3% of GDP in 1994 is testimony to the powerful stimulus provided to the hidden economy by the creation of new opportunities during business expansions.

d. The Tax Gap Path and the Deadweight Loss of Evasion

In 1969, as indicated in **Table 4.1**, when the tax/GDP ratio stood at 23.6%, the

---

[112] A simple examination of the data will help to make this point. During the last decade, the total tax to GDP ratio has risen from about 29% in 1984 to 35% in 1994. But the hidden economy has not shown such a progressive upward trend, as indicated in Figure 4.1. This has occurred in part because the illicit sector of the hidden economy, which represents about 40% of the hidden economy, and is composed of organised criminal activity, is not principally motivated by changes in the effective tax burden or tax mix, or changes in the statutory tax rates. Further, as indicated in the Report, the business cycle has an important positive influence on the level of the hidden economic activity and tax evasion. A careful examination of the evolution of the size of the hidden economy to GDP ratio (Table 4.6) indicates that the ratio was in decline in 1981, 1982, 1984, 1985, 1987, 1988, 1990, 1991, and 1992. The first years in which GST made a significant contribution to total indirect taxes were 1987 and 1988. In 1987, the indirect tax to GDP ratio jumped from 7.5% to 8.6%. During that year, the hidden economy to GDP ratio shrank from 11.3% to 9.8% of GDP -- a decrease of 13%, the second largest drop (after 1987) in the last 30 years. In 1988, when the indirect tax to GDP ratio jumped from 8.6% to 12%, the hidden economy to GDP ratio fell from 9.8% to 9.4%. The only other jump since then occurred in 1990 when the ratio rose from 11.2% to 12.4%. In 1990 the indirect tax to GDP ratio fell from 10.03% to 9.09%.

Table 4.2
Period Averages and Changes in New Zealand's Tax Burden, Hidden Economy and the Tax Evasion Gaps: 1970-94

Period	A Tax/GDP Ratio		B Hidden Economy/ GDP		C Total Tax Evasion Gap/GDP		D Soft Core Evasion Tax Gap/ GDP		E Hard Core Evasion Tax Gap/ GDP		F Cents Evaded Per $ Of Tax Collected	
	%	% chg	%	% chg	%	% chg	%	% chg	%	% chg	%	% chg
1970-74	25.5		7.75		1.99		0.97		1.02		7.8	
1975-79	29.3	14.9	8.58	10.7	2.51	26.1	1.34	38.2	1.17	14.7	8.6	10.3
1980-84	30.8	5.1	9.32	8.6	2.87	14.3	1.64	22.4	1.23	5.1	9.3	8.1
1985-89	32.2	4.6	9.83	5.5	3.17	10.5	1.88	14.6	1.29	4.9	9.8	5.4
1990-94	34.8	6.2	9.51	-3.3	3.31	5.1	1.93	2.7	1.40	8.5	9.5	-3.1

Source: Giles (1995); Giles and Caragata (1996)

Figure 4.2
The Tax Evasion Gaps in New Zealand - Total, Softcore and Hardcore: 1969-95

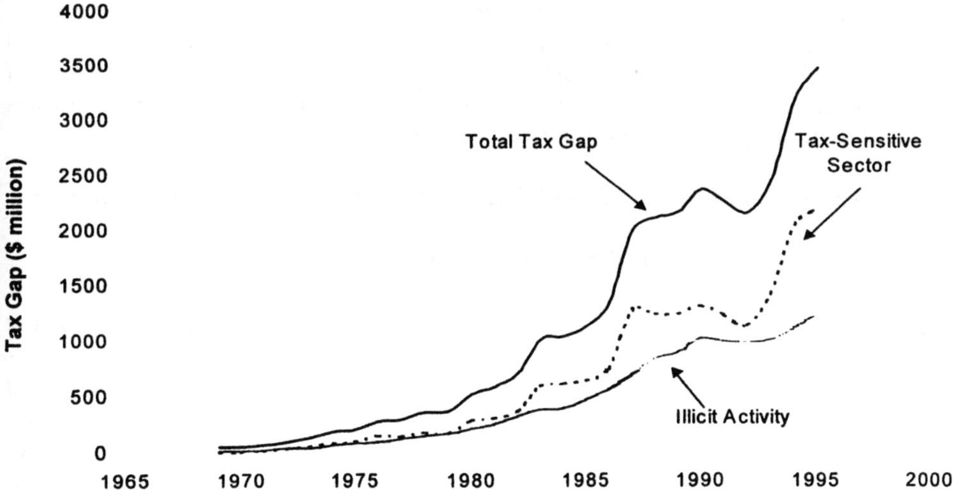

Source: Inland Revenue, 1996

total tax gap was 1.84% of GDP; thus the hidden economy evaded taxes of 1.8 cents per dollar of measured economic activity. Another way of looking at this, is that per dollar of tax paid, 7.8 cents were evaded in 1969.

The 7.8 cents is a deadweight loss, as Harberger (1964) recognised 30 years ago. While evaders escape tax and thus incur no deadweight loss directly, as free-riders on public expenditure, they create a distortion in the allocation of resources when they escape the tax net. Of course, tax evasion also creates an equity problem because the 7.8 cents burden is shifted to other taxpayers and/or less services are provided to taxpayers, and/ or other taxes could have been reduced by that amount if all taxpayers were compliant.

In 1979 when the tax/GDP ratio was 29.4%, the total tax gap was 2.36% of GDP. Thus, per dollar of taxes paid, 8 cents was evaded. By 1989, almost 34 cents were being taxed per dollar of measured national income, and per dollar of taxes paid, 9.6 cents was evaded. In 1994, the tax/GDP ratio rose to 34.9%, and per dollar of tax paid, 11.3 cents of tax was evaded.

This suggests that the tax gap is growing at a faster rate than the hidden economy. From 1969 to 1994, the tax evasion gap ratio to GDP increased by 114%, whereas, as we have already seen, the hidden economy rose by 45%. Using **Table 4.2**, the smoothing created by period averages narrows the gap somewhat: 22.7% increase in the early 1990s over the early 1970s for the hidden economy growth, versus 66.3% jump for the tax gap/GDP ratio. Meanwhile, the average value of the deadweight loss from tax evasion per dollar of tax revenue rose from 7.8 cents in the first half of the 1970s to 9.5 cents in the first half of the 1990s, an increase of 22%.

Thus, the opportunities for profit making in the hidden economy are growing faster than in the measured economy (this may, in part, be a statistical phenomenon since the hidden economy is much smaller than the measured economy). That, in turn, suggests that other factors, such as the rising level of the tax/GDP ratio, are exerting influence on the growth of the tax gap. As the level of evasion grows, so too does the deadweight loss of evasion.

e. *Tax Evasion Paths of the Illicit Sector and the Tax-Sensitive Sector*

The Tax-Sensitive Sector Evasion Tax Gap

Table 4.3 (See also **Figure 4.2**) sets out the learning paths of the total tax evasion gap, the tax-sensitive sector evasion tax gap and the illicit sector evasion tax gap over the period 1969-1994. **Table 4.2** provides the period averages. As we see in **Table 4.3**, in 1969 the tax gap/GDP ratio was 1.8%, and 48% of that gap was accounted for by the tax-sensitive sector evasion gap, which is the level of evasion arising from individuals outside of petty and organised criminal activity. Individuals and firms in the tax-sensitive sector evasion tax gap would be engaged in a narrow definition of illicit-activity (hiding income or transactions) for tax reasons alone.

Table 4.3
The Tax Evasion Gap Challenge: 1969-94

	A Total Tax Evasion Gap/GDP	B Tax-Sensitive Sector Evasion Tax Gap/GDP	C B/A (%)	D Illicit Activity Sector Tax Evasion Gap/GDP (A-B)
1969	1.84	0.89	48.4	0.95
1970	1.66	0.70	42.2	0.96
1971	1.78	0.76	42.7	1.02
1972	1.96	0.93	47.5	1.03
1973	2.10	1.09	51.9	1.01
1974	2.43	1.35	55.6	1.08
1975	2.44	1.27	52.1	1.17
1976	2.75	1.62	58.9	1.13
1977	2.36	1.23	52.1	1.13
1978	2.62	1.38	52.7	1.24
1979	2.36	1.19	50.4	1.17
1980	2.81	1.59	56.6	1.22
1981	2.69	1.47	54.7	1.22
1982	2.67	1.42	53.2	1.25
1983	3.21	1.93	60.1	1.28
1984	2.98	1.79	60.1	1.19
1985	2.81	1.61	57.3	1.20
1986	2.87	1.63	56.8	1.24
1987	3.57	2.30	64.4	1.27
1988	3.38	2.00	59.2	1.38
1989	3.22	1.86	57.8	1.36
1990	3.32	1.86	56.0	1.46
1991	3.16	1.74	55.1	1.42
1992	2.97	1.61	54.2	1.36
1993	3.26	1.90	58.3	1.36
1994	3.94	2.54	64.5	1.40

Source: Inland Revenue, 1996

Table 4.4
Current Value of the Hidden Economy, and the Tax Evasion Gaps ($million): 1969-95

	Hidden Economy	A Total Evasion Tax Gap	B Tax-Sensitive Sector Evasion Tax Gap	C Illicit Activity Sector Evasion Tax Gap (A-B)
1969	$348	$82	$40	43
1970	344	82	35	48
1971	391	101	43	59
1972	504	130	62	68
1973	632	160	83	77
1974	797	216	120	96
1975	812	238	124	114
1976	1,100	312	184	128
1977	1,145	323	169	155
1978	1,268	392	207	186
1979	1,363	400	202	198
1980	1,829	556	315	242
1981	2,030	621	339	282
1982	2,387	748	398	350
1983	3,262	1,044	628	416
1984	3,602	1,072	644	482
1985	3,890	1,167	668	498
1986	4,402	1,369	777	591
1987	6,419	2,033	1,310	723
1988	6,233	2,148	1,271	877
1989	6,477	2,202	1,272	930
1990	6,512	2,402	1,346	1,057
1991	6,443	2,290	1,261	1,029
1992	6,427	2,186	1,167	1,020
1993	7,256	2,475	1,442	1,032
1994	9,225	3,217	2,074	1,143
1995*	9,615	3,497	2,220	1,276

Source: Inland Revenue, 1996

By 1979, the tax-sensitive sector accounted for about 50% of the total tax gap, by 1989, 58% and by 1994, 65%. As indicated in **Table 4.2**, using period average data, the tax-sensitive sector has shown a strong increase over the period. This growth may be explained by several factors. In the 1970s, the period of strongest growth, New Zealanders began to take a more activist approach to tax matters as inflation rose, tax burdens rose and government intervention became the order of the day.

The process of tax activism continued into the 1980s and peaked with the stock market frenzy in 1987. The NZ crash, the worst in the OECD in terms of the length of recovery, removed a strong speculative element in the growth of tax-sensitive sector evasion activity that was only rekindled 7 years later by the strong economic recovery in 1994. Thus, in 1994 the tax-sensitive sector accounted for about 65% of the total tax gap, the peak for the last quarter of a century.

The Illicit Sector Evasion Tax Gap

In **Table 4.3** we see that in 1969 the illicit sector evasion tax gap reached almost 1% of GDP and accounted for about 52% of the total tax gap. Recall that the illicit sector evasion tax gap activity represents evasion arising from individuals in petty and organised criminal activity. Individuals and firms in the illicit sector evasion tax gap would be engaged in tax evasion as an indirect consequence of other illicit-activity. Tax evasion would not be their primary objective or motivation.

By 1973, the illicit sector fell below 50% of the total tax gap for the first time during the period analysed, and has stayed there ever since. This is probably due to the change in the incentive effects for evasion by individuals in the tax-sensitive sector, as discussed, but may reflect a more successful police campaign against petty and organised criminals. Since both hard and tax-sensitive sector evasion activities continued to grow relative to GDP, the issue of successful policing is at best moot.

By 1979, the illicit sector evasion tax gap rose to 1.17% of GDP, and accounted for about 50% of the total tax gap. A decade later in 1989, the illicit sector evasion gap was up to 1.36% of GDP, and contributed only 42% of the total tax gap. In 1994, the illicit sector evasion gap had reached 1.4% of GDP, but accounted for about 36% of the total tax gap. More modelling is required to examine illicit sector activity to determine if its dynamic behaviour has been adequately captured by our existing models. This would involve modelling components of the illicit sector such as fraud, illegal doings etc.

Summary

It seems that tax evasion activity is alive and well in NZ. Both the illicit sector (petty and organised criminal activity) and tax-sensitive sector (tax driven illicit-activity) have been on expansion paths over the last quarter of a century. Tax-sensitive sector evasion activity is outpacing illicit sector evasion activity, suggesting that there is wide recognition of the savings to be had by not paying taxes. The next section illustrates the magnitude and therefore the attraction of those savings.

4.7 The Stakes in the Hidden Economy

Table 4.4 presents the current annual value of the hidden economy, the total tax gap, the tax-sensitive sector evasion tax gap and the illicit sector evasion tax gap over the period 1969-95. **Table 4.5** presents period averages for the same data.

The stakes in the hidden economy are rising dramatically in nominal terms over time, and of course it is nominal dollars that are taxed, and nominal dollars that are saved through evasion. But perhaps it is more realistic to look at these numbers relative to GDP in order to provide some perspective. In current dollars, in 1969 our models place the value of the hidden economy at about $348 million. Ten years later, this amount had soared to $1.4 billion. By 1989, the hidden economy had reached roughly $6.5 billion. In 1995 the value is estimated at $9.6 billion.

This spectacular rise over the last 25 years or so reflects the growth of government intervention in the economy in the form of restrictions in the 1970s and early 1980s, the rising tax burden throughout the period, the presence of double digit inflation for 18 of 19 years from 1970-1988 (averaging 15% per annum), and changes in criminal activity.

The total nominal value of the tax gap over the period has jumped from $82.4 million in 1969 to $3.5 billion in 1995. The only year during which the tax gap exhibited a decline (over the previous year's activity) was in 1992 (a serious recession year). With the recovery, the increase in evaded taxes was spectacular in 1994, rising by 30% over the previous year.

The total value of the tax-sensitive sector evasion tax gap in 1995 was $2.2 billion, while the illicit sector evasion tax gap was about $1.3 billion. It is premature at this stage to set targets for reducing the two tax gaps. More work is needed to differentiate between the contribution of firms and individuals, and types of firms and individuals, to each tax gap and the nature of the constraints in dealing with these problems. Once information is developed about the probability profiles of avoiders and evaders among firms and individuals, targeting will be feasible.

From the government's perspective the value of the evaded taxes is also significant. The $3.2 billion in evaded tax in 1994 represents over 11% of total current tax revenue. This compares favourably with the Internal Revenue Service's estimate for the US of 20% in 1987 (Slemrod, 1992:1).

Thus, if all evaded tax were collected, this would permit the government to increase spending by $3.2 billion without raising taxes or borrowing. Or, perhaps the government could cut taxes by 4% of GDP without disrupting any spending

Table 4.5
The Stakes in the Hidden Economy and the Evasion Tax Gap ($ millions): 1970-94, 5-year averages

	Average Value of the:			
	Hidden Economy	Total Evasion Tax Gap	Tax-Sensitive Sector Evasion Tax Gap	Illicit Activity Sector Evasion Tax Gap
1970-74	$533.5	$137.8	$68.4	$69.4
1975-79	1,137.6	333.1	176.9	156.2
1980-84	2,621.9	808.2	464.7	343.5
1985-89	5,484.1	1,783.7	1,059.7	724.0
1990-94	7,172.7	2,514.0	1,457.9	1,056.1

Source: Inland Revenue, 1996

Table 4.6
Some Tax Mix Simulations for the Hidden Economy: 1969-94

Year	(T/GDP)	(H/GDP)						
		Actual	Control	Policy				
				1	2	3	4	5
	%	%	%	%	%	%	%	%
1969	23.62	7.77	7.59	7.02	6.20	5.91	5.69	5.35
1970	23.83	6.95	7.48	7.05	6.23	5.87	5.70	5.37
1971	25.66	6.95	7.61	7.11	6.21	5.81	5.62	5.25
1972	25.73	7.60	7.92	7.24	6.36	5.99	5.73	5.37
1973	25.30	8.29	8.24	7.5	6.65	6.32	6.03	5.68
1974	27.04	8.98	8.50	7.53	6.67	6.33	5.96	5.62
1975	29.40	9.31	8.75	7.33	6.50	6.18	5.65	5.33
1976	28.28	9.71	8.30	7.03	6.17	5.89	5.41	5.07
1977	28.24	8.36	8.11	6.75	5.94	5.66	5.15	4.82
1978	30.90	8.47	8.08	7.03	6.16	5.88	5.23	4.88
1979	29.42	8.04	9.13	7.52	6.63	6.39	5.79	5.44
1980	30.41	9.24	9.14	7.51	6.60	6.29	5.70	5.34
1981	30.56	8.80	9.55	7.71	6.81	6.55	5.88	5.53
1982	31.40	8.52	9.65	7.80	6.82	6.54	5.87	5.49
1983	31.99	10.03	9.45	7.60	6.58	6.27	5.61	5.21
1984	29.76	10.01	9.67	8.15	7.15	6.85	6.30	5.90
1985	30.03	9.37	8.92	7.61	6.54	6.18	5.70	5.28
1986	31.10	11.27	9.35	7.62	6.66	6.34	5.71	5.33
1987	31.64	9.81	9.43	7.83	6.73	6.37	5.80	5.37
1988	34.01	9.47	9.35	8.42	6.81	6.22	5.89	5.28
1989	31.99	10.03	9.54	8.36	6.88	6.39	5.97	5.41
1990	36.56	9.09	9.61	8.64	6.94	6.32	5.98	5.35
1991	35.53	8.89	9.36	8.32	6.64	6.07	5.71	5.08
1992	34.01	8.73	9.53	8.80	7.09	6.48	6.22	5.58
1993	34.13	9.56	9.80	9.12	7.40	6.76	6.52	5.88
1994	34.86	11.30	10.12	9.38	7.67	6.98	6.72	6.08
Mean	**30.30**	**8.96**	**8.96**	**7.77**	**6.66**	**6.26**	**5.83**	**5.39**

Source: Caragata and Giles, 1996

programs or running up deficits. It is clear that much is at stake in the existence and termination of tax evasion.

4.8 A Simulation Model Approach to Taxation and the Hidden Economy

a. Introduction

The aggregate response of (relative) underground activity to changes in the overall "tax burden" was measured (Giles & Caragata, 1996). Intuitively, one would expect that an increase in the tax burden would lead to an increase in underground activity, *ceteris paribus*. The precise form of this response or learning path, provides a basis for computing the elasticity between these two ratios.

The first objective was to determine the likely "threshold" size of the Hidden Economy - that is, the extent to which underground activity will take place even in the absence of taxation. This threshold is important in terms of distinguishing between tax-driven activity and petty and organised criminal activity in the hidden economy which has other motivations aside from tax evasion. The second objective was to determine what would happen if the tax/GDP ratio were raised to a very high level.

Third, the threshold also helps in evaluating the extent to which reductions in the tax/GDP ratio and/or the tax mix[113] can assist in minimising the size of the hidden economy and the tax gap. That minimum point suggests the existence of a best practice frontier (Caragata & Giles, 1996). Current performance divided by frontier performance describes the performance ratio and reveals the current health of the tax system with respect to the total tax gap.

There is little previous work simulating the effect of a tax cut on the size of unreported income (i.e. the tax gap). Clotfelter (1983:368), in a simple model, found that:

"for a taxpayer with a combined federal and state marginal tax rate of 0.40 [40%], which is about average for the sample, ... a 10% decline in this tax rate to 0.36 would result in an expected 5% to 8% decline in underreporting".

In Caragata & Giles (1996) sample period (1969-94), the average-marginal and average-average tax rates have mean values of 35% and 25% respectively, and the mean tax/GDP ratio value is 30%. The elasticity between the tax/GDP ratio and the size of the hidden economy is 0.67. Thus, reducing the aggregate tax burden from 30% of GDP to 27% (a 10% cut) is predicted to reduce the relative size of the hidden economy by 6.7%. Although these calculations are rather simplistic, this result seems to accord quite well with Clotfelter's (1983).

---

113 The major components of total tax revenue - namely, personal, indirect, corporate and "other" taxes.

Caragata & Small (1996)[114] have developed a non-linear two-equation *dynamic* model that examines the relationship between the growth of the measured economy, the hidden economy and the tax to GDP ratio. Their model predicts that an increase in the tax/GDP ratio will reduce growth in measured real activity, and increase growth in the hidden economy. These effects are found to be stronger, the smaller is the initial tax burden. In the case of the hidden economy, they find that a 20% tax to GDP ratio over the period 1968-1994, as compared to the actual levels that prevailed, would have resulted in a hidden sector 26% smaller than the historical figures measured by Giles (1996). This corroborates the findings of Caragata & Giles (1996).

b. Methodology[115]

(1) Aggregate Tax-Hidden Economy Model

Various simple functional relationships between Hidden Economy and GDP and Total Tax and GDP were considered. The tax to GDP ratio was *not* one of the causal variables adopted in the latent variable modelling that was used to construct the former series in Giles (1995), so the estimation of such relationships is not a redundant exercise. In each case, the proportional rate of growth in real GDP is included as a second explanatory variable in view of the highly cyclical nature of the hidden economy to GDP ratio (see Giles, 1996; 1996c, for further details).[116]

Initial experimentation with some simple quadratic and cubic relationships and a Fourier approximation in the spirit of Gallant (1981)[117] was unsatisfactory (see also Scully (1996a)). The next step was to test the Cumulative Normal, Logistic,

---

[114] The model used by Caragata & Small (1996) arises from the maximum likelihood estimation of a vector autoregression with non-stationary data and possible cointegration. The model uses data observed at an annual frequency over the period 1969-1995. Hypothesis tests reject the existence of a long run relationship between the output in the measured and hidden economies and the aggregate tax rate, allowing the direct modelling of the output growth rates in a dynamic setting. A two equation system is estimated to explain real GDP growth and hidden economy growth as functions of their own lags (the learning process) and the aggregate tax rate. In each equation, the tax to GDP ratio enters non-linearly through the use of a logistic function, similar to the one used by Giles & Caragata (1996). This non-linear relationship allows predictions to be made about the way in which output growth responds to the tax ratio at different levels of the tax burden. Although only a small percentage of variation in the growth rates is explained in the model, the estimated coefficients are statistically significant and the model is adequate as assessed through diagnostic tests for non-normality and serial correlation. The model predicts that increases in the tax to GDP ratio depress growth in real measured GDP and increase the rate of growth of the hidden economy. Furthermore, these effects are predicted to be stronger, the smaller is the tax burden. This suggests that the efficacy of fiscal policy has been reduced by the steady increases in the tax to GDP ratio over the last 30 years.

[115] Annual data for the (H/GDP) variable are available directly for the period 1968 to 1994 from the results of Giles (1996).

[116] The inclusion or exclusion of this growth rate variable has only negligible effects on the results which are reported below.

[117] Gallant, A. R., 1981, "On the Bias of Functional Forms and an Essentially Unbiased Form: The Fourier Flexible Form", *Journal of Econometrics*, 15, 211-245.

Gompertz and Extreme-value[118] functional forms which allow for non-linear growth in (H/GDP) as (T/GDP) grows. Emphasis was on finding a single point of inflection and positive "saturation" and "threshold" levels in the dependent variable. This would tell us the optimisation point for managing the size of the hidden economy within appropriate trade-offs, given that a reduction of tax to zero is unacceptable for various reasons. There is clear evidence that (H/GDP) and (T/GDP) are non-stationary but cointegrated, so the models were estimated using the actual values (rather than the first-differences) of the data (Giles & Caragata, 1996).

The results for each functional form were compared with respect to "t-values", R^2 (correlation between the actual and "fitted" values); a "goodness of fit" test for Normality; and the exact Durbin-Watson statistic. Very little difference was found between the results of the different functional forms, but on balance the Logistic function was preferred. The estimated coefficients are generally quite significant, the errors are normally distributed, and the residuals are free of autocorrelation (at least at the 1% significance level).

(2) Dis-aggregated Tax-Hidden Economy Model

With a refinement of the aggregate model, a logistic relationship between the H/GDP ratio and the component tax ratios to GDP was established, with the estimated parameters constrained to conform with the results of the aggregate estimated relationship. This new model provides the basis for investigating the effects of changes in both the tax burden and the tax mix.

Table 4.6 presents the results of a series of simulations of the impact of variations in the tax/GDP ratio and the tax mix and their impact on the size of the hidden economy. The actual time series of estimated values for the hidden economy in NZ appears under the column "actual" in **Table 4.6**. The simulation model generated a time series that very closely approximates the "actual" values estimated by the MIMIC Model. The simulated values appear under the column "control" in the same Table.

[118] Various constrained versions of the models were considered in each case without success, so these results are not reported here.

c. *Econometric Results*

(1) *The Zero-Tax Value of the Hidden Economy*[119]

The four functional forms that were employed established that with a zero growth rate in real GDP, and a zero "tax burden", the minimum threshold value for the size of the Hidden Economy is approximately 4.2% of measured output. This compares reasonably with the long-run (1968-94) average value of 8.8% for this ratio, 6.8% in 1968 (the smallest (estimated) value for the (H/GDP) ratio over our sample period), 11.3% in 1994 (the largest corresponding value) (Giles,1995). This remaining 4.2% is the size of the illicit sector of the hidden economy that is driven by motives other than tax. This figure might be described as "the natural rate of underground activity".

This suggests that, on average, over the long run, about 40% of the hidden economy is driven by tax considerations (constraints with attached costs), and the remaining 60% petty and organised criminal activity. But the weights vary. During a recession, the illicit sector (4.2%) will account for more of the total value of the hidden economy - 4/6.8 or 59% in 1968; while during the peak of an economic boom (1994: 4/11.3, or 37%), the illicit sector will become less important in the value of the hidden economy.

How realistic are these numbers for the illicit sector of the hidden economy? Much more research needs to be undertaken to measure the magnitudes of the different features of the unreported illicit sector economy. Nonetheless, a preliminary examination of the issue of theft could be of some value.

We suspect that the largest component of the illicit sector in the hidden economy is related to theft and fraud. Detailed statistics for NZ are not yet available. Data for the US is available from a survey 2,608 certified fraud examiners in United States in a 30 month study undertaken by the Association of Certified Fraud Examiners. Fraud and abuse losses in American businesses totals $400 billion annually. Managers and executives are responsible for 16 times more fraud and abuse than non-managerial employees. Men accounted for four times more of the losses than women, while those over 60 caused 28 times more of the losses than those 25 years and younger (ACFE, 1995:5;13).

The annual value lost by firms on account of fraud and abuse (including theft by employees, managers and customers) in the United States is about 6% of annual sales (ACFE, 1995:13). Since the ratio of sales to GDP is roughly 2.0 to

[119] A unit elasticity between the hidden economy ratio and the tax/GDP ratio occurs at a tax rate of approximately 44% of GDP. Note, that as the data for (H/GDP) and for (T/GDP) are expressed in percentage terms, these elasticities have to be interpreted with care. For instance, consider the situation in 1994, when (T/GDP) = 34.9% and (H/GDP) = 11.3%. For this tax ratio, the elasticity is 0.84. So, suppose that in 1994 the aggregate tax rate had been *cut* by 10% - that is (T/GDP) had been reduced from 34.9% to 31.4%. Then according to our results, (H/GDP) would have been reduced by 8.4% (as opposed to 8.4 percentage points) - that is, it would have fallen from 11.3% to 10.4%. Similarly, if (T/GDP) had been reduced to 20% in that year (a reduction of 42.7%), then (H/GDP) would have fallen to 7.2%.

2.5 to 1, this would imply that approximately 12-15% of GDP is lost annually to fraud, theft and abuse. In Australia's retail sector, it is estimated that 1% of sales per annum is lost owing to managerial, employee and customer fraud and theft. Thus, a range of 1-6% of total sales is used for estimating total theft and fraud from business. Theft from homes and apartments is not included in these estimates.

NZ has one of the highest burglar rates in the OECD, which may suggest a high propensity towards theft and fraud. But, a conservative estimate is that 1.4% of total sales are lost to theft and fraud in NZ per annum. This would work out to 3.5% of GDP (the ratio of total sales to GDP in NZ is roughly about 2.5:1). Recall that our 1994 estimate for the total size of the illicit sector hidden economy (where criminal activity is located) is 4.2% of GDP.[120]

Thus, excluding all other forms of criminal activity, such as protection rackets, illegal gambling, drug trafficking, prostitution and miscellaneous, theft from residential property, auto theft and theft from cars, and including only theft and fraud perpetrated against business in NZ, we have already accounted for 83% of the illicit sector of the hidden economy. We consider these estimates to be prudent and realistic.

(2)· Maximum Value of the Hidden Economy

As the tax/GDP ratio is raised to a maximum 100% of nominal GDP (and when there is no growth in real output), all four models indicated that the Hidden Economy would rise to *at least* between 30% and 40% of measured GDP.[121] (For the preferred Logistic functional form the finding was 38%). This suggests that the higher taxes are raised, the greater is the size of the hidden economy and the larger are the tax evasion and potentially preventable tax avoidance problems.

(3) Minimising the Size of the Hidden Economy: Tax Burden and Tax Mix Adjustments

A series of policy scenarios were examined to determine if a best practice combination of adjustments to the tax/GDP ratio and the tax mix existed that would minimise the value of the hidden economy and the tax gap. Those scenarios are depicted in **Table 4.6** and summarised below. **Table 4.7** provides supplementary information for each policy option by presenting the simulated or real ratios of personal, indirect and corpoprate tax to total tax and the tax/GDP ratio for each year. **Table 4.6** presents the consequences of these yearly options for the size of the hidden economy in that year.

---

120 These estimates exclude social welfare fraud against the government. Overseas estimates place that figure at about 10-12% of total benefit payments.

121 There are no significant inconsistencies in these results - asymptotic confidence intervals, constructed by taking two standard errors on either side of the simulated values, all overlap one another substantially. This last point holds regardless of the (T/GDP) ratio used in the simulations.

Table 4.7
Total New Zealand Government Expenditure, percentage of GDP: 1950-2000, 5-year averages

	Policy 1				Policy 2				Policy 3				Policy 4				Policy 5			
	TAX MIX: Values for share of personal and indirect taxes relative to total tax are switched TOTAL TAX BURDEN: Total actual tax burden is unchanged.				TAX MIX: Personal taxes are set to zero and indirect taxes are increased to compensate. TOTAL TAX BURDEN: Total actual tax burden is unchanged.				TAX MIX: Tax mix is unchanged. TOTAL TAX BURDEN: Total actual tax burden is halved.				TAX MIX: Values for the share of personal and indirect taxes relative to GDP are interchanged. TOTAL TAX BURDEN: Total actual tax burden is halved.				TAX MIX: Personal taxes are set to zero and indirect taxes are increased to compensate. TOTAL TAX BURDEN: Total actual tax burden is halved.			
	T/GDP	P/T	I/T	C/T	T/GDP	P/T	I/T	C/T	T/GDP	P/T	I/T	C/T	T/GDP	P/T	I/T	C/T	T/GDP	P/T	I/T	C/T
	%	%	%	%	%	%	%	%	%	%	%	%	%	%	%	%	%	%	%	%
1969	23.6	32.1	52.5	12.8	23.6	0.0	84.7	12.8	11.8	52.5	32.1	12.8	11.8	32.1	52.5	12.8	11.8	0.0	84.7	12.8
1970	23.8	31.5	46.6	19.3	23.9	0.0	78.2	19.3	11.9	46.6	31.5	19.3	11.9	31.5	46.6	19.3	11.9	0.0	78.2	19.3
1971	25.7	31.5	47.3	18.9	25.7	0.0	78.8	18.9	12.8	47.3	31.5	18.9	12.8	31.5	47.3	18.9	12.8	0.0	78.8	18.9
1972	25.7	30.3	51.5	16.5	25.7	0.0	81.8	16.5	12.9	51.5	30.3	16.5	12.9	30.3	51.5	16.5	12.9	0.0	81.8	16.5
1973	25.3	30.1	53.5	14.8	25.3	0.0	83.6	14.8	12.6	53.5	30.1	14.8	12.6	30.1	53.5	14.8	12.6	0.0	83.6	14.8
1974	27.0	27.5	55.4	15.5	27.0	0.0	82.9	15.5	13.5	55.4	27.5	15.5	13.5	27.5	55.4	15.5	13.5	0.0	82.9	15.5
1975	29.4	23.9	59.5	15.0	29.3	0.0	83.4	15.0	14.7	59.5	23.9	15.0	14.7	23.9	59.5	15.0	14.7	0.0	83.4	15.0
1976	28.3	26.1	60.0	12.1	28.1	0.0	86.1	12.1	14.1	60.0	26.1	12.1	14.1	26.1	60.0	12.1	14.1	0.0	86.1	12.1
1977	28.2	24.8	61.2	12.4	28.1	0.0	86.0	12.4	14.0	61.2	24.8	12.4	14.0	24.8	61.2	12.4	14.0	0.0	86.0	12.4
1978	30.9	23.5	64.1	11.2	30.9	0.0	87.5	11.2	15.5	64.1	23.5	11.2	15.5	23.5	64.1	11.2	15.5	0.0	87.5	11.2
1979	29.4	25.5	65.1	8.2	29.4	0.0	90.6	8.2	14.7	65.1	25.5	8.2	14.7	25.5	65.1	8.2	14.7	0.0	90.6	8.2
1980	30.4	24.8	62.9	11.3	30.4	0.0	87.7	11.3	15.2	62.9	24.8	11.3	15.2	24.8	62.9	11.3	15.2	0.0	87.7	11.3
1981	30.6	24.1	66.4	8.8	30.6	0.0	90.5	8.8	15.3	66.4	24.1	8.8	15.3	24.1	66.4	8.8	15.3	0.0	90.5	8.8
1982	31.4	25.2	65.9	8.1	31.4	0.0	91.1	8.1	15.7	65.9	25.2	8.1	15.7	25.2	65.9	8.1	15.7	0.0	91.1	8.1
1983	32.0	25.5	64.9	9.0	31.0	0.0	90.4	9.0	15.5	64.9	25.5	9.0	15.5	25.5	64.9	9.0	15.5	0.0	90.4	9.0
1984	29.8	27.9	64.3	7.2	29.0	0.0	92.2	7.2	14.5	64.3	27.9	7.2	14.5	27.9	64.3	7.2	14.5	0.0	92.2	7.2
1985	30.0	29.3	60.3	9.8	28.7	0.0	89.6	9.8	14.3	60.3	29.3	9.8	14.3	29.3	60.3	9.8	14.3	0.0	89.6	9.8
1986	31.1	25.2	64.0	10.3	29.9	0.0	89.2	10.3	14.9	64.0	25.2	10.3	14.9	25.2	64.0	10.3	14.9	0.0	89.2	10.3
1987	31.6	28.0	62.7	8.8	30.6	0.0	90.7	8.8	15.3	62.7	28.0	8.8	15.3	28.0	62.7	8.8	15.3	0.0	90.7	8.8
1988	34.4	35.3	52.9	11.2	33.9	0.0	88.3	11.2	16.9	52.9	35.3	11.2	16.9	35.3	52.9	11.2	16.9	0.0	88.3	11.2
1989	34.0	33.5	56.3	9.3	33.4	0.0	89.8	9.3	16.7	56.3	33.5	9.3	16.7	33.5	56.3	9.3	16.7	0.0	89.8	9.3
1990	36.6	34.4	51.4	12.9	36.1	0.0	85.7	12.9	18.0	51.4	34.4	12.9	18.0	34.4	51.4	12.9	18.0	0.0	85.7	12.9
1991	35.5	35.3	54.0	9.7	35.8	0.0	89.3	9.7	17.9	54.0	35.3	9.7	17.9	35.3	54.0	9.7	17.9	0.0	89.3	9.7
1992	34.0	37.6	51.7	10.3	33.7	0.0	89.3	10.3	16.8	51.7	37.6	10.3	16.8	37.6	51.7	10.3	16.8	0.0	89.3	10.3
1993	34.1	37.7	50.7	11.3	34.2	0.0	88.4	11.3	17.1	50.7	37.7	11.3	17.1	37.7	50.7	11.3	17.1	0.0	88.4	11.3
1994	34.9	36.2	50.1	13.6	34.5	0.0	86.3	13.6	17.3	50.1	36.2	13.6	17.3	36.2	50.1	13.6	17.3	0.0	86.3	13.6
Mean	30.3	29.5	57.5	11.9	30.0	0.0	87.0	11.9	15.0	57.5	29.5	11.9	15.0	29.5	57.5	11.9	15.0	0.0	87.0	11.9

P - personal, I - indirect, C - corporate, T - total actual tax burden. P+I+C equals less than 100% because "other taxes" are excluded.
Source: Inland Revenue, 1996

The policies are increasingly effective, in terms of reducing the size of the Hidden Economy relative to the measured economy, as we move from Policy 1 through to Policy 5.[122]

Policy 1 The *total tax burden is unaltered from its historical path*, but the tax mix is altered by interchanging the historical values for personal (50.1% in 1994) and indirect taxes (36.2%) as a share of total taxes. Personal income taxes were greater than indirect taxes in every year from 1968-94. So, Policy 1 involves, for example, in 1994, a significant (28%) *decrease* in direct, and an (38%) *increase* in indirect, taxes. Corporate taxes remain as they were. The tax/GDP ratio remains unchanged from its historical record.

The result is a decrease in the hidden economy from 11.3% of GDP to 9.38%, a reduction of roughly 2% points of GDP. *This would reduce the tax evasion gap by about 0.7% points, or about $700 million, thus increasing tax revenue without raising taxes.* This suggests the powerful impact of indirect taxes on modifying behaviour in the hidden economy.

Policy 2 The tax mix is changed by *setting personal taxes to zero* in every past period, and increasing indirect taxes to compensate, so that the *total tax burden is unaltered* in every year. This is a more extreme version of policy No. 1. Eighty-six percent of tax revenue in this simulation in 1994 would have been collected by indirect taxes. Corporate taxes are unchanged from the historical case.

Increasing indirect taxes from 50% to 86% of total taxes reduces the hidden economy relative to GDP by only one extra percentage point, from 9.38% in 1994 in policy No. 1 to 7.67% in Policy No. 2 in the same year. This suggests that there are diminishing returns in using indirect taxes as the main line of attack in controlling the hidden economy. Additional research needs to be undertaken to refine the preliminary estimate that the maximum share of indirect taxes would be below 50% of total taxes.

Policy 3 The *tax mix is unaltered*, but the *tax burden is halved* in each year from its actual record. The corporate tax mix is unchanged. Thus, in 1994, the tax/GDP ratio was cut to 17.3% from 34.9%, while 50.1% of taxes came from personal taxes, 36.2% from indirect and 13.6% from firms.

The result is a shrinkage of the hidden economy by 4.3 percentage points from 11.3% to 6.98%. Roughly speaking, for each

[122] The "control" time-path shows the predicted values of (H/GDP) with all of the data set to their actual historical values - this is the series of predicted values when the model is estimated. The "control" provides a bench-mark time-path against which the other simulation paths should be compared.

1 percentage point reduction in the tax/GDP ratio, the hidden economy declines by 0.25 percentage points. The result is close to the lowest level of the hidden economy over the last 25 years (6.98% (simulated) versus 6.95% (in 1970 and 1971)).

Policy 4 The total tax burden is halved and the historical values for the share of personal and indirect taxes relative to GDP are interchanged. This is a combination of Policy 1 and Policy 3, but corporate taxes are reduced by 50%.

The result is a marginal improvement over Policy 3. The hidden economy falls to 6.72% of GDP and the tax gap shrinks to about 2.4% of GDP. This suggests that tax evasion by individuals is a much more serious problem than evasion by firms. This is probably true if self-employed persons are classified as firms.

Policy 5 The tax mix is changed by *setting personal taxes to zero* in every past period, and increasing indirect taxes to compensate, but the total tax burden is halved. In this case, the hidden economy drops to the lowest among all the simulations: 6.08% in 1994.

The results suggest the following:

- If there is a sufficiently large reduction in the overall tax burden, with no change to the tax mix, then this can result in a greater reduction in underground activity than can be achieved by quite dramatic changes to that mix.
- A significant reduction (2 percentage points) in the hidden economy can be achieved without loss of tax revenue by placing stronger emphasis on using indirect taxes to collect tax revenue.[123]
- *Assuming total tax revenue is held constant, increasing* the share of total taxes derived from indirect taxes has a more potent effect in reducing the size of the hidden economy, as compared to raising the share of personal or corporate taxes. Further, if the total tax/GDP ratio is being reduced, there is more to be gained in reducing tax evasion by making deeper cuts to personal or corporate tax.
- A uniform 10% reduction in the tax/GDP ratio is roughly equivalent to altering the tax mix by interchanging the roles of personal and indirect taxes, in terms of the reduction in the relative size of the Hidden Economy.

(4) *Simulating the GST Shock on the Size of the Hidden Economy*

[123] This refers to a *static* best practice frontier where the sole objective is to reduce the amount of tax evasion, and where the desire is to sustain or increase the existing level of tax revenue. But a cut in all taxes is more potent in reducing tax evasion than is a shift in the tax mix. Thus, a dynamic best practice frontier is to be preferred over a static best practice frontier. A dynamic best practice frontier would involve a reduction in both the level of total tax (relative to GDP) as well as a shift in the tax mix to favour greater use of indirect tax.

In October 1986, sales taxes were abolished and the Goods and Services Tax (GST) was introduced, at an initial rate of 10%, subsequently raised to its present rate of 12.5% in 1989. Simultaneously, major changes were made to the personal income tax and corporate tax scales, with the effects of simplifying their structure and reducing the extent to which they were regressive. These changes affect the data from 1987 to 1994. GST has accounted for approximately 20% of total tax revenue on average since its inception, and about 25% of total tax revenue in recent years, and for the bulk of indirect taxes. If the GST had *not* been introduced, how might this have affected the relative size of the Hidden Economy?

- If all the potential revenue had been foregone, the weight of the tax mix would have shifted heavily in favour of direct taxes; but in this particular case the burden effect outweighs the mix effect, and the net result is a *fall* in H/GDP as compared to the current situation with GST;

- On the other hand, if the GST had *not* been introduced and if the foregone GST revenue had been recovered completely via increased personal and corporate taxes, *by apportioning the increase in taxes to personal and corporate tax according to their share of total tax*, the relative size of the Hidden Economy would have been *greater* than in the historical "control".

- *These results make intuitive sense. One would anticipate a rise in the Hidden Economy/GDP ratio if the tax burden on personal income increases, because the incentive to evade is stronger when income is under threat. Similarly, a rise in this ratio is also expected in the case of companies - small firms will be stimulated to evade and larger corporations will have a greater incentive to avoid, if there is a shift in the tax mix with less emphasis on a consumption tax to a tax mix which targets incomes more.*

Based on anecdotal evidence, Hotelling (1939a:152) concluded that excise taxes tended to promote more evasion and have higher collection costs than personal income taxes. Various reports would suggest that this problem still exists today. For example, "Sweden's high alcohol taxes have already led to a surge in 'beer traffic' between Sweden and Denmark, where taxes are substantially lower" (McIvor, 1996:3). Thus, there are two important distinctions that need to be made with respect to the evasion effects of taxation. There is the need to distinguish between (1) the evasion effects of excise taxes versus value added taxes, and (2) the evasion effects of personal income taxes as compared to value added taxes.

Research has not yet focused on a detailed examination of the difference between the evasion effects of excise taxes as compared to GST, but our work on GST for NZ suggests strongly that where GST has a higher share of total tax than direct taxes, if total taxes are held constant, the size of the hidden economy and tax evasion will be smaller than under a tax mix dominated by direct taxes. But, we agree with Smith and Hotelling that excise taxes promote smuggling and tax evasion.

(5) A Best Practice Frontier for the Tax/GDP Ratio Relative to the Hidden Economy

From this analysis, it is clear that higher tax burdens, as measured by the tax/GDP ratio, promote an ongoing increase in the size of the hidden economy and the tax evasion gap. Conversely, a reduction in the tax/GDP ratio will induce a reduction in the hidden economy and the tax evasion gap. At what point do diminishing returns in reducing the hidden economy set in as taxes are cut? Or, what level of cut in the tax/GDP ratio combined with a proxy for a best practice tax mix minimises the *relative* size of the hidden economy? At a point where diminishing returns arise, will a new unit reduction in taxes yield progressively smaller reductions in the size of the hidden economy.

Caragata & Giles (1996) have addressed this issue. Their data in Table 4 of that paper suggest the following. From the analysis earlier it seems that the hidden economy will shrink if the tax mix emphasises indirect taxes more heavily than direct taxes. The simulations described in **Table 4.7** of this Report show that proportions to total tax of personal and indirect taxes have been switched so, for example, in 1994, about 30% of tax is collected from personal tax (instead of 50%, as was the actual case) and 50% of tax was accounted for by indirect tax (instead of 30%, as was the case historically).

This mix is then coupled with a cut in the tax/GDP ratio of 10%, 20%, 30%, 40%, 50%, 60%, 70%, 80%, 90% and 100%. Recall that the objective is to search for the point at which diminishing returns set in, given this new tax mix, as we progressively simulate a tax cut. The results are as follows:

- the rate of change in the reduction of the hidden economy first begins to slow down as taxes are cut at a level of 25% in the tax/GDP ratio; this point is the first part of a range where deceleration on this curve[124] begins to appear;

- the next point where deceleration really becomes noticeable is about 17% of GDP; thereafter, progress in reducing the hidden economy is very slow; and

- to be cautious, we should take the average of these two points; the result is a tax/GDP ratio of *approximately 21%.*

The implications of this result are quite important. First, this is the first estimate of the best practice frontier in the tax/GDP ratio relative to the objective of reducing the size of the hidden economy. Previous work (Scully, 1995, 1996 and Caragata & Small, 1996) indicates that the reduction in the tax/GDP ratio promotes greater economic activity. The analysis of Caragata & Giles (1996) suggests strongly that the objective of reducing the size of the hidden economy is compatible with promoting economic growth.

---

[124] This curve is based on the percentage changes from one policy shock to another, on the progressive basis established above.

Second, shrinking the tax gap broadens the tax base, and ensures that the tax burden is more widely spread. Therefore, reducing the size of the hidden economy is a strong, positive contribution to fairness and equity. Third, this optimal frontier for the tax/GDP ratio is roughly in the same range as that discovered by Scully (1995,1996) for maximising economic growth (16.5-23.0%, with an average of 19.7%. Thus, *there is a strong compatibility between the objectives of maximising economic growth and minimising the size of the hidden economy.*

These two independent modelling exercises using different objective functions have reached the same general conclusion about the best practice size of the tax/GDP ratio. Hence, the existence of a best practice frontier between an average of 19.7% (Scully) up to 21% (Caragata & Giles) of the tax/GDP ratio is confirmed. This frontier maximises efficiency through growth and promotes fairness and equity through the reduction of tax evasion and potentially preventable tax avoidance and thus a broader sharing of the tax burden. The estimation of each of these approaches to the best practice frontier provides for changes in government spending and tax revenues because both models are dynamic, as is the Caragata & Small (1996) non-linear dynamic tax model which corroborated the results of the first two models. Thus, these empirically based econometric models treat tax revenue and government expenditure as fluctuating, as occurs in reality.

This research supports Clotfelter's (1983:373) conclusion that "...tax rates should be considered along with enforcement, tax simplicity, and information reporting as valid instruments for influencing tax evasion". On the other hand, the conclusions of this report with respect to the link between tax evasion and the preference for using indirect taxes to reduce the size of the tax evasion gap casts some doubt on Gordon and Neilsen's (1996) finding that "Denmark could reduce the real costs of avoidance activity by putting more weight on income rather than value-added taxes".

Modelling and analysis undertaken for this Report indicates the opposite. Although there is a generic difference between the sources of evasion and potentially preventable tax avoidance, both are quite sensitive, first, to the level of the effective tax rate (tax/GDP basis) and, second, to the tax mix (direct, indirect relative to GDP). Increasing the rate of income tax, while holding the level of tax constant, aggravates, rather than resolves, both potentially preventable tax avoidance and evasion problems. Such action also misses the fundamental nature of the incentive structure that shapes tax evasion and potentially preventable tax avoidance decisions by firms and individuals.

First, as discussed earlier, income is easier to disguise than consumption, in part because of higher transaction costs of disgusing income as compared to consumption. Second, people treat income as a personal possession or property right and are motivated to protect it accordingly. Third, the risks of getting caught for hiding income are probably lower than for hiding consumption because of the information problems in obtaining income data for those outside the PAYE (pay-as-you-earn) tax collection system. As well hidden income can be transferred out of the country for consumption abroad or laundered (e.g. declared as gambling earnings which are tax free).

Fourth, the rewards for disguising income are higher than for disguising consumption because of the higher tax burden on income. Finally, value added taxes pick up spending by those in the hidden economy, whereas the income tax does not, and, as a result, evasion is less than it would otherwise be and tax revenue is higher. Tax mix effects are best estimated when the total tax burden is held constant. When the total tax burden is changing simultaneously with the mix, it is the burden effect that will dominate over the tax mix effect on the incentive to evade.

Some caveats are in order. The value of any partial shift of the tax mix from direct to indirect taxes to reduce the tax evasion gap depends on other factors such as: (a) the type of indirect tax (purchase or manufacturers' tax versus value added tax– GST is preferred); (b) the degree of international exposure of the income and sales tax systems; and (c) the role of services in the economy (services are difficult to tax under both VAT and income tax systems).[125]

4.9 Findings, Conclusions and Implications

In NZ, the total level of taxes relative to GDP accounts for about 57% of the change in the size of the hidden economy and thus tax evasion. Inflation accounts for about 24% of the change, personal disposable income about 7.5%, regulation about 6.5% and unemployment about 5.3%. *If the level of taxes is lower, the size of the hidden economy and tax evasion will be lower. In the short term, where there is little change in the tax level, but it remains high, an increase in real disposable income will trigger a powerful tax evasion reaction by individuals and many firms. Since current tax evasion is a path-dependent learning process, it is likely a function of the lagged level of evasion.*

In 1969, about 24 cents per dollar of national measured income was collected in tax, and the hidden economy generated about 8 cents per dollar of measured economic activity. By 1994, the tax/GDP ratio rose to 35 cents per dollar of measured economic activity, and hidden economy activity hit about 11 cents per dollar of measured economic activity. The hidden economy rose (45.4%) at about the same rate as the tax burden (48%) over this period. In 1969 the illicit activity sector evasion tax gap was about 1% of GDP and accounted for about 52% of the total tax evasion gap. By 1994, the illicit activity sector evasion gap had reached 1.4% of GDP, but accounted for only 36% of the total tax evasion gap, indicating that the non-organised, tax-driven segment of the hidden economy is outpacing illicit activity sector evasion activity, and suggesting that there is wide recognition of the savings to be had by not paying taxes.

In effect, NZ has a growing tax evasion problem arising from individuals, the self-employed and, small firms and petty and organised criminal activity which appears to be based on widespread, rather than isolated, behaviour. A large part

[125] I thank Jack Mintz for pointing out these issues.

of this criminal activity is theft by employers, employees and customers. In 1994, NZ's hidden economy was estimated by our models to be $9.2 billion, or 11.3% of GDP, while the total tax evasion gap was $3.2 billion per annum, or about 4.0% of GDP, assuming the maximum estimate is both accurate and fully collectable, neither of which may be the case. More research is needed on this matter.

In general, about 30-40% of the size of the hidden economy is not driven strictly by a tax evasion motivation (based on a simulation model). If taxes are reduced to zero, this *illicit activity sector* of the hidden economy would remain. It is called the illicit activity sector of the hidden economy because it has more complex motivations than simply evading taxes. It is "the natural rate of underground activity". The *illicit activity sector* is composed of criminal activity such as theft, illicit gambling, protection rackets, prostitution, the manufacture and sale of illicit drugs, smuggling of weapons and drugs, money laundering etc. Such activity may lead to tax evasion, but tax evasion is not the driving force. The illicit activity sector could be interpreted as being essentially arising from value-driven (i.e. a social or market preference for non-conformist behaviour or criminal activity) rather than tax-driven incentives. The tax-driven part of the hidden economy is the *tax-sensitive sector* of the underground economy because it driven only by the motivation to evade taxes. Taxes are an additional cost of living for individuals and impose a higher cost of doing business for firms. Tax savings are high-powered money that offer a significant rate of return despite the transaction costs of tax advice and the risks of getting caught.

Thus, the hidden economy is composed of the illicit activity sector and the tax-sensitive segment. The tax-sensitive segment will modify its tax evasion behaviour if the rules of the game are made more punitive (tougher enforcement and penalties) and if tax rates are *reduced* and the tax mix is changed. It is doubtful that the criminal element will cease its behaviour because of more punitive tax rules, but it may adjust its behaviour. Both the illicit activity sector and tax-sensitive sector expand and contract with the normal business cycle.

Unchecked, the hidden economy can pose a serious threat to fiscal and monetary policy (Caragata, 1995). Revenue forecasting and government expenditure are constrained if a rising segment of the population is not paying tax. This will promote larger than necessary deficits that will have important implications for investor confidence, the balance of payments and the exchange rate. This will ultimately affect the efficacy of monetary policy. At the same time, the control of inflation becomes more problematic when activity in the hidden economy is not immediately responsive to changes in policy by the central bank. It is therefore imperative to discover the range for tax rates and the tax mix which minimise the propensity to evade and avoid. This can be achieved by developing a better understanding of the incentive structures that shape the development of the unreported economy.

Large cuts in the tax/GDP ratio have a more significant impact on reducing the hidden economy and the tax gap than significant changes to the tax mix. A 2 percentage point cut in the hidden economy can be achieved without loss of tax revenue by placing stronger emphasis on using indirect taxes to collect tax revenue. In fact, in this option, about 0.7 percentage points of the tax gap is removed. But, a cut in the total tax burden (relative to GDP) has a more potent effect on reducing the hidden economy and tax evasion than does a shift in the tax mix to favour greater use of indirect tax. Finally, a combination of both these options has a greater effect than either option alone in reducing both the hidden economy and tax evasion. We also surmise that when the total tax burden is changing simultaneously with the mix, it is the burden effect that will dominate over the tax mix effect on the incentive to evade, until the optimal tax level is reached. At that point, the mix will become dominant.

More research is required to determine the simulated limits of shifting the tax mix towards indirect taxes. The initial conclusion is that a tax mix weighted more heavily towards indirect taxes will be more successful in minimising tax evasion for several reasons. First, income is easier to disguise than a sales transaction. Second, because income tax is more complex than a sales tax, various factors can be used to adjust income (deductions can be inflated, transfer prices manipulated, equity disguised as debt and vice versa, financial structures redesigned etc).

Third, taxpayers are more motivated to protect their income from all incursions such as taxation because income is a personal possession and a tax on such income is a direct threat to a personal possession, whereas a tax on a consumption item is not. Fourth, income tax evasion carries a higher reward and a lower risk of getting caught than sales tax evasion because there is a greater information deficiency problem for the tax authority with respect to personal income outside of PAYE schemes, as compared to GST where detailed records are required to be kept.

As a result of these elements of control, possession, reward and risk, the opportunities and constraints favour the choice of income tax evasion as compared to consumption tax evasion. Hence, individuals and small business probably devote more learning time to minimising income as compared to indirect taxes, which reinforces their preference for income tax evasion.

There are diminishing returns in relying on indirect taxes to reduce the hidden economy and the tax gap. More research is also needed to identify the constraints that prevent the tax gap from being closed. What remains to be learned about the incentive structures that affect learned behaviour in the underground economy? Can we learn more about the diminishing returns of adjusting the tax revenue streams? At what tax rate does tax evasion began to accelerate?

This analysis has presented an estimated range for the best practice frontier in the tax/GDP ratio relative to the objective of reducing the size of the hidden economy. The range is 18% to 24%, with an average estimate of 21% of GDP. The objective of reducing the size of the hidden economy and the tax gap is compatible with promoting economic growth. Shrinking the tax gap reduces tax evasion and potentially preventable tax avoidance, broadens the tax base, and ensures that the tax burden is more widely spread. This provides an important boost to fairness and equity.

This best practice frontier for the tax/GDP ratio for minimising tax evasion is roughly in the same range as that discovered by Scully (1995,1996) for maximising economic growth. Thus, there is a strong compatibility between the objectives of maximising economic growth and minimising the size of the hidden economy. These two independent modelling exercises using different objective functions have reached the same general conclusion about the best practice size of the tax/GDP ratio. Hence, the existence of a best practice frontier between 19%-23% of tax/GDP ratio appears to be confirmed. This best practice frontier maximises efficiency through growth and promotes fairness and equity through the reduction of tax evasion and potentially preventable tax avoidance and thus a broader sharing of the tax burden.

In the introduction to his 1992 book of edited articles on *Why People Pay Taxes*, Joel Slemrod, a leading US tax economist highlighted a key thread running through all the articles, the need to abandon the stick of punishing tax evasion and to offer the carrot of encouragement for compliance:

"If there is a persistent theme to the essays presented in this volume, it is a change in perspective away from deterring non-compliance towards positive encouragement for compliance – an emphasis on the 'carrot' for compliance rather than the 'stick' for non-compliance. Positive attitudes toward the tax system and pleasant, efficient contacts with the tax collection agency can increase compliance. This insight is especially important because, from the tax collection standpoint, it is extraordinarily expensive to arrange an enforcement regime so that, from a strict cost-benefit calculus, non-compliance does not appear attractive to many citizens. It follows that methods that reinforce and encourage taxpayer's devotion to their responsibilities as citizens play an important role in the tax collection process" (Slemrod, 1992:7).

What is wrong with this analysis? At, first sight, nothing, because this view is in harmony with the shift in thinking in the current generation from emphasising punishment to stressing persuasion in all types of compliance problems. Moreover, tax authorities impose high compliance costs which can be reduced by more selective auditing. Greater selectivity will mean no compliance costs for many taxpayers and that will promote good will. But this simple choice may be unrealistic because it ignores crucial systemic changes. In particular, over the past 30 years, the average size of government (measured in terms of tax revenue relative to GDP) in 28 OECD countries has risen by about 46%, from 26.3% of GDP in 1966 to 38.4% of GDP in 1994.[126] Of course, this is a conservative estimate since most countries have deficits rather than balanced budgets.

Most available evidence indicates that this expansion of the role of government in the economy has been accompanied by a larger hidden economy and thus more tax evasion. A professional review of compliance problems cannot, and should not, therefore, ignore the impact of the level and the mix of taxes relative to the size of the economy. Unfortunately, scholars sometimes just treat the level

---

[126] For New Zealand the tax to GDP ratio rose from 24.7% to 37% of GDP from 1965-1994, an increase of 49.8%

and mix of taxes as given. Such a static view precludes valuable insights and minimises the potential for making more than marginal reductions in the level of tax evasion.

When the total tax burden is higher and economic growth rises, taxpayer concerns about income property rights, the savings in the minimisation and value for money in government spending and the propensity for tax evasion, all increase. This does not justify tax evasion. It is illegal and punishable by fines and imprisonment. These factors, however, explain the very behaviour the tax department is trying to curb, and so they must be recognised in responses to reduce tax evasion. In effect, when tax burdens are too high, the carrot (if focused only on moral and the stick are probably ineffective in reducing tax evasion in any significant way. In that case, the only recourse is to cut taxes.

5. THE REVENUE POTENTIAL OF THE NEW ZEALAND TAX SYSTEM

5.1 The Dimensions of Potential Revenue

Current Versus Potential Revenue

Current revenue could be expanded quite considerably in several ways without adjusting tax rates in order to reach *potential revenue*. In the static dimension, the tax/GDP ratio, the tax mix and any behavioural effects are held constant; estimated potential revenue is the total of current revenue plus the dollar value of the tax gap. The tax gap is composed of both illicit sector and tax-sensitive sector evasion in the hidden economy, as well as potentially preventable avoidance (with the latter not yet having been estimated). Thus, in the case of static revenue, we want a snapshot of the difference between current revenue and potential revenue.

Dynamic revenue estimates do not hold constant the tax/GDP ratio, the tax mix or current tax law. They also incorporate the behavioural responses of individuals and firms to changes in the rates and mix. Unfortunately, currently there is a bias in Keynesian-based macro-econometric models that emphasises the demand side consequences of tax changes and tends to ignore or under-estimate some or all the supply side consequences.[127] Auerbach (1996) has provided some useful insights into this issue during federal budget-making exercises in the United States. He observes that

> "it is common for revenue estimates to incorporate projections of behavioural responses in particular affected markets or transactions. For example, the revenue estimate of a change in the capital gains tax rate does incorporate predicted changes in capital gains realisations and shifts in the composition of income, but does not explicitly include changes in aggregate output or investment that might result from the tax change. In other words, the existing methodology directly accounts for some 'micro' behavioural responses to taxation, but no 'macro' responses" (Auerbach, 1996:144; see also Feldstein, 1996a).

In the short term, an increase in rates may increase the amount collected. But various studies have indicated that as tax rates are raised, the greater is the level of tax avoidance and evasion. As a result, the revenue collecting efficiency of the tax system begins to diminish, and the weaker the economy becomes as it bears the increased tax burden. The extent to which a tax cut will replace existing tax revenue as a result of higher growth is still a matter for discussion and debate. But, Branson & Lovell (1997) estimate that moving from a tax/GDP ratio of 35% currently to an optimal growth maximising level of 22.5% for New Zealand would lead to a reduction in revenue of only 6%, given the tax-driven economic expansion. Purchasing power in the non-government sector would rise by about 27%.

There are two dimensions to revenue generation in a dynamic context. First, there is the revenue response that rises or falls with the level of economic activity, which in turn responds to the tax/GDP ratio and the tax mix. Second,

[127] See Spiro (1996) for comments on a related issue in a Canadian context.

there is the change in the potentially preventable tax avoidance/evasion response to the change in the tax/GDP ratio and the tax mix.

All of this raises the question about what should be the objective of government with respect to tax revenue. Should the aim be to maximise (regardless of constraints) or to optimise (given constraints)? And should that focus be a short run perspective, a long run perspective, or both?

As John Stuart Mill noted in "Considerations on Representative Government" in *Essays on Politics and Society* (v. 19, Collected Works p. 441), "the interest of the government is to tax heavily; that of the community is to be as little taxed as the necessary expenses of good government permit". This different set of community versus individual objectives leads to a tension between revenue maximisation and revenue minimisation that is subsequently reshaped by various factors, e.g. interest group pressure, discussed elsewhere in this Report. Tax authorities have a mandate to maximise revenue under current law. It would probably be wise to revisit that objective given constraints, including financial and human resource limits, that prevent tax authorities from closing the tax gap between current and potential revenue.

Revenue-Maximising Tax Rates and their Complications

It is conceivable, of course, that government could continue to increase its revenue relative to GDP even though the deadweight loss of government taxation was placing an ever-increasing burden on the economy and constraining or reducing economic growth. The analysis in this Report suggests that the peak in the growth rate relative to the tax rate is reached long before the peak in tax revenue. Of course, this would be true theoretically because government could possibly raise taxes to 100% of GDP (i.e. the equivalent of complete state ownership). But that 100% could never be reached because of the growth of "illegal" activity would rise and the hidden or black economy would become huge.

Nonetheless, at what point could we expect revenue maximisation to occur? Scully (1996:10) has addressed this question and concluded that for New Zealand:

"Utilising the coefficients in the growth (CPI) equation, the tax-maximising tax rate is 57.8 percent [of GDP]. While New Zealand has never reached this level of taxation, some northern European nations have."

Thus, the tax-maximising rate estimated by Scully for New Zealand is about 2.9 times the growth-maximising tax rate (58% divided by 20%). Obviously, this raises the question: is the economy and society sustainable at a tax rate of 58% of GDP, and for how long? Equally, is efficient government and social consensus sustainable with a growth-maximising tax/GDP ratio of 20%?

In a similar analysis of 103 countries for data in 1980, Scully (1991:7) concluded that "at tax rates higher than 43.2 percent governments could actually raise more revenue by lowering their tax rates".

Lindbeck (1986:31) has speculated about this revenue-maximisation level and its implications in the case of Sweden where, at the time of his writing, the government expenditure to GDP ratio "including transfer payments" about 65%, compared with about 45 percent in the UK, and 33% in the US. Sweden is generally considered to be one of the most heavily intervened economies in the world.

Lindbeck expressed concerns about the negative implications of the size of government for: (1) real rates of return in the private sector, (2) the role of the family in society, (3) the crowding out of *collective goods (such as justice, defence, culture and research)* because lobbying by vested interests reshapes government spending patterns, (4) the standard of ethics in a society that deprives individuals of more and more of their earnings and then places stiffer and stiffer penalties in response to tax evasion that has arisen in response to higher taxes and more regulations; and (5) the inefficiency that rises as the economy struggles to cope with government demands for revenue. More specifically, he noted that:

"...it hardly seems possible to avoid serious problems concerning economic efficiency, the freedom of choice of the family, and the protection of the individual against the state without keeping total public spending within certain bounds. My guess, built on Swedish experience, is that the various problems discussed here become serious if public spending rises substantially above 50% of GDP, since then the after-tax rates of return start to fall rapidly for every additional increase in the tax rates. If the expansion of welfare-state spending cannot be stopped in time, there is, in my judgement, a severe risk that other types of public spending will instead be cut substantially" (Lindbeck, 1986:31).

Of course, there are at least two important *time-related issues* that need examination regarding these matters. First, there is the length of time that a country remains at, or near, its tax-revenue maximisation levels. Lets call this *high altitude time*. More cross-country research is needed to determine the extent of the negative social, ethical and economic effects of taxation at progressively higher levels of tax/GDP ratios. Second, there is the *transition time* that is needed to de-couple the economy from its addiction to high spending government. If it took 30 years for the tax/GDP ratio to rise to its current level, it may take 10-20 years or more to bring the ratio back down to more realistic levels, given the adjustment problems.

Freeman (1995:20) has examined Sweden in this light. After expenditures reached an incredible 70% of GDP in the early 1990s, Sweden experienced "macroeconomic collapse". In response the government started to unwind the welfare state (Lindbeck,1995:12). Freeman concluded that descent from such high altitudes of the welfare state can have high costs in the short term because of the inflexibility in such systems (given labour and capital markets constraints and the interdependence of work and benefits and high taxes). One could also add to this the deadweight loss of high altitude taxes which create sluggishness and the deadening effect of bureaucratic dominance of the decision-making process etc). This suggests great difficulty in adjusting to changing economic environments. Caragata & Small's (1996) model of New Zealand growth – tax relationships confirms the existence of this sluggish response of growth to tax cuts at high altitudes. The economy is more responsive at lower tax altitudes.

Until the 1990s, Sweden's high altitude welfare state appears to have worked for a long time when domestic markets could be protected because of exchange rate controls, capital and labour market restrictions, and where benefits were dependant on working, taxes were highly progressive and wages were compressed, and high prices were ensured because markets were cartelised. When economic change forces these constraints to become looser, it appears that the welfare state begins to unravel because the tight linkages between economic agents implied by the numerous market constraints make the system inflexible. The adaptability of high altitude welfare states appears to be less than those at lower altitudes. Thus, there is "some evidence that countries with high welfare-state expenditures do more poorly on some economic country outcomes than do other advanced countries" (Freeman, 1995:18).

More research is needed on the transition time required to bring all categories of government spending to more realistic levels, even if optimal tax levels are not reached. Does the duration of time spent at high altitudes affect the transition time and the quality of the progress? In other words, are transition times smoother and faster when one starts to cut government expenditure at lower levels? One factor which will slow down the transition time is the share of the adult population dependant on government for their income:

"in the early 1990s, a large majority of the adult population in Sweden received practically their entire income from the public sector, either by way of transfer payments or as factor incomes from public sector employment (apart from state-owned corporations)." (Lindbeck, 1995:14)

These last two points are particularly important. There are existing constraints (including inherited obligations with respect to interest on national debt, existing superannuation commitments, and the impact of demographics on the education and health system) that prevent any rapid movement by government to more optimal levels of tax. In addition, there are always equity questions about which each generation needs to develop a consensus.

Revenue maximisation objectives can lead to serious economic problems. Tanzi & Schuknecht (1997), who are with the International Monetary Fund, have compared the economic performance (growth rates, gross fixed capital formation, inflation, unemployment, debt) and social performance (life expectancy, infant mortality, education and income distribution) for 17 small, medium and large OECD countries. They conclude that "there is no evidence" that countries with big governments have out-performed the countries with medium and small sized governments. Moreover, there appears to be an optimal range beyond which the return on government size (and thus spending) clearly indicate diminishing returns:

"the large increase in public spending in some of these [17 OECD] countries does not seem to have contributed much to social welfare. This leads us to conclude that by the time countries reach the level of public spending shown by the small governments, namely between 30 and 40 percent of GDP [with an average of 34.6% of GDP], much of the potential social gain from public spending has been obtained. Spending beyond that level does not contribute that much" (Tanzi & Schuknecht, 1997:167).

5.2 Static Potential Revenue Under Existing Rules

a. Introduction

The performance ratio for revenue conservation is current tax revenue divided by potential tax revenue, under existing law. The hidden economy has a pro-cyclical relationship with the measured economy. Thus, during the course of an upturn in the business cycle, the growth rate of actual tax revenue will start to run behind the growth of tax evasion, and thus fall behind potential tax revenue at an accelerating pace until the economy slows down. Thus, during business cycle upturns the revenue performance ratio (current divided by potential performance) will deteriorate and the Tax Authority could, innocently but wrongly, be perceived as being less efficient in collecting revenue than was the case during the previous trough in economic activity. In fact, a cyclical adjustment probably needs to be made at the tax gap estimate.

These are complex issues that require additional research. But there are other constraints that impede complete elimination of the hidden economy and tax evasion as well as potentially preventable tax avoidance. The principal constraints are information deficiencies and the lack of financial resources. Tied in with the information constraint is the understanding that there are justifiable limits to intrusion that protect privacy and private property rights.

b. Estimating Static Potential Tax Revenue

The following exercise is a preliminary attempt to define the current maximum value of potential tax revenue, and take into consideration the fact that *some* tax revenue is probably uncollectable. This is particularly true of criminal activity in the hidden economy. Asset seizure laws, however, have the potential of helping correct the problem of collecting unpaid tax.

To review, the total tax evasion gap, unadjusted for risk, averaged 3.3% of GDP over 1990-94 (about $3.2 bn) and rose to 3.9% of GDP ($3.5 bn) in 1994, the long term high. **Table 5.1** provides a gross annual estimate of static potential tax revenue in NZ over the period 1969-1994. The hypothetical assumption in the simulation is that the tax authority has the ability to collect all outstanding tax liabilities stemming from evasion. Potentially preventable tax avoidance has not yet been estimated. In 1994, total tax revenue collected was $28.2 billion (rounding will be used throughout this exercise). The tax gap ($3.2bn) plus revenue collected implies a potential revenue level of $31.4 billion. The tax gap equals 11.4% of current revenue and about 10% of potential revenue (given rounding) in 1994.

Assuming no constraints, it is estimated that, roughly 6.6% more revenue was collectable in 1970, 8.4% in 1980, 8.4% in 1990 and 10% in 1994 (**Table 5.1**).

Table 5.1
Gross Estimate of Static Potential Tax Revenue for New Zealand ($ millions) (assumes that 100% of tax evasion and tax avoidance can be captured): 1969-94

	A Total Revenue Collected	B Total Evasion Tax Gap	C Total Potential Revenue	D Performance Ratio Actual/Potential (A/D)	E Performance Gap (D-A)
1969	1,059	82	1,141	0.93	7.00
1970	1,181	82	1,263	0.94	6.00
1971	1,445	101	1,546	0.93	6.00
1972	1,707	130	1,837	0.93	7.00
1973	1,927	160	2,087	0.92	8.00
1974	2,395	216	2,611	0.92	8.00
1975	2,865	238	3,103	0.92	8.00
1976	3,185	312	3,497	0.91	9.00
1977	3,485	323	3,808	0.92	8.00
1978	4,626	392	5,018	0.92	8.00
1979	4,990	400	5,390	0.93	7.00
1980	6,020	556	6,576	0.92	8.00
1981	7,050	621	7,671	0.92	8.00
1982	8,798	748	9,546	0.92	8.00
1983	10,097	1,044	11,141	0.91	9.00
1984	10,431	1,072	11,503	0.91	9.00
1985	11,914	1,167	13,081	0.91	9.00
1986	14,236	1,369	15,605	0.91	9.00
1987	17,408	2,033	19,441	0.90	10.00
1988	21,528	2,148	23,676	0.91	9.00
1989	22,864	2,202	25,066	0.91	9.00
1990	26,105	2,402	28,507	0.92	8.00
1991	25,979	2,290	28,269	0.92	8.00
1992	24,795	2,186	26,981	0.92	8.00
1993	25,974	2,475	28,449	0.91	9.00
1994	28,187	3,217	31,404	0.90	10.00

Source: Inland Revenue, 1996

This 10% macro estimate of the tax gap has been confirmed by Giles (1997:16) using audit corporate taxpayer databases of tax evaders and non-evaders. It should not be assumed that the total tax evasion gap could be closed, given information constraints, scarce financial resources, and scarce skilled auditing and tax policy resources.

Table 5.2
Gross Estimate of Static Potential Tax Revenue for New Zealand (% of GDP), (excluding legal tax minimisation)

	a Total Tax	b Potential Tax Evasion Gap		a + b Revenue		Performance Ratio (current/potential)	
		100%	70%*	100%	70%	100% Gap Closure	70% Gap* Closure
1970	23.9	1.7	1.2	25.6	25.1	93.4	95.2
1975	29.3	2.4	1.7	31.7	31.0	92.4	94.5
1980	30.4	2.8	2.0	33.2	32.4	91.6	93.8
1985	28.7	2.8	2.0	31.5	30.7	91.1	93.5
1990	36.2	3.3	2.3	39.5	38.5	91.6	94.0
1991	35.6	3.2	2.2	38.8	37.8	91.8	94.2
1992	33.8	3.0	2.1	36.8	35.9	91.8	94.2
1993	34.2	3.3	2.3	37.5	36.5	91.2	93.7
1994	35.0	3.9	2.7	38.9	37.7	90.0	92.8

* Risk adjusted tax gap. This adjustment takes into consideration various information, resource, time, political and other constraints that impede perfect tax collection. It assumes that 70% of illicit-activity sector criminal tax evasion and 70% of the tax-sensitive sector tax evasion among individuals, the self-employed and small firms, can be eliminated.

Source: Inland Revenue, 1997

These estimates should be adjusted for the risk or probability of collection. Current guesstimates suggest that it is prudent to assume that only about 70% of the gross tax evasion gap is actually collectable. Taking this assumption into consideration produces what can be referred to as a risk-adjusted tax evasion gap[128].

Using this risk-adjusted basis, the tax gap would fall from 3.9% to 2.7% of GDP in 1994 (**Table 5.2**). On this basis, roughly 4.8% (as compared to 6.6%) more revenue could have been collected in 1970, 6.2% in 1980 (as compared to 8.4%), 6.0% in 1990 (as compared to 8.4%) and 7.2% in 1994 (as compared to 10%).

[128] 100% minus 30% equals 70%. The tax gap is the difference between what can be collected theoretically and what is collected in practice. The risk-adjusted tax gap reduces the amount that is theoretically collectable because of constraints.

Another way of reducing the tax gap, of course, is to cut the tax burden. Caragata & Giles (1996) estimate that the hidden economy could shrink from about 11% of GDP to around 7% of GDP if the tax burden is cut to 21% of GDP. This would shrink the dollar value of the amount of tax evasion in NZ and the tax gap, with a lag to accommodate changes in the incentive structure of companies and individuals.

Currently, about $500 million per annum is collected in audits by Inland Revenue. Thus, this is the numerator in the performance ratio measuring Inland Revenue's success in closing the *total* tax gap. The denominator is either $4.5 billion (unadjusted basis) or $3.1 billion (adjusted for the feasibility of collection). On an unadjusted basis, the performance ratio is 0.11, with a performance gap of 89%. On an adjusted basis, the performance ratio is 0.16, with a performance gap of 84%.

This result compares favourably (using identical classifications for the numerator and denominator) with a recent IRS estimate for the U.S. for individual taxpayers (*and excluding firms*):

"the gross tax gap as a percentage of the 'true" tax liability... for Tax Year 1992 range(s) from 16.9 to 17.3 percent" (Thomas et. al., 1996:v).

Twenty years ago in 1976 an IRS study indicated that the tax gap was 7% to 9% of *reported* income, or slightly less in terms of *reportable* income (Clotfelter, 1983:363). A decade later, in 1987 the IRS reported that non-compliance by both firms and individuals had reached 20% of potential revenue (Slemrod, 1992:1). Obviously, the tax evasion problem in the U.S. has grown, assuming the numbers are accurate. Thus, overall, the evidence seems to suggest that the US has a more serious problem with tax evasion than New Zealand, even though New Zealand has a higher tax/GDP ratio.

c. *Options for Closing the Tax Evasion Gap*

There is a range of policies that can be considered to deal with tax evasion arising from petty and organised criminal activity and from other sources of tax evasion. Options include:

- improved teamwork within government,
- asset seizure laws, perhaps not as draconian as the anti-racketeering laws (RICO[129]) in the United States, which permit Napoleonic Code type seizure and auctions of the proceeds of crime and hence provide a non-tax source of tax revenue,
- tougher money-laundering laws,
- carefully targeted tax policy laws that anticipate criminal methods,
- public education,
- a review of ethical standards,

[129] Racketeer Influenced and Corrupt Organizations Act. Among other things, in civil cases, this law permits the award of damages three times larger than in normal civil lawsuits.

- a reasonable tax rate level[130] and appropriate tax mix,
- adequate resources for tax and social policy design, police and tax audit enforcement and public education,
- increasing the use of the *deduction at source* approach[131] (e.g. PAYE),
- controlling inflation,
- minimising government regulations with high compliance costs,
- ensuring that taxpayers get value for money in government expenditures, and,
- perhaps a more rapid move towards a cash-less society.

The longer tax evasion habits are ingrained, the harder they will be to change. Further analysis is needed to determine the appropriate combination of these and other options for dealing with the problem.

d. Conclusions

There is a strong argument that if a debt is not collectable, then it should be written off. In this case, the issue is a matter of assessing the management performance of the tax authority. It should not be held responsible for collecting the uncollectable. Precisely where the line should be drawn requires considerably more work on risk profiling. All high-risk cases need to be assessed rigorously for their long term versus short term revenue generating potential.

5.3 Dynamic Revenue Potential: Long Term Tax Revenue Generation

We can expect that, at some point in an upward path of the statutory tax rate, taxpayer resistance begins to set in and output losses rise more steeply. After that point, the tax burden changes from being an *acceptable* to an *unacceptable* cost of living for individuals and a cost of doing business for firms. Taxpayers begin to step up significantly their potentially preventable tax avoidance and evasion activities, indicating one type of substitution effect, or reduce their production in one type of business or another perhaps by shifting to other jurisdictions (indicating an output loss to the economy). It is too early to say whether resistance rises faster or at the same rate as the increase in the statutory tax rate (and/or the intensification of loophole closing by government which raises effective tax rates).

As a result, after that point the revenue collected from a marginal increase in the statutory tax rate should increase but at a diminishing rate. This would be the revenue-optimising point, and the related rate would be the optimal statutory tax rate with a revenue-optimisation objective. This suggests that as the statutory tax rate moves up, for example, into the mid-to-upper thirties or early forties, the gap between actual and expected tax revenue could widen.

---

[130] High tax evasion is a signal that people want lower taxes. But lower taxes will not eliminate tax evasion, rather evasion will be better controlled and less widespread.

[131] *Deduction at source* (including PAYE programs for salary and wage earners, and interest and dividend withholding taxes) is the lynchpin of the modern tax system because it ensures high levels of "voluntary compliance".

Feldstein and Feenberg (1995) investigated the 1993 increase in the U.S. marginal tax rate from 31% to 36% for those with income between $140,000 and $250,000 and an increase from 31% to 39.6% for incomes above $250,000. Their preliminary conclusion, using a dynamic model, was that the expected additional annual tax revenue from the tax increase was $19.3 billion. Actual tax revenue from the tax increase was only $8.4 billion. Thus, the marginal performance ratio, actual divided by potential revenue, was 43.5%. Feldstein and Feenberg (1995:21) concluded that the 1993 increase in the marginal tax rate was "a very inefficient way of increasing revenue".[132]

This indicates that if the marginal rates were even higher, the performance ratio would drop further. As well, it suggests that, if the marginal tax rate is set below 36%, the marginal revenue performance ratio will be higher than 43.5%. In turn, this implies, at least in an American context, that the best practice level for the marginal tax rate on personal income where the performance ratio approaches 1.0 is below 36%. Thus, increasing returns or efficiency of revenue collection improves below rather than above a statutory tax rate of 36%. Some new research in a NZ context should be undertaken on this matter.

At a best practice tax rate, potentially preventable avoidance and evasion would be minimised, deadweight losses would be significantly reduced and revenue-generating efficiency of the economy would be maximised. Such analysis also needs to consider the equity constraints imposed by the political system and the utility of government expenditures on social and economic infrastructure. Elsewhere, Feldstein (1995:9) concluded that if the actual behavioural responses of taxpayers to existing tax cuts are properly taken into consideration in revenue estimations "lower marginal tax rates would involve much less revenue loss than is traditionally assumed".

Spiro (1996:14) examined the impact of tax cuts on the labour force participation rate and employment growth in Canada over the period 1967-1994. At the same time, he calculated the revenue effects of a $1 billion dollar tax cut, and concluded that the resultant growth in output and incomes would lead to tax revenue that would recapture 76% of the tax cut. This is a useful hypothesis for future research.

A cut in all taxes is more potent in reducing tax evasion than is a shift in the tax mix. Thus, a dynamic best practice approach is to be preferred over a static best practice approach in order to assess properly the long run effects of tax changes. A dynamic best practice frontier would involve a reduction in both the level of total tax (relative to GDP) as well as a shift in the tax mix to favour greater use of indirect tax. This finding lends some support to Bill Archer, Chairman of the House Ways and Means Committee in the United States who stated recently that:

---

[132] Their analysis hinges not only on the level of the top marginal tax rate, but also on the fact that the rate is part of a progressive rate structure. Raising the top rate alone is more distortionary than raising the overall schedule, in a static context. The distortion relates to the size of the marginal rate increase, and there is very little income in the U.S. tax base subject to the rate increase. Thus the 'cost-benefit' ratio is very high.

"in the area of getting at the underground economy, I would score the flat tax a zero, maybe a one [out of ten].... [As for a consumption tax] ...if you're in the illegal drug business and want to buy a Mercedes with your ill-gotten gains, you're going to pay your share of the cost of government. So I would score a properly designed consumption tax somewhere between eight and ten in the underground economy" (Archer, 1996:1829).

In Scully's (1996) tax and growth model, Caragata & Giles' (1996) hidden economy simulation model, and Caragata & Small's (1996) non-linear dynamic model, the level of government expenditure fluctuates. All estimations in the Health Report concerning the best practice frontier implicitly treat government expenditures as dynamic. Thus, as taxes are cut, the models predict that there is a high probability that economic growth will increase, thus generating more investment and employment, while tax evasion will be reduced.

These two factors may very well lead to less revenue loss than expected, but more research is required to sort out the net revenue effects of tax cuts. Some preliminary research on this matter has been undertaken in New Zealand. Branson & Lovell (1997) estimate that reducing the current tax burden in New Zealand from 35% of GDP to 22.5% of GDP will reduce the nominal amount of revenue by 6%, but increase the purchasing power of the rest of the economy by 27%.

5.4 Conclusion

If the tax system is held constant, potential tax revenue is composed of three elements: (1) current tax revenue received (including the results of audit investigations); (2) tax evasion by firms and individuals in the hidden economy; and, (3) potentially preventable corporate tax avoidance. If the tax rates and the tax mix are being changed, potential revenue is composed of each of these three elements, plus two others (4) the change in tax revenue arising from the change in the level of economic activity as a result of the change in the tax regime; and, (5) the results of behaviour modification on potentially preventable tax avoidance and evasion caused by the change in taxes. These latter factors require complex modelling which is left to future research. Therefore, the current estimate used for current potential revenue ignores the behavioural responses of taxpayers.

In the short term, an increase in rates may increase the amount collected. But various studies have indicated that as tax rates are raised, the greater is the level of potentially preventable tax avoidance and evasion, the less revenue is collected, and the weaker the economy becomes as it bears the increased tax burden. The extent to which a tax cut will replace or increase existing tax revenue that is sacrificed in a tax cut is still a matter for discussion and debate, and also should be the subject of future research.

6. THE EFFICIENCY EFFECTS OF TAXATION

6.1 Introduction

This section explores several important economic efficiency consequences of taxation. In particular, we are interested in the impact of taxes on economic growth, deadweight loss and employment. Other issues such as the impact of taxes on investment and competitiveness await future research.

In a dynamic context, a healthy tax system would have tax levels, tax rates and a tax mix that optimise economic efficiency (including economic growth, compliance costs and employment), and minimise tax evasion and potentially preventable avoidance and tax administration costs given a (inter-generational and intra-generational) politically determined equity constraint. As constraints (including equity constraints) change across time, these optimal or frontier tax levels, rates and mix will also change, albeit perhaps slowly. Up to the best practice point, for a given period of time, the tax system and related government expenditures are creating increasing returns to economic growth as a result of the contributions to social and economic expenditure; after that point or range there are positive, but diminishing returns. At some point in a range, the costs from increasing the tax/GDP ratio exceed the benefits of additional expenditures (assuming balanced budgets) resulting in negative returns. Conversely, there is a point beyond which cuts in the tax/GDP ratio create decreasing returns as the cost of lost expenditure outweighs the benefits of lower taxes.

The gap between the current and the potential efficiency performance of the economy, given the presence of taxes, is *the tax-driven economic efficiency gap, other things being equal.* The closer the economy is to the optimal efficiency performance point or range, taking into consideration all the above efficiency factors (in terms of the tax/GDP ratio and the tax mix), the healthier is the tax system. But, efficiency is not the only objective of the tax system.

Early Assessments of the Optimal Tax Rate

(1) Lessons From 6000 Years of Taxation

There is an ancient Asian proverb that stresses the benefits of moderate, as opposed to high, taxation: "It is not the heavy taxed nation that executes great deeds, but the moderately taxed one". Charles Adams chose this epigram to end his book *For Good and Evil: The Impact of Taxes on the Course of Civilisation* in 1993. He emphasised the need to develop a balanced approach to tax rates, tax authority intrusions, penalties and equality in his review of 6000 years of taxes from the dawn of recorded civilisation in the Tigris and Euphrates plains tom the present.

Historically, the standard range of tax has been from about 5-20% of income, with sales taxes generally between 1%-15%, and sometimes higher. In his foreword to this book Alvin Rabushka of Stanford University's Hoover Institution noted that a 10% flat tax "is well-grounded in several thousand years of history of Israel, Rome,

Greece and ancient China" (Adams, 1993:xii). Rabushka (one of the modern creators of the flat tax) went on to observe that Adams' book recorded several lessons from tax history:

"First, good tax systems go bad unless citizens are able to restrain their governments, which have a normal propensity to adjust their spending to their innate voracious appetites, not their wallets. Second, civilisation tends to self-destruct from excessive taxation. Third, moderation is an important principle in the design and implementation of any tax system. The principle of moderation includes the choice of tax rates and penalties for evasion, the intrusiveness of tax collection, and the need to treat taxpayers equally by avoiding severe progressivity or regressivity" (Adams, 1993:xiii).

(2) Adam Smith

In his *Lectures on Jurisprudence*, Adam Smith gave a hint at his concept of an optimal tax rate. He suggests that if the tax burden is more than 20% of GDP, the taxpayers would be justifiably upset:

"No doubt the raising of a very exorbitant tax, as the raising as much in peace as in war, or the half or even the fifth of the wealth of the nation, would, as well as any gross abuse of power, justify resistance in the people" (p. 187).

Inflation and Exchange Rate Stability

Following on from an earlier suggestion from Keynes[133], Clark (1945) undertook a cross-country (France, Belgium, Britain, Japan, Italy, and Norway) examination of the optimal level of tax with respect to a combined objective function of stabilising domestic prices and ensuring that the exchange rate is neither under-valued nor over-valued. The analysis covered the 1920s and 1930s. Clark observed that "excessive taxation, levied for payment of interest on public debt" would promote higher inflation, lead to the over-valuation of the country's currency and eventually require a devaluation. He presented cross-country data for the optimal level of tax related to these objectives, indicating that "... the critical limit of taxation is about 25% of the national income, or possibly rather less" (Clark, 1945:376).

In NZ, national income represented about 86% of GDP over the last 10 years. Thus 25% of national income would be equal to about 21% of GDP, recalling that national income excludes indirect taxes and transfers and thus is smaller than GDP. Assuming an error of plus or minus 20%, Clark's optimal range for the tax/GDP ratio for stabilising exchange rates and inflation would be between 17% and 25% of GDP. This provides further support that the optimal tax rate range, from an efficiency perspective, is between 15% and 25%, with a mid-point at 20% of GDP.

[133] Keynes, J.M., 1926, *The Nation and Athenaeum*, January 9: "The level of the franc is going to be settled in the long run, not by speculation of the balance of trade, or even the outcome of the Ruhr adventure, but by the proportion of his earned income which the French taxpayer will permit to be taken from him to pay the claims of the French rentier" .

An Efficient Level for the Expenditure to GDP Ratio

In a survey of the spending patterns for 17 OECD countries from 1913 to 1990, Tanzi & Schuknecht (1997) found that there is an upper limit to the efficient provision of services and benefits by government and that relatively smaller government is more effective at achieving standards for less cost than larger governments. They note that "...by the time countries reach the level of public spending shown by the small governments, namely between 30 and 40 percent of GDP [with an average of 34.6% of GDP], much of the potential social gain from public spending has been obtained. Spending beyond that level does not contribute that much" (Tanzi & Schuknecht, 1997:168). In their longer background paper on the subject, the same authors concluded that

> "over the long run, total public expenditure could be reduced to, perhaps, under 30 percent of GDP without sacrificing much in terms of social or economic objectives" (Tanzi & Schuknecht, 1995:25).

Their analysis compared the economic performance (growth rates, gross fixed capital formation, inflation, unemployment, debt) and social performance (life expectancy, infant mortality, education and income distribution) for 17 small, medium and large OECD countries. They observe that "there is no evidence" that countries with big governments have out-performed the countries with medium and small sized governments (Tanzi & Schuknecht, 1997:167). More particularly they concluded that:

> "...the social indicators improved the most between 1870 and 1960 when the welfare state was still in its infancy. The expansion of public expenditure and of the welfare state during the last three decades has yielded limited gains in terms of social objectives while possibly damaging the countries' economic performance". (Tanzi & Schuknecht, 1995:25)

6.2 Taxation, Economic Growth and Deadweight Loss

a. *Introduction*

As was established earlier, there is a wedge between pre-tax and post-tax prices created by taxes. This price difference distorts the choice of the mix of inputs for producers and the mix of items in the consumer's basket. Second, there is also a direct production loss that is perhaps just as, if not more, important. This is an empirical matter. There is a long-standing tradition in welfare economics that the maximisation of output is one measure of welfare:

> "...the maximisation of total physical output may be considered as the most narrow type of a concept of maximum total welfare. It is concerned only with the possibility of increasing the output of some commodities without diminishing the output of any other commodity, regardless of who is to get the commodities" (Lange, 1942:225).

One should be cautious of interpreting Lange's comments as meaning that *technical* efficiency is less important than allocative efficiency. Results presented in this section suggest that the *technical* efficiency losses arising from taxation are very large. While this section of the Report examines the efficiency (rather than the equity) effects of taxation, it should be apparent that a rapidly expanding economy provides more jobs, a faster introduction of high technology employment opportunities, and a broader range of employment choices as incomes rise and investment and consumption patterns become more sophisticated.

Economic growth and improved productivity contribute to enhanced resource allocation and equity by generating new employment. But, obviously, other important factors, such as taxes, affect equity outcomes, and there are other important considerations involving equity besides employment (e.g. educational opportunity funded by taxes, especially for those caught in *generations of poverty)*. The equity consequences of taxation will be reviewed at a later stage when resources are available.

In the case of NZ, one might hypothesise that, because NZ has one of the most neutral tax systems in the developed world[134] allocative inefficiency from taxation is currently likely to be less than in those other countries, and in all probability less than the output loss caused by taxes. This suggests, but does not prove that, with respect to the deadweight loss of taxation in NZ, more attention should be focused on the dynamic efficiency losses rather than the static allocative efficiency losses.

Diewert & Lawrence (1994) investigated the *static* allocative inefficiency arising from the deadweight loss of the taxation of consumption and labour income in NZ over the period 1972-1991. Their analysis was a pioneering contribution to assess the distortions created by taxation in NZ. Their key findings were that:

"...the marginal excess burdens associated with labour and consumption taxation have increased from 5 per cent to over 18 per cent and from 5 percent to 14 per cent, respectively, over the last 20 years...(T)he costs of allowing average [effective] tax rates to continue to increase are becoming increasingly high. Conversely, the New Zealand economy would reap large benefits from reduced government spending and taxation" (Diewert & Lawrence, 1994:78).

This analysis was subjected to a thorough econometric review by Small (1995) who estimated confidence intervals for each of the annual *static* deadweight loss estimates for labour and consumption by Diewert & Lawrence over the period 1972-1991. Small's confidence interval estimates are presented in **Table 6.1**.

A comparison of the confidence intervals for consumption and labour *static* deadweight losses does not support any conclusion about the relative size of these effects, but it is clear that the estimates by Diewert & Lawrence for labour taxation are measured less precisely than those for consumption taxation (for all time periods, the confidence intervals of the former span those of the latter) and their relative magnitude cannot be unambiguously determined. It is suggested that consumption taxes and production subsidies have broadly similar deadweight losses. The conclusion by Diewert & Lawrence that deadweight

[134] "These reforms created one of the least distorting tax systems in the OECD area, the lowest OECD producer subsidy equivalent in agriculture, substantial trade liberalisation, and a more efficient public sector" (OECD, 1993:13).

Table 6.1
Estimates of Deadweight Loss from the Taxation of Consumption and Labour: 1972-1991

Year	Deadweight Loss		80% Confidence Intervals			
	Consumption	Labour	Consumption		Labour	
			Lower Bound	Upper Bound	Lower Bound	Upper Bound
1972	0.049	0.053	0.0008	0.1106	0.0005	0.1162
1973	0.049	0.053	0.0007	0.1395	0.0005	0.1497
1974	0.053	0.057	0.0004	0.1540	0.0003	0.1630
1975	0.071	0.075	0.0005	0.1641	0.0004	0.1818
1976	0.063	0.063	0.0006	0.1728	0.0004	0.1807
1977	0.070	0.073	0.0005	0.1667	0.0003	0.1695
1978	0.075	0.081	0.0008	0.1673	0.0006	0.1684
1979	0.065	0.067	0.0011	0.1721	0.0008	0.1725
1980	0.077	0.080	0.0010	0.1688	0.0007	0.1716
1981	0.075	0.079	0.0009	0.1725	0.0008	0.1732
1982	0.081	0.083	0.0011	0.1840	0.0008	0.1890
1983	0.077	0.083	0.0011	0.1949	0.0007	0.2135
1984	0.071	0.080	0.0011	0.2220	0.0007	0.2495
1985	0.076	0.088	0.0011	0.2562	0.0005	0.2981
1986	0.084	0.100	0.0013	0.3047	0.0006	0.3671
1987	0.099	0.121	0.0010	0.3368	0.0002	0.4067
1988	0.116	0.139	0.0009	0.3728	0.0001	0.4743
1989	0.126	0.157	0.0007	0.3906	0.0001	0.4836
1990	0.137	0.183	0.0002	0.3435	0.0000	0.4349
1991	0.137	0.183	0.0004	0.2382	0.0001	0.2756

Source: deadweight loss (marginal excess burden) - Diewert and Lawrence (1994); confidence intervals - Small (1995).

Figure 6.1
Direct and Indirect Components of Total Tax Revenue as a Percentage of GDP and the Real GDP Growth Rate (9-year moving average) in New Zealand: 1918-1995

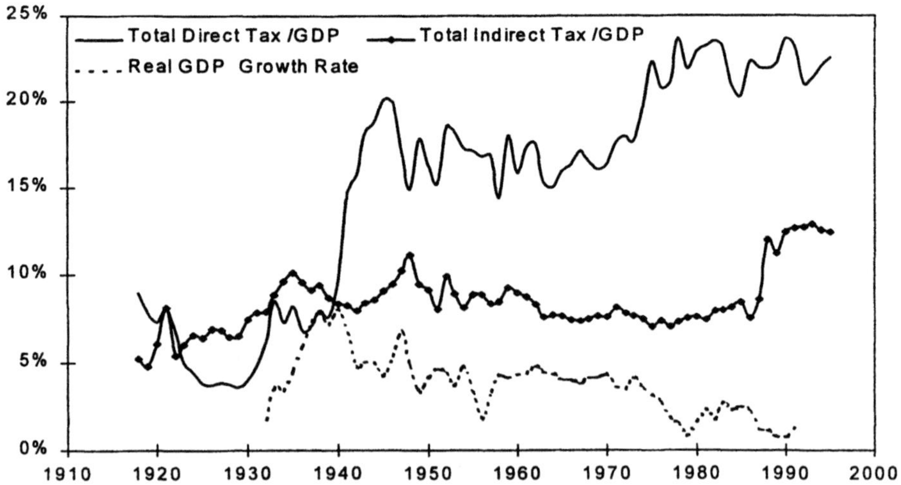

Source: NZ Institute of Economic Research, Inland Revenue, Treasury

losses from labour taxation (at an original point estimate of 18%) exceed those from taxation of general consumption is sensitive to the inclusion of a linear spline in the consumption sector model. Removal of this spline reduces the estimated deadweight loss from labour taxation to below 10% (Small, 1995:27-28).

In summary, a careful review suggests that Diewert & Lawrence probably over-estimated somewhat the *static* deadweight loss arising from the taxation of labour income, while they may have under-estimated the *static* deadweight loss arising from the taxation of consumption. This view would be consistent with the decrease in the statutory tax rate for personal income in the mid-1980s, and the introduction and then increase of GST in 1987 and 1989, recognising that a change in the statutory rate has some effect on the effective tax rate basis for calculating deadweight loss.

b. The Tax/GDP Ratio and Economic Growth

(i) Literature Review

At the outset, it needs to be pointed out that the Report's analysis of the relationship between taxes and growth is not designed to explain historical rates of growth in NZ[135], which of course can be due to many causes. Rather the purpose of this analysis is to assess the role of the tax level and tax mix in explaining why economic output and economic growth have under-performed their potential.

There is increasing interest by policy makers in the determination of the actual (as opposed to theoretical) relationships between the overall tax burden and economic growth. An original assessment[136] of this issue comes from Scully (1991) who estimated an econometric relationship between total taxes (as well as the tax mix) relative to GDP and economic growth for 103 countries for the period 1960-80. He concluded that:

> "on average, countries reach their maximum economic growth rates when they take no more than 19.3 percent of GDP in taxes; (as well) the economic growth rate tends to zero and then becomes negative once taxes consume more than 45 percent of GDP; (finally) the specific rates that maximise economic growth are an income tax rate of 11.9 percent, a sales tax rate of 4.6 percent and trade taxes equal to 9.4 percent" (Scully, 1991).

Previously, Manas-Anton (1987:218), in a study of 39 developing countries, examined the link between personal and corporate income and economic growth and reached the tentative conclusion that

---

[135] Factors and opportunities that helped to promote economic growth in the post-war period included New Zealand's competitive advantage in producing food after the War, the contributions of growing physical capital and human capital development, the spillover effect of importing new technology, and the initial boost from various government new spending programs etc. Constraints which have impeded past economic growth in New Zealand include labour market rigidities, high tariff and non-tariff barriers, barriers to foreign capital inflows, rising inflation, disincentives to work generated by government transfers, poor quality of government investment etc (e.g. Think Big projects).

[136] Manas-Anton (1987) had earlier presented work on the link between the level of personal income tax and corporate income tax and economic growth in developing countries.

"...while there is some evidence supporting a negative relationship between output growth rates and the reliance of a country on income taxes, this relationship can not be asserted with much confidence".

An alternative view was presented by Ferleger & Mandle (1993) who make the very legitimate case that government spending on social and economic infrastructure (roads, bridges, airports, education etc) promote economic growth. But they rely on statistical comparisons of *changes* in the tax to GDP ratio and productivity growth in the US, Japan and the OECD without using significance tests. As a result, for example, they reached the conclusion that Japan's impressive productivity growth rate was assisted by its rising tax burden (20% of GDP in 1970 versus 30.6% in 1989):

"These data suggest, contrary to commonly held expectations, that productivity growth may be positively, not negatively correlated with increasing tax burdens" (Ferleger and Mandle, 1993:14).

This conclusion misses the point that there are differences in quality across government spending categories and that taxes generate deadweight losses[137] Further, there is a debate in the economic literature about the importance of the impact of government spending on infrastructure on economic growth and productivity performance, with some studies suggesting a very important positive effects, and others a negligible, positive effect. Morrison & Schwartz (1996) critiqued the methodology of these earlier studies and analysed the impact of public infrastructure investment on manufacturing firms in the US. They concluded that "infrastructure investment provides a significant return to manufacturing firms and augments productivity growth".

It is obvious that government expenditures on key aspects of social and economic infrastructure can contribute to an improvement in economic performance, but there are counteracting forces at work as government intervenes in the economy through rising taxes, regulations and expenditure. At some point, diminishing returns from government intervention expenditure set in. The literature on the efficiency of public infrastructure investment appears to miss this point:[138]

"Economic theory suggests that up to some level government expenditures increase the productivity of private economic resources. The provision of national defence and a judicial system protect private property and individual rights. Other publicly provided goods, such as infrastructure, also enhance private productivity. Thus, up to some point, government expenditure acts as a positive

---

[137] Other problems with their analysis, include the following: (1) they ignore the fact that Japan's tax/GDP ratio was consistently well below the U.S. until 1989, just prior to its asset price deflation; and (2) they do not undertake an analysis of the cumulative effect of dynamic and static deadweight loss of taxes for all countries. What the authors also could not know is that by 1996, the reduction of taxes had become a principal strategy of Japan's new government in promoting economic growth, and that a similar perspective has now been adopted by the governments of Britain, Germany and Ireland. *Financial Times of London*, "Japanese PM Says High Corporate Tax Hindering Recovery", 14 November 1996; *Financial Times of London*, "Kohl Seeks to Calm Tax Fears", 19 August 1996.

[138] Corsetti & Roubini (1996) correctly criticise the presupposition in some parts of the economic literature that assume or assert that "government spending [is] useless and [involves] unproductive consumption of economic resources". But, the quality and level of government spending are at issue, not government spending per se. What taxpayers want is value for money not excuses to keep raising taxes regardless of the consequences.

externality on private economic activity...Beyond some optimal size of government. increased taxation acts as a negative externality on the private sector" (Scully, 1996:4-5).[139]

The World Bank has also begun to grapple with this problem. Its 1997 World Development Report emphasises the value of having an "effective state" that facilitates rather than impedes higher levels of economic performance. The Report on "The State in a Changing World" (World Bank, 1997), concludes that a large part of the problem in economic development is that as the state grows in size it develops an internal co-ordination problem that impedes communication and prevents coherent, stable policy development. As well, this growth of the state creates an external deadweight loss because of various forms of government intervention, notably regulation. The result is poor credibility, less investment, notably foreign investment, less economic growth and employment and a lower standard of living.

In a cross-country study examining the impact of 14 independent variables on the growth in GDP per capita, the World Bank (1997:170) analysis concludes that the size of government (measured by government consumption divided by GDP) has an important and consistent negative relationship with the standard of living. But;

"when evaluating the consequences of government for growth, it is not simply size that is relevant. Bad policies, as represented by overvalued currencies and pervasive trade restrictions, hold down a country's growth, while the quality of government can exert a positive effect on performance". (World Bank, 1997:171)

The World Bank has identified five core functions[140] for successful, governments to undertake, rather than markets and private associations. Those functions are:

- establishment of the rule of law and the protection of property rights;
- the development of effective non-distortionary, macroeconomic policy;
- investment in basic economic and social infrastructure;
- the provision of a social safety net for those in need; and
- environmental protection.

Without the establishment of "an effective state", according to President of the World Bank, James Wolfensohn, "sustainable development, both economic and social, is impossible" (World Bank, 1997).

[139] In one of the first attempts to approach the question of the "optimum size of governments", Buchanan & Tullock (1971:113) theorised that "the answer is given by a comparison between the additional decision-making costs involved in moving from a lower to a higher level and the spillover costs that remain from retaining the activity at its lower level". While this is a useful beginning one needs to decompose the costs. First there are the opportunity costs (gains) of raising (lowering) taxes. Second, there are the transitional costs (gains) associated with higher (less) public debt and higher (lower) debt service payments. In addition, there are the (positive or negative) effects of the adjustment in the country's credit rating and the higher (lower) costs imposed on domestic borrowers in international markets. This chapter examines only the opportunity costs issue. Chapter 3, dealing with the history of government expenditures in New Zealand, sketched out some initial details with respect to the other factors. Clark (1945) is probably the first author who grappled with the issue of the optimal size of government.

[140] See also Stern, N, and Stiglitz, J., 1997, *A Framework for a Development Strategy in a Market Economy: Objectives, Scope, Institutions and Instruments*, No. 20 London: European Bank for Reconstruction and Development, EBRD Working Paper.

The work in the optimal tax theory literature linking taxes and growth has been summarised by Roubini & Milesi-Ferretti (1994).[141] They conclude that higher taxes on capital and labour (human capital) income will reduce the growth rate. But this concept of optimality is heavily constrained by various assumptions. Thus they are unable to identify specific optimal tax rates that maximise the growth rate in a practical way:

"Formally, in the absence of constraints on the ability of the government to borrow and lend, the optimal tax problem yields a solution that involves initially high taxes on both human and physical capital. This allows the government to accumulate a sufficient quantity of assets to finance government expenditure in the long run without any further recourse to taxation. In practice, this is not a realistic solution, for a number of reasons" (ibid: 26).

The practical problems with this theoretical approach include the fact that: (1) over the long term, governments cannot usually commit themselves to the same policy (time inconsistency), (2) in the short-term, governments may be spendthrifts and thus not consider inter-generational interests, and (3) there are usually restrictions on the ability of governments to borrow and lend. As a result, their second best alternative requires that "human and physical capital should be taxed similarly if they both contribute to accumulation and long-term growth" (Roubini & Milesi-Ferretti, 1994:27). While this is a helpful step forward, it is a long way from providing specific details about the best practice policy frontier, as compared to Scully's econometric analysis using long time series data. As Engen & Skinner (1996:10) conclude:

"ultimately one needs to consider the empirical record to make informed judgements about whether tax policy exerts a strong influence on economic growth".

The central problem is that these two strands of literature in economics have tended to ignore each other, even though many of the same authors (e.g. Hotelling, Stern, Stiglitz, Atkinson, Dixit, Diamond and Mirrlees) have worked in both areas. As Stern (1992:274;293) noted:

"the theory of optimal taxation has not had a great deal to say about dynamics and the theory of growth has been reticent on taxation. This has clearly not been because the developers of one have been ignorant of the other - the number of authors who have contributed to both is striking. Rather the reason include the following: dynamic optimising models are more difficult analytically than static ones; we know much less about the dynamic behaviour of individuals; and there are important logical and theoretical problems that arise for dynamic models that do not appear in the static".

In his recent empirical work, Scully (1995) focused on the relationship in the United States between growth and federal, state and local taxes as a percentage of GDP over the period 1929-1989. He concluded that real growth rates in the U.S. decline when the tax/GDP ratio rises beyond about 23%. This assessment places the opportunity cost of taxes at about 7 percentage points of GDP given the current tax/GDP ratio of 30% of GDP in the U.S. and suggests the need for a re-

[141] Diewert (1983:178) contributed an early insightful speculation: "Could the large unexplained portion of [1950s' and 1960s'] productivity decline [in the Western economies] be explained by the rapid growth in government programs, discriminating tax policies, hidden barriers to trade and regulatory activities that had the effect of increasing distortions within the world economy?"

examination of the optimal size of government in the United States as well as abroad. In a similar study for NZ, Scully (1996), to be examined below, focused on the nature of the relationship between the observed growth rate of economic output and the size of the overall tax burden as measured by the ratio of total taxes to measured GDP.

How do taxes act to engender lower economic growth? Engen & Skinner (1996:4-5) have sketched out a theoretical framework which helps to fill this gap:

"First, higher taxes can discourage the investment rate[142], or the net growth in capital stock,[143] through high statutory tax rates on corporate and individual income, high effective capital gains taxes, and low depreciation allowances. Second, taxes may attenuate labour supply growth, by discouraging labour force participation and hours of work, or by distorting occupational choice or the acquisition of education, skills, and training. Third, tax policy has the potential to discourage productivity growth by attenuating research and development and the development of venture capital for 'high tech' industries; activities whose spillover effects can potentially enhance the productivity of existing labour and capital. Fourth, tax policy can influence the marginal productivity of capital by distorting investment from heavily taxed sectors into more lightly-taxed sectors with lower overall productivity. And fifth, heavy taxation on labour supply can distort the efficient use of human capital by discouraging workers from employment in sectors with high social productivity but a heavy tax burden".

While this theoretical framework helps us to understand the way in which taxes affect economic growth, it is not designed to locate the frontier tax level and tax mix. That is an empirical question which papers by Scully (1996, 1996a, 1996b), Caragata & Small (1996, 1996a) and Branson & Lovell (1997) were developed to answer.

There is strong support, however, for the view that that high income tax rates lower the rate of economic growth (Becker, 1985; Feldstein, 1974; Judd, 1985; Sato, 1967; and Stiglitz, 1978). In addition, empirical work by a number of authors has demonstrated that in the United States there is an inverse relationship between the level of taxation and the rate of economic growth as suggested in **Figure 6.1** (Grossman, 1987; Peden & Bradley, 1989; Peden, 1991, and Scully, 1995).

---

[142] "...consensus estimates of the impact of the user cost of capital on investment indicate that...pursuing a monetary policy that would reduce expected inflation and switching from an income tax to a consumption tax ...would significantly stimulate investment...(M)ost recent studies imply a high long-run elasticity of the capital stock to the user cost of capital, so that tax policy clearly has the potential to have a powerful effect on equipment investment and the capital stock in the long run" (Hassett & Hubbard, 1996:46).

[143] In the short run, a change in tax which lowers the cost of capital, other things being equal, would tend to raise the price of labour and the capital - labour ratio for a fixed level of output. This would tend to have a negative effect on demand for labour, depending on the elasticity of substitution between the two factors. Over the long run, however, a tax cut, which induced a decrease in the cost of capital, would promote investment, employment and growth. Thus, the long run consequences of a tax change affecting the cost of capital may be quite different than the short run effects, and much more important. Vickrey (1993:3-4) called the corporate income tax "the most serious hurdle in the way of private capital formation". He observed that "unlike most other, the corporation tax inflicts a double whammy on the economy in that it both extracts income from the stream of purchasing power and reduces the recycling of savings through investment. If imposed on a revenue-neutral basis it causes unemployment, while if the budgetary adjustment is made to maintain employment constant, its burden can be thought of as falling on future wage earners, who will have less capital with which to work".

In a study of 3000 firms' investment decisions across 14 countries, Cummins, Hassett & Hubbard (1995) concluded that in all but two countries (Spain and the Netherlands) changes in corporate tax policy have a statistically significant inverse correlation with the investment behaviour of firms. Thus, as taxes increase, investment tends to fall and adjustment costs are small (about 5-10 cents per investment dollar). Moreover, in some countries, notably Canada, Japan, the UK and the US, investment behaviour is very sensitive to changes in cash flow (see also Kaplan & Zingales, 1995). Finally, in their review the tax-growth literature, Engen & Skinner (1996:33-34) conclude that

"...tax policy does affect economic growth. There is enough evidence linking taxation and output growth to make reasonable inference that beneficial changes in tax policy can have modest effects on output growth. The implied effects from the 'bottom-up" micro-level studies, and the "top-down" cross-country regressions, are quite close in magnitude: a major tax reform reducing all marginal rates by 5 percentage points, and average tax rates by 2.5 percentage points, is predicted to increase long term growth rates by between 0.2 and 0.3 percentage points. Whether these effects on output growth are permanent (lasting forever) or transitory (lasting perhaps 10-15 years) is difficult to determine, both because our data sources do not extend for a lengthy period, but also because tax regimes themselves generally have such short half-lives".

The issue of the longevity of the impact of tax cuts is an important one. Scully (1996) argues that the effects are cumulative across time, and have important consequences for estimating the magnitude of the deadweight loss of tax. This point has been recognised in a recent OECD study:

"In the two endogenous growth models the tax effects on economic growth are generally small, but not negligible. In one of the models, a tax reduction by 1 per cent of GDP accompanied by a similar cut in transfers to guarantee deficit-neutrality increases annual growth of GDP by between roughly one-half and one decimal point. But permanent growth effects of this size are nevertheless significant given that they imply ever-compounding effects on the level of output. Also applying these findings to the increase of about 10 percentage points in the OECD tax-to-GDP ratio (weighted average) that has occurred since 1960 would imply a reduction in growth in the OECD area by around ½ to 1 percentage point. Thus, up to one-third of the growth deceleration in the OECD (from around 5 percent in 1965-73 to around 2 percent in 1989-95) would be explained by higher taxes. In some European countries, tax burdens increased much more dramatically than the OECD average, which would imply correspondingly larger effects on their growth rates" (Leibfritz, Thornton & Bibbee, 1997:49).

Scully's model reports that the long run average tax/GDP ratio for New Zealand in the post war period of 28% is 8 percentage points above the optimal tax rate of 20%. This implies a 2 percentage point reduction in growth from 5% to 3%. Thus, for each percentage point reduction in the average tax/GDP ratio, the average growth rate would likely rise by 0.25 percentage points.

A parallel approach has been taken by Barro (1995). Inflation is commonly treated in economics like a tax[144] on production and income. Barro's study of 100 countries over the period 1960-1990 concludes that there is an inverse relationship between inflation and growth and investment, and this negative response deepens as

[144] Keynes in chapter 2 of his 1923 *A Tract on Monetary Reform* appears to have been the first modern economist to have viewed "inflation as a method of taxation".

inflation rises above 10-20%. Thus, deviations from optimal monetary policies generate deadweight losses. Feldstein (1996) reached a similar conclusion.

Scully's (1995) research suggests that in the United States, at times when the tax/GDP ratio has been less than about 22%, the effect of an increase in taxation on the real growth rate of GDP is positive, whereas when the tax/GDP ratio rose above, approximately, 22%, the effect on growth is negative. The rationale is as follows:

"By providing public goods, including law and order, national defence, and income distribution that expands the gains from exchange (the scope and membership of the constitutional agreement) government expenditures act as a positive externality on the growth rate. Beyond that level, taxes act as a negative externality" (Scully, 1995:71).

Peden (1991:168-69) examined the link between the evolution of macro productivity performance in the US economy over the period 1929-1986. He found that government expenditure up to 17% of GNP improves the productivity performance of the American economy, but expenditures above that level reduced "the growth of productivity". Thus, government expenditures on social and economic infrastructure can add considerably to the productivity and productive efficiency of an economy, but beyond a certain point there are diminishing returns. Thus, beyond a frontier point, the government's contributions to growth are still positive, but progressively less. Finding that point is important in terms of establishing an equilibrium or balance in the relations between government and the market.

Even if that point is recognised by governments, this does not mean that they would be unwilling to trade-off some economic growth for other objectives. But there are always limits and constraints that need to be identified. In particular, it is important to identify the marginal trade-offs between revenue, equity and efficiency[145]. For each one percentage point change in efficiency, what is the impact on revenue and equity? For each one percentage point adjustment in equity, what is the impact on revenue and efficiency? As Feldstein (1996a:26) has argued, "the central public finance question facing any country is the appropriate level of spending and therefore of taxes".[146] Our exploration of optimal tax rates relative to optimal expenditure levels is designed to provide preliminary answers to that question.

What is of greater long-term benefit to an economy: an increase in government expenditures, or a tax cut? Recent work in New Zealand by Hall and Rae (1996)

---

[145] A utilitarian approach (Kaplow, 1994) would advocate maximising total utility subject to an equity constraint, but not a constraint requiring income distribution equality across all taxpayers because of the negative effect such a constraint would have on the incentive to work, and thus on investment and productivity. Brown & Heal (1979:573) point out that, under conditions of increasing returns, which are prevalent in reality, equity and efficiency cannot be treated as independent dimensions. Instead, their inter-dependence needs to be studied because of their relative effects on each other: "...once one admits increasing returns... one can no longer judge between alternative distributions purely in terms of equity".

[146] In New Zealand, the development of a majority consensus in 1984 that the government needed to reduce its scale and scope was crucial in determining the scale and scope of the subsequent economic reforms (Cangiano, 1996).

compared the long run growth implications of choosing between a 3 percent increase in the public debt to GDP ratio based on either an increase in government spending or a tax cut of the equivalent amount. The preferred policy is the tax cut (especially one which is distributed between employers as well as employees), rather than the increase in government spending largely because:

"The major reason for the different dynamic responses of the two policy rules is that a tax shock does not have such as direct impact on output, compared with the spending shock. Instead, the shock works primarily through the consumption function and consumption smoothing ensure that spending does not rise by the full amount of the shock. This is partly because the short run marginal propensity to consume is less than unity, and partly because households respond to expected future income and thus take the future path of the economy into account when making spending decisions. Consumption smoothing implies that the tax cut will lead to some increase in household savings. At least initially, and this can be seen in the private debt figures and the current account balance.." (Hall and Rae, 1996:12-13).

In general, a tax cut will therefore have less of an upward effect on the exchange rate and interest rates and thus lead to less crowding out than will an increase in government expenditure of a similar amount. This boosts investor confidence and subjects the economy less to a boom and bust cycle. Moreover, the redistribution of income has important opportunity costs:

"government spending is more about redistributing, rather than creating, wealth. The redistribution tends to flow from the business and export sectors to those using government services" (Rae, 1996:5).

Or, one might add, beneficiaries. There appears to be a growing consensus that even short-term government spending in the context of a *budget deficit* (not necessarily a budget surplus) may not be so advantageous (e.g. because of consequential higher interest rates and a higher exchange rate). Alan Blinder of Princeton University who has recently stepped down as Vice-Chairman of the Board of Governors of the Federal Reserve System has noted that this idea has "taken hold in policy circles from Washington to Brussels". He went on to say that:

"deficit reduction, we are told, promotes economic growth in the short-run. How can that be? I can think of two coherent lines of reasoning that lead to the unconventional conclusion that a *credible* change in fiscal policy that promises lower *future* budget deficits can stimulate the economy by producing lower long term real interest rates today. The first is a (Keynesian) flow-equilibrium argument: promises of future fiscal contraction create rational *expectations* of lower real short rates in the future which, via term structure, lead to lower long-term interest rates today. The second is an argument involving long-run stock equilibrium: expectations of lower future public government debt lead to lower long term rates today", (Blinder, 1997:242).

Yet only one empirical example of this wisdom (Clinton's 1993 budget) has been substantiated. Thus, while the idea may have merit the jury is still out and more research is awaited.

This analysis of the link between taxes and growth suggests that cutting expenditures rather than raising taxes is probably the preferred strategy for deficit reduction. It also suggests strongly that a 'first best' economy is not an economy without taxes, as theory would have it. Government expenditures on law and order, defence, and economic and social infrastructure do make important contributions to productivity that are necessitated by the fact that there are economies of scale and general savings to be found in pooling funding to provide many key services. Government acts as an appropriate channel for pooling this funding, and offers economies of scale that are unavailable in the private sector to undertake more efficiently certain activities. But diminishing returns inevitably set in. Identifying that point is the focus of this section of the Report on the Health of the Tax System.

(ii) A Review of Empirical Trends

Earlier in the Health Report it was noted that World War II marked the arrival of a new era in taxation in NZ. The tax/GDP ratio vaulted almost 10 percentage points from about 16% in the 1930s to about 26% in the 1940s. This represented the most important systemic tax shock to the NZ economy in the Twentieth Century. As indicated in **Figure 3.1**, a new plateau for the tax/GDP ratio was established during World War II, and this was largely due to the significant jump in the direct tax to GDP ratio (**Figure 3.3**), in general and also to the jump in the ratio of direct to indirect taxes (**Figure 3.4**) and thus the rise in the personal tax/GDP ratio (**Figure 3.5**).

It is clear from the graphs that this shift in the tax burden and tax mix created strong path dependence for the tax system itself that has persisted through to 1996. The key question is, what was the long-term impact of this shift on the incentive structure and behaviour of individuals and firms and the output path of the economy? Economic theory and empirical evidence suggest that there were also production losses and distortions in consumers' choices and the pattern of investment as a result of these large jumps in the tax burden and changes in the tax mix.

But how large were the losses? One insight is that NZ's per capita real gross domestic product fell from a rank of 4 in 1950 to a rank of 19 in 1992 among the OECD nations (Summers & Heston, 1991). But, of course, the tax burden could not have been the only source of the decline. Other important factors included the decline in the terms of trade, Britain's entry into the European Community and the excessive regulation of the NZ economy.

Figure 6.1 combines an illustration of the long-term trend for the real growth rate with the changes in the tax/GDP ratio and the indirect tax/GDP ratio. It is clear that, in the post-war period and until recently, the rate of economic growth[147] has been in secular decline while the level of taxation has been secularly rising. This graphic illustration suggests, but does not prove, that there is a link between the increase in the tax burden and the long-term decline in the real growth rate.

(iii) Aggregate Deadweight Loss of Taxation in New Zealand

---

[147] The growth rate series has been smoothed by a nine-year moving average to eliminate the usual noise in growth rates. Results in this section are based on the use of the CPI deflator. Despite its disadvantages (it excludes investment goods and government services and overweights goods that are also exported), the results are similar to those derived from the use of the GDP deflator.

A parsimonious model[148] of the growth-maximising tax-rate was developed by Scully (1996)[149] for NZ covering the period 1927-94. Increases in the tax/GDP ratio up to t^* advance the growth rate at a decreasing rate, while increases in the tax/GDP ratio beyond t^* reduce the growth rate at an increasing rate. Assumptions in the model included: (1) only two sectors in the economy, government and the private sector, each of which produces goods; (2) government spending is financed exclusively by taxes; (3) not all government services are public goods; and (4) some of the previous period's output is consumed.

Estimation and tests yielded the following. Tests for unit roots indicate that the data are stationary. Minor problems with heteroskedasticity and autocorrelation were found. Corrections for both did not lead to important changes in the coefficients. The coefficients are of the right sign and are statistically significant in a one-tail test above the 99% level. The growth-maximising tax rate for NZ (over the period 1927-1994) was found to be 19.7% of GDP (for more technical details see Scully, 1996). Assuming an error of plus or minus 20%, the range around the 19.7% estimate would be 15.8%-23.6% of GDP.

The actual tax/GDP ratio in 1995 was about 34-35%, hence the growth maximising rate is 14% points, or roughly 42%, lower. If maximisation of the growth rate is the only objective, then reducing the tax/GDP rate to this level would be a policy objective. This may not be the case, for a variety of different reasons. There will be several different objectives that governments take into consideration, aside from the maximisation of economic growth, such as increasing spending on health, education or various social benefits in order to correct perceived existing deficiencies. Thus, there are diminishing returns and increasing costs to government expenditure. But there are also long term benefits arising from a good part of government spending on health, education and economic infrastructure. The care with which that spending is chosen is of national importance.

---

[148] This model has achieved some recognition in North America. A study linking rising taxes with higher unemployment by a tax official in the Ontario government in Canada concluded: "The goal of tax policy is not to maximize government revenue, but to maximize economic well-being. The results here have a bearing on the marginal cost of public funds raised through taxation. The estimates on the responsiveness of the labour force participation rate...provides supporting evidence for those studies that claim that the marginal cost of collecting a dollar of tax revenue is considerably greater than one dollar. The other side of the benefit cost calculation is the benefits that accrue from government spending on vital services such as infrastructure, health care, and education. There is considerable evidence that these government services also contribute to economic growth. The challenge for public policy is to find the optimal point where the marginal cost of a dollar of government revenue matches the marginal cost of a dollar of government spending. An ingeniously simple framework for measuring this point has been devised by Gerald Scully of the University of Texas [Scully, 1995]. Scully recognizes that, up to a certain point, higher taxes can have a positive impact on real GDP growth because of the useful government services they purchase. However, like most good things, these services are subject to the law of diminishing returns" (Spiro, 1996:15).

[149] Scully's analysis involves an economy with a public sector and a private sector, exhibiting constant returns. The latter feature of the model is supported statistically by the data. With this constraint, and using the empirical estimates for the models' parameters, positive growth paths emerge. The empirical basis of the model is crucial, misleading results could be obtained if arbitrary values were assigned to the parameters. The rate of growth is a function of the tax rate, and Scully's model facilitates a calculation of the value of the latter rate which maximises output growth.

With such multiple objectives, rather than just growth maximisation, the political process may well prefer a tax rate above 20% or 25% of GDP. The intent here is not to advise on policy. Rather it is to use performance benchmarks for measuring the current consequences of taxation. The optimal range for the tax/GDP ratio in a multi-objective policy framework cannot be identified until all the research on equity and efficiency has been completed.

Scully's range of 16%-23% for the optimal tax rate for New Zealand is very similar to the two other ranges estimated in the *Working Papers on Monitoring the Health of the Tax System*. The range estimated by Branson & Lovell (1997) was 18%-27%. The range estimated by Caragata & Small range was 13.4%-15.5%. All three results are statistically similar and suggest that an optimal tax/GDP ratio for New Zealand is in the range of 15%-25% of GDP.

(iv) International Comparisons and Corroboration

Growth Maximising Tax Rate

The growth-maximising tax rate for NZ does not differ much from the growth-maximising tax rates in some other nations for which long-term data were available (Scully, 1996). For the same model as is estimated for NZ, the growth-maximising tax rate for the United States (1929-89) was 21.5% of GNP. Growth-maximising tax rates for Denmark (18.5%), Finland (18.9%), Italy (20.1%), Sweden (16.6%), and the United Kingdom (25.2%) were estimated over the period 1927-88, yielding an average of 20.1%. All of the t-tests were highly significant.

The deadweight losses for NZ were found to be \$2.69 in 1994 (**Table 6.2**) and \$2.51 on average for the period 1990-94 (**Table 6.2**) for each real dollar of tax revenue. Scully (1995) found a \$2.17 average deadweight loss for the United States over the period 1949-89 for each dollar of real tax revenue (Scully, 1995).

The results for NZ were compared with the United States (Scully, 1996). On an annualised, per capita basis, the losses were estimated to be roughly similar: US\$9,985 for Americans and NZ\$6,675 for New Zealanders. With a purchasing power adjustment, per capita real GDP is about 63% of that in the U.S. Thus, taking the per capita income differential into account, the wealth losses are similar.

Additional research was undertaken to cross-check Scully's results. Caragata & Small (1996) have studied the relationship between the aggregate tax rate and growth in the measured and hidden economies. Although their time series analysis does not support the existence of a long run linear relationship between all three of these variables, they do find evidence of a dynamic non-linear relationship. Their estimates suggest that at current levels of taxation, a reduction in taxes of 3% (that is reducing the tax to GDP ratio from 30% to 29% (i.e. one percentage point)) would lead to an increase in the growth rate of real GDP of 0.3% and a reduction of 0.1% in the growth rate of the hidden economy.

The findings corroborate Scully's (1996) contention of the size of the output lost over the last 50 years as a result of the tax to GDP ratio being above 20%. Caragata & Small (1996) estimate that the output loss in 1994 from this policy to be $64 billion real 1992 dollars, so that GDP would have been 80% higher than it was if the tax burden on the economy had been around 20% of GDP, about a third less than at present, roughly over the last 30 years.

(v) Issues in the Models

The tax-growth model picks up the average relationship between the tax rate and the growth rate. The explanatory power of the model, which is highly aggregate and very simple, explains no more than about 15% of the variation in one plus the growth rate divided by one minus the tax/GDP ratio (i.e. RGDP/(1-(tax/GDP))). Thus, the business cycle can create asymmetries where the change in the tax to GDP ratio does not seem to be related to the change in the growth rate; the weakness is in short term variations. Thus, the current growth in the NZ economy up to end of 1995 has come from a combination of the consequences of structural adjustment, including improved competitiveness, and overseas demand, and not from an earlier tax cut. It remains to be seen what effect the current tax cut has on economic growth and tax revenue.

Since much less than half of the variation in RGDP/(1-(tax/GDP)) ratio is explained it means that other things are going on, including changes in the terms of trade, changes in regulatory environment, inflation and a variety of other macro variables. To control for those other factors would require a sophisticated structural model that is not possible given the state of macro economic theory. As a result, we commissioned Branson and Lovell (1997) to address this problem. Their model, which is very different to Scully's, yields a growth-maximising tax rate that, at 22.5% of GDP, is very similar to Scully's (1996) 20% of GDP estimate.

It is possible that Scully's model overstates the effect of taxes on growth, but we doubt it. In the case of the NZ economy, growth has been declining, tax/GDP has been rising and there are no other obvious trends that could destroy this correlation. For example, the deterioration in the terms of trade is not secular over the entire period 1927-1994, whereas the tax/GDP ratio has risen progressively.

Branson & Lovell (1997) have contributed a number of valuable findings that help to substantiate the negative effects of tax on economic performance:

- The optimal tax rate for New Zealand over the period 1946-1995 is 22.5%, and 20% over the period 1928-1995. Direct taxes are between 15 and 22 times "more damaging to economic growth than indirect taxes are" (Branson & Lovell, 1997:11), and "while adjustments to the tax mix can be expected to have marginal impacts on the rate of economic growth, reductions in the tax burden can be expected to have major impacts on the rate of economic growth" (Branson & Lovell, 1997:13); "on average over the period [1946-1995], a one percent reduction in the tax burden has 6.3 times as large a favourable impact on economic growth as does a one percent reduction in the ratio of direct to indirect taxes"(Branson & Lovell, 1997:13).

- "A one percent reduction in the tax burden can be expected to generate a greater than one percent increase in the rate of economic growth. The implication is that the tax burden is a high powered variable" (Branson & Lovell, 1997:12)... "It is interesting to note that Caragata (1995) reached a similar conclusion that tax savings are 'high-powered money' which have a dramatic effect on incentive structures" (Branson & Lovell, 1997:23).

- "in 1995 the output gap constituted 16% of real GDP and 47% of real tax revenue. These figures provide perhaps the clearest indication of the cost of maintaining a sub-optimal tax structure, or the potential benefits of adopting an optimal tax structure – one sixth of real GDP or 60% of real tax revenue"(Branson & Lovell, 1997:14).

- "the Treasury's tax receipts would decline by 5.9% per annum, on average during the period [1946-1995]. However, since real GDP would rise by 16% on average, the remainder of the economy would enjoy a 27% increase in purchasing power. The impact of moving to an optimal tax structure would have been even greater in 1995; real GDP would have increased by 16.4%, tax revenue would have declined by 10.8%, and the remainder of the economy would have reached a 31% increase in purchasing power. Thus the second consequence of adopting an optimal tax structure is that government would account for a smaller share of a larger economy" (Branson & Lovell, 1997:15).

- Branson & Lovell (1997:15) have developed a modified effective tax rate that incorporates both the actual amount paid relative to GDP and the opportunity cost that arises because economic growth is less when the actual effective tax rate is above the optimal effective tax rate: "in 1995 the modified effective tax rate was 51.4%, whereas the actual effective tax rate was 35%. By adding the opportunity cost of foregone output to the actual cost of taxes the modified effective tax rate provides an alternative view of the burden of taxation in New Zealand."

An issue arising from this analysis is whether or not high tax economies are doomed to low growth or growth slowdown owing to high taxes or to a maturation process which apparently is typical of the advanced economies. Those are experimental questions that require empirical estimation. We anticipate that mature economies can perform closer to their economic frontiers by improving productivity and efficiency through a reduction in the tax level. Caragata's and Small's (1996:26) results suggest that the impact of a tax reduction is smaller, the greater is the tax/GDP ratio.

"Tax cuts are less effective at higher levels of the tax/GDP ratio (e.g. over 35%) as compared to lower levels (e.g. 25%) in promoting economic growth (and possibly in generating tax revenue) and reducing the size of the hidden economy (and related tax evasion)."

This finding may reflect the fact that the cumulative effect of the deadweight loss of taxation makes the economy more sluggish and less responsive to remedial efforts. The deadweight loss grows with the rise in the effective tax rate (e.g. tax/GDP ratio) and declines as the effective tax rate declines. The Caragata & Small (1996) finding may help to explain why there appears to be a correlation between more "mature" economies and slower rates of economic growth. That is to say, there may be a spurious link between "maturity" and real growth because the real link between higher taxes and slower growth is ignored or obscured.

Finally, Caragata & Small (1996:26) have concluded that the timing of tax cuts during the course of a business cycle is very important. They note that "tax cuts enhance economic growth more when they are applied well before a recession begins." This makes sense because the closer to the business cycle trough, the weaker is investor and consumer confidence. The introduction of an appropriately sized tax cut perhaps mid-way between the peak and the expected trough could reshape the economic downturn.

Making the connection between growth performance and the level and mix of taxation has taken about a hundred years of analysis by economists because the tax burdens and government expenditures have grown slowly over long periods of time and many factors (e.g. war, energy shocks, exchange rate crises, economic restructuring and market liberalisation, and business cycle variations etc) have tended to make tax changes and the increase in tax burdens less noticeable.

Other factors which have helped progress in this area include the development of good quality long time series data bases and small powerful computers in the last 15 years, and some new contributions in econometrics and efficiency analysis beginning in the late 1970s and early 1980s (Granger causation, cointegration methodology, stochastic frontier estimations and Data Envelopment Analysis etc).

It now seems conceivable that so-called 'mature' economies can get a second wind involving a higher rate of economic growth by making judicious modifications to their total tax burden and tax mix. A significant reduction of the total level would promote savings, investment, R&D, growth and employment. It should be recalled that it took decades for the tax/GDP ratio to reach its high current level, and so we should expect that it may take decades for the ratio to drop back to optimal levels.

(vi) The Costs of Performing Below the Best Practice Frontier

The cost of deviating from the best-practice potential policy performance can be expressed either as a cumulative loss or current loss. Cumulative losses are like historic, or sunk, costs that can never be recovered. They provide information about the lessons to be learned concerning the magnitude of mistakes that were previously made in tax policy development. Hence, cumulative losses are important for reviewing past policy. Current losses may be annual aggregates or annual per capita estimates.

Because cumulative losses are sunk, for current policy making purposes and for assessing the current health of the tax system, it is preferable to think of the current rather than the cumulative losses arising from taxation because at the margin, the former are the costs that can be changed. Current losses hold the potential for applying the stop-loss rule. The stop-loss rule is irrelevant for cumulative losses because they are a sunk cost of previous policy choices embedded in the tax legislation. This does not mean that the potential gain is not large, it just means that the cumulative deadweight loss does not define the potential. The potential gain is defined by the gap in the current year between current and potential output.

On the other hand, because estimates of cumulative losses involve long-term estimates of the consequences of tax policy mistakes, they provide useful guidelines for the long-term risk assessment of tax policy. Current loss estimates provide the basis for short-term risk assessment of tax policy.

(vii) Cumulative Deadweight Losses

Over the period 1927-94, the growth-maximising tax rate is 19.7% of GDP. At that rate, economic growth would advance at 5% per annum and compound. This compares with an actual average real growth rate since WW II of 3.1%. The (real) output gap between the two growth rates, actual versus potential, describes the basis for calculating the cumulative deadweight loss of taxation in NZ over the period. The output gap divided by the amount of real tax revenue describes the deadweight loss per dollar of real revenue (**Table 6.2**).[150]

[150] Table 6.2 summarises the salient factors in one approach to the analysis of the deadweight loss of taxation in New Zealand. Very briefly, the stimulus or independent variable is the tax/GDP ratio (column A). The economy responds to the level and change in taxation, among other factors, and generates a real economic output path (Column B). Were taxes to be set at a growth maximising rate of about 20% of GDP the path of real growth would exhibit a better performance (potential output - Column C). The ratio of actual to potential output is the performance ratio (B/C) (Column D). The output or performance gap is the distance required to travel so that actual performance meets potential performance (C-B). The output gap is the gross deadweight loss of taxes (E). If E is divided by F (real tax revenue per annum), the result is a measure of the marginal deadweight loss per unit of tax revenue raised (E/F). This is one measure of the cost relative to the benefits of taxation. This assumes that each dollar of tax revenue contributes one dollar of benefit to the economy and that there is no waste in government.

Table 6.2
Annual Estimates of the Output-Based Deadweight Loss of Taxation in New Zealand: 1970-94

Year	A Tax/GDP Ratio	B Actual RGDP (NZ$ billion)	% Change	C Potential RGDP (NZ$ billion)	% Change	D Performance Ratio (B/C)	E Output Gap (C-B) (NZ$ billion)	% Change	F Real Tax Revenue (NZ$ billion)	G Deadweight Loss per $ of Tax Revenue (E/F) (NZ$)
1970	23%	43.6	6%	61.6	8%	71%	18.0	11%	10.1	1.78
1971	25%	46.3	6%	66.3	8%	70%	20.0	11%	11.4	1.76
1972	26%	47.7	3%	69.2	4%	69%	21.5	7%	12.3	1.75
1973	23%	55.4	16%	81.4	18%	68%	26.0	21%	13.0	1.99
1974	26%	56.1	1%	83.4	2%	67%	27.3	5%	14.8	1.85
1975	29%	54.6	-3%	82.3	-1%	66%	27.7	1%	15.8	1.75
1976	27%	56.8	4%	86.6	5%	66%	29.8	8%	15.2	1.96
1977	27%	58.7	3%	90.7	5%	65%	32.0	7%	15.8	2.02
1978	30%	54.6	-7%	85.5	-6%	64%	30.9	-4%	16.6	1.85
1979	28%	57.2	5%	90.6	6%	63%	33.4	8%	16.2	2.06
1980	29%	57.7	1%	92.7	2%	62%	34.9	4%	16.9	2.07
1981	29%	58.1	1%	94.5	2%	62%	36.4	4%	17.0	2.14
1982	30%	61.1	5%	100.6	6%	61%	39.5	9%	18.3	2.15
1983	31%	58.0	-5%	96.7	-4%	60%	38.7	-2%	18.3	2.12
1984	29%	61.8	7%	104.4	8%	59%	42.6	10%	17.9	2.38
1985	29%	65.7	6%	112.4	8%	58%	46.7	10%	18.9	2.48
1986	30%	65.5	0%	113.5	1%	58%	48.0	3%	19.6	2.46
1987	31%	68.3	4%	119.9	6%	57%	51.6	7%	20.9	2.47
1988	34%	67.2	-2%	119.4	0%	56%	52.2	1%	22.8	2.30
1989	33%	68.7	2%	123.8	4%	56%	55.0	5%	23.0	2.40
1990	36%	67.2	-2%	122.5	-1%	55%	55.4	1%	24.3	2.28
1991	36%	64.5	-4%	119.1	-3%	54%	54.6	-1%	23.1	2.36
1992	34%	64.7	0%	121.1	2%	53%	56.4	3%	21.8	2.58
1993	34%	66.7	3%	126.4	4%	53%	59.7	6%	22.6	2.65
1994	34%	70.6	6%	135.5	7%	52%	64.9	9%	24.2	2.69

Note that this analysis utilises an earlier data set, hence the slight discrepancy between the tax/GDP ratios of this table and those presented elsewhere in this report. It is anticipated that replication of this analysis with the revised data set will provide deadweight loss estimates of very similar magnitudes.

Source: Scully (1996), adapted by Inland Revenue

Actual real GDP (CPI deflator) in 1994 (in 1988 dollars) was $70.6 billion, while cumulative output over the period was $2.2 trillion over the past 48 years. Other things being equal, if the growth-maximising tax rate had been in effect throughout the period, real GDP in 1994 would have been $135.5 billion, and cumulative output would have been $3.3 trillion over the half century of time analysed.

The divergence in the paths of real GDP versus potential GDP under a growth-maximising tax regime and with the same business cycle is depicted in **Figure 6.2** (using Scully's (1996) model). The cumulative difference between actual and potential would be $1.16 trillion. Thus, the efficiency loss to the economy due to taxation above the optimal level, then, is about 33% or, using the current position as a base, the economy could have increased output by about 88% over the current level with the same resources had the level of taxation remained at 19.7% of GDP.

The accumulated real total taxes (1988 dollars) of New Zealanders over the period 1946-1994 was $618.6 billion. Thus, on average, over the entire period each dollar of tax was associated with an average $1.88 deadweight loss of private wealth ($1.16 trillion/$618.6 billion). This long term average estimate understates current annual estimates of deadweight loss per dollar of real tax revenue collected, as indicated in **Table 6.2**.

(viii) Average and Cumulative Data: 1946-1994

Table 6.2 examines the behaviour of aggregate annual deadweight loss over the last 25 years. Over the period, the performance ratio (actual output divided by potential output) has declined steadily from 0.71 in 1970 to 0.52 in 1994, while the output gap has risen from $18.0 billion to $64.9 billion. Dividing the output gap by real tax revenue, we obtain the deadweight loss per dollar of real tax revenue. In 1970 the deadweight loss was $1.78 per $1.00 of tax revenue. By 1994, the amount had risen to $2.69.

(ix) Yearly Marginal Changes (5-year averages) and Cumulative Data

Table 6.3 presents a summary of the average output loss arising from average tax/GDP ratios for given five-year periods. Over the period 1946-49, the tax/GDP ratio was 27.5%, the peak level until the late 1970s. Between the last half of the 1940s and the first half of the 1990s, the average tax/GDP ratio rose 29.6%. Over the same span, the average annual real deadweight loss (arising from tax-induced drops in output) rose from $1.1 billion to $58.2 billion. This dramatic shift, in relative terms, meant that the average annual deadweight loss per dollar of real tax revenue jumped from $0.22 to $2.51 over the period.

Thus, the output-related deadweight loss of taxation in NZ has been rising steadily over the period despite the 1980's reductions in the personal and corporate statutory tax rates. Such reductions would normally suggest that the deadweight loss might fall. But, the deadweight loss is not calculated using

Figure 6.2
Potential versus Actual Output and the Output Gap - consequences of tables: 1946-94

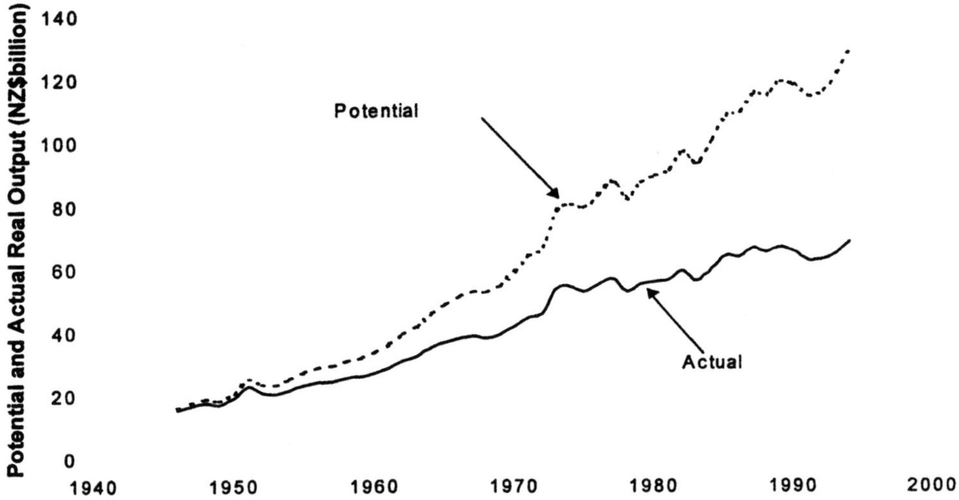

Source: Scully (1996)

Table 6.3
Average Output Consequences of Average Tax/GDP Ratios: 1946-94

Years	Average Tax/GDP Ratio	Deadweight Loss Average Annual Output Gap (NZ$ billion)	Average Deadweight Loss per $ of Tax Revenue (NZ$)
1946-49	27%	1.1	0.22
1950-54	26%	2.8	0.48
1955-59	25%	5.2	0.78
1960-64	24%	9.0	1.16
1965-69	24%	14.4	1.53
1970-74	25%	22.5	1.83
1975-79	28%	30.8	1.93
1980-84	30%	38.4	2.17
1985-89	31%	50.7	2.42
1990-94	35%	58.2	2.51

Source: Scully (1996), adapted by Inland Revenue

statutory tax rates. It is calculated using effective tax rates, including the tax/GDP ratio. That ratio has continued to rise in the 1990s largely because tax collection has become more efficient owing to tax reform and improved auditing, and because of the strong economic recovery.

The longer a country remains at a high level of tax, the greater is the loss because the negative effect of taxation is cumulative. Another way of looking at the same issue is that the benefit of a tax cut of 1 percentage point of GDP rises across time, even when the tax/GDP ratio is fixed, because of the cumulative gains.

(x) Current Deadweight Losses

Deadweight losses[151] are the efficiency costs to the economy of actual performance falling below best practice performance as a result of a sub-optimal tax regime. These costs include lost output and distortions in the patterns of consumption and investment both at present (static estimate) and over the long term (dynamic estimate).

Thus, deadweight losses are the opportunity cost of taxes and comprise sunk or irretrievable costs as well as the current efficiency costs of taxes. It is only current losses that are important for evaluating policy in the *short run* because they can be recovered, whereas sunk costs stretching back over time cannot be undone or recovered.

The current cost estimates of taxation in terms of economic growth were modelled by Branson & Lovell (1997). Their approach modelled the rate of growth of real GDP for 1946-95 as a function of the tax burden (normalised by DEA-derived efficiency scores[152]), the tax mix, and second order variables.[153] In

---

[151] An Illustration of the Aspects of Current Deadweight Loss: There are many dimensions to the deadweight loss of taxation, as this simple example from the United States illustrates. In 1991, a 10% Luxury Tax was imposed on small aircraft and pleasure boats, jewellery, furs, and luxury automobiles. The expected tax revenue, as estimated by the Congressional Joint Tax Committee, was $6 million. The actual amount of tax revenue received before repeal of the Act in 1993 was $53,000. Fortune Magazine commented as follows: "This sad tale provides an unusually clear example of one of the foggier concepts of economics: the 'deadweight loss' inherent in taxes. A deadweight loss reflects a cost imposed on some individuals without any offsetting benefit to others - a pure economic inefficiency. ...The all too-real luxury tax had all the elements" (Norton, R, 1993, "American's Screwed-Up Tax Code, FORTUNE, Sept., p. 62). The types of distortions created were as follows: (1) *Production distortion*: e.g. Beech Aircraft Corp sold 80 fewer planes than expected, at a loss of $130 million; this also affected the timing of the next investments for these firms, (2) *Consumption distortion*: people who would have liked to buy new airplanes did not buy them and (3) *Resource allocation distortion*: workers who would have been employed building the airplanes were idle (e.g. 480 employees at Beech Aircraft lost their jobs).

[152] These reflect the "efficiency" of the economy in differing years, relative to "peer" (comparable) years, in terms of whether the growth rate produced could have borne a higher burden (or, conversely, whether a higher growth rate could have been achieved for the given burden). The observed tax burden is normalised in order to correct for the fact that in these years the relationships observed between growth rates and tax burdens under-represent those possible at these *levels* of growth or burden.

[153] It is thought that the existence of an outlier, necessitating inclusion in the model of a dummy variable for 1952, is attributable to the effects upon GDP of the "Waterfront" industrial dispute of 1951.

the first stage, the linear programming model eliminated the effects of the non-tax factors on the real growth rate and was used to construct a *best-practice economic growth frontier*. In the second stage, variations of the real growth rate were explained by variations in annual values of the normalised tax burden and the tax mix (indirect tax divided by direct tax).

This model assessed the impact of a one-off "shock" to the tax regime, specifically the move to the optimal tax burden and tax mix, without accumulating the output effects over time, where estimates of the optimal tax burden and tax mix for each year of the sample period were generated.

The average observed tax burden for the period 1946-95 was 28%. The average optimal tax burden was estimated to be 22.5% of GDP, ranging from an optimum of 17.9% in 1958 to 27.0% in 1993. The average observed tax mix in to terms of the ratio of indirect to direct tax for this period was 0.47 (a tax mix of 68% direct tax and 32% indirect tax). The average optimal ratio of indirect to direct tax was estimated to be 0.54 (implying 65% direct tax and 35% indirect tax), ranging from an optimum of 0.47 (68% direct tax and 32% indirect tax) in 1951 to 0.56 (64% direct tax and 36% indirect tax) in 1990.

The average elasticities produced by the model coefficients suggest that altering the tax burden has a greater impact upon the growth rate than an equivalent change in tax mix by a factor of 6.28. The estimated annual output gap constituted on average 16.84% of GDP over the period 1946 to 1995. The cumulative effects of the deadweight losses were not taken into consideration. A comparison of the optimal GDP derived from this model and observed GDP is presented in **Figure 6.3**.

This output gap resulting from sub-optimal tax regimes can also be expressed in terms of deadweight loss per dollar of real tax revenue. The Branson & Lovell (1997) estimate a current deadweight loss for 1995 of $0.47 cents per dollar of tax revenue. These results are consistent with Scully's estimates.

Similar model specifications were applied to a longer data series, 1928-95. The inclusion of three dummy variables was found to be necessary due to the presence of outliers (the depression of 1931-32, 1952) and a difference in the nature of the growth-taxation relationship pre-1946. The findings of this second model, in terms of optimal tax burden, optimal tax mix, potential GDP and the output gap, were consistent with those derived for the shorter time series.

(xi) Findings

There was a more or less steady increase in the tax burden over the last 25 years, although the increases were largely in the first half of the 1970s and the latter part of the 1980s and the early 1990s. With lag effects, this means that deadweight losses (using Scully's estimate – **Table 6.2**) would be higher in the 1980s and 1990s, which the data confirm. The output gap in the 1980s was larger than that of the 1970s. The first half of the 1990s witnessed an

Figure 6.3
Current Cost Estimated of the Deadweight Loss of Taxation - observed and optimal real GDP: 1946-95

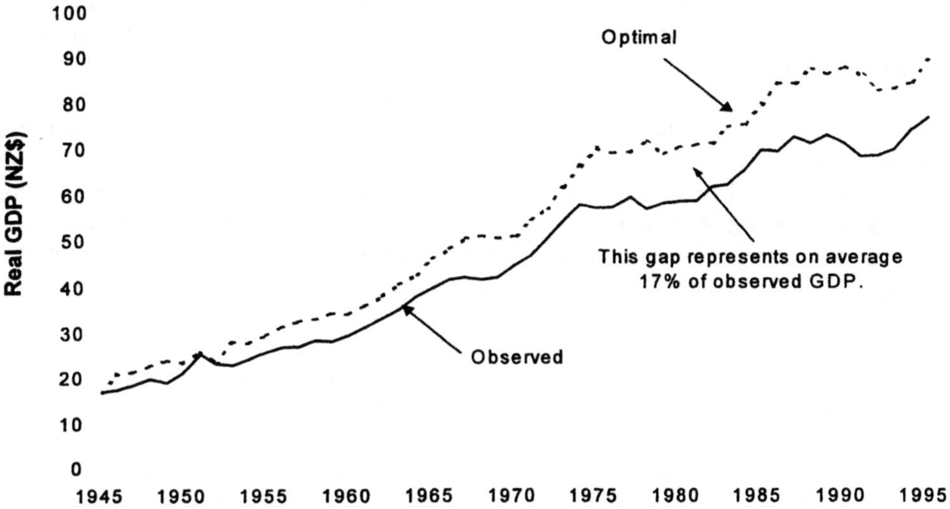

Source: Branson and Lovell (1997)

Table 6.4
Growth Maximising and Actual Tax Rates and Tax Mix for New Zealand: 1970-94

Tax Type	Optimal Rate % of GDP	Actual Rate 1993 % of GDP	Optimal Mix % of Total Tax	Actual Mix 1993 % Of Total Tax
Property	0.6	0.1	3.5	0.3
Personal	7.1	17.3	37.1	50.7
Company	3.1	3.9	16.3	11.3
Import	2.4	0.8	12.9	2.2
Other Indirect	5.7	12.1	30.0	35.4
Direct	11.3	21.3	55.7	62.3
Indirect	9.0	12.9	44.3	37.7
All Taxes	19.8	34.2	100	100

Notes:

Property tax consists of estate duty, gift duty and land tax.
Personal tax consists of income tax and social security payments.
Company tax includes that paid by non-residents.
Import tax refers to customs duty.
Other indirect tax consists of excise duties on alcohol and tobacco, motor vehicle and petrol taxes, motor vehicle fees and road user charges, sales tax, gaming duty, payroll tax, energy resources levy, stamp duties, other taxes, and, since 1987, GST.
The optimal rates by tax type cited are the averages of four separate estimations, hence the discrepancy between their sum and the optimal all taxes rate. See Scully (1996a) for further details.

Source: NZ Institute of Economic Research, Inland Revenue, Treasury, Scully (1996a)

accumulation in the output gap that was similar to the 1980s. It is too early to factor in the implications of the 1996 tax cut.

The cumulative deadweight loss is $2.69 for each dollar of additional tax. This deadweight loss varies with the tax rate. In 1946, a dollar of taxes was associated with a 13 cent loss of private wealth. In 1994, a dollar of taxes was associated with a $2.70 loss of private wealth. Lower tax rates are associated with lower deadweight losses. This implies that for each dollar of tax revenue, the benefits should be roughly around $2.70. It is important to point out, however, that this estimate is based on the assumption that optimal tax rate could have been in place since 1946, just after WW II. While this long run perspective is useful for setting the upper limit on the long run benefits expected from taxes, it does not indicate the current amount of the annual benefit that could be obtained by switching to the optimal rate at the beginning of a new year. The current costs as we shall see shortly, according to Branson & Lovell (1997), are just less than 50 cents per dollar of tax. This difference between current and sunk costs was discussed earlier.

The discovery of a best practice range of useful estimates for the tax to GDP ratio should not be taken as the discovery of a 'constant' that holds across time and countries. The best practice tax frontier will vary across time and countries, depending on the length of the time series used in the estimations. But, we anticipate that the range is not enormous. An examination of the optimal tax rate for the US (22%), Denmark (19%), Finland (19%), Italy (20%), Sweden (17%), and the UK (25%) over a 60 year period indicates that the range is probably roughly between 16%-25% of GDP, with a mid point of 20.5%. Five models developed for this Report suggest that the optimal range for the tax/GDP ratio in New Zealand is between 15% and 25% of GDP. Thus, for New Zealand, Scully's (1996) estimate of 20% must be considered a very good estimate.

(xii) Conclusions

The higher the tax/GDP ratio, and the longer a country stays at the higher ratios, the greater the long term output losses and the greater the risks of smothering economic growth. The effect is cumulative. The longer an economy remains at a high tax/GDP ratio, the more necessary is a cut in taxes because of the cumulative nature of the costs. But, as Caragata & Small (1996) suggest, a tax cut is less effective at those high levels because of the expected sluggish response due to the cumulative effect of the deadweight loss and the constraints on firms' incentive structures (e.g. the high transaction costs of adapting to more efficient performance).

When adjustment comes after years of accumulating deadweight losses, the structural adjustments will have to be significant. The deadening effects of high taxes can be countered by potentially preventable tax avoidance and evasion (Italy), productivity increases (earlier in Germany, 1945-65) or competitive exchange rate devaluations (earlier in Sweden), but eventually economic progress will require a reduction of taxes from such high levels, as is now currently evidenced in Germany.

Scully's (1996) results describe a growth-maximising tax rate of 20% of GDP for NZ. This estimate has been checked by four other models for NZ and by estimates for other countries and has been found to be very reasonable. A somewhat higher figure (21% of GDP) has been found for minimising the size of the hidden economy, in terms of diminishing returns in tax cuts. The figures are mutually supporting, in terms of arriving at an estimate roughly in the same range using two completely different models.

6.3 The Tax Mix and Economic Growth

There tends to be a bias in the formal optimal tax design theoretical literature against the use of a hybrid tax system, incorporating both direct and indirect taxes. Instead, the debate focuses on the binary choice between a system based on the taxation of income, or a system based on the taxation of expenditures. There seems to be a growing preference among academics, in the US at least, for consumption-based taxes *(ironically, the U.S is one of the few OECD countries without a GST or VAT)*. Unfortunately, much of the debate ignores the fruitful opportunity of examining the trade-offs between the two generic types of taxes empirically, as they affect objectives to maximise economic growth, employment, and minimise tax evasion and avoidance, compliance costs and administration costs.

Alm (1996) has also noted that there are good practical reasons why countries prefer a hybrid tax system:

"Both direct and indirect taxes should be levied. Use of both taxes allows each tax to be imposed at lower marginal tax rates, which reduces distortions and, most likely, non-compliance. Use of both taxes also gives the government more flexibility to achieve its equity and its revenue-yield goals, especially given the limitations that administrative considerations impose on the scope and even the use of some taxes. The optimal tax mix guidelines are the most uncertain and the most in need of additional research."

The following material should be treated with caution. The objective is only to determine the location of the frontier for the tax mix and the impact on growth and employment. The objective is not to advocate a movement to that frontier, although movement toward the frontier would certainly improve real per capita income. The purpose of the analysis in this section, as elsewhere, is to provide decision-makers with more information about the costs and benefits of moving away from the current policy position.

As indicated in **Table 6.4**, if the tax mix in 1993 is compared with the estimated growth maximising tax mix, the gap between current performance and the frontier for personal, company and indirect taxes can be estimated as follows. Keep in mind that the following calculations of the best practice frontier are not based on adjustments to the statutory rates for personal, indirect or corporate taxes. *The calculations are looked at in effective tax rate terms (tax/GDP ratio) or in revenue mix terms (shares of total tax revenue).*

In 1993, the personal tax/GDP ratio was 17.3% as compared to a growth maximising rate of 7.1%, hence the ratio of actual to potential is 17.3/7.1 or 2.44.

That is, the personal tax rate in 1993 was almost two and a half times as high as it needs to be if the objective of policy is to maximise the growth rate. That is, a 59% cut ([1 – 1/2.44] * 100) would bring the personal tax/GDP ratio close to the efficient growth maximising target, assuming that is what policy makers felt comfortable doing, and, of course, *they may very well not.* The implications of this finding for the personal statutory tax rate need to be examined.

In 1993, the ratio of company tax to GDP was 3.9%, versus a growth maximising rate of 3.1% of GDP. The actual to potential ratio, or performance ratio is 3.9/3.1, or 1.26. That is, if the value of company taxes were reduced by 21% ([1 – 1/1.26] * 100), economic growth would have a better chance of being optimised. The implications of this finding for the corporate statutory tax rate need to be examined

In 1993, the indirect tax/GDP ratio was 12.9% as compared to a growth maximising rate of 9%, hence the ratio of actual to potential (the performance ratio) is 12.9/9, or 1.43. That is, the indirect tax rate is about 30% ([1 – 1/1.43] * 100) higher than it needs to be if the objective of policy is to maximise the growth rate, assuming that is what policy makers felt comfortable doing, and, of course, *they may very well not.* The implications of this finding for GST statutory tax rate need to be examined. For all direct taxes, the existing rate was 21.3% of GDP as compared to a frontier rate of 11.3%, indicating that a 47% cut in direct taxes would help promote the maximisation of economic growth.

Another way of looking at the current versus potential rates is to examine the tax mix relative to total tax revenue.[154] Caution is again necessary here. The growth maximising tax rate (19.8% of GDP) is about 42% lower than the rate of 34.2% of GDP in 1993. Thus, if maximising growth is the sole objective, and it may not be, then all rates for personal, corporate and indirect taxes relative to GDP would fall at the frontier. But, the mix would also change, and some revenue streams (namely, property taxes, company taxes and import tariffs) would have their *relative* share of total tax revenue rise, *but not their absolute value*, in order to create a more optimal balance of revenue sources.

In 1993, the personal tax/total tax ratio was 50.7% as compared to a growth maximising ratio of 37.1%, hence the ratio of actual to potential is 50.7/37.1 or 1.37. That is, the personal tax revenue contribution to total revenue is about 27% ([1 – 1/1.37] * 100) higher than it needs to be again *if* the objective of policy is to maximise the growth rate.

The company tax/total tax ratio was 11.3% in 1993 as compared to a growth maximising rate of 16.3%, hence the ratio of actual to potential is 11.3/16.3 or 0.69. That is, assuming the total tax/GDP ratio (and thus all taxes) were reduced by 42%, then the share of that new, lower total accounted for by corporate tax payments would need to be 44% higher if the objective of policy is to maximise

[154] These actual numbers and the optimal estimates relative to total tax revenue differ somewhat from the typical way of construing a tax mix (personal, indirect, corporate) because they include tariffs, which are a source of government revenue, and property taxes, hence the shares relative to total mix will differ from those used elsewhere in the text.

the growth rate. Note that this basis for comparison was made in 1993. Data for 1994 indicates that this gap is closing. That is to say, in 1994 taxes paid by incorporated firms rose in nominal terms by 30% over the 1993 level. The change for unincorporated firms has not yet been calculated. This suggests that a period average, covering at least a full business cycle is perhaps more useful when identifying the optimal tax rate in empirical analysis.

In 1993, the indirect tax/total tax ratio was 37.7% as compared to a growth maximising ratio of 44.3%, hence the ratio of actual to potential is 37.7/44.3 or 0.85. That is, the indirect tax contribution to total tax revenue needs to be about 18% higher if the objective of policy is to maximise the growth rate. Again, this is a relative increase in the share of total revenue while a tax reduction to the frontier rate is occurring.

In 1993, the direct tax/GDP ratio was 62.3% as compared to the frontier growth maximising tax rate of 55.7% of GDP. Thus, the ratio of actual to potential is 62.3/55.7, or 1.12. Direct tax burden is about 11% higher than it needs to be if the objective is to maximise economic growth.

This analysis suggests some important conclusions. First, the personal tax/GDP ratio appears to be the greatest impediment to growth maximisation in two out of three of our in-house models. A growth-maximisation strategy would require about a 60% cut for the personal tax/GDP from 1993 levels, only if that was the strategy that government wanted to pursue, and holding other objectives, such as equity considerations constant. If equity and other considerations are introduced, it would not affect the frontier rate of the tax/GDP ratio for growth maximisation, rather it would affect the willingness of politicians to move to such a frontier. A second best option is to move toward that frontier by cutting taxes, but cutting taxes on firms and consumption less so they gradually receive more weight in the tax mix.

Second, a growth maximisation strategy would require a cuts in the ratios of company tax to GDP (21%) and indirect tax to GDP (30%) from 1993 levels. Because the personal tax/GDP ratio would shrink so much, under a growth-maximising scenario even though the company and indirect tax/GDP ratios would also shrink, they would shrink much less. As a result, their share of total tax would actually rise if the objective were an overall tax burden which maximised the real growth rate. Third, the current settings for indirect and company tax, while not perfect, must be considered to be relatively more realistic than the personal tax/GDP setting.

What does the literature say about the optimal mix? Unfortunately, the literature, which has remained formal in its approach, tends to focus on the choice between a tax system based solely on income and one based solely on expenditure or consumption tax. While theoretical, as opposed to empirical, in approach, there seems to be very strong support that a tax system based on consumption tax will enhance economic efficiency for various reasons, including the fact that savings are not taxed under such a system. But that is not the original position in welfare economics.

Hicks' (1941:41) analysis of the consumer surplus led him to draw certain conclusions about the optimal theory of taxation: "a tax on commodities lays a greater burden on consumers than an income tax". Since his focus was on static analysis, he tended to ignore the effect on income and thus on savings.[155] Subsequent debate in optimal tax theory focused on the choice between *equal* indirect taxes across all commodities and income tax. Little (1951) specified that under Pareto optimum conditions, one could not judge between the two. Corlett & Hague (1953) shifted the emphasis to favour the application of *unequal* indirect taxes across commodities[156] as opposed to the use of an income tax.

Since that time, the weight of theory has favoured consumption tax over income tax. Kotlikoff and Jorgenson found that switching from an income tax to a consumption tax based system will enhance economic growth (Boskin, 1996). Engen & Skinner (1996:19) commenting on a cross-country regression study by Mendoza, Milesi-Ferretti & Asea, conclude that evidence "suggest(s) that income taxation is more harmful than broad-based consumption taxes".

A second Inland Revenue New Zealand working paper (Branson & Lovell, 1997) also examined the optimal tax mix where the objective is to maximise economic growth. They conclude that, on average, a mix of 65% direct and 35% indirect is optimal for maximising economic growth in NZ at an average optimal tax/GDP ratio of 22.5%.

In summary, two working papers (Scully, 1996; and Branson & Lovell, 1997) with a growth maximisation objective firmly support the viability of a hybrid tax system composed of both income and consumption tax in preference to a tax structure without either income tax or consumption tax. Similar strong support for the hybrid system comes from Caragata & Giles (1996) when the objective is to minimise tax evasion. They found that a mix of 33% direct and 67% indirect would most efficiently minimise the size of the hidden economy and tax evasion.

On the other hand, with an objective of finding an inflection point in the link between growth and the tax/GDP ratio, Caragata & Small's (1996a) non-linear model estimated that at a tax/GDP ratio of 20%, tax policy would have its most powerful effect on (in terms of accelerating) economic growth when the tax mix is 28% direct tax and 72% indirect. Their model found no turning point in the relationship between growth and direct taxes. The relationship was always negative. This implies that a tax mix with zero direct taxes and 100% indirect taxes would maximise economic growth.[157]

---

155 "In the terminology of my Value and Capital, income effects are to be neglected" (Hicks, 1941a:109). This of course does not mean that they should be neglected, as Hicks (1941:231) noted in his discussion of the dynamic income effects of price changes.

156 Commodities "most complementary" to leisure would have the highest tax rates, while commodities "most substitutable" for leisure would have the lowest rates.

157 The conclusion to be drawn from this model is that in the transition to an optimal tax mix, a 28% (direct) and 72% (indirect) tax split would best accelerate the rate of economic growth. In the long run, the growth-maximising mix in this model is 0% direct and 100% direct. Nonetheless, there are measurement errors in this model which make the conclusions both tentative and subject to caution.

These models all suggest that a much more rigorous, dynamic analytical framework is required, than is typically used, when specifying that a flat income tax is to be preferred over an expenditure tax, or vice versa, as the sole basis for taxation. In the transition period, a hybrid tax system can optimise efficiency if the level of the aggregate tax burden and the tax mix are simultaneously set at the appropriate levels assuming that the anticipated empirical consequences of taxation are assessed with some precision.

In summary, 2 models (Scully, 1996; and Branson & Lovell, 1996) with a growth maximisation objective suggest that the short and long run optimal mix should favour direct over indirect taxes, while 1 model (Caragata & Small, 1996) with the same objective (in the long run, but not the short run) and another model (Caragata & Giles, 1996) with an objective of minimising tax evasion suggest that the mix should favour indirect taxes. A preliminary assessment of these results suggests that NZ will experience more economic growth and lower tax evasion if the tax/GDP ratio were reduced. As well, given trade-offs between growth and tax evasion objectives, a rough balance of direct and indirect taxes in the tax mix would seem, at this preliminary stage, to offer a useful best practice frontier against which to benchmark policy progress.

Scully (1997), in reviewing these models, recommends focusing only on the first two models, if growth maximisation is the objective, and recommends averaging the Scully (1996) and Branson & Lovell (1997) results. This recommendation would lead to an indirect/direct tax ratio averaging 0.61. This would imply that direct taxes would mean that direct taxes would account for 62% of the total tax burden and indirect taxes 38%, under a growth-maximising optimum. This result is similar to the current mix in 1995 of 36% indirect and 64% direct.

Of course, efficiency is not the only objective in taxation. Given an equity constraint, and objectives of minimising tax evasion, compliance costs and administration costs, the settings for the tax/GDP ratio and the tax mix could be quite different than with objectives or maximising efficiency and minimising tax evasion. More research is required.

6.4 Taxation and Employment

a. Introduction

Economics is still in the early stages of understanding the linkage between taxation and employment. The analysis and findings in this section, therefore, should be considered preliminary rather than definitive. Macro-econometric models tend to have a demand-side emphasis that leads them to under-estimate the incentive effects and benefits from income tax cuts. This finding was highlighted in a recent study of the Canadian tax system covering the period 1967-94, which concluded that:

"higher personal direct taxes and personal income taxes were found to have a significant negative impact on the labour force participation rate and employment growth. It appears that actual job losses caused by past tax increases were roughly twice as large as predicted by Keynesian demand-oriented macro models". (Spiro, 1996:1)

This suggests the need for a more comprehensive and systematic analysis of the responsiveness of labour markets to tax changes. In particular, there is a need to examine the interactive effects of tax changes on the supply of labour and on firms' willingness and ability to hire. The evidence and analysis presented below suggests two important, preliminary findings. The first has been confirmed with econometric testing, the second finding is partly confirmed by econometric evidence (Caragata, 1996), but part of the analysis is still at the pre-testing stage (Caragata, 1997).

First, there is an inverse relation between a change in the total level of taxes, on the one hand, and the change in labour force participation, and employment generation, and a positive relationship between unemployment rates and taxes, that are confirmed across countries (Spiro, 1996; Scully, 1996b; Scully, 1996c). Thus, lower taxes will generate more labour participation, greater employment growth and less unemployment.

Second, there is a difference between the way that revenue and profit generating efficient and inefficient firms respond to taxes (Caragata, 1996)[158]. Profit and revenue efficient firms have high cash flow and good credit ratings. This permits them to borrow and invest more freely and frequently and, therefore, allows the firms to take greater advantage of the interest deduction and depreciation provisions of the tax system to lower their effective tax rates. As a result, more efficient firms engage in the normal substitution of capital for labour, hence generating redundancies. But the savings is reinvested and promotes an expanding economy which generates more demand for labour. Thus, one must be careful to distinguish between the short term and the long-term effects of the interaction between taxation and the incentives to employ labour.[159]

Less efficient firms, on the other hand, do not have the same cash flow and credit rating advantages and therefore neither invest as much or as frequently, nor do they have low effective tax rates - unless they go through sustained periods of loss. Less revenue and profit efficient firms do not have the normal capital-labour substitution. They hypothesise that less efficient firms face a difficult substitution choice between labour and taxes (and also between R + D and taxes) (Caragata & Heiler, 1997). [160]

---

[158] Revenue-generating efficiency is defined for these purposes by using the accounting concept of the activity ratio (sales divided by net assets) which is a component of RONA - the return on net assets. More revenue-efficient firms generate more sales per unit of net assets than less revenue efficient firms. This concept of financial performance efficiency is only a partial measure and is not to be confused with comprehensive measures of input-output efficiency used in microeconomic literature.

[159] Another important feature of this analysis involves the need to distinguish between the short term and the long-term consequences of government spending on employment. Government spending tends to create jobs and growth in the short term, but if not carefully chosen, it creates less growth and employment over the longer term because of the deadweight loss of taxation.

[160] Some conditional support for this idea has been presented by Engen and Skinner (1996:32) who summarise the results of a Princeton University Working Paper that quantifies the labour hiring decisions by self-employed workers: "...a 6 percentage point decline in the marginal tax rate

Less efficient (in terms of revenue and profit generating efficiency) firms (and, notably, smaller new entrants to markets) may, over the course of the year (given provisional tax requirements), substitute taxes (which are often a non-discretionary, periodic cost) for new labour. Thus, inefficient firms may postpone or reduce hiring because of the need to meet tax obligations. Whether or not they actually shed labour because of this tax trap[161] remains to be seen. Given the predominance of the under-utilisation of capacity, the marginal cost of current production is largely based on changes in variable costs. This helps to explain the labour-tax payment trade-off that occurs for more inefficient firms.

In brief, as taxes rise the incentive to invest and to hire falls and the less efficient firms (as defined) may reduce output. Simultaneously, taxes reduce the incentive to participate in the labour force. More efficient firms (as defined) may absorb the tax shock more easily because they are already utilising interest deductibility and depreciation, more actively than inefficient firms, in order to reduce their effective tax rates. Inefficient firms (including new market entrants), on the other hand, may not have so much freedom of choice and flexibility. It is possible that a similar tax and R & D expenditure trade-off may exist for firms that are less efficient at generating revenue and profits.

Thus, new tax shocks are most felt by inefficient firms, including small firms. Small firms are the principal source[162] of employment growth outside the manufacturing sector (Davis, Haltiwanger & Schuh, 1996). It would appear that the tax system favours revenue and profit (per unit of assets) efficient firms at the expense of firms which are less efficient in these terms, including new small firms. This is an observation rather than a judgement. Few would suggest that the reverse (i.e. favouring inefficient firms) policy should be in place. But this dilemma does raise

---

of [an]... entrepreneur in the top tax bracket increased by 11 percent the likelihood of hiring at least one employee. However, the magnitude of these effects, and their impact on aggregate employment, are not well enough understood to hazard a numerical estimate of their growth effects". Tanzi (1996:20) also notes that "...to the extent that part of [the] incidence [of social security taxes] may fall on the enterprises (because of the existence of minimum wages and other constraints that reduce the possibility of shifting them on to labour), they reduce the demand for labour and may also encourage both enterprises and workers to engage in underground economic activities."

[161] The tax trap arises because inefficient firms do not have the cash flow or the credit ratings to take advantage of opportunities to borrow and invest, both of which permit the firm to more readily exploit the provisions of the tax system that favour investment (interest deductibility and depreciation). As a result, less efficient firms operate well below the production frontier partly because they cannot exploit those normal benefits offered by the tax system. Because those firms have to pay more taxes than they would if they were more efficient, they cannot so readily afford to hire labour and invest so as to produce more cash flow and become more efficient. Hence, the link between inefficiency and higher effective tax rates creates a tax trap.

[162] A study for Statistics Canada in 1994 estimated that over the period 1984-88 just over 54% of the new jobs created were provided by firms with 19 or less employees. Further, as reported in Spiro (1996:5) "in the 1981-84 period, which spans a deep recession, total employment in the Canadian economy fell by 277,000 jobs, but employment in small [19 employees and under] firms rose by 97,000. Tax policy measures that influence the viability of small business can have a profound impact on job creation".(see Picot, G., Baldwin, J., and Dupuy, R., 1994, *Have Small Firms Created a Disproportionate Share of New Jobs in Canada? A Reassessment of the Facts*, Statistics Canada Research Paper Series No. 71, Ottawa: Statistics Canada, November).

the issue of the costs of such a tax system, and the extent to which new entrants are marginalised or deterred by the tax system.

The combined effect of those efficiency differences plus a tax increase creates a lower rate of employment generation that is only offset by economic growth. That is to say, making the economic pie larger may tend to offset the effects of the tendencies for firms to shed labour given their interaction with the tax system. On this account, there is also a greater need for more information about the costs of the current tax system.

b. Unemployment: An OECD-Wide Problem

The development of new jobs and the reduction of unemployment is one of the principal social issues of the 1990s. Many OECD countries are experiencing persistently high unemployment above 10%. These rates are quite out of line with experience earlier in the post-war period. Those levels are roughly double what they were 20 years ago[163], and in 1992, are about four times the 1965 level.[164]

A general explanation for this trend is the presence of lower real growth rates in each of the OECD countries as compared to 20 years ago. [165] [166] As indicated in **Table 6.5**, this is also NZ's experience. Using the GDP deflator basis, in the 1950s and 1960s, real growth averaged about 3.8% per annum, whereas in the 1970s and 1980s it was only about 2.3% per annum, dropping off in the period 1990-94 to less than 1%. Of course, since then growth has generally been much stronger.

Over a somewhat similar period, Browne and Leeflang (1996:5) report that "the overall tax rate on employed labour throughout the European community grew by about one-fifth". Using a different measure, the average personal tax/GDP ratio, from **Table 3.3**, for fifteen[167] European countries for which data are available, the average personal tax/GDP ratio rose from 14.4% in 1965 to 24.8% in 1992, an increase of 72%. This suggests, but does not prove, that there may be a link between taxation, growth and employment.

The experience in NZ is somewhat different (as indicated in **Table 6.5**), but, nonetheless, unemployment has been very high until recently. For most of the three decades following World War II, NZ had virtually no visible unemployment, although hidden unemployment was present because of the significant role played by state-owned enterprises and government departments in making work.

---

[163] *Economic Report of the President*, Washington, D.C: USGPO, 1996,p.399.

[164] Austria (1965,1.9% versus 5.3% in 1992); Belgium (1965, 1.8%, versus 10.4% in 1992); Denmark (1965, 2% versus 11.3 in 1992); Finland (1965, 1.4% versus 13.1% in 1992); France (1965, 1.4%, versus 10.3%); Germany (1965, 0.3% versus 7.7% in 1992); Greece (1965, 5.6% versus 8.7% in 1992); Ireland (1965, 4.7% versus 15.5% in 1992); Italy (1965, 5.3%, versus 8.8% in 1992); Netherlands (1965, 0.5%, versus 5.4% in 1992); Norway (1965, 1.8%, versus 5.9%); Sweden (1965, 1.2%, versus 5.3%); OECD, *OECD Economic Outlook*; ILO, *Bulletin of Labour Statistics and Yearbook of Labour Statistics.*

[165] *Economic Report of the President*, Washington, D.C: USGPO, 1989,p.434

[166] *Economic Report of the President*, Washington, D.C: USGPO, 1996,p.402

[167] Austria, Belgium, Denmark, Finland, France, Germany, Greece, Iceland, Ireland, Italy, Luxembourg, Netherlands, Norway, Sweden, and Switzerland.

Table 6.5
Economic Indicators: 1951-94

Period	Unemployment Rate %	Employment Growth %	Tax Rate (Tax/GDP) %	Growth Rate (CPI) %	Growth Rate (Real GDP) %
1951-59	0.02	1.83	25.6	3.48	3.69
1960-69	0.19	2.10	23.7	4.11	3.98
1970-79	0.60	2.42	26.5	3.55	2.62
1980-89	4.35	0.36	30.5	1.93	2.03
1990-94	9.20	0.82	34.7	0.60	0.70

Source: Statistics New Zealand

Table 6.6
Taxation Shocks and Labour Market Responses - cross country comparisons (for a 1% point increase in the tax/GDP ration and per billion dollars of taxes in the local currency)

	New Zealand (1951-94)	Canada (1967-94)	USA (1950-95)
Labour Force Participation Rate (%)	-0.43	-0.55% -0.87	-0.21% - 0.28
Estimated Drop In Labour Force Participation	11,900	115,000**	506,200
(per $1bn of Tax in Local Currency)	17,526		6,900
Change in Employment Growth Rate (%)*	-2.6	-1.98	-0.7
Potential Job Loss	42,470	236,700	872,000
(per $1bn of Tax in Local Currency)	51,540	35,000	11,947
Change in the Unemployment Rate (%)	+ 0.87		+ 0.47
Unemployment Increase	15,900		623,400
(per $1bn of Tax in Local Currency)	19,300		8,500

* The growth rate of employment is equal to the growth rate of the labour force participation rate times the growth rate of the working age population.
** Estimated from Spiro's co-efficient - 0.57

Source: Scully (1996b; 1996c) and Spiro (1996)

In the 1980s, with the onset of structural adjustment and the movement towards a more market-based economy, unemployment levels rose to an average of 4.4% in the 1980s and to 9.2% in the first 5 years of this decade. In August 1996, the unemployment rate had fallen to 6.1%, although it has been stable at that level for a year. At the same time, as indicated in the Table, employment growth has also exhibited a similar downward pattern, although there was a modest upturn in the 1990s. Over the period 1965-1995, in NZ, the personal tax/GDP ratio rose from 9.7% to a peak of 21% in 1982, and declined thereafter to 17.4% in 1995, a drop of 17% over the 1982 peak.

c. Current Explanations are Unsatisfactory

Many possible explanations have been offered by economists for the high unemployment levels in OECD countries. The key contenders include: (1) the role of minimum wages (more generally, incomes policy), (2) collective bargaining and the role of union power, (3) efficiency-wage theory, (4) job search models that examine the imbalance between flows into and out of the labour market, (5) employment protection schemes and other labour market rigidities, (6) unemployment benefits, (7) structural deficient aggregate demand to suppress inflation, (8) fiscal policy[168] and *(9)* structural adjustment, tariff reduction and deregulation that lead to the redeployment of labour. But, so far, there are no widely accepted views because of their inability to meet certain critical tests:

"Persistent unemployment, like that plaguing Europe since the early 1980s, has been a persistent problem for economic theory." (Greenwald and Stiglitz, 1995:219; cf Phelps, 1994)

Recently, in Europe, a considerable degree of attention has been focused on the link between the tax cost of labour combined with the "hidden costs of employment". A review of these costs in 17 European countries by Deloitte Touche Tohmatsu has revealed that, in rank order, personal tax liability (which is factored into the wage bill) is the most important cost, followed by: (1) social security cost; (2) redundancy cost; (3) collective labour agreements; (4) defined benefits in kind; (5) limitations of deductibility for corporate tax purposes; (6) company pension plans; (7) providing a working place; (8) payroll administration; (9) overtime payments; (10) payroll taxes; and (11) company savings plans (Browne and Leeflang, 1996:5).

The Deloitte's study was a statistical, rather than an econometric, exercise, and did not present confidence intervals along with the analysis. But some useful working hypotheses can be established from the data. Across all countries, there is no clear relationship between the level of an employee's personal tax and social security costs (per average annual wage) and the unemployment rate. But, second, for some countries, there does appear to be a strong link, while for others there is not:

---

[168] For example, Phelps (1994) notes that if there is an inverse relationship between the wage rate and the interest rate, then fiscal imbalance can lead to higher interest rates and higher unemployment.

"Finland, for instance, which has the second highest unemployment rate after Spain, levies the highest income tax rate on the average wage, in our study. In this instance, there may well be a correlation between the two as such high rates may act as a disincentive to work ... Belgium, Denmark, Italy and France also have high unemployment and high employment costs. France and Italy have particularly high social security rates and the personal tax costs for Danish employees [are] almost as much as in Finland. In contrast, some countries with high unemployment have low employment costs. Spain, for instance, has a fairly average wage, low tax and social security costs and yet has the highest unemployment rate in our survey. Greece and Ireland also have fairly low employment costs and high unemployment rates. To some extent this reflects a need in these countries to counteract high unemployment rates with reduced income tax rates" (Browne and Leeflang, 1996:12).

A similar survey of statistics (Zee, 1997:233-35) for 1993 for a broader range of countries (OECD, developing economies and transition economies - former communist countries) also suggests "no clear pattern". For example, Belgium (45.3%), Denmark (49.2%), Finland (46.5%), France (43.8%), Italy (41.1%), Netherlands (46.7%) all had high tax/GDP ratios and had unemployment rates higher than 7%. In contrast, some countries with tax/GDP ratios over 40% (Austria, 42.5%; Luxembourg, 48.6%, Norway, 46.4% and Sweden, 51.9%) had unemployment rates in 1993 below 5%, except for Norway where the rate was 5.7%. Nonetheless, this IMF study also made an extensive survey of the literature of the relationship between taxation and employment and concluded that:

"...while taxation is but one of many factors (under some circumstances it may arguably not even be a dominant factor) that can directly affect unemployment, it is an important determinant of market distortions in general, and labour market distortions in particular, with a consequent negative influence on the functioning of labour markets" (Zee, 1997:251)[169].

Some econometric analysis of these data might yield some useful results. Perhaps more importantly, the Heads of State of Government at all meetings of the European Council of the European Union since 1994 and in the aftermath of the European Commission's 1993 White Paper on *Growth, Competitiveness and Employment* have reiterated the "need to reduce taxes on labour in the fight against unemployment in Europe".[170]

Third, the unemployment rate is not the only labour market variable that needs to be considered. Also important are the labour force participation rate and the growth rate of employment. An econometric approach to the examination of the link between taxation and unemployment rates, employment growth rates and labour force participation rates would offer some useful refinements to this type of analysis.

---

[169] In its theoretical analysis the paper concluded that there are both long run and short consequences to the decrease in taxes on the "rental price" of capital. In the short term, this could have an adverse impact of employment because of the substitution effects, but in the long run "such a tax cut is likely to stimulate investment and produce a favourable impact on economic growth and employment prospects" (Zee, 1997:229). In its recommendations, the paper suggests the value of shifting the tax mix somewhat away from "employer payroll contributions to other tax bases such as consumption [in] OECD countries..." (Zee, 1997:251).

[170] Private communication from the Directorate General XXI, Customs and Indirect Taxation, European Commission, Brussels.

d. *Objectives and Methodology*

Given theoretical problems in explaining unemployment and employment generation a reduced form model was considered more appropriate than a structural model (Scully, 1996b). The rationale for this choice is provided by Sims (1980) and Maasoumi (1986).[171] Various assumptions used in the model include the following:

- real growth rate of other inputs, mainly net capital formation, is 5% per annum;
- labour's share is about two-thirds of output and other inputs receive the remaining third (based on empirical evidenced in OECD countries); and,
- holding the growth of the real money supply and the change in real interest rates constant.

Tests were undertaken for Granger causality, unit roots and cointegration (Scully, 1996b;appendix). The NZ results[172] indicate that the tax variables Granger cause the employment variables, that all of the variables are integrated of order 1 and are cointegrated.

Analysis focused on two levels. The impact of the tax/GDP ratio on the labour force participation rate, the employment growth rate and the unemployment rate was examined for NZ and the results were compared with those for the United States and Canada, where data were available (**Table 6.6**). This was followed by an analysis of the impact of direct and indirect taxes on the labour force participation rate, the employment growth rate and the unemployment rate for NZ alone.

The more aggregate approach using the tax/GDP ratio was designed to test for the inverse relationship between taxes and employment, and to assist in determining if a best practice frontier or setting for the tax/GDP ratio, which minimised employment losses and maximised labour force participation and employment growth, could be identified. The decomposition of the tax/GDP ratio into the components of the tax mix was designed to determine the efficient tax mix which offered a similar best practice frontier.

e. *Labour Force Participation Responses to Tax Changes*

The labour force participation rate describes the proportion of the population engaged in the labour force. For NZ, the labour force participation rate was 62.8% based on a labour force of 1.728 million and a working age population of 2.752 million in 1995.

---

[171] Blanchflower and Oswald (1995:163-64) provide additional justification for using a reduced form model to assess new and difficult empirical questions and for not using a structural neo-classical model in their examination of the *wage curve* which links changes in local not aggregate unemployment to changes in wages: "employees who work in areas of high unemployment earn less, other things constant, than those who are surrounded by low unemployment". In effect, the reduced form model provides a useful tool when existing paradigms ignore key relationships that can be observed in reality. In this case, the wage curve is intended to replace the labour supply curve.

[172] Similar results were developed for the U.S. data (Scully, 1996c).

In NZ, over the period 1951-94, (**Table 6.6**) a 1 percentage point increase in the tax/GDP ratio lowers labour force participation by 0.43%. In Canada, the tax coefficient lies between -0.55 and -0.87, whereas in the U.S. the range is -0.21 and -0.28.[173] Several conclusions can be drawn from these results, which were all statistically significant.

First, there is a strong inverse relationship between tax and labour force participation that is consistent across countries. Second, this suggests that the willingness to supply labour to the market is very responsive to changes in the tax burden. Third, the lowest responsiveness, among the three countries, occurs in the US (which has the lowest overall statutory tax rate), followed by NZ (the second lowest), and then Canada (the highest). This implies that the elasticity rises in response to a change in the statutory rate. Some additional research needs to be undertaken on this matter. Fourth, this suggests that Canada, which has the highest elasticity, has a relatively greater potential problem with labour disguising its participation in the hidden economy. If the experiences of these 3 countries are representative, the findings are very important for tax policy in other countries. If not, they are remain important for these 3 countries.

For NZ, taking 1994 GDP ($82.4 billion) as a starting point, a 1 percentage point increase in the tax/GDP ratio is equal to $824 million. In response to such a hike in taxes, labour force participation would drop by 11,900 individuals. If the tax shock were $1 billion, then the decline in labour force participation would reach 17,526. By comparison, for each 1 percentage point decrease in the tax/GDP ratio, in Canada 115,000 people would withdraw from the labour, while in the U.S. 506,200 less individuals would participate in the work force.

f. Employment Growth Responses to Tax Changes[174]

Employment growth is related to the change in the labour force participation rate, but is not coincident with it. The effect of an increase in the tax rate is negative, quite substantial, and statistically significant, and consistent across the three countries. For all taxes as a share of GDP, a 1 percentage point increase lowers NZ's employment growth by 2.6%. The effect of a 1 percentage point increase in direct taxes is larger (a reduction in employment growth of 4.0%). The effect of an increase in indirect taxes is also substantial. Each 1 percentage point increase lowers employment growth by 3.7%.

In 1995, in NZ 1.61 million were employed. A 1 percentage point increase in overall taxation eliminates 42,470 jobs over a five year period. A 1 percentage point increase in direct taxes eliminates 64,320 jobs. A 1 percentage point increase in indirect taxes costs 58,930 jobs. Spiro found that a 1 percentage point increase in total taxes out of GDP cost Canada a 1.98% decline in employment

---

[173] Control variables included the percentage change in real wages or the percentage change in real compensation, the change in the unemployment rate, the change in the growth rate of the real money supply, the change in the real interest rate, and a time trend.
[174] Regressions were run relating the percentage change in employment to changes in various tax rates, holding the growth in the real money supply and the change in the real interest rate constant.

growth. Canadian employment was 13.3 million in 1994. This amounts to a loss of 236,700 jobs. For the United States, a 1 percentage point tax increase reduces job formation by 0.7% or by 872,000.

g. Unemployment Rate Responses to Tax Changes

Increased levels of taxation adversely affect labour force participation and employment growth. Does increased taxation raise the unemployment rate? If so, it would mean that fiscal policy is working opposite its intended purpose of reducing unemployment.

Table 6.6 presents the results of regressions for New Zealand linking the change in the unemployment rate to the change in the tax/GDP ratio, holding other effects, previously discussed, constant. In NZ, a 1 percentage point increase in the tax/GDP ratio raises the unemployment rate by 0.87%. By comparison, for the United States, the effect of a 1 percentage point increase in the tax/GDP ratio raises the unemployment rate by 0.47%. Thus, the unemployment rate is much more sensitive to a tax change in NZ than in the U.S.

To assist in understanding the NZ results, recall (**Table 6.5**) that during 1960-69, the unemployment rate averaged 0.2% and the tax rate was 23.7% of GDP. In 1990-94, the unemployment rate increased 9 percentage points to 9.2% and the tax rate increased 11 percentage points to 34.7% of GDP, representing an increase in the total tax burden facing the economy of 46% over approximately 30 years. Multiplying the coefficient by the change in the tax rate (0.87 times 11%) yields a 9.5 percentage point increase in the unemployment rate, which is close to what actually occurred.

In terms of the number of unemployed in NZ, a 1 percentage point increase in the tax/GDP ratio raises unemployment by 15,900 after four years.

h. Tax Mix Changes and Employment Effects

The following analysis should be seen as preliminary. Since additional research is required to test these results, caution should be exercised in drawing firm conclusions. The choice of tax mix may be quite important in shaping the incentives to supply and hire labour, but consistent with the results of the other models presented in this report, the impact of the level of taxes on economic activity is much more important than the impact of the tax mix. This modelled finding challenges Engen & Skinner's (1996:36) view that "the composition of the tax system is probably as important for economic growth as is the absolute level of taxation".

A change in the balance of direct and indirect taxes can have a significant effect on *labour force participation*, employment growth and the unemployment rate. Both direct and indirect taxes are inversely related to labour force participation, but the link with direct taxes is only weakly significant, whereas the impact of indirect taxes is much more significant. This suggests that a tax system weighted more toward direct taxes would promote more labour force participation.

Recall that in NZ, for all taxes as a share of GDP, a 1 percentage point increase lowers *employment growth* by 2.6%. The effect of a 1 percentage point increase in direct taxes is larger (a reduction in employment growth of 4.0%). The effect of an increase in indirect taxes, also, is substantial. Each 1 percentage point increase lowers employment growth by 3.7%. This indicates that direct taxes play a slightly more important role in shaping the demand for labour. A 1 percentage point increase in the direct tax/GDP ratio in NZ eliminates 5,390 more jobs than a similar rise in the indirect tax/GDP ratio.

In terms of the number of unemployed in NZ, a 1 percentage point increase in the overall tax rate raises *unemployment* by 15,900 after four years. The effect of a 1 percentage point increase in direct taxes is a little larger (16,700). A 1 percentage point increase in indirect taxes as a share of GDP would raise unemployment by about 17,400 after two years.

In summary, the effect of the total tax burden on labour force participation rates, unemployment rates and employment generation is more important than the impact of the tax mix. Indirect taxes have a less negative impact on employment generation than direct taxes. Direct taxes have a less negative impact on unemployment rates and labour force participation rates than indirect taxes.

This brief analysis suggests that lowering direct taxes (as compared to indirect taxes) is a more fruitful way of promoting labour force participation and reducing unemployment. This is consistent with the previous finding of Scully (1996), Branson & Lovell (1997), and Caragata & Small (1996a) that personal taxes have been found to be more detrimental than indirect taxes to long term economic growth.

i. Deadweight Loss in Labour Markets

The tax increase-induced loss of labour force participation, lowered employment growth, and increased unemployment can be converted into GDP never produced. **Table 6.7** below presents the deadweight loss for a 1 percentage point increase in the tax/GDP ratio measured by the relevant GDP base (i.e. 1994 GDP times lag length). For all taxes, the loss from the tax-induced change in labour force participation is 0.26% of GDP, from lowered employment growth is 0.55%, and from increased unemployment is 0.26%. The total deadweight loss from all employment effects is 1.07% of GDP. This is equivalent to 6.2 cents per dollar of personal tax revenue.

These results can be contrasted with those for the United States. The lost GDP calculations were 0.14% (change in the labour force participation rate), 0.35% (change in the employment growth rate), and 0.25% (change in the unemployment rate), for a total deadweight loss of 0.74%. The U.S. deadweight loss in employment effects of taxation per unit change in the tax/GDP ratio is 69% of the NZ deadweight loss. The US tax/GDP ratio (29%) is 85% of NZ's tax/GDP ratio (34%). This difference could explain half of the difference between the two countries. The remaining 16 percentage points may be explained by imperfections in NZ's labour markets, or in structural differences (e.g. scale of plant and scope of products across sectors).

Table 6.7
Percentage Deadweight Loss of GDP for a One Percent Increase in Taxation, by Type of Tax

Variable	All Taxes	Direct Taxes	Indirect Taxes
DLFPR	0.26	0.22	0.47
DEmp. Growth	0.55	0.84	0.77
DUnemp. Rate	0.26	0.27	0.57
Total	1.07	1.33	1.81

Notes:
DLFPR change in the labour force participation rate
DEmp. Growth change in the employment growth rate
DUnemp. Rate change in the unemployment rate

Source: Scully, 1996, Taxation and Employment

j. Conclusions

The principal findings in this analysis confirm that, in NZ, Canada and the United States, there is an inverse relationship between the tax/GDP ratio, on the one hand, and the labour force participation rate and employment growth rate, on the other hand, and a positive correlation with the unemployment rate. Thus, taxes have an important effect on the supply of labour and the demand for labour. This suggests that the level of tax may be undermining the objectives of economic policy.

In NZ, a 1 percentage point increase in the tax/GDP ratio appears to have its strongest impact in labour markets on employment growth (tax co-efficient -2.6), although the impact on labour force participation (-0.43), and the unemployment rate (0.87) are also strong results. Thus, a 1 percent increase in the tax/GDP ratio in NZ lowers employment growth by over 42,470 workers, decreases labour force participation by 11,900 workers and increases the unemployment rate by about 15,900. All results were statistically significant, and tests indicated Granger causation, no unit roots, stationarity and cointegration.

A 1 percentage point increase in the tax/GDP ratio induces a deadweight loss in labour force participation on the order of 0.26% of GDP, a deadweight loss from lowered employment growth of 0.55% of GDP, and from increased unemployment is of 0.26% of GDP. The total deadweight loss from all employment effects is 1.07% of GDP. Thus, for each $1.00 of tax there is a deadweight loss of $1.07 in labour markets.

The choice of tax mix is quite important in shaping the incentives to supply and hire labour. Both direct and indirect taxes are inversely related to labour force participation, but the link with direct taxes is only weakly significant, whereas the impact of indirect taxes is much more significant. This suggests that a tax system weighted more toward direct taxes would promote more labour force participation. But the level of the tax/GDP ratio is probably more important. A growth-maximising tax rate for the period 1951-94 was estimated to be 20.9%. At that rate, the annual increase in the growth rate of employment would be higher than the actual estimate of 2.3% that NZ experienced during the period.

In brief, as taxes rise they reduce output and the incentive to invest and to hire. Simultaneously, they reduce the incentive to participate in the labour force. More efficient firms (in terms of revenue and profit generating efficiency) can absorb the tax shock more easily because they are already utilising interest deductibility and depreciation more actively than inefficient firms, in order to reduce their effective tax rates. Inefficient firms (including new market entrants), on the other hand, do not have so much freedom of choice and flexibility.

Thus, new tax shocks are most felt by inefficient firms, including small firms. Small firms are the principal source of employment growth. It would appear that the tax system favours efficient firms (as defined) at the expense of inefficient firms (as defined), including new small firms, and that the combined effect of those efficiency differences plus a tax increase generate a synergistic reduction in employment that is only offset by economic growth. That is to say, making the economic pie larger offsets the effects of the tendencies for firms to shed labour given their interaction with the tax system.

As the role of government has grown significantly over the last three decades it has created had a wider and deeper range of effects on the economic performance of individuals, firms and the economy. Those effects are just now becoming better understood, but there is still a long way to go in assessing these impacts. One of the natural consequences of greater government intrusion is the onset of a society that prefers less risk and less personal responsibility. There is also a greater propensity for fraudulent use of government transfers and tax evasion. Thus, as government expands it creates both benefits and costs.

Perhaps the most important fiscal trade-off that must be managed most carefully in the latter part of the 20th century is the conflict between real social need (arising from abuse, incapacitation, poverty and discrimination) versus free-riding[175] by undeserving individuals who wish to live at the expense of others. If the voting population becomes dominated by individuals living on tax-based transfers rather than private sector income earning individuals, then there will be the real risk that those who are socially dependent will always out-vote those who create wealth. The result could be that taxes would remain high.

This discussion is not helped by ideologues of the left who argue for big government or those on the right who argue for small government. What is required is rigorous cost benefit analysis and risk assessment to clarify the nature of the impacts of the difficult choices that governments must make. Where

[175] A somewhat cynical view of the role of the state in this matter was provided by Frederic Bastiat, a 19th century French commentator who said: "The state is the great fictitious entity by which everyone seeks to live at the expense of everyone else".

social needs are real, they must be met with appropriate budget provision. Where the needs are not real, then they would not be met. Of course, there is an enormous information problem in determining legitimate from illegitimate needs.

Another important task is to ensure that current tax burdens do not undermine the country's economic performance, and that appropriate limits are placed on the level of government expenditure. Where deficits become large and perpetual, the current generation lives at the expense of future generations. Protecting the rights of future generations of voters from being victimised by current political mandates is a serious challenge to democratic institutions. What is the long run fiscal viability of today's political promises and programs?

For New Zealand, the legacy of the great intervention in the period 1975-1993 when taxes and debt reached historic highs and growth was virtually stagnant is a painful reminder of the insensitivity of a previous generation to the current generation of voters. Taxes have long term and short effects and both need to be given equal consideration in estimating the health of the tax system.

7. REVIEW AND ASSESSMENT OF THE HEALTH OF NEW ZEALAND'S TAX SYSTEM

7.1 Introduction

The principal objective of this Report is to determine whether the health of the tax system is improving or deteriorating, given the diverse impacts of taxation on the behaviour of individuals, firms and the economy. Because this is the first such report, the reader should exercise caution in drawing firm conclusions in view of the fact that the research will likely continue in the academic community and re-estimations of the models employed and use of revised data from Statistics NZ could change some of the results. Thus, this is an initial contribution to what can be expected to be a long debate.

All findings reported herein should be considered preliminary rather than definitive. Results are presented for the impact of the tax level and mix on: (1) the size of the hidden economy and tax evasion, the tax gap and potential revenue; (2) tax payment behaviour of corporations; and (3) economic growth and employment (the dynamic deadweight[176] loss or efficiency effects).

7.2 Measuring the "Health" of the Tax System

Measuring the health of the tax system means calculating the gap between current tax system performance and potential best practice tax system performance and the different consequences of each.

Ensuring a healthy tax system requires closing the gap between current tax policy practice (and related consequences) and "best practice" tax policy and its related consequences. This is known as the efficiency, or performance, ratio. The gap between the two is the performance gap, or the potential for improvement. At this stage of analysis, given research constraints, best practice has been defined to be that point where economic growth is maximised simultaneously with the minimisation of tax evasion. Minimising tax evasion and maximising growth both require lower tax/GDP ratios; thus, these objectives are complements rather than substitutes.

It should be emphasised that this first attempt is inevitably preliminary and incomplete. Ideally, models should also be developed to study the impact of taxes on (1) equity (intra-generational and inter-generational), (2) dynamic revenue performance, (3) compliance costs, (4) competition, including market entry and international competitiveness, and (5) administration costs. Future research should also involve detailed risk profiling of the taxpaying behaviour of firms and

[176] Static deadweight loss includes the allocative efficiency losses (distortions of consumption and investment patterns) and the technical (output) efficiency losses arising from taxation at a point in time. If these allocative and technical efficiency losses are examined across time, they become estimates of dynamic efficiency losses. There is a very long, rich academic tradition supporting this distinction that goes back to English case law (The Case of Monopolies in 1588), and which was further developed by Adam Smith, Dupuit (1844), Hotelling (1938), Hicks (1941), (Corlett & Hague, 1953), Musgrave (1959), and more recently by Tullock (1967) Bergson (1973), Ballard (1990), Dahlby (1996).

individuals. Final outputs for constructing a report on the health of a tax system should include indices for efficiency, equity, effective tax rates, compliance (representing weighted strengths and weaknesses in the corporate and personal tax bases), and *corporate* revenue forecasting variance.

Using multiple objectives, rather than a single objective, is the proper basis for establishing the overall best practice tax system. This will require calculations of complicated trade-offs, notably between equity and efficiency.

The analytical focus in the Report is on the *best practice* (frontier or level) or "optimal" level of the total tax/GDP ratio, and the tax mix (direct and indirect taxes relative to GDP). However, the optimal tax rate depends on the policy objective being sought. Comprehensive optimal tax rates and an optimal tax mix would:

- *minimise* the size of the hidden economy, the levels of tax evasion (illicit non-payment of tax) and legal tax minimisation (permissible within the bounds of the law), compliance costs and administration costs,
- *maximise* economic growth and employment, and
- *optimise* both revenue and equity given political preferences.

Meeting equity objectives may require a tax level higher than under the other two objectives. Thus, trade-offs are necessary. The variety of trade-offs required indicate the need for more research, so readers should be cautious about drawing premature conclusions from this Report concerning the optimal tax/GDP ratio and the optimal tax mix related to any specific objective. In particular, research on the role of equity in defining an optimal level of tax is incomplete, but very important for final policy considerations. As well, in a world dominated by *resource, information, financial, demographic and political* constraints, an optimal tax rate and an optimal tax mix will require even more trade-offs. Thus, any final optimal tax level and tax mix will be a second or third best solution.

Identifying optimal tax rates and an optimal mix enables an assessment of the extent to which new policy choices make things better or worse. This provides the basis for a comprehensive evaluation of the health of the tax system since the information is useful for both cost benefit analysis and risk assessment of new tax policy choices, and for clarifying the value of proposals for changing the tax system.

7.3 Key Findings on the Total Tax Level and Tax Mix

The total tax level in New Zealand is near a 100 year high. (Figure 7.1)

In 1996 the tax/GDP ratio (35%) almost matched the historic high of 36%[177] set in 1991, the peak for the last 100 years. This compares to 12% in the 1920s, 26% in the 1940s and 31% in the 1980s. Thus, over the last 70 years, the ratio has almost tripled.

[177] Excludes local taxes.

Figure 7.1
Total Tax Revenue as a Percentage of GDP in New Zealand (with Decade Averages): 1918-95

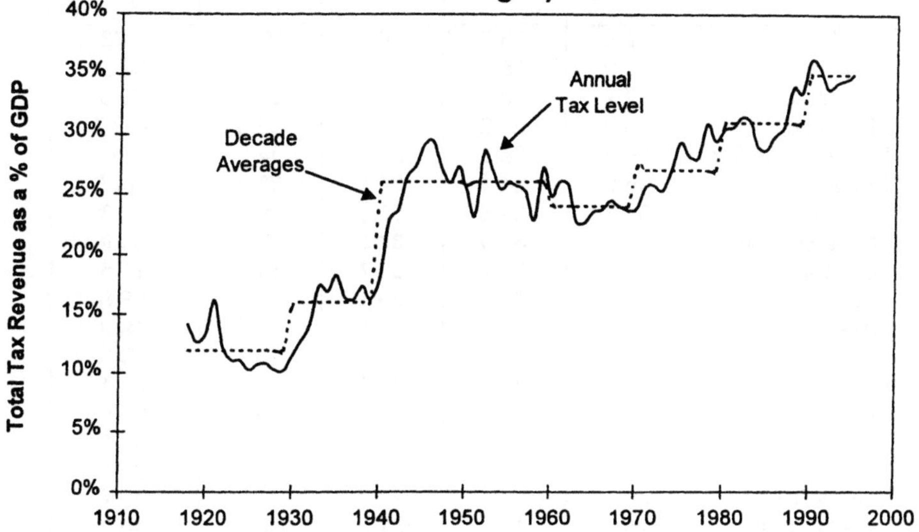

Source: NZ Institute of Economic Research, Inland Revenue, Treasury

Figure 7.2
Direct and Indirect Components of the Tax Mix as Percentages of GDP in New Zealand: 1918-95

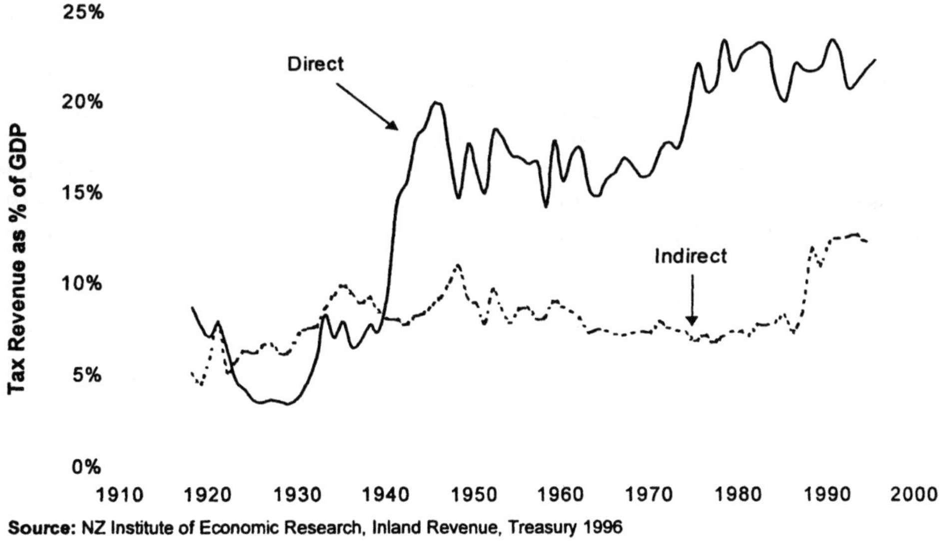

Source: NZ Institute of Economic Research, Inland Revenue, Treasury 1996

Table 7.1
Total Tax/GDP Ratios: Selected OECD Countries (incl. local taxes)%

Country	1970	1980	1990	1994	% change 1994/1970
USA	27.4	26.9	26.7	27.6	0.73
Japan	20.0	25.4	31.3	27.8	39.0
Australia	24.2	28.4	30.8	29.9	23.6
Portugal	16.2	25.2	31.0	33.0	103.7
United Kingdom	36.9	35.3	36.4	34.1	-7.6
Spain	16.9	24.1	34.4	35.8	111.8
Canada	31.3	31.6	36.5	36.1	15.3
New Zealand	**27.4**	**32.9**	**37.6**	**37.0**	**35.0**
Germany	32.9	38.2	36.7	39.3	19.5
Italy	26.1	30.2	39.1	41.7	59.8
Austria	35.7	41.2	41.3	42.8	19.9
France	35.1	41.7	43.7	44.1	25.6
Netherlands	37.0	46.3	43.6	45.9	24.1
Belgium	35.7	44.4	44.8	46.6	30.5
Finland	32.5	36.9	45.4	47.3	45.5
Sweden	39.8	48.8	55.6	51.0	28.1
Denmark	40.4	45.5	48.7	51.6	27.7
OECD AVG	**29.5**	**34.1**	**37.0**	**38.4**	**30.2**

Source: OECD, Revenue Statistics, 1996

New Zealand's tax/GDP ratio has been rising faster than the OECD average.[178]

As indicated in **Table 7.1**, only the UK and the US have had either no growth in the total tax burden relative to GDP, or a reduction, over the period 1970-94. All other countries experienced growing tax burdens. The total tax burden has grown much more rapidly in Spain (112%), Portugal (104%), Italy (60%) and Finland (46%) than in other OECD countries over the period. The average tax/GDP ratio for 18 OECD countries has risen from 29.5% in 1970 to 37% in 1990 and 38.4% in 1994. Taxes in 12 OECD countries in 1994 were at their highest level in the last 25 years, those for Australia, Canada, New Zealand and Sweden were close to their 1990 peak, and those for Japan and the UK were well below their 1990 peak. Business cycle effects will play some role in these changes.

In brief, the average tax burden of these 18 OECD countries grew by 30% in the last 25 years. NZ's tax burden rose by a slightly larger amount, 35%, over the same period. Since 1984 when the economic reforms began, the tax/GDP ratio (excluding local taxes) in NZ has risen by 6 percentage points. Of this amount 73% has been accounted for by the introduction of GST, with remaining 27% coming from corporate taxes.

[178] All OECD comparisons, including those with NZ, include local taxes.

New Zealand's 1988 tax cuts did not cut the total tax burden, but the 1996 and 1998 tax cuts likely will. The reforms in the 1980s improved the efficient allocation of resources, whereas the 1990's tax cuts are designed to improve the growth potential of the economy, and probably will.

After the personal tax cuts in 1987-88, when the top statutory rate on personal income dropped from 48% to 33%, the total tax burden still went up because of the introduction of GST and the closing of corporate tax loopholes. Thus, in New Zealand, the tax/GDP ratio rose from 30% in 1985 to 32% in 1989. The principal benefits of the 1980s tax reforms were the:

(1) reduction of distortions in the pattern of investment as a result of the removal of accelerated depreciation allowances, special industry concessions (e.g. films) and special export incentives,
(2) reduction in tax favouritism toward debt through the introduction of the imputation regime which removed the double taxation of dividends, and
(3) reduction of avoidance by the closure of loopholes (fringe benefit tax; the Controlled Foreign Corporation regime and the Foreign Investment Fund regime, and in 1991, the elimination of tax benefits on schemes involving redeemable preference shares).

The tax cuts beginning in 1996 were targeted at improving the incentives for individuals to work, invent, invest, produce and save by raising after-tax disposable income. In brief, the 1980s' tax reforms improved the allocative efficiency of New Zealand, while the 1990s' tax cuts, assuming they are implemented, are likely to improve the technical and dynamic efficiency of the economy.

The tax mix has been dominated by direct taxes since World War II. (Figure 7. 2)

Before World War II the tax mix was dominated by indirect taxes. Since then the reverse has been true. The peak in the dominance of direct taxes came in the 1970s, when $2.68 on average was raised in direct income taxes on firms and individuals for every dollar of indirect taxes (**Table 7.2**). By the 1980s, on average, only $1.85 in direct taxes was collected per dollar of indirect tax, largely because of the introduction of GST.

By 1995, largely with the help of GST, this ratio had fallen to $1.81 to $1, a level comparable to the 1940s. Thus, at present, about 64% of taxes are collected via direct taxes and about 36% via indirect taxes. This current mix may not bring NZ to the *best practice* tax policy frontier or level is close to the growth-maximising mix (Scully, 1996a; Branson & Lovell, 1997). But if tax evasion and equity preferences are taken into consideration, an alternative mix is probably required.

Within direct taxes, the dominance of personal taxes over corporate taxes peaked in 1987, when $7.15 in personal taxes was raised for every dollar of corporate taxes. By 1995 this ratio had fallen to $3.42 to $1.00. In 1995 the corporate tax/GDP ratio, at 5.1%, was just short of the high of 5.7% in 1957. Overall, the tax mix has become more balanced in the last decade as indicated in **Table 7. 2.**

Table 7. 2
Trends in the Tax Mix

Period	Direct Taxes Divided by Indirect	Personal Taxes Divided by Corporate
1890s	$0.20	--------
1900s	$0.55	$0.50 (1918-19)
1920s	$0.78	$0.51
1930s	$0.77	$1.72
1940s	$1.85	$2.33
1950s	$1.93	$2.52
1960s	$2.08	$2.22
1970s	$2.68	$4.10
1987	$2.57	$7.15
1988	$1.83	$4.74
1980s	$1.85	$6.38
1990s	$1.77	$4.43
1995	$1.81	$3.42

Source: Inland Revenue, 1996

Table 7.3
Personal Tax to GDP Ratios in OECD Countries (%)*

Country	1980	1990	1994	% change 1994/1980	
France	5.4	5.2	6.2	14.8%	(no)
Japan	6.2	8.4	6.4	3.2%	(no)
Spain	4.9	7.5	8.1	65.3%	(no)
Austria	9.5	8.7	8.4	-11.6%	(yes)
Netherlands	11.8	11.0	9.3	-21.2%	(yes)
United Kingdom	10.5	10.4	9.4	-10.5%	(yes)
USA	10.5	10.1	9.8	-6.7%	(yes)
Germany	11.3	10.1	10. 4	-8.0%	(yes)
Italy	7.0	10.3	10.6	51.4%	(no)
Australia	12.5	13.2	12.0	-4.0%	(yes)
Canada	10.8	14.9	13.4	24.1%	(no)
Belgium	15.6	14.3	14.5	-7.1%	(yes)
New Zealand	**20.3**	**17.4**	**16.6**	**-18.2%**	**(yes)**
Finland	14.3	17.5	17.5	22.4%	(no)
Sweden	20.0	21.4	18.7	-6.5%	(yes)
Denmark	23.5	25.6	27.7	17.9%	(no)
OECD Average	**12.1**	**12.9**	**12.4**		

* (excludes social security taxes)
yes: country's personal tax/GDP ratio dropped
no: country's personal tax/GDP ratio did not drop

Source: OECD Revenue Statistics, 1996

The strengthening of New Zealand's corporate tax regime has considerably enhanced the collection potential for company taxes.

NZ's corporate tax/GDP ratio is currently among the highest in the OECD and its corporate tax regime is much more efficient now at extracting tax, largely as a result of the tax policy (which closed loopholes) and audit changes since the mid-1980s.

Over the period 1980 to 1994, nine OECD countries experienced a drop in the personal tax/GDP ratio, while 7 countries witnessed an increase (**Table 7.3**). The largest drop was experienced by the Netherlands (21%), followed by NZ (18%), Austria (12%), UK (11%), Germany (8%), Belgium (7%), US (7%), Sweden (7%), and Australia (4%). The largest increase over the period was evidenced by Spain (65%), followed by Italy (51%), Canada (24%), Finland (22%), Denmark (18%), France (15%), and Japan (3%) (these results are rounded). The decreases were largely attributable to the significant drops in marginal income tax rates[179] and the reduction of the number of tax brackets.

It should be noted that NZ's tax burden on personal income is much higher than in most other OECD countries only if social security taxes are excluded. In many countries, these other taxes are an effective substitute for income taxes. When they are treated as taxes on personal income, NZ's personal tax/GDP ratio is below the OECD average.

Why are Tax Burdens at Historic Highs?

There are several explanations on both the revenue side and the expenditure side that explain why taxes have continued to grow after World War II.

During World War II, many OECD governments experienced a large increase in tax revenue because of new taxes and increased taxes used to finance the war effort. The initial success that big government had in the introduction of the welfare state in the 1930s and in the management of the war gave rise to growing confidence that government could solve many problems. Governments gradually imposed higher levels of tax in part to pay for nationalisation of industries, new infrastructure developments, and new social programs. This path cut by expanding government was reinforced by the baby boom demand for hospitals and then education facilities. Rose (1985) proposed a *law of inverse tax reform* to explain what happens as government becomes dependent on larger revenue streams. In essence, the more important the revenue source, the more difficult it is to make all but small changes: [180]

[179] The top marginal rate for the US fell from 70% to 28% in 1986, but was subsequently raised to 39.6% by President Clinton. For the UK, there was a drop from 83% to 40%, and for Australia, 60% to 47%.

[180] "The amount of change that can purposefully be introduced into a national tax structure varies inversely with its effect on total tax revenue. The more money that a tax raises, the greater its inertia force, whether in motion (a force against repeal) or stationary (a force against adoption). Conversely, the less money raised by a tax, the easier it is to alter because it will have virtually nil effect on total revenue. From a revenue perspective, tax reform is about fringe tuning; it must leave the core of revenue secure" (Rose, 1985: 316).

Rose (1985:305) also observed that new types of taxes are generally not large revenue producers: "the motive for their adoption is not to increase revenue but to promote economic activity, simplify the administration of taxation, or occasionally advance what is perceived as greater horizontal or vertical equity. Very occasionally, a new tax may balloon up, producing large revenues after it has been in effect for decades or, in the case of income tax, a century."

In New Zealand, an exception to this rule occurred with the introduction of GST. However, this was because taxpayers were promised and received a simultaneous cut in high marginal tax rates on personal income. Rose also observed that inherited obligations, the risk averse nature of politicians, among a few other factors, were most useful in explaining why taxes remain high. Each of these factors offers a partial explanation, but there are more factors that need to be analysed. What are the full range of such factors?

A complementary approach is to explain why expenditures rise and remain high. Lindbeck (1995) links the disconnection between paying tax and receiving benefits combined with an habituation to benefits by *the majority* on the demand side, and the on-going, repetitive nature of expenditure systems:

> "...in the same way that the combination of specific benefits and general financing, strengthened by the recursiveness [sequential nature of the budget process] of the spending process, all help to explain the expansion of the welfare state, the same factors all help to explain why it is politically difficult to reverse the process. An unwinding of welfare-state spending could be expected to be particularly difficult in societies where a large share of the electorate is financed by the public sector (i.e. tax-financed rather than market financed)" (Lindbeck, 1995:14).

Key factors influencing the current high level of taxes include the ambitions of politicians and bureaucrats, competition for votes and voter response, pressure group activity, crisis management, inherited obligations, risk minimisation, tax revenue buoyancy, the ratchet effect, information deficiency, tax reform fatigue and future constraints.

There appear to be at least 12 key factors that help to explain the move to high taxes in New Zealand during the last 30 years, and why taxes relative to GDP have stayed high. First, very briefly, the 6 key factors promoting higher spending and taxes are:

(1) external and domestic crises which require government intervention and additional, or perhaps extraordinary, financing;
(2) political and bureaucratic ambitions, combined with the competition among political parties for votes and the response of voters; [181]
(3) the short time horizon of politicians and bureaucrats: normally 1-3 years;
(4) tax revenue buoyancy (the joint upward effect of inflation and economic growth on taxes);
(5) pressure group activity lobbying for more government handouts and regulation favouring the group; and
(6) future constraints such as demographic trends that influence spending e.g. on superannuation and health.

---

[181] See for example Stigler (1971), Niskanen (1971) and Buchanan and Tullock (1972).

Second, there are at least 6 factors that help to ensure that taxes remain high:

(1) inherited obligations (e.g. social programs and debt servicing);
(2) the ratchet effect (it is easier to raise something than to lower it given downward constraints);
(3) risk aversion by politicians and bureaucrats (in the face of public and media criticism);
(4) taxpayer information deficiency (so that taxpayers do not have the facts about the effects of tax);
(5) tax reform fatigue among politicians and bureaucrats who tire of major changes; and
(6) the de-motivation of taxpayers who are distracted, alienated, tired of major tax reform, or evading tax because they are fed-up, opportunistic, or both.

The most important factors are the confluence of the ambitions of politicians, the competition for votes, the lobbying of pressure groups and bureaucrats, and the response of voters. But, it is external and domestic crises that have triggered the big jumps in tax revenue in New Zealand because they provide significant new opportunities for this confluence of factors to operate. Tax revenue requirements often go up during a crisis as government determines what new solutions are required to address the new problems.

The development of domestic and international constraints can force governments into a financial *crisis management* cycle, where first they borrow to raise spending to resolve a problem, and then need to raise taxes to pay for on-going debt service costs. The domestic constraints in New Zealand have included: (1) paying down the debt incurred during World War II; (2) rewarding soldiers for military service; (3) pursuing more comprehensive social and education policies; and (4) coping with the rising indebtedness stemming from the Think Big energy projects, transfers and subsidies. The international constraints that affected government expenditure included: World War II, the Korean War, the Vietnam War, the Cold War, the loss of preferential access to the UK market when it joined the EC, and the two energy crises.

Inherited obligations stem from past fiscal commitments (including interest payments) or from past commitments to new programs that require consistency and reliability of tax revenue to finance.[182]

Risk minimisation has been an important factor in maintaining high tax burdens because politicians prefer "keeping out of trouble" by avoiding the blame for, and controversy over, expenditure cutting programs (Rose, 1985:306-7).

Tax revenue buoyancy arises when tax revenue grows faster than GDP as a joint effect of economic growth, inflation and the type and rate of tax. These factors brought many people into higher tax brackets and raised more tax in the 1970s and 1980s. This "buoyancy" is a major reason for the emphasis by

[182] (Rose, 1985:304; 312)

policymakers on personal income tax, social security taxes, VAT, and sales taxes (Rose, 1985:309-10).

The ***ratchet effect***[183] is a result of *tax revenue buoyancy,* as well as political ambitions built on increasing rather than decreasing expenditures and related interest group pressure. In NZ, for example, taxes on personal income jumped considerably because of World War II and never came down afterwards. In the 1970s once the political parties began to compete for votes, they fostered the development of new lobby groups that promoted more spending.

Information deficiency plays a role in sustaining high tax burdens because it takes a considerable effort and expense to locate, assemble and analyse information about the efficiency, compliance and revenue consequences of tax changes, and the real benefits of expenditures.

Tax reform fatigue: A multiplicity of small changes and growing tax system complexity can overwhelm taxpayers, tax professionals, and politicians, reducing support for change.

Future constraints: In the future, three other factors *may* combine to restrain any downward trend in the tax/GDP ratio: (1) demographics: future social security obligations as the baby boom generation retires after the turn of the century; (2) equity considerations; and (3) the greater risk absorption role played by government as economies become more open.[184]

Total Government Expenditure Trends: 1950-2000[185]

The government expenditure to GDP ratio in New Zealand was very stable for 25 years (from 1950-1974) at an annual average of about 28%. We speculate that this level and this consistency in the government's share of the economy made an important contribution to the average 4.4% per annum real economic growth during the period. The de-stabilisation in the New Zealand economy in the 1970s and 1980s was in part created by a massive (56%) increase in the value of government expenditure relative to GDP within only 12 years (1975-87).

If we split the last half-century into two periods, before *versus* after 1975, the expenditure to GDP ratio remained below 30% in the first period, and then sky-

---

[183] (Rose, 1985:305; 314)

[184] Experience suggests that "public spending is a risk-reducing instrument on which there is greater reliance in more open economies" (Rodik, 1996:3). The quality of that spending, of course, is another matter, but it is clear that interest groups apply pressure to secure regulatory intervention to minimise the risks of external shocks. The recent policy changes in NZ appear to have reduced the need for such shock absorption, but only time will tell.

[185] How do trends in New Zealand government expenditures relative to GDP compare with other OECD governments? Over the period 1960 to 1990, for 17 OECD governments there has been a significant jump in the level of government participation in the economy (Tanzi & Schuknecht, 1997:165). In 1960 the average expenditure to GDP ratio for these countries was 27.9%, but by 1990 this had risen to 44.9%, an increase of 61%. By comparison, New Zealand climbed from 26.9% to 41.3%, for an increase of 53.5%. Thus, the role of government, during this 30 years period was advancing at a slightly lower rate than the OECD average. Nonetheless, New Zealand still advanced from 13th in 1960 to 11th place among these countries.

rocketed from 1975-1987, gradually declining until now. Over the 25 years from 1950-1974, the ratio of government expenditures to GDP was remarkably stable, staying between 26% and 29% for 23 or 25 years. It seems likely that this degree of stability, at this level, played an important role in ensuring New Zealand's 4.4% per annum growth rate for the period.

On a decade by decade basis, in the 1950s, the government expenditure to GDP ratio averaged about 27.8%, in the 1960s about 27.5%, in the 1970s about 34%, in the 1980s about 39.5%, and 36.7% in the first half of the 1990s. For the last half of the decade, the figure is expected to be 34% of GDP.

Even under the reformist Labour Government (1984-90), expenditures were not cut, rather they were reallocated as government corporatised and privatised parts of the public sector, liberalised and de-regulated the private sector, and had to cope with the transitional expenditures for the big leap in unemployment, the rising superannuation bill bequeathed by the Muldoon government, and higher public debt service payments. The expenditure to GDP ratio also remained high (at about 38%) for the first 2 years of the National government in 1991-92.

The expenditure/GDP ratio rose by 56% over the period 1974-1987, peaking at 44.2%. By any measure, this is a massive and quick increase in the role of government in a short period. Such a shift in the balance of power between the market and the government was bound to have important long term negative consequences. This great intervention was strategically unplanned and not managed in a scientific fashion. That is to say, there was no proper cost benefit analysis and risk assessment of the potential long term consequences of this major increase in government intrusion in the economy.

In 1974-75, the expenditure to GDP ratio rose to 34.9%, an increase of 23% over the previous year. The immediate causes were the government's response to the economic consequences of first energy crisis in 1973-74, continuing problems related to New Zealand's loss of preferential access to the UK market along with the, and, perhaps most importantly, the expenditure consequences of the strong competition for votes by the Labour and National parties using a more activist social policy agenda.

The initial expenditure jump in New Zealand in the last half of the 1970s was principally caused by new spending on transfers, secondarily by current expenditures, and thirdly by the energy projects.

From the end of March 1975 until 30 March 1979, social security transfers relative to GDP recorded the largest rise among the three major categories of expenditure, increasing by 47%. Current expenditures jumped by 32% and capital expenditures by 15%. Thus, the principal cause of the big spend-up in the late 1970s was social policy spending, subsidies (including energy prices) and not capital spending on energy projects. In other words, the government was borrowing (increasingly overseas) to finance consumption, not long term profitable investment.

As a result of this major increase in government's share of the economy, the somewhat careless expenditures from 1975-1992 eliminated much of the gains of the previous 25 years, sharply reducing the per capita income of New Zealanders, and brought the country close to a debt crisis given the response of creditors after 1984. The general consequences were higher inflation, increased regulation, lower growth (a drop of perhaps as much as 2 percentage points), an increase of 50% in the national debt, a two and a half times increase in interest payments, a major credit rating downgrade, and a massive (67%) devaluation of the exchange rate. The government's higher share in the economy was unsustainable.

The cost of the 56% increase in the size of government was approximately $100 billion in terms of lost growth of GDP, higher debt and higher interest payments, a lower credit rating and a weak currency. This should be considered a rough estimate requiring further modelling refinements.

If we stop the clock back in 1993 and add up the cost of this great intervention period, rounding off, we would add possibly as much as $34 billion in foregone economic wealth as a result of lower growth rates, $29 billion in higher total public debt, and $37 billion in financing costs on the public debt over the period 1975-1993 (19 years). This represents an estimated cost of $100 billion for the mistakes made in government intervention in the 19 years from 1975-1993. This represents a loss of $5.3 billion per year, or $1500 per person in New Zealand per year. This should be considered a rough estimate, based on one set of assumptions, that requires modelling refinements. The estimate does not explicitly include the higher borrowing costs owing to the reduction in New Zealand's credit rating, and the higher costs of importing owing to the currency devaluation, although it could be argued that these factors are captured in the growth rate loss mentioned above.

New Zealand has still not recovered its triple A credit rating that it lost when it was first down-graded in April 1983 by Standard & Poor's. This means that the government is still paying an interest premium on foreign loans, as are many private sector New Zealand borrowers in overseas markets. Likewise the exchange rate has also not recovered to its 1982 pre-crisis level.

Long Term Future Expenditure Requirements and the Tax/GDP Ratio

Given expected (including superannuation) expenditures, and assuming no cuts, the tax/GDP ratio over the next 50 years can be expected to range between 30%-38% of GDP.

Various expenditure to GDP scenarios were prepared by NZIER for the 1997 interim report of the Retirement Income Periodic Review Group. Those scenarios make a number of assumptions about the budget balance and the level of public debt. In general, the model results indicate that superannuation payments, a major part of future government expenditures over the next 50 years, will not begin to have an important impact on government budgets until between 2015 and 2020 when the baby boom generation begins to retire.

After 2020, government operating expenditure[186] (including superannuation, health, education, social welfare and other core activities, but excluding debt servicing costs and capital expenditures) is expected to rise gradually to between 36%-40% of GDP by 2050. This projection assumes no expenditure cuts from current levels.

Future cost benefit analysis of government programs should explore the gap between the growth maximising tax rate floor of about 20% for the tax/GDP ratio and the maximum expected expenditure ceiling of about 38% of GDP to determine ways of reconciling the two (in the context of various scenarios for national fees, national debt and economic growth).

In the interim, 1998-2015, there is the potential for a lengthy period of a stable expenditure to GDP ratio between 29%-33%, as compared to about 34% in 1997. This leaves scope for reducing the public debt and lowering taxes and fees over the next 10 years without harming government's major social policy objectives. The gap between these tax/GDP ratios and the growth–maximising tax rates of 20-23% of GDP, identified elsewhere in this Report, is the basis for an analysis of the opportunity cost (in terms of reduced growth and wealth generation) of remaining at these levels of expenditure (assuming a balanced budget). Ultimately, while tax policy must be responsive to expenditure policy, expenditure policy must be fiscally responsible because of the deleterious effects that rising taxes have on growth, employment, investment, tax avoidance, tax evasion and ethical standards in the country.

What are the Current Concerns about Taxes in Major OECD Countries?

One of the principal themes in this Report is that high taxes have negative effects on growth, employment and tax evasion. Are there similar concerns in other countries?

Governments in OECD countries are increasingly concerned about the impact of taxes on labour force participation, technological innovation, savings and investment.

In 1996 NZ introduced a package of tax cuts affecting personal income, reflecting a desire to promote sustainable economic growth and to improve the overall efficiency performance of the economy by improving incentives to work, save and invest[187]. Similar pressure for reducing direct taxes to promote investment, growth and employment is building in key OECD countries with both

[186] These projections are based on Treasury's Long Term Fiscal Model and exclude capital expenditure.

[187] Countries are now much more sensitive to the need to keep tax burdens in line with those in other countries, as evidenced by the wave of cuts to statutory tax rates and the reductions of the number of tax rates in most OECD countries following UK and US moves in the 1980s. Denmark (1987), Sweden (1991), Norway (1992) and Finland (1993) have all reduced tax on capital income to 30% or less in order to maintain their tax competitiveness vis-a-vis each other. In 1989, for example, Germany faced serious problems when it imposed a 10% withholding tax on interest that triggered a massive outflow of funds to Luxembourg which has no such tax. (Denmark faced a similar problem in 1988 with respect to the Netherlands). (*Financial Times*, 24 December 1996, p2).

moderately high tax/GDP ratios (Japan: 28%) and high tax/GDP ratios (Germany: 39%; and France: 44%).

In Britain, in July 1997 the new Labour government lowered the starting rate on personal income tax to 10%.[188] As well, the tax on corporate profits was cut by 2 percentage points to 31%, while the rate for small business was also reduced by 2 percentage points to 21%. But, overall, with the utility tax and the elimination of refundable dividend tax credits for pension plans and non-resident investors, the tax burden will likely go up. Ireland, which has had its first-ever budget surplus, has cut the standard rate of income tax by one percentage point to 26%, while corporate tax will fall by 2 percentage points to 36%. In 1996, former Prime Minister Alain Juppe said that France needed to lower its tax burdens on individuals to improve economic performance: "We need to give additional purchasing power to all those who are holding back from spending or investing because their tax burdens are too great. We need to encourage those who work, who invent, who create, who invest - in summary those who make the country tick". In the 1997 French national elections, the Socialists took over and soon raised the corporate income tax rate to 41.6% from 36.6%. This emergency two-year increase is designed to reduce the public sector deficit to 3% of GDP and help France meet its fiscal targets for the planned single European currency.

In Germany in 1996, Chancellor Helmut Kohl raised the need to lower taxes (worth about US$16.3 billion) beginning in 1999 in order to improve employment growth and competitiveness. He said that his " 'first and most important goal' was to lower the excessive burden of taxes to help the individual citizen, boost the economy and create jobs". This sentiment was supported later in the year by prominent economic institutes and industrial associations in Germany: "Germany faces higher industrial unemployment in the new year, with 90,000 job losses in construction alone, unless incentives to industry are created by lower taxation and reduced labour cost, economic institutes and industrial bodies warned yesterday".

Germany's plans to cut taxes recently fell victim to political positioning prior to the September 1998 election, to party rivalry over amendments in the Bundesrat (the Upper House controlled by the Social Democrats) and to weaker economic performance and lower tax revenue. No substantive changes are expected before the election. By August 1997 concern over the delay led the Bundesbank, Germany's central bank, to put pressure on the German Government to

"...correct the mistakes of the past' by lowering taxes and social security levies, cutting bureaucracy and continuing efforts towards wage moderation and labour flexibility. This would enable Germany to participate successfully in the competition among advanced industrial nations to present themselves as attractive investment locations...In its tax criticism the bank dismissed arguments that the necessary shift in the burden from income to consumption taxes would be unfair. Instead, the present opaque system helped those adept at tax avoidance, it said".[189]

---

[188] The sources for the following country by country analysis are the *Financial Times* (4 August 1997; 3 July 1997, p17; 23 January 1997; 6 Sept. 1996; 22 July 1997; 19 Aug. 1996; 23 Dec. 1996; 30 July 1997; 8 Oct. 1996, p.15).
[189] *Financial Times* 14 August 1997. p.2.0

In the United States, a new tax cut package was agreed in mid-year between the President and the Congress. The tax savings, which are affordable given the booming economy, will cost the Treasury about 0.3% of GDP per annum. The cuts include special tax credits for families with children, students, and retirement saving, as well as a reduction of the capital gains tax rate from 28 to 20%. A bipartisan committee has been set up to examine potential cuts in entitlements programs (health, welfare, social security, food stamps etc).

The proposed new German tax reform strategy is one that New Zealand adopted 11 years ago: much lower income tax rates with a broader base, higher indirect taxes, and simplification of the tax system. According to the Minister of Finance, Theo Waigel, Germany "...must get rid of everything that hollows out the tax base and makes fools of those who pay their taxes honestly".[190] The need for lower taxes is also a concern in Japan. In late 1995 Prime Minister Tomiichi Murayama observed that Japan's corporate tax rate was too high[191]: "We recognise... that a high corporate tax in comparison with international standards is problematic".[192] The total tax burden faced by Japanese companies is about 50% of profits, with 37.5% going to the national government and 12.5% of profits going to local government. In August 1997 Japan's Ministry of Finance proposed a reduction in the national corporate tax rate from 37.5% to 35% in order to improve business competitiveness. Pressure is on the government to increase the value added tax from 3% to 5% in order to reduce the fiscal deficit.

Implications of High Tax Rates

Higher taxes have long and short term effects that policy decisions need to take into consideration, including the impact on international relativities, and fairness to wage and salary earners. Higher taxes do not guarantee balanced budgets.

High marginal tax rates yield little revenue, promote increased tax evasion and legal tax minimisation, and create inefficiency by reducing the incentives to work, hire, invent, save and invest. As well, inflation-related bracket creep drags too many taxpayers into higher tax brackets. Finally, growing international capital mobility has sensitised countries to the need to avoid being at a competitive disadvantage with other countries in terms of tax burdens on mobile capital.

Higher tax burdens do not guarantee that governments will balance the budget and that debt will be reduced. OECD countries now all have both higher tax/GDP ratios, fiscal deficits and public debt than they did in the 1960s, 1970s, and

---

[190] *Financial Times*, 8 October 1996, p.15. Germany proposes to cut the top marginal rate of income tax from 53% to 39%; the lowest marginal rate would fall from 26% to 15% for earnings between US$8-12,000, the tax rate for small business and retained earnings of large firms would drop between 10-12 percentage points to 35%, while the rate for distributed earnings for large firms would fall to 25% from 30%. If approved, the changes would take effect in January 1998, with final effect 1 year later. These are Germany's lowest tax rates in 50 years. The VAT would rise 1 percentage point to 16%. (*Financial Times*, 24 January 1997). Although the top rates for income tax on business profits and corporate tax on retained earnings would be cut to 40 per cent from 46.7 per cent and 45 per cent respectively, business would be faced with less generous depreciation and loss carry-forward rules (*Financial Times* 23 June 1997).

[191] At 87% of GDP Japan's gross public debt is also very high.

[192] *Financial Times*, 14 November 1995.

1980s. This is a key reason why the Fiscal Responsibility Act in New Zealand is so important.

The global economy began to become a reality within the last twenty years given the liberalisation of exchange rates, capital market controls, and foreign investment legislation. In this changing regulatory environment, businesses and portfolio investment have become much more mobile. In response, governments have altered the tax mix, giving more emphasis to tax on less mobile factors, notably labour (including social security, payroll and consumption taxes).

While more research is necessary about the impact of higher tax burdens in the last 25 years, the preliminary messages are that: (1) we must take seriously all of the short and long term incentive effects of higher taxes, including the effects on taxpayer honesty and tax evasion, work, production, inventions and investment; (2) high tax rates do not guarantee balanced budgets; (3) corporate and personal tax rates should be close to each other and must be sensitive to what is done in other countries; and (4) tax rates must be fair to wage and salary earners. The general implications are that politicians need to ensure that people get value for money when they spend taxpayers' money. The remaining sections of this Report outline some of the key incentive effects of tax on tax evasion and growth and employment.

7.4 Key Findings on the Hidden Economy and Tax Evasion

Enhanced compliance is dependant first and foremost on lower tax burdens, and then on the credibility of government expenditures, an appropriate penalties regime, and scientific audit selection.

Key factors promoting tax compliance include providing evidence that there is a reduction of tax evasion (some progress has been made in this area), ensuring that government provides value for money in its expenditures (some progress), lower tax burdens (some progress), a tough but fair penalties regime (introduced in 1997), tough but fair and realistic disclosure requirements regime (not currently an issue), requiring deductions at source (well in hand), and introducing a scientific-based audit selection approach based on risk analysis of all taxpayers using the taxpayer databases (some initial models have been developed but much more progress is possible). The key to compliance is to ensure that the tax burden is set at the right level with the right mix of direct and indirect taxes and to ensure the implementation of scientific audit selection, based on probability analysis of highest to lowest risk taxpayers. If the tax burden is set low enough the credibility of government expenditures and the penalties regime are no longer serious issues.

The scale of NZ's hidden economy grew until recently, but lies in the lower part of the range estimated for overseas countries. The tax-sensitive sector of the hidden economy, which generates tax evasion from the non-reporting or under-reporting of income and transactions, is larger than the illicit-activity sector in the hidden economy, which arises from organised and petty criminal activity, including white collar crime.

While fluctuating considerably over the last 25 years, NZ's hidden economy, based on modelled estimates (Giles, 1996), grew by about 3.5 percentage points of measured GDP, jumping from 7.8% of GDP in 1969 to just over 11% in 1994, or about $9.2 billion (**Figure 7.3**), and, it is estimated, fell to about 10.8% in 1995. The long run average (1969-94) has been estimated at 8.8% of measured GDP, but it is *not* a good indicator of current trends. These macro estimates of the size of hidden economic activity have been corroborated by estimates using audited taxpayer databases for evaders and non-evaders (Giles, 1997:15-16). Caragata & Small's (1996) non-linear model confirm that an increase in the tax/GDP ratio increases the size of the hidden economy and reduces economic growth in New Zealand.

The total value of goods and services produced in the hidden economy is accounted for by both under-reporting and non-reporting of income and transactions by the *tax-sensitive sector*, and by the non-reporting of income and transactions in the *illicit sector*. Tax-sensitive sector activity is largely the evasion activity of individuals, the self-employed and small businesses, although some larger firms may be involved. The illicit-sector activity involves petty and organised criminal activity.

This is an estimate of the value of the goods and services subject to theft[193] and fraud against private business and persons, related income not reported by employers, and various types of criminal activity including illegal drug activity, prostitution, and protection rackets. This analysis is, therefore, an assessment of the *benefits of crime* rather than the *costs of crime*[194] (excluding fraud against government which is implicitly recorded in the total value of government transfers), and the non-reporting of income for purposes of tax evasion.

During the period 1990-94, the average size of the hidden economy was 9.5% of GDP (about $7.1 billion). The increase in the size of the hidden economy, to around 11% of GDP in 1994, reflects historically high tax levels and the fact that the hidden economy rises and falls with the business cycle. The decline in 1995, to just under 11% of measured GDP, reflects slower economic growth.

Most overseas studies of the hidden economy took place 15-20 years ago when inflation first began to be a serious problem. At that time, the estimated range for the size of the hidden economy in OECD countries was between 7% and 16% of GDP (Giles, 1996). Higher tax burdens, higher inflation and more government regulation, combined with improving economic growth, since the late 1970s

---

[193] According to security industry specialists, "research in the United Kingdom indicates that only a small portion of retail theft is actually discovered by apprehending the culprit and that staff theft is an even bigger problem than customer theft". NZ faces a similar problem (Steeman, 1995:6). Thus, a considerable amount of theft and fraud is not reported in the measured economy and thus becomes a basis for financing activity in the hidden economy.

[194] This contrasts with an NZIER report, which deals with the costs of crime. Those costs largely, but not exclusively, deal with the costs to victims and government (Yeabsley, Duncan and Mears, 1995). Their estimate of $5 billion per annum is not comparable to the estimate of about $4 billion per year in this Report. The NZIER estimate, for example, includes $900 million for road-related deaths and injuries, and $298 million for the psychological and other costs incurred by victims of crime such as homicides. Some of their figures, however, do get at the benefits. The Serious Fraud Office estimates that white-collar crime is well above $700 million per year. Shoplifting is very conservatively estimated by NZIER at $300 million per year.

appear to have raised that range to between 10%-25% of measured GDP by the mid-1990s. This would mean that most western economies are probably experiencing a larger hidden economy and higher tax evasion than 20 years ago.

New Zealand's hidden economy and tax evasion problems are near the low-end of the present estimated range for the OECD. At 11% of GDP in 1995 New Zealand's hidden economy (and thus its tax evasion problems) is near the low-end of the estimated range for the OECD. Relative to GDP, New Zealand's underground economy is larger than estimates for Switzerland and Austria (7%), just below the size of the hidden economy in Canada,[195] Britain, Japan, the USA, Australia, the Netherlands, Germany, France, Ireland and Denmark (11%-15%), and much lower than Norway and Sweden (about 18% of GDP), and Belgium, Spain and Italy (22- 26% of GDP).[196]

Preliminary estimates suggest that, in 1994, tax-sensitive sector activity reached a value of about 7.3% of measured GDP (about $5.9 billion) in 1994, and an average of 5.5% of GDP ($4 billion) over the period 1990-94. Illicit sector activity reached an estimated 4% of measured GDP in 1994, or $3.3 billion, and an average of 4% of GDP over the 1990-94 period. The ratio of total taxes divided by measured GDP multiplied by the level of hidden activity yields estimates of the level of tax evasion.

There appears to be a long-term upward trend for tax evasion. The chief causes of the rising hidden economy and tax evasion, in order of importance, would appear to be historically high and rising tax burdens, inflation, rising disposable income (given the recent strong growth in NZ), and an apparent change in ethical standards. IRD prosecutions are estimated to have reduced the growth in tax evasion.

The principal causes (Giles, 1996) of the upward trend in New Zealand's hidden economy are estimated to be a tax/GDP ratio (excluding local taxes) increase of 12 percentage points (from 24% of GDP in 1968 to about 34.6% in 1994), rising inflation until the late 1980s[197], increased government regulation and, more recently, rapidly rising disposable income[198] as the economy recovered from the serious recession of 1991-92. It would also appear that these changes may have helped to induce changes in ethical standards. As the modelling indicates (Giles,1996), the key determining factor affecting the size of the hidden economy is the tax level, and not the rate of inflation. The change in the level of disposable income, that fluctuates with the business cycle, acts as an explosive catalyst resonating with public reaction to the rising level of tax and regulation (and inflation when it is a problem) to generate more hidden economic activity and tax evasion. These causal relations are discussed further below.

---

[195] Another recent estimate for Canada placed the size of the hidden economy between 8-11% of GDP (Spiro, 1994).

[196] *The Economist*, "Light on the Shadows", 3 May 1997 p. 63-64.

[197] The fact that low inflation in the last 5 years has not led to an appreciable drop in the size of the hidden economy underlines the importance in the tax burden's effect on informal economic activity.

[198] Short term adjustments are generally most responsive to changes in disposable income.

In the hidden economy, the tax evasion problem caused by individuals, the self-employed, small firms and criminal activity is growing. Total tax evasion also fluctuated over the last 25 years, but rose by 2 percentage points of GDP, from 1.8% of GDP in 1969 to 3.9% in 1994, and averaged 3.3% of GDP over the period 1990-94 (about $2.5 billion per annum). Tax evasion is increasingly dominated by *tax-sensitive sector evasion* (by individuals, the self-employed and small businesses), as compared to *illicit-activity sector evasion* (by criminal elements) (**Table 7.4**). More research is needed to refine the estimates.

Extensive modelling suggests that the rising aggregate tax burden relative to total GDP is the most significant factor promoting tax evasion, followed in order of importance by inflation, changes in the level of *per capita* disposable income, unemployment rates, and the degree of regulatory intrusion by government. In addition, changes in measured real GDP would appear to cause similar changes in the size of the hidden economy. On the other hand changes in the size of the hidden economy appear to have only a mild effect on the size of measured GDP (Giles, 1996).

Econometric evidence (Giles, 1996) suggests that the hidden economy is pro-cyclical. It expands when the business cycle improves, and declines relatively when there is an economic downturn. This important finding suggests that acceleration in the size of the hidden economy can sometimes (if there is no change in taxes, regulations or inflation) be caused largely by rising opportunities to make and disguise income, assuming that tax rates are held constant and inflation is reasonably stable. Thus, when explosive growth takes place, as occurred in 1993-1995, hidden economy activity and tax evasion should be expected to rise unless taxes are lowered, inflation is stable, and regulation reduced.

The size of the hidden economy and IRD prosecutions, which historically have a high conviction rate, have been modelled (Giles, 1996b). The results indicate that IRD takes a pro-active, rather than reactive, approach to offences against the Revenue Acts, and that these prosecutions shrink the size of the hidden economy and tax evasion. The 1997 penalties regime should also help.

But, for New Zealand, a hidden economy just below 11% of GDP is still large. Unreported activity reduces government revenue significantly. Reducing tax evasion can be viewed as an alternative source for raising tax revenue, instead of raising taxes. But there are other important implications of the hidden economy. Tax evasion is patently unfair to honest taxpayers because it leads to an inequitable distribution of the tax burden.[199] The longer high levels of tax evasion persist, the greater is the threat to public confidence in the tax system, and the higher is the risk that tax evasion will become more widespread.

Addressing the problem will most likely require some combination of: (1) public education, (2) higher ethical standards (tax evasion is illegal – it is not a sporting

[199] For this reason public support for enforcement is generally strong.

activity), (3) a reasonable tax rate level[200] and appropriate tax mix, (4) adequate resources for tax and social policy design, police and tax audit enforcement and public education, (5) more comprehensive use of the *deduction at source* approach[201] (e.g. PAYE), (6) minimising inflation, (7) minimising government regulations with high compliance costs, (8) ensuring that taxpayers get value for money in government expenditures, (9) tougher asset seizure laws for criminal property, and (10) perhaps a more rapid move towards a cash-less society. The longer tax evasion habits are ingrained, the harder they will be to change. This implies that there will be a lag effect when the total tax burden is lowered.

7.5 Sources of Tax Evasion

Tax-sensitive sector evasion by individuals and small firms has been rising more rapidly than illicit-activity sector tax evasion by criminals. (Table 7.4)

Tax-sensitive sector tax evasion, among individuals, the self-employed and small business, is motivated solely by the potential savings from eliminating or reducing tax burdens. Illicit-activity sector tax evasion is connected to criminal activity (including organised crime), which is motivated by factors which are generally more important to criminals than tax savings. Tax-sensitive sector tax evasion rose from 0.9% of GDP in 1969 to 2.5% in 1994, while illicit-activity sector tax evasion rose from about 1% of GDP (1969) to 1.4% (1994).

In 1969 tax-sensitive sector evasion accounted for 48% of the total tax evasion gap, while illicit-activity sector evasion accounted for 52%. By 1994 tax-sensitive sector evasion had risen to 64% of the total tax evasion gap, while illicit-activity sector evasion slipped to 36% (**Table 7.4**). The shift in emphasis is probably attributable to rising economic opportunities for individuals and firms coupled with their response to the rising total tax burden and higher marginal tax rates.

How viable are the estimates of the size of the criminal activity? Overseas studies suggest that 1% to 6% of total sales, or 2.5-12% of GDP, is lost by private business each year from managerial, employee and customer theft and fraud. A very preliminary analysis suggests that about 1.4% of sales, or 3.5% of GDP, is a working hypothesis for NZ pending further research.

The modelled estimate of the illicit-activity sector of the hidden economy is 4.2% of GDP, and thus if fraud and theft alone represent 3.5% of GDP, then roughly 83% of the activity in the illicit sector of the hidden economy is based on theft and fraud.

This would mean that other forms of criminal activity (such as protection rackets, illegal gambling, drug trafficking, prostitution and miscellaneous theft from

[200] High tax evasion is a signal that people want lower taxes. But lower taxes will not eliminate tax evasion; rather evasion will be better controlled and less widespread.

[201] For example, a contractor's withholding tax. Deduction at source (including PAYE for salary and wage earners, and interest and dividend withholding taxes) is the lynchpin of the modern tax system, because it ensures high levels of compliance.

Figure 7.3
The Size of the Hidden Economy as a Percentage of GDP - Annual Estimates and 5-Year Moving Averages: 1968-94

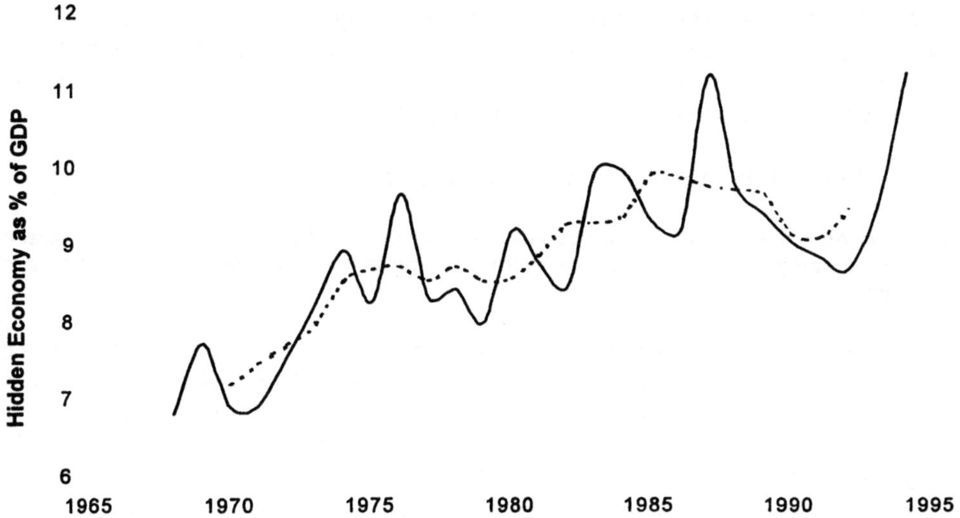

Source: Giles, 1996

Table 7.4
The Tax Evasion Gap Challenge: 1969-94

	A Total Tax Evasion Gap/GDP	B Tax-Sensitive Sector Evasion Tax Gap/GDP	C B/A (%)	D Illicit Activity Sector Tax Evasion Gap/GDP (A-B)
1969	1.84	0.89	48.4	0.95
1970	1.66	0.70	42.2	0.96
1971	1.78	0.76	42.7	1.02
1972	1.96	0.93	47.5	1.03
1973	2.10	1.09	51.9	1.01
1974	2.43	1.35	55.6	1.08
1975	2.44	1.27	52.1	1.17
1976	2.75	1.62	58.9	1.13
1977	2.36	1.23	52.1	1.13
1978	2.62	1.38	52.7	1.24
1979	2.36	1.19	50.4	1.17
1980	2.81	1.59	56.6	1.22
1981	2.69	1.47	54.7	1.22
1982	2.67	1.42	53.2	1.25
1983	3.21	1.93	60.1	1.28
1984	2.98	1.79	60.1	1.19
1985	2.81	1.61	57.3	1.20
1986	2.87	1.63	56.8	1.24
1987	3.57	2.30	64.4	1.27
1988	3.38	2.00	59.2	1.38
1989	3.22	1.86	57.8	1.36
1990	3.32	1.86	56.0	1.46
1991	3.16	1.74	55.1	1.42
1992	2.97	1.61	54.2	1.36
1993	3.26	1.90	58.3	1.36
1994	3.94	2.54	64.5	1.40

Source: Inland Revenue, 1996

residential property, auto theft and theft from private cars) would account for only 17% of illicit sector activity. This suggests that the estimate of the size of illicit-activity sector in the hidden economy should be considered conservative.

More research is required to distinguish between evasion by individuals and firms, to develop risk profiles of firms engaging in tax evasion and legal tax minimisation, to estimate systematically the strengths and weaknesses of the corporate tax base, to develop scientific tax audit selection using systematic risk profiling, and to improve forecasting of corporate revenue. All of these can be achieved using taxpayer data and probability analysis.

7.6 Tax Evasion Responses to Tax Changes

A cut in the tax/GDP ratio is more potent than a change in the tax mix (direct vs. indirect tax) in reducing tax evasion. GST is more powerful than income taxes in curtailing tax evasion.

A cut in the total tax burden (relative to GDP) appears to have a more potent effect on reducing the hidden economy and tax evasion than does a shift in the tax mix to favour greater use of indirect tax. A combination of both of these options has a greater effect than either option being applied alone in reducing both the hidden economy and tax evasion (Caragata & Giles, 1996). A combination of a reduced tax/GDP ratio and a tax mix favouring indirect taxes, along with improved tax policy and tax auditing, would reduce tax evasion more than any single measure. This suggests it is important to develop multi-faceted approaches to solve complex problems.

Any increase in taxation, regardless of type, would increase the size of the hidden economy. But, for a given dollar value of tax increase, some taxes have less of an effect than others on the hidden economy. Thus, if GST had not been introduced in New Zealand 1986, the size of the hidden economy would have been less relative to GDP than it was following the introduction of GST. However, if the GST had not been introduced and the equivalent revenue had been obtained instead from increased personal or corporate taxes, the relative size of the hidden economy would have been greater than under the GST option. Thus, a tax mix emphasizing indirect taxes increases the hidden economy less than a mix emphasizing direct taxes, holding the total tax take constant (Giles & Caragata, 1996).

In general, there appear to be more opportunities and fewer constraints for individuals and firms to minimise income tax as compared to indirect tax. First, personal income is often easier to disguise than a sales transaction, although, of course, there are exceptions. Second, because income tax is more complex than a sales tax, various factors can be used to adjust income (deductions can be inflated, transfer prices manipulated, equity disguised as debt and vice versa, financial structures redesigned etc). Third, taxpayers are more motivated to protect their income from all incursions such as taxation because income is a personal possession (and therefore treated as a property right) and a tax on such income is perceived to be a direct threat to a personal possession. By contrast, a tax on a consumption item is not. Fourth, income tax evasion carries a higher reward and a lower risk of getting caught than sales tax evasion because there is a greater information deficiency problem for the tax authority with respect to personal income outside of PAYE schemes, as compared to GST where detailed records are required to be kept (Caragata, 1997).

As a result of these elements of control, possession, reward and risk, the opportunities and constraints favour the choice of income tax evasion as compared to consumption tax evasion. Hence, individuals and small business probably devote more learning time to income tax evasion instead of indirect tax evasion, reinforcing their preference for, or the hope for higher rewards from, income tax evasion. Finally, a GST collects tax on spending in the measured economy based on earnings in the hidden economy.[202]

The NZ experience with the introduction of GST indicates evasion is more easily controlled as the share of indirect taxes in the total rises. This experience is different from Canada for a number of important reasons. The GST in Canada was not compensated by simultaneous income tax cuts and GST was visibly displayed on all items for sale. This was not the case in NZ.

In Canada a number of factors combined to generate resentment about the new GST. First, Canada introduced a 7% GST in 1991 without providing simultaneous cuts in personal income tax. In 1986 when NZ introduced the GST, income tax rates were simultaneously reduced.[203] Second, GST charges were not embedded into the marked sales price of goods in Canada. By contrast, in New Zealand, in the majority of cases, the GST is embedded in the marked price of goods. The visibility of Canada's GST meant there was a constant reminder of the tax. On the other hand, the *relative* GST effect on consumption in Canada was magnified by a much lower US-Canadian dollar exchange rate than is the case today.

Informal evidence suggests that as a result of the introduction of GST in Canada, border smuggling and tax evasion increased. In Canada there is a long, undefended border that is quite permeable to smuggling activity. As well, a very large percentage of Canadians live within 300 kilometres of the US border. As a result of the introduction of GST, many Canadians took advantage of lower cross-border tax-inclusive prices in the US and smuggled items back to Canada to avoid federal GST and high provincial sales taxes. New Zealand, by contrast, has no other country bordering the territorial boundary.

The hidden economy poses threats that require a serious response. Reducing tax evasion is another way of raising revenue. Given constraints, perhaps as much as 70% of the tax gap can be eliminated.

---

[202] These results are supported by empirical models (based on New Zealand data) developed by Caragata and Giles (1996). Their findings contradict the general equilibrium model results of Kesselman (1993:131) whose work is theoretically speculative, based on unrealistic assumptions and not empirical: "...changing the tax mix will have little or none of the claimed anti-evasion or distributional effects. Increased indirect taxes on evaders' consumption purchases will be shifted onto suppliers in the compliant sector. Evaders will end up evading less income taxes but evading more indirect taxes".

[203] For personal income taxpayers the top marginal rate fell from 66% to 33%. There were also changes to the corporate tax scale.

Unchecked, the hidden economy and tax evasion can pose a serious threat to fiscal and monetary policy and to the credibility of the tax system and government.[204] As unreported activity and tax evasion grow, the government has less control over economic management (higher deficits because of evaded taxes and less control over the money supply) and risks having to pay a high price later when greater intervention is needed.

There may also be a potential threat to the integrity of the police, the judiciary and politicians because of the rising level of hidden economic activity *if bribery becomes common*. In addition, reducing tax evasion could permit an increase in government spending or a reduction in taxes.

The total tax evasion gap, unadjusted for risk, averaged 3.3% of GDP over 1990-94 (about $2.5 billion) and rose to 3.9% of GDP in 1994. It should not be assumed that the total tax evasion gap could be closed, given information constraints, scarce financial resources, and scarce skilled auditing and tax policy resources. Assuming no constraints, it is estimated that, roughly 6.6% more revenue was collectable in 1970, 8.4% in 1980, 8.4% in 1990 and 10% in 1994 (**Table 7.5**). This 10% macro estimate of the tax gap has been confirmed by Giles (1997:16) using audit-tax payer data bases of tax evaders and non-evaders.

Table 7.5
Gross Estimate of Static Potential Tax Revenue for New Zealand (% of GDP), (excluding legal tax minimisation)

	a Total Tax	b Potential Tax Evasion Gap		a + b Revenue		Performance Ratio (current/potential)	
		100%	70%*	100%	70%	100% Gap Closure	70% Gap* Closure
1970	23.9	1.7	1.2	25.6	25.1	93.4	95.2
1975	29.3	2.4	1.7	31.7	31.0	92.4	94.5
1980	30.4	2.8	2.0	33.2	32.4	91.6	93.8
1985	28.7	2.8	2.0	31.5	30.7	91.1	93.5
1990	36.2	3.3	2.3	39.5	38.5	91.6	94.0
1991	35.6	3.2	2.2	38.8	37.8	91.8	94.2
1992	33.8	3.0	2.1	36.8	35.9	91.8	94.2
1993	34.2	3.3	2.3	37.5	36.5	91.2	93.7
1994	35.0	3.9	2.7	38.9	37.7	90.0	92.8

* Risk adjusted tax gap. This adjustment takes into consideration various information, resource, time, political and other constraints that impede perfect tax collection. It assumes that 70% of illicit-activity sector criminal tax evasion and 70% of the tax-sensitive sector tax evasion among individuals, the self-employed and small firms, can be eliminated.

Source: Inland Revenue, 1997

204 Caragata (1995) examined the impact of these problems which, among other factors, contributed to the subsequent crisis in Albania.

These estimates should be adjusted for the risk or probability of collection. Current analysis suggests that it is prudent to assume that only about 70% of the gross tax evasion gap is actually collectable. Taking this assumption into consideration produces what cab be referred to as a risk-adjusted tax evasion gap[205].

Using this risk adjusted basis, the tax gap would fall from 3.9% to 2.7% of GDP in 1994 (**Table 7.5**). On this basis, roughly 4.8% (as compared to 6.6%) more revenue could have been collected in 1970, 6.2% in 1980 (as compared to 8.4%), 6.0% in 1990 (as compared to 8.4%) and 7.2% in 1994 (as compared to 10%).

Another way of reducing the tax gap, of course, is to cut the tax burden. Caragata & Giles estimate that the hidden economy could shrink from about 11% of GDP to around 7% of GDP by if the tax burden is cut to 21% of GDP. This would shrink the dollar value of the amount of tax evasion in NZ and the tax gap. Caragata & Small (1996) confirm that a lower tax burden will shrink the size of the hidden economy.

7.7 Trends in Corporate Tax Payments

Legal tax minimisation increased during the 1970s and 1980s, as a result of a combination of tax planning activities by firms, tax concessions provided by government and access to new offshore tax havens. This trend was reversed in the late 1980s as a result of audit improvements and tax policy changes.

The level of regulation, inflation and total taxes increased significantly over the last 25 years. This provided a strong incentive for firms to minimise their tax burdens through legal methods, as opposed to tax evasion. Of course, along with motive goes opportunity. Thus, legal and accounting tax advisers imported tax planning methods from abroad and helped firms take advantage of the growing number of tax havens and low tax jurisdictions that arose to compete for off-shore business activity (e.g. Malta, Gibraltar, Panama, Cayman Islands, Singapore, Hong Kong, Luxembourg, Cyprus, Ireland, Switzerland and the Cook Islands etc).

In addition, partly in response to the combined effects of high tax rates and high inflation, governments in New Zealand until the mid-1980s provided various forms of tax relief to companies operating in New Zealand. Those tax concessions included specific incentives to (i) encourage investment in capital and research and development; and (ii) to protect industry from the impact of high levels of inflation and the oil shocks. Further, the opening of the economy beginning in 1984 exposed weaknesses in the tax-base that had existed for the past 50 years. In particular, firms responded to the reduction of subsidies and tax incentives, and reduced trade protection and deregulation by intensifying tax

[205] 100% minus 30% equals 70%. The tax gap is the difference between what can be collected theoretically and what is collected in practice. The risk-adjusted tax gap reduces the amount that is theoretically collectable.

planning activities. Tax savings are a valuable basis for reducing current operating costs and improving cash flow.

In response, beginning in the mid-1980s, tax policy reform broadened the tax-base, closed loopholes and reduced the double taxation of dividends by introducing imputation, while Inland Revenue's improved (but non-scientific) audit methods reduced the opportunities and increased the cost of tax minimisation. As a result, NZ's level of corporate income tax relative to GDP is now close to its post-war peak, and among the highest in the OECD (**Figure 7.4**). From the late 1970s until 1992 NZ either matched or under-performed on corporate tax revenue collection relative to the OECD average. Before and since that period NZ's performance has been well-above the OECD average. This suggests that New Zealand currently has a reasonably tough corporate tax regime, despite the fact that our statutory rates are much lower than many OECD countries. Nonetheless, there is a puzzling trend among publicly listed firms and non-resident controlled firms that bears much closer examination.

In 1982, as indicated in **Figure 7.5** roughly 29% of publicly listed and non-resident controlled corporate taxpayers (TTPs) in a sample of about 500 firms were zero-taxpayers (ZTPs).[206] By 1991, the depth of the worst recession in post-war New Zealand, about 43.5% of these incorporated firms paid no tax. However, at most about one-third of the 43.5% can be explained by the consequences of structural adjustment, the stock market crash of 1987 and the long recession in 1990-1991, since these factors entered after 1982 when the ratio of ZTPs to TTPs was already at 29%. Why are so many companies in the ZTP zone? There are two ways of testing that; first, by examining corporate taxpayer data (a random sample of independent entity firms from different sectors and with different scale) in NZ, and second, by comparing NZ performance with overseas behaviour.

The publicly listed and non-resident controlled firm data were compared with the corporate taxpayer (independent entity) data for the period 1991-1995 (**Figure 7.5**). At the beginning of the period, the rate of zero taxpaying for the publicly listed and foreign firms was 1.7 times greater than the independent entity firms. This gap continuously narrowed so that by 1995 the results for the two data bases were exactly the same: 27% of all firms on each data base were zero taxpayers in that year. The gap between the two data sets in earlier years needs to be explored further, so caution is advised.

The next step was to compare the NZ firms (publicly listed and foreign controlled) with similar firms overseas listed on Standard and Poor's Compustat Global Vantage Database in 18 OECD countries. The results (**Figure 7.6**) reveal that during recessions (1982) and (1992) the ratio of ZTPs to total corporate taxpayers in the sample is about 14%-17%. Over the entire period, OECD

[206] This data is in a public domain data base created by Inland Revenue from publicly listed firms and firms required to file annual reports in the Companies Office.

Figure 7.4
Taxes on Corporate Income as a Percentage of GDP - New Zealand and the OECD Average: 1965-94

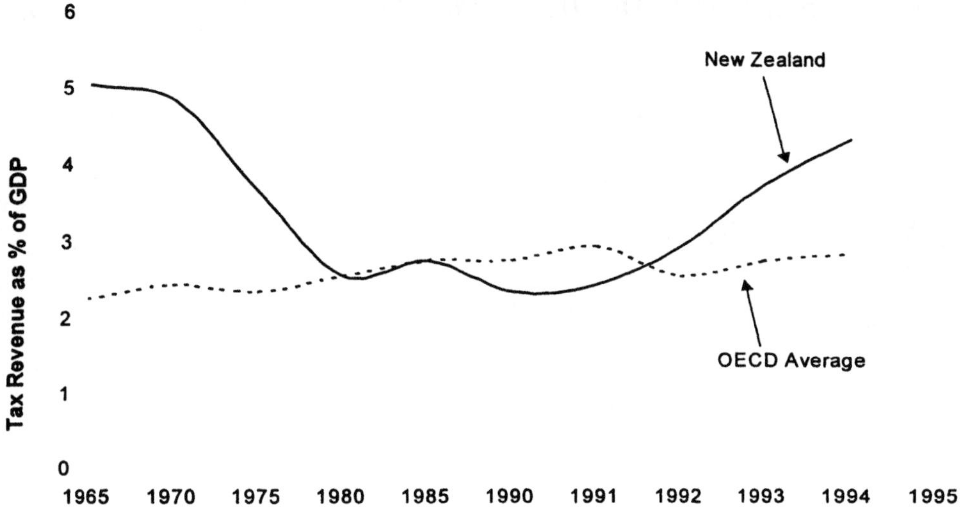

Source: Revenue Statistics 1965-95, OECD, 1996

Figure 7.5
The Ratio of Zero to Total Corporate Taxpayers by Frequency: FIRST* database, 1991-95, 671 companies; NZCDB, 1982-95, 507 (average p.a.) companies**

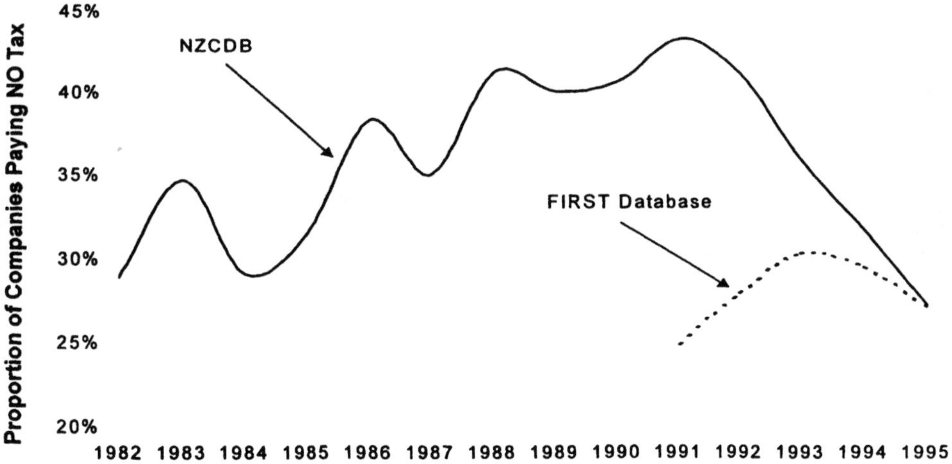

Source: * FIRST - Inland Revenue's taxpayer database of all taxpayers in New Zealand; **NZCDB - New Zealand Corporate database of all public and foreign-owned companies in New Zealand, 1997

Figure 7.6
The Proportion of Corporate Taxpayers Paying No Tax: a comparison of companies in New Zealand (1982-95) with the average for companies in 18 OECD countries (1982-92; 1993-95 estimated)

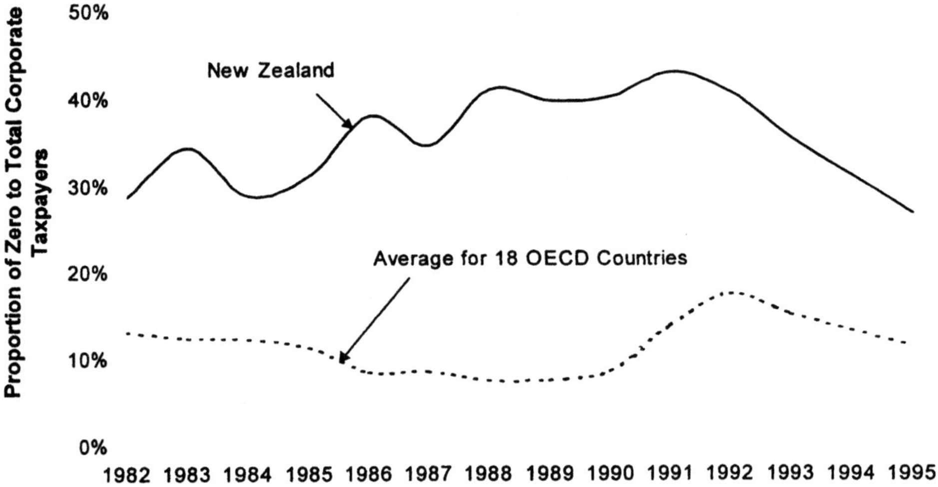

Source: New Zealand Corporate Database, Compustat's Global Vantage Database, Inland Revenue, 1997

Figure 7.7
Net Profit and Taxes: Median Value ($ thousands) of Deciles Sorted by Sales, 6570 companies, FIRST Database

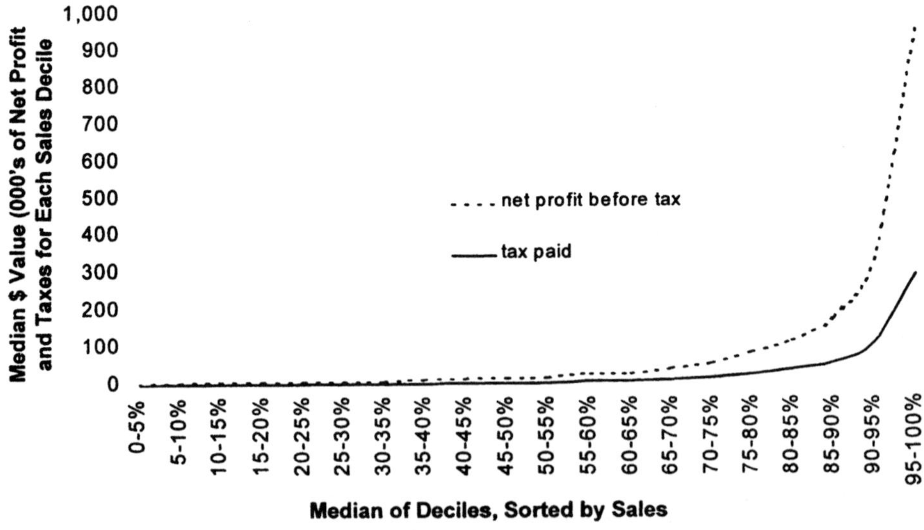

Source: Inland Revenue

average is about 13%. In New Zealand, the long run average is about 35%, or about two and a half times the OECD average. This analysis suggests that there may be a problem that needs deeper exploration.

The remaining explanations lie in legitimate commercial reasons such as reduced demand or financial mismanagement and some degree of potentially preventable tax avoidance. It is unlikely that the firms captured in this sample of incorporated firms are engaged in evasion to any significant degree. Past experience in NZ and overseas indicates that evasion is more the province of small firms and the self-employed, with inevitable exceptions. Additional research is needed to sort out the extent to which normal commercial behaviour and strategic tax behaviour are responsible for this situation. The first place to look is the relationship between the efficiency performance of firms and their taxpaying behaviour.

Normal commercial activity often brings about reduced effective tax payments for firms. More successful firms, in terms of their turnover, tend to pay a smaller proportion of pre-tax net profits in taxes than firms which are less successful. More successful firms have higher cash flow and better credit ratings, and can take better advantage of interest deductions and depreciation allowances in the system. Thus, it is normal for more successful firms to benefit more from relieving provisions in the tax system than less successful firms. Therefore, one should be cautious about assuming that more successful firms should always have high effective tax rates.

Analysis for 6,570 companies from the FIRST data for 1993-95 suggests that companies tend to pay a smaller proportion of their pre-tax net profit in taxes as their sales increase. This result is significant at the 95% confidence level for the economy as a whole. In effect, as companies generate more sales their profits tend to grow more rapidly than their tax burdens. This is depicted in **Figure 7.7** by the steeper slope for the profits curve than for the tax curve.

The result is also significant at the industry level for (i) agriculture & mining; (ii) manufacturing; and, (iii) personal & community services. The result holds, but is not significant, in the (i) retail trade, (ii) finance, insurance & property services, and, (iii) business service industries. Successful companies in the (i) construction, (ii) wholesale trade, and, (iii) transport, communication & storage industries tend to pay a larger proportion of their profits in taxes, although this result is not significant. Further refinements of this analysis, such as improving the functional form of the equations are expected to improve the significance of these results.

These results suggest that more successful companies, in terms of their turnover, are able to utilise the deductions available in the tax system to a far greater extent to minimise their tax burden than their less successful competitors. Companies that are more successful (in terms of greater turnover) generally have better cashflow, a broader and more flexible asset portfolio and a better credit rating. Thus, these companies have more opportunity to manipulate their portfolio to maximise their use of the tax instruments such as depreciation and interest expenses and thus minimise their tax burdens.[207]

Other analysis suggests that companies that more efficient at generating revenue and profit have a higher probability of paying no tax. For inefficient companies, the probability of paying no tax is relatively insensitive to changes in economic growth. However, the efficient companies tend to minimise their tax burden to a far greater extent during periods of low economic growth and recessions.

Preliminary analysis suggests that an increase in the growth of taxes relative to GDP leads to a rise in the rate of company failure (receiverships and liquidations) relative to GDP. The result is significant at the 10% significance level (one-sided t-test). At the mean, a 1% increase in the rate of growth of taxes relative to GDP, results in an increase of 4.6% in the number of company failures per dollar of nominal GDP. Forty-one percent of this effect occurs in the first year after the increase in the growth rate of the tax burden (relative to GDP), and the remainder of the impact is felt in the second year. More research should be undertaken on this issue.

These results suggest that *successful* companies are likely to carry a lower relative tax burden because more efficient firms will have more opportunities to take advantage of deductions. For inefficient companies, the probability of paying no tax is relatively insensitive to changes in economic growth. However, the efficient companies tend to minimise their tax burden to a far greater extent during periods of low economic growth and recessions.

The public needs to be cautious about making accusations against firms that legitimately have lower effective tax rates. Normal commercial behaviour, through both inefficient and efficient performance, can lead to lower effective tax rates (e.g. increases in the level of sales will outpace the rate of growth of taxes). More research is needed to explore these findings in order to differentiate between normal commercial reasons and strategic reasons for low or zero taxpaying behaviour.

7.8 Key Findings on Economic Growth and Employment

Real growth rates are more affected by changes in the total level of taxes than by changes in the tax mix [the balance between direct (personal and corporate income tax) and indirect (GST and excise) taxes].

Real growth rates are much more sensitive to changes in the tax/GDP ratio than to changes in the tax mix. Higher taxes are associated with less economic growth, more unemployment and higher tax evasion. But higher taxes may provide greater equity, at least in the short term, and greater security (if physical or national security is an issue). Nonetheless, one needs to be cautious about presuming that increasing taxes will promote long term equity. The opposite may

[207] For the original development of these concepts and some preliminary evidence see Caragata (1996).

be the case if higher taxes promote greater unemployment as a result of reduced economic growth.

Economic growth is a very important factor in promoting greater long-term income distribution by generating more employment, but so is new government spending on education and training, and health. These issues are complex, and the equity-efficiency trade-off requires much further examination than has been possible here.

The link between maturity and slower growth in OECD countries may be spurious. High tax burdens may be the real problem. But the higher the burden, the less effective are tax cuts in promoting growth. Therefore, sustained tax cuts over a long period of time may be an appropriate option for dealing with constraint, assuming that it right.

As economies become more mature, they are generally expected to have slower growth, but how much of a role do higher taxes have in generating slower growth? The link between maturity and slower growth may be spurious because OECD countries have higher tax burdens than less developed countries. But just as mature corporations can be re-engineered to improve performance, so too can countries. One way of re-engineering them is to reduce their costs, such as high tax burdens relative to GDP. Caragata & Small's (1996:26) results suggest that the impact of a tax reduction on growth and tax evasion is smaller, the greater is the tax/GDP ratio:

"tax cuts are less effective at higher levels of the tax/GDP ratio (e.g. over 35%) as compared to lower levels (e.g. 25%) in promoting economic growth (and possibly in generating tax revenue) and reducing the size of the hidden economy (and related tax evasion)."

At higher levels of tax the economy is possibly more sluggish and less responsive to remedial efforts. This suggests the need for a sustained series of tax cuts across time in order to realise the long term growth effects of tax cuts. A one off tax cut at a high level is insufficient. It took decades for taxes to get this high, and it may take a few decades to bring them back down to optimal levels from the perspective of promoting growth and employment.

Tax cuts enhance economic growth more when they are applied well before a recession begins, and perhaps can be used to reshape the expected severity of the downturn. Of course, estimating downturns and the time to the next recession is very difficult.

As well, Caragata and Small (1996:26) concluded that the timing of tax cuts during the course of a business cycle is very important. They note that "Tax cuts enhance economic growth more when they are applied well before a recession begins." This makes sense because the closer to the business cycle trough, the weaker is investor and consumer confidence. The introduction of an appropriately-sized tax cut perhaps mid-way between the peak and the expected trough could reshape the economic downturn, assuming that it is possible to get the timing right given the information problems involved.

Tax cuts are to be preferred over expenditure increases where the objective to promote long term stable growth.

Recent work in New Zealand by Hall and Rae (1996) compared the long run growth implications of choosing between a 3 percent increase in the public debt to GDP ratio based on either an increase in government spending or a tax cut of the equivalent amount. In general, a tax cut will have less of an upward effect on the exchange rate and interest rates and thus lead to less crowding out than will an increase in government expenditure of a similar amount. This boosts investor confidence and subjects the economy less to a boom and bust cycle. Moreover, the redistribution of income has important opportunity costs because "government spending is more about redistributing, rather than creating, wealth. The redistribution tends to flow from the business and export sectors to those using government services" (Rae, 1996:5).

An optimal level of total tax, which maximises economic growth, is probably located in a range between 15% and 25% of GDP.

Work by Scully (1996), using a reduced form model,[208] concluded that economic growth is 2 percentage points per annum lower than if the tax/GDP ratio were set at 20% (with a range of 15.8%-23.6%)[209] (**Figure 7.8**). Work by Branson & Lovell (1997) suggests that, on average over the period 1946-1995, the annual level of economic output is 17% below what it would have been if the tax/GDP ratio had been at an average optimal level of 22.5% of GDP (with a range of 18%-27%) over the period 1946-1995. When that time period was extended to 1928-1995, the average optimal tax rate was 20%, almost exactly the same as Scully's, but based on an entirely different model. Caragata & Small (1996) developed 3 models that identified a growth-maximising tax rate in New Zealand over the period 1967-1994 that averaged about 15% of GDP (with a range of 13.4%-15.5%). These results are consistent with an OECD study that concluded that:

"up to one-third of the growth deceleration in the OECD (from around 5 percent in 1965-73 to around 2 percent in 1989-95) would be explained by higher taxes. In some European countries, tax burdens increased much more dramatically than the OECD average, which would imply correspondingly larger effects on their growth rates" (Leibfritz, Thornton & Bibbee, 1997:49).

These results for New Zealand[210] (Scully's range of 16%-23%; Branson & Lovell's range of 21%-25%; and Caragata & Small range of 13.4-15.5%) are all statistically similar (**Figure 7.9**) and suggest that an optimal tax/GDP ratio for New Zealand is in the range of 15%-25% of GDP. Interestingly, a 50 year old study by a highly regarded Australian economist, Colin Clark, suggested that if the objective is to minimise inflation and stabilise the exchange rate, the optimal tax rate is likely in the range of 21% of GDP (with a range of 17%-25%, assuming an error of plus or minus 20%).[211]

---

[208] Such reduced form approaches are common in the literature.

[209] For a similar period for the US, Peden (1991:169) determined that the productivity-maximising level of government expenditure relative to GNP was 17% over the period 1929-1986.

[210] It needs to be recalled that these estimates of growth-maximising tax rates ignore equity.

[211] Following a suggestion from Keynes, Clark (1945) undertook a cross-country (France, Belgium, Britain, Japan, Italy, and Norway) examination of the optimal level of tax with respect to a combined objective function of stabilizing domestic prices and ensuring that the exchange rate is neither under-valued nor over-valued. He determined that "the critical limit of taxation is about 25% of the national income, or possibly rather less" (Clark, 1945:376). This would be equal to about 21% of GDP in New Zealand.

Figure 7.8
Potential versus Actual Output and the Output Gap - consequences of tables: 1946-94

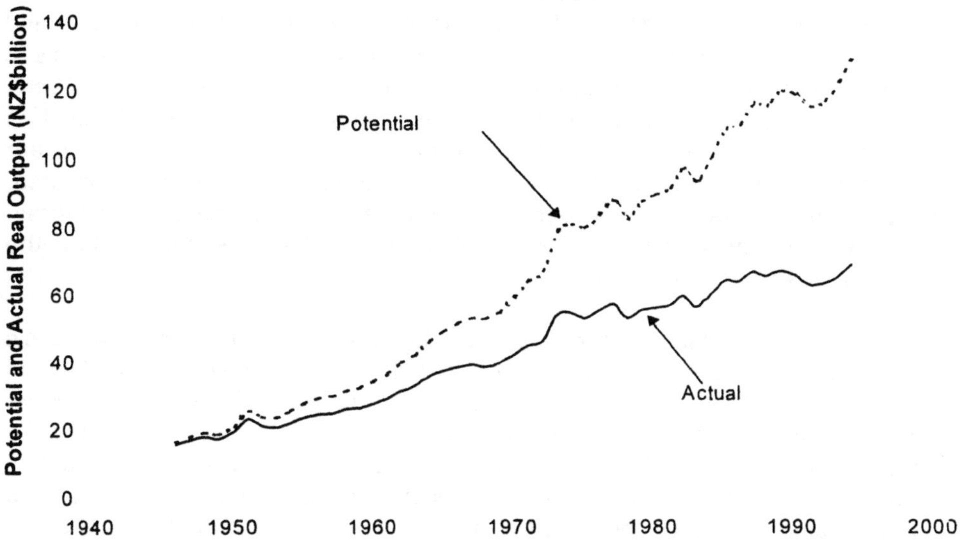

Source: Scully (1996)

Figure 7.9
A Comparison of Optimal vs Actual Total Tax to GDP Ratios given Specific Objectives of Growth Maximisation and Minimisation of Tax Evasion

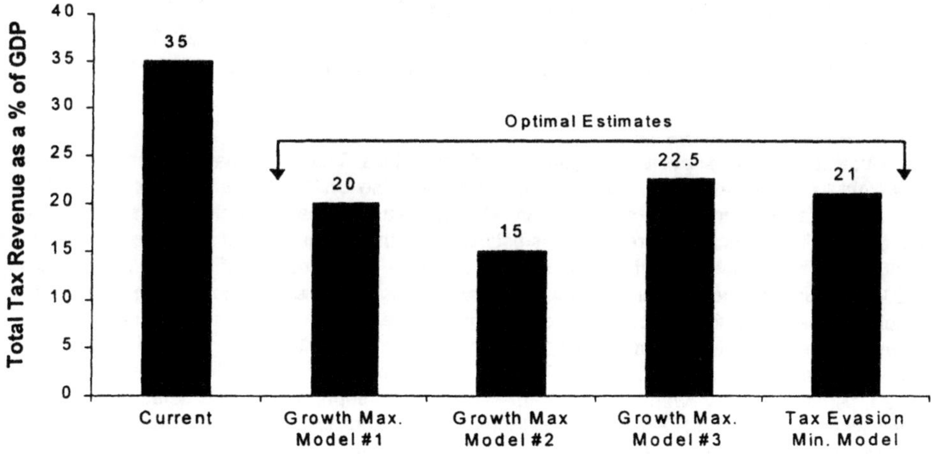

Growth Model #1: Scully; Growth Model #2: Caragata and Small; Growth Model #3: Brankson and Lovell; Tax Evasion Min Model: Giles and Caragata.

Source: Inland Revenue

Dynamic deadweight loss is the performance cost of taxes. Higher taxes mean less efficient performance. Cumulative deadweight loss indicates the long-term cost of tax increases, while current deadweight loss indicates the benefits of tax cuts.

Dynamic deadweight losses (output losses in the context of the dynamic analysis employed in this research) [212] are the efficiency costs to the economy of tax burdens arising from the fact that potential performance is less than best practice performance owing to the tax burden. These costs include lost output and distortions in the patterns of consumption and investment both at present (static estimate) and over the long term (dynamic estimate). Thus, deadweight losses are the opportunity cost of taxes and represent the sunk, or irretrievable, cost as well as the current efficiency costs of taxes. It is only current losses that are important for tax policy aimed at tax cuts because they can be recaptured, however sunk costs stretching back over time cannot be undone or recovered. Cumulative deadweight losses, nonetheless, can signal a warning about the long-term costs of tax increases.

Scully (1996) found that the *cumulative* deadweight loss of sub-optimal tax levels since 1946 in NZ amounted to $2.64[213] per dollar of tax revenue by 1994. In brief, the real long run cost to the economy of sub-optimal taxes is far higher than the tax revenue that is generated. A separate model developed by Caragata & Small (1996) corroborated this result.[214] Bird (1991:8) notes that "...the real economic cost of raising a dollar in taxation and *transferring it to someone else* may be as much as two or three times the recorded amount of the tax burden as usually measured" (emphasis added).

This suggests that the government might consider trying to obtain about $2.70 in additional long run economic and social benefits for each dollar of tax collected and spent so that long run costs and benefits are balanced. This deadweight loss or opportunity cost approach should provide some incentive for more rigorous analysis of the value of government expenditure. Branson & Lovell (1997) estimate that the *current* deadweight loss costs for 1995 are $0.47 cents per dollar of tax revenue. These results are consistent with Scully's estimates.

---

[212] An illustration of the aspects of *dynamic* deadweight loss: There are many dimensions to the deadweight loss of taxation, as this simple example from the United States illustrates. In 1991, a 10% Luxury Tax was imposed on small aircraft and pleasure boats, jewellery, furs, and luxury automobiles. The expected tax revenue, as estimated by the Congressional Joint Tax Committee, was $6 mn. The actual amount of tax revenue received before repeal of the Act in 1993 was $53,000. Fortune Magazine commented as follows: "This sad tale provides an unusually clear example of one of the foggier concepts of economics: the 'deadweight loss' inherent in taxes. A deadweight loss reflects a cost imposed on some individuals without any offsetting benefit to others - a pure economic inefficiency. ...The all too-real luxury tax had all the elements" (Norton, R, 1993, "American's Screwed-Up Tax Code", *FORTUNE*, Sept., p. 62). The types of distortions created were as follows: (1) Production distortion: e.g. Beech Aircraft Corp sold 80 fewer planes than expected, at a loss of $130 mn; this also affected the timing of the next investments for these firms; (2) Consumption distortion: people who would have liked to buy new airplanes did not buy them; and (3) Resource allocation distortion: workers who would have been employed building the airplanes were idle (e.g. 480 employees at Beech Aircraft lost their jobs).

[213] This estimate has subsequently been refined to an estimate of $2.69.

[214] These results challenging the existing paradigm that deadweight loss estimates are small have been anticipated by Usher (1991) and Feldstein (1995; 1996a).

Higher taxes reduce the rate of employment generation.

Scully (1996a) also concluded that a tax rate of 20% of GDP would promote a higher employment generation rate than occurs under the current tax/GDP of 35%. A one percentage point increase in the tax/GDP ratio appears to have its strongest negative impact in labour markets on employment growth, but its impact on labour force participation and the unemployment rate are also strong. A one percentage point increase in the tax/GDP ratio in NZ lowers employment growth by over 42,000 workers, decreases labour force participation by 17,500 workers, and increases unemployment by about 15,900.[215]

A one percentage point increase in the tax/GDP ratio induces a reduction of GDP through the reduced participation of the labour force. The deadweight loss in labour force participation is about 0.26% of GDP, the deadweight loss from lowered employment growth of 0.55% of GDP, and the deadweight loss from increased unemployment is about 0.26% of GDP. The total deadweight loss from all employment effects is, therefore, approximately 1.07% of GDP. These results for New Zealand are consistent with results for the US (Scully, 1996a) and for Canada (Spiro, 1996).

7.9 'Best Practice' Tax Policy Frontiers and Their Implications

Estimates of the growth-maximising tax rate (relative to the size of the economy) for other countries are similar to the New Zealand estimates.

Three models (**Figure 7.9**) were developed to examine the link between the maximisation of economic growth and taxation. They all indicate that the existing tax/GDP ratio is too high if economic growth is to be maximised. Scully (1996) modelled a growth-maximising tax rate of 20% of GDP for NZ. He also estimated the growth-maximising tax rate for the US (1929-89) at 22% of GNP, as well as GDP-based growth-maximising tax rates for Denmark (19%), Finland (19%), Italy (20%), Sweden (17%), and the UK (25%) over the period 1927-88. The average for these countries is 20%. All of the test results were highly significant. Earlier in a study of 103 countries for the period 1960-80, Scully (1991) concluded that they would maximise growth rates, on average, when their tax to GDP ratio no more than 19.3% of GDP.

Branson & Lovell (1997) derived an average optimal tax/GDP ratio of 23% of GDP. Analysis by Caragata & Small (1996) estimated that the growth maximising tax rate for New Zealand is 15% of GDP. Caragata & Giles (1996) developed a different model for NZ estimating a tax evasion-minimising optimal tax rate of 21% of GDP. These results all suggest that the best practice tax to GDP ratio is well below the current rate of 35%. Future research should concentrate on adding more precision to the optimal frontier for the tax/GDP ratio, given the multiple objectives of government, including equity constraints, compliance cost minimisation, tax evasion minimisation and then minimisation of Inland Revenue administration costs. More research is also needed for examining the optimal level of expenditure:

[215] All results were statistically significant, and tests indicated Granger causation.

"the large increase in public spending in some of these [17 OECD] countries does not seem to have contributed much to social welfare. This leads us to conclude that by the time countries reach the level of public spending shown by the small governments [an average of 35% of GDP], much of the potential social gain from public spending has been obtained. Spending beyond that level does not contribute that much" (Tanzi & Schuknecht, 1997:167; see also Tanzi & Schuknecht, 1995).

An optimal tax rate that takes into consideration both efficiency and equity has not yet been calculated so current estimates should be considered preliminary. For this reason we emphasise growth-maximising tax rates or evasion minimising tax rates per se, rather than optimal tax rates.

Without the work on equity and compliance costs, no definitive conclusion can be reached, but a preliminary estimate is that the optimal tax/GDP ratio that would best benefit New Zealand by optimising efficiency and promote voluntary taxpayer compliance is within a range of 15%-25% of GDP.

Two models we have developed for New Zealand with a growth-maximisation objective favour a tax mix that is weighted more heavily by direct taxes. Another model with a similar objective suggested an emphasis on indirect taxes instead. A fourth model with an objective of minimising tax evasion also called for an optimal mix weighted more heavily by indirect taxes.

Before discussing the mix, it is important to recall that all of the models indicate that the total tax burden is far more important than the mix in its impact on economic growth and tax evasion. In terms of the optimal mix, Scully (1996) concluded that a mix of 57% direct tax and 43% indirect tax would maximise economic growth at a tax/GDP ratio of 20%. Branson & Lovell (1997) concluded that, on average, a mix of 65% direct and 35% indirect is optimal for promoting economic growth in NZ at an average optimal tax/GDP ratio of 23%.

Caragata & Small's (1996a) non-linear model estimated that at a tax/GDP ratio of 20%, tax policy would have its most powerful effect on (in terms of accelerating) economic growth when the tax mix is 28% direct tax and 72% indirect. Their model found no turning point in the relationship between growth and direct taxes. The relationship was always negative. This implies that a tax mix with zero direct taxes and 100% indirect taxes would maximise economic growth.[216] Finally, Caragata & Giles (1996) found that a mix of 33% direct and 67% indirect would most efficiently minimise the size of the hidden economy and tax evasion.

In summary, 2 models with a growth maximisation objective suggest that the optimal mix should favour direct over indirect taxes, while 1 model with the same objective (in the long run) and another with an objective of minimising tax evasion suggest that the mix should favour indirect taxes. A preliminary assessment of these results suggests that NZ will experience more economic growth and lower tax evasion if the tax/GDP ratio were reduced. As well, given

[216] The conclusion to be drawn from this model is that in the transition to an optimal tax mix, a 28% (direct) and 72% (indirect) tax split would best accelerate the rate of economic growth. In the long run, the growth-maximising mix in this model is 0% direct and 100% indirect. Nonetheless, there are measurement errors in this model which make the conclusions both tentative and subject to caution.

trade-offs between growth and tax evasion objectives, a rough balance of direct and indirect taxes in the tax mix would seem, at this preliminary stage, to offer a useful best practice frontier against which to benchmark policy progress. Further research is needed to refine the conclusions.

7.10 Summary Scorecard: Economic, Compliance and Revenue Health of the Tax System in New Zealand (Table 7.6)

Current Versus Potential Revenue

In 1994, total tax revenue collected was 35% of GDP (excluding local taxes), while the tax evasion gap was about 3.9% of GDP unadjusted for risk. Thus, total potential revenue was about 39% of GDP, assuming all of the evasion is collectable. On an *unadjusted* basis, the performance ratio (current divided by potential revenue) was 0.86 in 1994, and the performance gap, or potential for improvement, was 14 percentage points. Given constraints, it is more likely that only about 70% of the tax gap (2.7% of GDP) can be collected, but this should not be used as an excuse to stop at 70%. As a result, total potential revenue (adjusted for risk) would have been about 38% of GDP in 1994 (**Table 7.6**).

On an *adjusted* basis, the performance ratio (current divided by potential revenue) was 0.90 in 1994, and the performance gap, or potential for improvement, was 10 percentage points. This result, which includes tax evasion by both firms and individuals, is much better than the 17% estimate by the US Internal Revenue Service calculated in 1996 for individual taxpayers, and the 20% for both companies and individuals estimated by the IRS for 1987 (Slemrod, 1992:1). More research is needed to determine the extent to which potentially preventable avoidance should be factored into the tax gap. Thus, this current estimate of the tax gap may be conservative and performance in closing the gap may be less efficient than presented here (**Table 7.6**).

The Hidden Economy, Tax Evasion, Tax Gap and Potential Revenue

The hidden economy fluctuated considerably over the last 25 years, but grew by about 3 percentage points of GDP, jumping from 7.8% of GDP in 1969 to 11.3% (about $9.2 billion) in 1994 (**Figure 7.3**). Currently, an average of about $500 million per annum is collected in audits by Inland Revenue. The 1994 total for the tax evasion gap on an *unadjusted* basis is 3.9% of GDP, or $3.2 billion, implying an actual/potential revenue performance ratio of 0.90, and a performance gap of 10 percentage points (**Table 7.6**). The tax evasion gap has a performance ratio of 0.16 and a performance gap of 84% points. That is, about 16% of the tax evasion gap is currently being closed, and another 84% remains to be captured.

Adjusted for a 70% probability of success in collection, the performance ratio is 0.93, with a performance gap of 7 percentage points. In that case, the tax evasion gap is 2.7% of GDP, or $2.2 billion (**Table 7.5**). On an unadjusted basis, the performance ratio is 0.22, with a performance gap, or potential for improvement, of 78 percentage points (**Table 7.6**).

The general trends in tax system health are as follows. The size of the hidden economy and relative degree of tax evasion have been increasing until 1995 when they declined somewhat. Tax-sensitive sector evasion, except for the recession in the early 1990s, showed strong growth relative to GDP since the early 1980s and peaked in 1994. Illicit-activity sector tax evasion expanded modestly since the early 1980s and peaked in 1990.

Economic Growth and Employment

The long run average tax/GDP ratio of 28% in the post war period (1946-1995) helped produce a long run average real growth rate of 3%, as compared to a 5% potential average real growth if a growth maximising tax rate of 20% of GDP had been adopted instead. The performance ratio is 0.60 and the performance gap is 40 percentage points. A lower tax/GDP ratio would, therefore, be expected to promote higher economic growth as well as employment. The total tax burden appears to have its strongest impact in labour markets on employment growth, although the impact on labour force participation and the unemployment rate are also strong (**Table 7.6**).

Scorecard Summary

A scorecard approach was developed to examine the performance ratios and gaps for the current versus potential impact of taxation on static potential revenue, the tax gap, economic growth and employment. The aim in the analysis was to determine the tax policy frontiers which optimise tax revenue, maximise economic growth, and minimise tax evasion.

The results indicate that NZ is doing quite well with respect to the efficiency of tax revenue generation, probably because of the tax policy and audit changes of the last ten years. On the other hand, there is room for much improvement with respect to tackling the growing evasion problem among both tax-sensitive sector evaders (individuals, the self-employed and small firms) and illicit-activity sector evaders (criminal elements). There is also considerable scope for improvement with respect to the economic growth and employment consequences of taxation.

In general, the NZ tax system is in a moderate state of health with room for improvement in all areas. Some of those gains could be realised by reducing the total level of tax and favouring a tax mix that is equally sensitive to both growth maximisation and tax evasion minimisation objectives. Objectives of reducing taxpayer compliance costs and tax administration costs reinforce the need for such changes in the tax system. Equity constraints, however, would tend to work in the opposite direction. Further research work is needed to reconcile these issues. Initial work by Scully & Stroombergen (1997) indicates that there is some loss of equity as the tax burden is reduced.

One of the factors driving higher tax/GDP ratios over the last 20 years was the high level of fiscal deficits and resultant debt (due to higher transfers and government consumption). Now that the budget economy is in surplus and the public debt is reducing, one might assume that the government has resolved its efficiency problems. That is not clear. More analysis needs to be undertaken to determine how the optimal tax level (the floor) and the current and the optimal expenditure levels (the ceiling) can be made to converge. This will require innovative thinking about the role of government in the economy, and about the optimal level of both expenditure and tax given foreseeable constraints such as health and superannuation commitments.

Table 7.6
Summary Scorecard: Economic, Compliance and Revenue Health of the Tax System in New Zealand

	Performance (% points) Ratio	Gap
Perfect Score =	100%	0%
1. MAXIMISING STATIC POTENTIAL REVENUE AND MINIMISING THE TAX GAP, 1994		
1.1 Unadjusted Basis (assumes that 100% of the total tax gap is collectable)		
(a) Actual/Potential Revenue (25% of GDP divided by 39.9% of GDP)	86	14
(b) Actual/Potential Tax Gap ($0.5bn divided by $4.5bn)	11	89
1.2 Risk Adjusted Basis (assumes that 70% of the total tax gap is collectable)		
(a) Actual/Potential Revenue (35% of GDP divided by 38.9% of GDP)	90	10
(b) Actual/Potential Tax Gap ($0.5bn divided by $3.2bn)	16	84
2. MINIMISING THE HIDDEN ECONOMY A tax/GDP ratio of 30% from 1969-1994 yielded a hidden economy of 11.3% of GDP in 1994, versus a potential of 7.5% of GDP: 11.3/7.5=1.51	151*	34**
3. MAXIMISING POTENTIAL GROWTH WITH GROWTH MAXIMISING TAX RATE The long run average tax/GDP ratio of 28% yields a long run average real growth rate of 3%, versus a potential of 5% with a tax of GDP ratio of 20%: 3% divided by 5% is the performance ratio	60	40

* This number is greater than 100 because the preferred position is lower. For the other indicators the preferred position is higher.

** In percent rather than percentage points.

Source: Inland Revenue, New Zealand, 1997

APPENDIX 1

WORKING PAPERS ON MONITORING THE HEALTH OF THE TAX SYSTEM

1. Financial Ratios and Tax Policy Development: Investigating Accuracy Issues of the New Zealand Corporate Data Base, June 1995, Chris Gillion, Daniel Aldersley, Patrick Caragata (Inland Revenue, NZ).
2. Effective Tax Rates for Corporations: A New Econometric Approach to Assessing Their Tax Payment Behaviour, Revised December 1995, Ewen McCann (Inland Revenue, NZ) John Small (University of Auckland), Patrick Caragata (Inland Revenue, NZ).
3. Monitoring the Tax Mix, Tax Shocks and Potential Economic Impacts: The PIC Model, June 1996, December 1995 (August 1996 revised), Patrick Caragata (Inland Revenue, NZ) and John Small (University of Auckland).

3a Monitoring the Tax Mix, Tax Shocks and Potential Economic Impacts: The PICO-DISC Model Theoretical Framework, June 1995, Patrick Caragata (Inland Revenue, NZ).

4. An Analysis of the Determinants of Deadweight Loss of Taxation in New Zealand, June 1995, John Small (University of Auckland).
5. Measuring the Size of the Hidden Economy and the Tax Gap in New Zealand: An Econometric Analysis, July 1995, December 1995 (revised), David Giles (University of Victoria, Canada).
6. The Relationship Between the Corporate Statutory and Effective Tax Rates: A Non-Parametric Approach, July 1995, Chris Gillion, Patrick Caragata, Ewen McCann (Inland Revenue NZ) and John Small (University of Auckland).
7. Optimal Cost Structures and Corporate Performance: Combining Learning Curve and Frontier Approaches to Economic Efficiency and Increasing Returns, July 1995, December 1995 (revised) Patrick Caragata (Inland Revenue, NZ).
8. Cost Structures and Economic Performance in the New Zealand Electrical Distribution Industry, July 1995, revised December 1995, Daniel Aldersley (Inland Revenue, NZ) and David Petterson (McCallum and Petterson, NZ).
9. Income and Tax Distributions for Individual New Zealand Taxpayers: 1991-1994, July 1995, Paul Dunmore, University of Victoria, Wellington, New Zealand.
10. An Endogenous Effective Tax Rates Model, April 1996, Ewen McCann (Inland Revenue NZ), Alan Rogers (University of Auckland), Ewen McCann, Patrick Caragata (Inland Revenue NZ).
11. Determinants of Effective Tax Rates in Zealand, 1981- 1994, December 1995, Ewen McCann, Chris Gillion, Patrick Caragata (Inland Revenue NZ).
12. Equity Effects of the New Zealand Personal Income Tax System, December 1995, Michael Dunn (Inland Revenue NZ).
13. Policy Indexes for New Zealand, December 1995 Gerald Scully (University of Texas at Dallas).
14. Taxation and Economic Growth in New Zealand, December 1995 Gerald Scully (University of Texas at Dallas).
15. Effective Tax Rates: Zero Tax Payments and the Migration of Firms Across Tax Bands, December 1995, Alan Rogers (University of Auckland), Patrick Caragata (Inland Revenue, NZ).
16. The Marginal Costs of Taxation in New Zealand: A Sensitivity Analysis of the Diewert and Lawrence Model, December 1995, John Small (University of Auckland).
17. A Latent Variables Approach to the Estimation of the Deadweight Loss of Taxation in New Zealand, December 1995, Johannah Dods, Ewen McCann (Inland Revenue, NZ).
18. Cost Efficiency in New Zealand's Electrical Supply Industry, 1982-1994, May 1996, Gerald Scully (University of Texas at Dallas).
19. The Impact of the Revenue and Profit Efficiency Performance of Firms on Taxation, November 1996, Patrick Caragata (Inland Revenue, NZ).
20. The Growth-Maximising Tax Mix in New Zealand, August 1996 Gerald Scully (University of Texas at Dallas).
21. The Learning Path of the Hidden Economy: Tax and Growth Effects in New Zealand, David Giles (University of Victoria, Canada) and Patrick Caragata (Inland Revenue, NZ), November, 1996.

22. Simulating the Relationship Between the Hidden Economy and the Tax Mix in New Zealand, Patrick Caragata (Inland Revenue, NZ) and David Giles (University of Victoria, Canada), November, 1996.
23. Taxation and Employment in New Zealand, Gerald Scully (University of Texas at Dallas), August 1996.
24. Tax Burden Effects on Output Growth in New Zealand: A Non-Linear Dynamic Model, Patrick Caragata (Inland Revenue) and John Small (Auckland University) December 1996.
25. The Tax Burden, The Tax Mix and Output Growth in New Zealand: A Tax Mix Model, Patrick Caragata (Inland Revenue) and John Small (Auckland University) December 1996.
26. *Establishing Risk Profiles of Corporate Tax Behaviour: FIRST System Data Base*, Anna Heiler (Inland Revenue, NZ), May 1997.
27. *Risk Profiling of Corporate Taxpayers: New Zealand Corporate Data Base*, Shee Boon Law (Inland Revenue, NZ), May 1997.
28. Modelling The Tax Compliance/Non-Compliance Profiles of Audited New Zealand Firms: Evidence from the ORACLE Database, David Giles (University of Victoria, British Columbia), May 1997.
29. Taxation and Bankruptcy: Corporate Taxpayer Behaviour Distress Prediction for Inland Revenue, Paul Dunmore (Victoria University of Wellington) and Shee Boon Law (Inland Revenue), May 1997.
30. A Growth Maximising Tax Structure for New Zealand: Johannah Branson (University of Exeter) and Knox Lovell (University of Georgia, Athens), May 1997.
31. Regulation and Growth: A Growth-Sensitive Regulatory Index for New Zealand, Anna Heiler (Inland Revenue), Adolph Stroombergen (BERL), Knox Lovell (University of Georgia, Athens), Patrick Caragata (Inland Revenue) March 1997.
32. Government Intervention and Economic Growth in New Zealand Johannah Branson (University of Exeter), Anna Heiler (Inland Revenue) and Knox Lovell (University of Georgia, Athens), May 1997.
33. The Equity-Efficiency Trade-Off in New Zealand: A Preliminary Analysis, Gerald Scully (University of Texas at Dallas), and Adolph Stroombergen (BERL).
34. The Taxation and Labour-Hiring Trade-Off in New Zealand, Patrick Caragata and Anna Heiler (Inland Revenue, NZ), May 1997.
35. Reconciling Different Estimates of the Optimal Tax Mix, Gerald Scully, (University of Texas at Dallas), May 1997.
36. The Life-Cycle Analysis of Corporate Taxpaying Behaviour: Implications of Integrating the Learning Curve and the Production Frontier: A Preliminary View, Patrick Caragata (Inland Revenue) and Knox Lovell (University of Georgia, Athens), May 1997.
37. Towards the Development of a Tax Avoidance Model for New Zealand, Patrick Caragata and Anna Heiler, (Inland Revenue, NZ), May 1997.

APPENDIX 2

DIFFERENT APPROACHES TO MEASURING EFFECTIVE TAX RATES

The approach taken to effective tax rate measurement depends on the purpose at hand. One of the purposes in this Report is to lay the foundation for developing an index number approach to estimating aggregate effective tax rates by illustrating, through statistical analysis, how different pockets of homogeneity arise in skewed distributions. This report should be considered a pre-testing exercise for the application of a data envelopment analysis approach to constructing an effective tax rate index. This approach will be cross-checked by an econometric estimation.

Up to now, there have been three different types of effective tax rates used in the literature. First, *effective or marginal corporate statutory tax rates* (MSTRs) are used largely in the financial literature. The MSTR measures the ratio of tax paid relative to assessable income per dollar of additional income or (typically interest) expense in order to assess the tax utility of increasing or decreasing debt (Altshuler & Auerbach, 1990; and Mintz 1988).

Second, the *average effective tax rate* (AETR), which is used in the financial, economics and accounting literatures, divides average tax paid by accounting profits during a specified period. AETRs are used to help estimate the amount of subsidies and incentives provided by government because it is a post-depreciation estimate of the tax burden, or (Grubert & Mutti, 1991) to assess the impact of the tax system on investment. Unfortunately, the AETR overestimates the actual tax burden because firms investing in new capital will drive down average effective tax rates when fast write-offs for investment are available. As well, firms also use AETRs as a signal to determine the amount of foreign sourced income to remit to the home country, or the amount that it will defer. The lower the AETR in the home country, the greater the likelihood of a high level of remission. On the other hand, the higher the AETR in the home country, the greater the likelihood of deferral. The AETR also affects the use of tax credits because the amount the home country will credit its MNEs for foreign taxes paid is based on the average amount they pay (AETR) in the host country within a given period.

Third, *effective marginal corporate tax rates on capital* (EMCTRs) are used in the theoretical economics literature and in the assessment of business decisions to invest and to produce. The theoretical work of King and Fullerton (1984) for closed economies and Boadway, Bruce and Mintz (1984) for open economies provides a theoretical methodology that yields an estimation of the marginal change in tax paid relative to pre-tax accounting profits on the investment (e.g. OECD, 1991) on a disaggregated basis not only for a firm but for individual activities. The intent of these measures is to provide an indication of how investment is affected by taxation without the measure being distorted by the existence or economic rents or losses etc. More recent work has extended this analysis to the impact of the tax system on the decision to produce. (McKenzie, Mintz & Scharf, 1993).

In summary ETRs have been applied to the analysis of many specific cases: e.g. losses carried forward, depreciation charges, tax credits. But existing ETR methods are not reliable for the calculation of the actual amount of tax paid by *all* firms and in assessing corporate tax payment behaviour for a number of reasons. *From a tax authority's perspective*, there are six basic problems with the current calculation of effective tax rates that either do, or would, build bias into the assessment of tax payment behaviour of firms: (1) hypothetical or normative assumptions; (2) the use of arithmetic calculations of the ETR; (3) the implicit assumption that ETR sample data are normally distributed; (4) the use of econometric techniques that run regressions using the ratio of tax paid to a base (e.g. accounting profits) instead of using the levels of the numerator and the denominator; (5) the bias in favour of using tax paid relative to accounting profits, as opposed to retaining that approach but also using tax paid relative to total corporate revenue, total corporate costs and total corporate assets, and finally, (6) the absence of an index number approach to effective tax rates that weights the disaggregated pockets of homogeneity in order to assess more accurately the source, magnitude and direction of changes.

First, some approaches (e.g. the King-Fullerton model) use a number of unrealistic assumptions, notably: the absence of transfer pricing and thin capitalisation, fixed rates of return, no inflation and fixed exchange rates, and the substitutability of investments. These assumptions prevent the use of this approach for accurate estimations of the amount of tax paid and the impact of a tax policy change on tax payment behaviour. Second, the use of the AETR applies arithmetic calculations across firms which can be inaccurate because firms are able to modify either accounting profits, assessable income or both, as a result of tax planning, or avoidance and evasion activity.

Third, where panel data or cross section data are employed, typically the use of the AETR employs the assumption that financial ratios across time and across firms are represented by a normal distribution. Gibrat (1931) Simon and Bonini (1958) and Dunmore (1994a, 1994b) have investigated this issue and demonstrated that all financial variables are not normally distributed. This includes effective tax rates. Thus, the *mean* of the sample AETR data cannot be used to draw valid inferences about the central tendency of the population. The appropriate approaches are the *median* or the "*andrews*" (Dunmore, 1994a), or some variation or modification of these metrics.

Fourth, some analysts (Porcano, 1986; Higgins, 1989; Collins & Shackleford, 1994) have used econometric techniques that run regressions using arithmetically calculated ratios of tax paid relative to a base (e.g. accounting profits) instead of using the levels of the numerator and the denominator. The problem with this approach is that it uses a parametric test (the mean) to describe a non-parametric distribution when it is not applicable, with the result that erroneous inferences are made. Some authors (e.g. Collins and Shackleford, 1994:12) trim the long right tail of the distribution, thereby eliminating many data entries, and thus important information, from the analysis. Trimmed and untrimmed samples yield different results.

Finally, there is a very strong bias in favour of using tax paid relative to accounting profits, as opposed to retaining that approach but also using tax paid relative to total corporate revenue, total corporate costs and total corporate assets. Some tax authorities, notably the U.S. Internal Revenue Service, have periodically used tax paid and net income relative to total corporate revenue and total assets when comparing the tax burdens of resident and non-resident controlled firms. Similar data were presented to the U.S. House Ways and Means Committee in the early 1990s when the debate the tax burdens on resident-controlled versus non-resident controlled firms first surfaced (See e.g. Graham, 1992; Goldberg, 1990; and Matthews, 1992).

In summary, if a tax authority wishes to be both accurate and fair, it cannot afford to make mistakes in its calculations of ETRs. Thus, it must take a strictly empirical approach, preferably using panel data. In assessing the revenue impact of tax rates and tax regulations, a tax authority should avoid using theoretical or normative calculations of the effective tax rates. Where possible and desirable, it should use econometric rather than arithmetic calculations. Finally, it should use a broad range of bases (accounting profits, revenue, costs and assets) in order to enhance the precision of the estimations across taxpayer types.

ABOUT THE AUTHOR

Patrick James Caragata received his PhD in political economy from the University of Toronto in 1981. His doctoral thesis was subsequently published by the Centre for Resource Studies at Queen's University in Canada as *National Resources and International Bargaining Power* in 1984. Over the period 1981-1983 he was Manager International Policy with both the Canadian Chamber of Commerce and the Canadian Council International Chamber of Commerce, and Associate Executive Director of the Canadian Committee of the Pacific Basin Economic Council. From August 1983 to August 1986 he was Senior Economist International in charge of the country risk analysis group at the Toronto-Dominion Bank in Toronto. From September 1986-March 1988, at the request of the Canadian government, he was seconded to Investment Canada in Ottawa and wrote three major papers on the investment implications and risk of the Canada-US Free Trade Agreement for the Canadian Government. During that time he also produced a 200-page report for Investment Canada on *International Trends in Merger Activity in the Twentieth Century: A North American Perspective*.

In June 1988 he moved to New Zealand and became chief economist at the Ministry of Energy where he redesigned the royalty regime for petroleum. His book *Resource Pricing: Rent Recovery Options for New Zealand's Energy and Mineral Industries (1989)* is now used at the Resources Institute at the East West Centre in Honolulu and the Harvard Institute for International Development as a standard reference tool for designing resource royalties in Asia and Latin America.

In 1991 he became Chief Tax Policy Adviser with Inland Revenue in New Zealand. He redesigned the petroleum mining taxation regime in 1991, and worked extensively on international tax issues for several years. In 1994 he initiated the work to monitor the Health of the Tax System. As Special Adviser, Taxation Economics he led the production of 37 working papers and the Report on the Health of the Tax System in September 1997.

Dr. Caragata has been a consultant for the World Bank's Foreign Investment Advisory Service in Sri Lanka in 1994 and for the IMF in Albania in 1995. In the latter case, it was his work in Tirana, Albania in December 1995 that first blew the whistle on the investment pyramid schemes whose collapse led to the rioting in early 1997.

In October 1997 Dr. Caragata was appointed managing director of McCallum Petterson Financial Diagnostics Ltd in Wellington. This company specialises in providing risk assessment and company performance analysis services to business. The focus is on diagnosing the potential for bankruptcy and fraud and assessing the financial health of companies and their potential for performance improvement in areas such as cost structure management and debt management. The company is part of the McCallum Petterson Group of companies specialising in forensic accounting, asset valuation, venture capital and turnaround management.

His e-mail address is Patrick@mpforensic.co.nz in Wellington New Zealand.

Index

REFERENCES

Aigner, D.J., Schneider, F., and Ghosh, D., 1988, "Me and My Shadow: Estimating the Size of the Hidden Economy From Time Series Data", in Barnett, W.A., et al. (eds), *Dynamic Econometric Modelling: Proceedings of the Third International Symposium in Economic Theory and Econometrics,* Cambridge: Cambridge University Press, pp.297-334.

Alesina, A., and Perotti, R., 1994, "The Welfare State and Competitiveness", NBER Working Paper Series, No.4810, Cambridge, Ma: National Bureau of Economic Research.

Alm, J., 1996, "What is an 'Optimal' Tax System", *National Tax Journal*, v., XLIX, March pp.

Alm, J., McClelland, G.H., and Schulze, W.D., 1992, "Why Do People Pay Taxes", Journal of Public Economics, vol. 48, pp. 21-38.

Altshuler, R. and Auerbach, A., 1990, "The Importance of Tax Law Asymmetries: an Empirical Investigation", *Quarterly Journal of Economics,* vol. 105, pp. 61-86.

Anderson, F., 1997, "Scully Growth Theory Caned", *The National Business Review,* 4 July, p. 2

Andvig, J.C., 1981, "Ragnar Frisch and Business Cycle Research During the Interwar Years", History of Political Economy, Vol. 14, No. 4.

Archer, B., 1996, "Goals of Fundamental Tax Reform", *Tax Notes*, March 26, pp. 1827-30.

Arrow, K.,1959, "Toward a Theory of Price Adjustment", in Abramovitz, M.A., *The Allocation of Resources*, Stanford: Stanford University Press.

Arrow, K.J., 1962, "The Economic Implications of Learning By Doing", *Review of Economic Studies*, vol. 29, June, pp. 155-173.

Asher, H., 1956, *Cost-Quantity Relationships in the Airframe Industry*, R-291, Santa Monica, California: The RAND Corporation.

Association of Certified Fraud Examiners (ACFE), 1995, Report to the Nation: Occupational Fraud and Abuse Austin, Texas.

Auerbach, A.,J., 1996, "Dynamic Revenue Estimation", *Journal of Economic Perspectives*, vol. 10, no. 1, Winter, pp. 141-157.

Auld, D.A.L., and Wilton, D.A., 1988, "The Impact of Progressive Income Tax Rates on Canadian Negotiated Wage Rate", *Canadian Journal of Economics*, vol. 21, May, pp. 279-84.

Ballard, C. L., 1990, "Marginal Welfare Cost Calculations", *Journal of Public Economics*, v. 41, (263-276).

Ballard, C. L., and Fullerton, D., 1992, *Journal of Economic Perspectives*, v. 6, no. 3, Summer, (117-131).

Barro, R. J., 1995, Inflation and Economic Growth, *Bank of England Quarterly Bulletin*, May, (166-76).

Bass, F.M., and Scully, G.W., 1995, *Convergence of Living Standards*, School of Management, University of Texas at Dallas, February.

Baumol, Wm. 1991, "Towards a Newer Economics: The Future Lies Ahead", *Economic Journal*, vol. 101, January, pp.1-8.

Becker, R.A., 1985, "Capital Income Taxation and Perfect Foresight", *Journal of Public Economics*, vol.26, March, pp.147-67.

Bergson, A., 1973, "On Monopoly Welfare Losses", *American Economic Review*, vol. LXIII, December, pp. 853-870.

Bird, R. M., 1991, "More Taxing Than Taxes: An Introduction", in Bird, R. M., (ed) *More Taxing Than Taxes: The Taxlike Effects of Nontax Policies in LDCs*, San Francisco: Institute for Contemporary Studies.

Bird, R.M., 1992, *Tax Policy & Economic Development*, Baltimore: Johns Hopkins University Press.

Blanchflower, D.G., and Oswald, A.J., 1995, "An Introduction to the Wage Curve", *Journal of Economic Perspectives*, vol. 9, No. 3, Summer pp. 153-167.

Blinder, A., 1997, Is There A Core of Practical Macroeconomics That We Should All Believe?", *AEA Papers and Proceedings*, v. 87, no. 2, pp. 240-243.

Blundell, R., 1995, "Tax Policy Reform: Why We Need Microeconomics", *Fiscal Studies*, vol. 16, no. 3, pp. 106-25.

Boadway, R., Bruce, N. and Mintz, J., 1984, "Taxation, Inflation and the Effective Marginal Tax Rate in Canada", *Canadian Journal of Economics,* vol. 17, pp. 62-79.

Branson, J.H., and Lovell, C.A.K., 1997, *A Growth Maximising Tax Burden and Tax Mix for New Zealand*, March, Working Paper No. 30, Working Papers on Monitoring the Health of the Tax System, Wellington: Inland Revenue.

Brash, D.T., 1996, *New Zealand's Remarkable Reforms*, Fifth Annual Hayek Memorial Lecture, London: Institute of Economic Affairs, 4 June.

Britton, S., LeHeron, R., and Pawson, E., 1992, *Changing Places in New Zealand: A Geography of Restructuring*, Christchurch: New Zealand Geographical Society, Canterbury University.

Boskin, M.J., (ed) 1996, *Frontiers of Tax Reform*, Stanford: Hoover Institution Press.

Browne, T.M., and Leeflang, K.W., 1996, *The Hidden Costs of Employment: A Comparative Study of Income Tax and Additional Employment Costs Across Europe*, London; Deloitte Touche Tohmatsu International.

Buchanan, J.M., and Tullock, G., 1971, *The Calculus of Consent: Logical Foundations of Constitutional Democracy*, Ann Arbour: University of Michigan Press.

Buchanan, J.M., 1974, *The Limits of Liberty: Between Anarchy and Leviathan*, Chicago: University of Chicago Press

Buchanan, J.M., 1975, "Taxation in Fiscal Exchange", *Journal of Public Economics*, vol. 6. No.1/2, pp. 17-30.
Buchanan, J.M., 1993, "The Political Efficiency of General Taxation", *National Tax Journal*, vol. XLVI, no. 4, December, pp. 401-410.
Burgenmeier, 1994, "The Misperception of Walras", *American Economic Review*, vol. 84, no. 1, March, pp. 342-352.
Caragata, P.J., 1995, *The Integration of the Formal and Informal Financial Sectors in Albania*, Mission Report for the International Monetary Fund, Washington D.C., December. (Confidential).
Caragata, P.J., 1995a, *Optimal Cost Structures and Corporate Performance: Combining Learning Curve and Frontier Approaches to Economic Efficiency and Increasing Returns,* Working Paper No. 7, Working Papers on Monitoring the Health of the Tax System, Wellington, NZ: Inland Revenue, December (revised).
Caragata, P.J., 1996, *The Impact of the Revenue and Profit Efficiency Performance of Firms on Taxation*, Working Paper No. 19, Working Papers on Monitoring the Health of the Tax System, Wellington, NZ: Inland Revenue, November.
Caragata, P.J., and Heiler, A., 1997, *The Labour-Taxation Trade-off for Inefficient Firms*, Working Paper No. XX, Working Papers on Monitoring the Health of the Tax System, Wellington, NZ: Inland Revenue, forthcoming.
Caragata, P.J., and Giles, D.E.A., 1996, *Simulating the Relationship Between the Hidden Economy and the Tax Mix in New Zealand,* Working Paper No. 22, Working Papers on Monitoring the Health of the Tax System, Wellington, NZ: Inland Revenue, November.
Caragata, P.J. and Small, J., 1996, *Tax Burden Effects on Output Growth in New Zealand: A Non-Linear Dynamic Model,* Working Paper No. 24, Working Papers on Monitoring the Health of the Tax System, Wellington, NZ: Inland Revenue, December.
Caragata, P.J., and Small, J., 1996a, *The Tax Burden, The Tax Mix and Output Growth in New Zealand: A Tax Mix Model,* Working Paper No. 25, Working Papers on Monitoring the Health of the Tax System, Wellington, NZ: Inland Revenue, December.
Carlsson, B., 1972, "The Measurement of Efficiency in Production: An Application to Swedish Manufacturing Industries", *Swedish Journal of Economics*, vol. 74, no. 4, pp. 468-485.
Chapple, S., 1997. "One From the X-Files? Scully on Taxation and Economic Growth", *Update*, July, Wellington: New Zealand Institute of Economic Research. P. 1
Chapple, S., 1997a, "IRD Tax Papers Need to be Taken With a Grain of Salt", *The National Business Review*, 18 July.
Chapple, S., 1997b, "One From the X-Files: A Critical Assessment of Professor Scully's "Taxation and Economic Growth in New Zealand", August, Wellington: New Zealand Institute of Economic Research. Contract No. 1282
Clark, C., 1945, "Public Finance and Changes in the Value of Money", *Economic Journal*, December, 371-389.
Clark, J.M., 1923, *Studies in the Economics of Overhead Costs*, Chicago: University of Chicago Press.
Clark, J.M., 1940, "Toward a Concept of Workable Competition", *American Economic Review*, vol.XXX, June, no. 2, pp. 242-256.
Clark, J.M., 1961, *Competition as a Dynamic Process*, Washington, D.C.: The Brookings Institution.
Clotfelter, C.T., 1983, "Tax Evasion and Tax Rates: An Analysis of Individual Returns", *Review of Economics and Statistics*, vol. LXV, no. 3, August, pp.363-373.
Coase, R.H., 1937, "The Nature of the Firm", *Economica*, vol. 4, November, pp. 386-405.
Coase, R.H., 1992, "The Institutional Structure of Production", American Economic Review, vol. 82, no. 4, September 713-719.
Colander, D., 1992, "Retrospectives: The Lost Art of Economics", *Journal of Economic Perspectives*, vol. 6, no. 3, Summer, pp. 191-198.
Colgate, P., 1991, *Databases for Taxation Modelling*, Report to the Inland Revenue Department, Wellington: New Zealand Institute of Economic Research.
Collins, J. H. and Shackelford D.A. 1994. *Using Financial Statement Information to Compare the Corporation Income Tax Systems of Canada, Japan The United Kingdom and the United States.* Mimeo, Kegan-Flager Business School, University of North Carolina, Chapell Hill, NC, Price Waterhouse.
Cook, D., 1997, *Fiscal Modelling: Policy Change Scenarios*, Report for the Periodic Group, June, Wellington: NZ Institute of Economic Research.
Cook, D., 1997, *Fiscal Modelling: Combination Policy Scenarios*, Report for the Periodic Group, May, Wellington: NZ Institute of Economic Research.
Cook, D., and Briggs, P., 1997, *Fiscal Modelling: Middle Ground Scenarios*, Report for the Periodic Group, May, Wellington: NZ Institute of Economic Research.
Corlett, W.J., and Hague, D.C., 1953, "Complementarity and the Excess Burden of Taxation", *Review of Economic Studies*, vol. 21, no. 1, pp. 21-30.
Corsetti, G., and Roubini, N., 1996, Optimal Government Spending and Taxation in Endogenous Growth Models, NBER Working Paper Series, No.5851, Cambridge, Ma: National Bureau of Economic Research.
Crawford, J.R., 1944, *Estimating, Budgeting and Scheduling*, Burbank California: Lockheed Aircraft Corporation.

Crawford, J.R., (n.d.) *Learning Curve, Ship Curve, Ratios, Related Data*, Burbank California: Lockheed Aircraft Corporation.

Crocombe, G.T., Enright, M. J., and Porter, M.E., 1991, *Upgrading New Zealand's Competitive Advantage*, Auckland: Oxford University Press.

Cummins, J.G., Hassett, K.A., and Hubbard, R.G., 1995, "Tax Reforms and Investment: A Cross-Country Comparison", NBER Working Paper Series, Working Paper 5232, August, Cambridge, MA: National Bureau of Economic Research.

Dahlby, B., 1996, Commentary on Erwin Diewert and Denis Lawrence, 'The Marginal Cost of Taxation in New Zealand", *Canadian Journal of Economics*, XXIX, Special Issue, April.

Davis, S.J., Haltiwanger, J.C., and Schuh, S., 1996, *Job Creation and Destruction*, MIT Press: Cambridge, Massachusetts.

Delionback, L.M., 1987, "Learning Curves and Progress Functions", in Stewart, R.D., and Wyskida,R.M., 1987, *Cost Estimator's Reference Manual*, New York: John Wiley.

Diewert, W.E., 1981, "The Measurement of Waste Within the Production Sector of an Open Economy", *Scandinavian Journal of Economics*, vol. 85, no. 2, pp. 159-179.

Diewert, W.E., 1981a, "The Measurement of Deadweight Loss Revisited", Econometrica, Vol. 49, No. 5, September, 1225-1244.

Diewert, W.E., and Lawrence, D.A., 1994, *The Marginal Costs of Taxation in New Zealand*, Canberra: Swan Consultants (prepared for the New Zealand Business Roundtable).

Downie, J., 1956, "How We Should Control Monopoly: II", *Economic Journal*, vol. 66, December, pp. 574-77.

Downie, J., 1958, *The Competitive Process*, London: Gerald Duckworth & Co.

Dunmore, Paul, 1994a, *The Cross Sectional Distributions of Financial Ratios: Theory Evidence and Implications. Mimeo*, Prepared for the New Zealand Inland Revenue Department, Wellington, New Zealand: Victoria University.

Dunmore 1994b, *Some Issues Pertinent to the Validity of Tax-Burden Inferences*, Prepared for the New Zealand Inland Revenue Department, Wellington, New Zealand: Victoria University.

Dupuit, J., 1844, "De La Mesure de l"Utilite des Travaux Publique", Annales des Ponts et Chaussees, 2nd Series, vol. 8, (On the Measure of the Utility of Public Works, English Translation in *International Economic Papers*, no.2. (1952).

Easton, B., 1997, "Baths, Hogwash and Taxes", *Listener*, 12 July, p. 57.

Engen E.M., and Skinner, J., 1996, *Taxation and Economic Growth*, NBER Working Paper Series, No. 5826. Cambridge, Ma: National Bureau of Economic Research.

Evans, L., Grimes, A., Wilkinson, B., and Teece, D., 1996, "Economic Reform in New Zealand 1984-1995: The Pursuit of Efficiency", *Journal of Economic Literature*, vol. XXXIV, December, pp. 1856-1902.

Fair, R.C., 1993, Testing Macroeconometric Models", *AEA Papers and Proceedings*, vol. 83, no. 2, May, pp.287-293.

Fare, R., Grosskopf, S., and Lovell, C.A.K., 1983, "The Structure of Technical Efficiency", *Scandinavian Journal of Economics*, 85 (2), pp.181-190.

Farrell, M.J., 1957, "The Measurement of Productive Efficiency", *Journal of the Royal Statistical Society*, Series A. General, vol. 120, no. 3, pp.253-81.

Feige, E.L., 1982, "A New Perspective on Macroeconomic Phenomena: The Theory and Measurement of the Unobserved Economy in the United States: Causes, Consequences and Implications", in Walker, M., (ed) *International Burden of Government*, Vancouver: Fraser Institute, pp. 112-136.

Feldman, A.M., 1983, *Welfare Economics and Social Choice Theory*, New York: Free Press.

Feldstein, M., 1974, "Incidence of a Capital Income Tax in a Growing Economy with Variable Savings Rates" *Review of Economic Studies*, 41, October, pp. 505-13.

Feldstein, M., 1976, "On the Theory of Tax Reform", *Journal of Public Economics*, vol. 6, pp. 77-104.

Feldstein, M., 1995, *Tax Avoidance and the Deadweight Loss of the Income Tax*, Working Paper No. 5055, National Bureau of Economic Research, Cambridge, MA: National Bureau of Economic Research.

Feldstein, M., 1995a, *The Behavioural Responses to Tax Rates: Evidence From TRA86*, NBER Working Paper Series, Working Paper 5000, February, Cambridge, MA: National Bureau of Economic Research.

Feldstein, M., 1996, *The Costs and Benefits of Going From Low Inflation to Price Stability*, NBER Working Paper Series, Working Paper 5459, February, Cambridge, MA: National Bureau of Economic Research.

Feldstein, M., 1996a, "How Big Should Government Be?" NBER Working Paper Series, Working Paper 5868, December, Cambridge, MA: National Bureau of Economic Research.

Feldstein, M. and Feenberg, D., 1995, *The Effect of Increased Tax Rates on Taxable Income and Economic Efficiency: A Preliminary Analysis of the 1993 Tax Rate Increases*, Working Paper 5370, National Bureau of Economic Research, Cambridge.

Fisher, F.M., 1983, *Disequilibrium Foundations of Equilibrium Economics*, New York: Cambridge University Press.

Forsund, F.R., and Hjalmarsson, L., 1974, "On the Measurement of Productive Efficiency", *Swedish Journal of Economics*, vol. 76, pp. 141-154.

Forsund, F.R, and Hjalmarsson, L. 1987, *Analyses of Industrial Structure: A Putty Clay Approach*, Stockholm: The Industrial Institute for Economic and Social Research.

Frankel, J., 1993, "Quantifying International Capital Mobility in the 1980s", in Frankel J., 1993, *On Exchange Rates*, Cambridge Mass: M.I.T. Press.

Frantz, R., 1985, "X-Efficiency Theory and Its Critics", *Quarterly Review of Economics and Business*, vol. 25, No. 4, Winter.

Freeman, R.B., 1995, "The Large Welfare State as a System", *AEA Papers and Proceedings*, vol. 85, No. 2, pp. 16-21

Frenkel, J.A., 1993, "Top Economist Ponders a Changing World", *Finance & Development*, December pp. 2-5.

Frey, B.S. and Weck-Hanneman, H., 1984, "The Hidden Economy as an 'Unobserved' Variable", *European Economic Review*, vol. 26, pp.33-53.

Frisch, R., 1939a, "The Dupuit Taxation Theorem", *Econometrica*, vol. 7, April, pp. 145-150.

Frisch, R., 1939b, "A Further Note on the Dupuit Taxation Theorem", *Econometrica*, vol. 7, April, pp. 156-7.

Fullerton, D., 1991, "Reconciling Recent Estimates of the Marginal Welfare Cost of Taxation", *American Economic Review*, vol. 81, no.1, pp. 302-308.

Gibrat, R., 1931, *Les Inegalites economiques*, Paris: Libraire du Recuil Sirey; reproduced in 1957 in *International Economic Papers*, as "On Economic Inequalities", vol. 7, p.53-70.

Giles, D.E.A., 1996, *Measuring the Size of the Hidden Economy and the Tax Gap in New Zealand: An Econometric Analysis*, Working Paper No.5 (rev), Working Papers on Monitoring the Health of the Tax System, Wellington NZ: Inland Revenue, December.

Giles, D. E. A.,1996a, "Causality Between the Measured and Underground Economies in New Zealand", to appear in *Applied Economics Letters*.

Giles, D. E. A., 1996b, "The Hidden Economy and Tax-Evasion Prosecutions in New Zealand", to appear in *Applied Economics Letters*.

Giles, D. E. A., 1996c, "Testing for Asymmetry in the Measured and Underground Business Cycles in New Zealand", to appear in *Economic Record*.

Giles, D.E.A., and Caragata, P.J., 1996, *The Learning Path of the Hidden Economy: Tax and Growth Effects in New Zealand*, Working Paper No. 21, Working Papers on Monitoring the Health of the Tax System, Wellington, NZ: Inland Revenue, August .

Giles, D.E.A., 1997, Modelling the Tax Compliance/Non-Compliance Profiles of Audited New Zealand Firms: Evidence from the ORACLE Database, Working Paper No.28, Working Papers on Monitoring the Health of the Tax System, Wellington NZ: Inland Revenue, May.

Goldberger, A.S., 1972, *Structural Equation Methods in the Social Sciences*, Amsterdam: North-Holland.

Gordon, R.H., and MacKie-Mason, J.K., 1993, *Why is There Corporate Taxation in a Small Open Economy? The Role of Transfer Pricing and Income Shifting*, University of Michigan and NBER, November, (mimeo).

Gordon, R.H., and Nielsen, S.B., 1996, *Tax Avoidance and Value-Added Vs Income Taxation in an Open Economy*, NBER Working Paper 5527, Cambridge, Mass.

Granger, C.W.J., 1969, "Investigating Causal Relations by Econometric Models and Cross Spectral Methods", *Econometrica*, vol. 37, pp. 434-438.

Greenwald, B.C. and Stiglitz, J.E., 1995, "Labour-Market Adjustments and the Persistence of Unemployment," *American Economic Review Papers and Proceedings*, vol. 85, no. 2, May, pp.19-225.

Griffith, R., 1996, "A Note on the Taxation of Capital Income in the Czech Republic and Poland", *Fiscal Studies*, vol. 17, no. 3, pp. 91-103.

Grosse, A.P., 1953, "The Technological Structure of the Cotton Textile Industry", in Leontief, W., 1953, *Studies in the Structure of the American Economy*, New York: Oxford U. Press.

Grossman, P.J., 1987, "The Optimal Size of Government", *Public Choice*, vol. 56, 193-200.

Grubert, H., and Mutti, J., 1987, "The Impact of the Tax Reform Act of 1986 in Trade and Capital Flows", in *Compendium of Tax Research*, Washington D.C.: U.S. Treasury Department.

Grubert, H., Goodspeed, T., and Swenson, D., 1991, "Explaining the Taxable Income of Foreign-Controlled Companies in the United States", in Giovanni, A., Hubbard, R.G., and Slemrod, J., *Studies in International Taxation*, (eds), University of Chicago Press, pp. 237-270.

Grubert, H. and Mutti, J. 1991. "Taxes, Tariffs and Transfer Pricing in Multinational Corporate Decision Making." *Review of Economics and Statistics*, vol. LXXII no.2, May, pp. 285-293.

Guesnerie, R., 1977, "On the Direction of Tax Reform", *Journal of Public Economics*, vol. 7, pp. 179-202.

Gutmann, P.M., 1977, "The Subterranean Economy", *Financial Analysts Journal*, vol. 33, November-December.

Haavelmo, T., 1956, *A Study of the Theory of Economic Evolution*, Amsterdam: North Holland.

Hahn, F.H., 1970, "Some Adjustment Problems", *Econometrica*, vol. 38, January, pp. 1-17.

Hahn, F.H., 1973, *On the Notion of Equilibrium in Economics*, Cambridge: Cambridge U.Press.

Hall, V.B., and Rae, D., 1996, "Fiscal Expansion, Interest Rate Risk Premia, and Wage Reactions: Some Illustrative Simulations with NBNZ-DEMONZ", Working Paper 14, *The GSBGM Working Paper Series*, Wellington: Victoria University .

Harberger, A.C., 1954, "Monopoly and Resource Allocation", *American Economic Review*, vol. 44, May, pp. 77-87.

Harberger, A.,C., 1962, "The Incidence of the Corporation Income Tax", *Journal of Political Economy*, vol. 70, pp. 215-240.

Harberger, A.C., 1964, "Principles of Efficiency: The Measurement of Waste", *American Economic Review*, vol. 54, pp. 58-76.

Harberger, A.C., et al. 1992, "Interface Between Economic Techniques and Economic Policy", Contemporary Policy Issues, vol. 10, July.

Harberger, A.C., 1993, "The Search for Relevance in Economics", Richard T. Ely Lecture, *AEA Papers and Proceedings*, vol. 83, no.2, May, pp. 1-16.

Hassett, K.A. and Hubbard, R.G., 1996, "Tax Policy and Investment", NBER Working Paper Series, Working Paper 5683, December, Cambridge, MA: National Bureau of Economic Research.

Haynes, J., 1895, "Risk as an Economic Factor", *Quarterly Journal of Economics*, pp. 409-449.

Heckscher, E.F., 1918, *Svenska produktionsproblem*, Stockholm: Bonnier.

Hicks, J.R., 1939, "The Foundations of Welfare Economics", *Economic Journal*, vol. 49, December, pp. 696-712.

Hicks, J.R., 1940, "The Valuation of Social Income", *Economica*, vol. 7, May, pp. 105-124.

Hicks, J.R., 1941, *Value and Capital: An Inquiry into Some Fundamental Principles of Economic Theory*, Oxford: Clarendon Press. Second edition.(originally published in 1939).

Hicks, J.R., 1941a, "The Rehabilitation of Consumer's Surplus", *Review of Economic Studies*, vol. 8, pp. 108-116.

Hicks, J.R., 1947, "The Empty Economy", *Lloyds Bank Review*, vol. 5, July, pp. 1-13.

Higgins, M.M. (Year) "An Empirical Analysis of the Relationship Between Corporate Effective Tax Rates and Book Effective Tax Rates With an Analysis of the Financial Characteristics the Influence Corporate Effective Tax Rates." *Ph.D. Thesis University of Tennessee*. Knoxville.

Hill, R., and Kabir. M., 1995, *Currency Demand and the Underground Economy in Canada,1991-1993*, Department of Economics, University of New Brunswick (mimeo).

Hines, J.R. (Jr.) and Hubbard, R.G., 1990, "Coming Home To America: Dividend Repatriations by U.S. Multinationals", in Razin. A., and Slemrod, J., (ed) *Taxation in a Global Economy*, Chicago: University of Chicago Press.

Hirsch, W.Z, 1952, "Manufacturing Progress Functions", *Review of Economics and Statistics*, vol. 34, May, pp. 143-155.

Hirsch, W.Z., 1956, "Firm Progress Ratios", *Econometrica*, vol. 25, pp. 136-143.

Hotelling, H., 1932, "Edgeworth's Taxation Paradox and the Nature of Demand and Supply Functions", *Journal of Political Economy*, vol. 40, no. 5, October, pp. 577-616.

Hotelling, H., 1938, "The General Welfare in Relation to Problems of Taxation and of Railway and Utility Rates:, *Econometrica*, vol. 6, July, pp. 242-269.

Hotelling, H., 1939a, "The Relation of Prices to Marginal Costs in an Optimum System", *Econometrica*, vol. 7, April, pp. 151-55.

Hotelling, H., 1939b, "A Final Note", *Econometrica*, vol. 7, April, pp. 151-55.

Houston, J.P., 1976, *Fundamentals of Learning*, New York: Academic Press.

Hubbard, R.G., and Slemrod, J., (eds), *Studies in International Taxation*, Chicago: U of Chicago Press.

Hull, C.L., 1943, *Essentials of Behaviour*, New York: Appleton.

IMF, 1995, *Taxation and Unemployment*, Washington: Fiscal Affairs Department, International Monetary Fund.

Ijiri, Y., and Simon, H.A., 1974, "Interpretations of Departures from the Pareto-Curve Firm-Size Distributions", *Journal of Political Economy*, vol. 82, pp.315-331.

Jackson, L. Fraser, 1997, *Taxation and Economic Growth: A Critique of Scully*, University of Victoria, Wellington.

Joreskog, K., and Goldberger, A.S., 1975, "Estimation of a Model With Multiple Indicators and Multiple Causes of a Single Latent Variable", *Journal of the American Statistical Association*, vol. 70, pp. 631-639.

Joreskog, K., and Sorbom, D., 1993a, *LISREL 8: Structural Equation Modelling With the Simplis Command Language*, Chicago: Scientific Software International.

Joreskog, K., and Sorbom, D., 1993a, *LISREL 8:User's Reference Guide,* Chicago: Scientific Software International.

Judd, K.L., 1985, "Redistributive Taxation in a Simple Perfect Foresight Model", *Journal of Public Economics*, vol. 28, October, pp. 59-83.

Kaldor, N., 1980, "Memorandum of Dissent", in *Reports on Taxation*, Vol. 1, London: Duckworth.

Kaplan, S.N., and Zingales. L., 1995, "Do Financing Constraints Explaikn Why Investment Is Correlated With Cash Flow?", NBER Working Paper Series, Working Paper 5267, February, Cambridge, Ma: National Bureau of Economic Research.

Kaplow, L., 1994, "A Fundamental Objection to Tax Equity Norms: A Call for Utilitarianism", NBER Working Paper Series, Working Paper 4961, February, Cambridge, MA: National Bureau of Economic Research.

Kaplow, L., 1996, "How Tax Complexity and Enforcement Affect the Equity and Efficiency of The Income Tax", *National Tax Journal*, vol. XLIX, no. 1, March, pp. 135-150.

Kay, J. A., 1990, "Tax Policy: A Survey", *Economic Journal*, vol. 100, March, pp.18-75.

Kesselman, J.R., 1993, "Evasion Effects of Changing the Tax Mix", The Economic Record, v. 69, no. 205, June pp 131-48.

Keynes, J. Maynard, 1923, *A Tract on Monetary Reform*, London: Macmillan.

Keynes, J. Neville, 1891, 1917, *The Scope and Method of Political Economy*, 4th Edition, London: Macmillan.

King, M. and Fullerton, D. 1984. "*The Taxation of Income From Capital.*" Chicago: U. of Chicago Press.

Kirman, A.P. 1992, "Whom or What Does the Representative Individual Represent?", *Journal of Economic Perspectives*, vol. 6, vol. 2, Spring, pp. 117-136.
Klepper, S., and Nagin, D., 1989, "The Anatomy of Tax Evasion", *Journal of Law, Economics and Organization*, vol. 1, pp. 1-24.
Koop, G., Osiewalski, J., and Steel, M.F.J, 1997, "Modeling The Sources of Output Growth in a Panel of Countries", Tilburg, Netherlands: Department of Econometrics, Tilburg University.
Kryzaniuk, M., and Musgrave, R., 1963, *The Shifting of Corporate Income Tax*, Baltimore: Johns-Hopkins Press.
Law, S. B., 1997, *Risk Profiling of Corporate Taxpayers*, Working Paper No. 27, Working Papers on Monitoring the Health of the Tax System, Wellington, New Zealand: Inland Revenue, May.
Lange, O., 1942, "The Foundations of Welfare Economics", *Econometrica*, vol. 10, July-October, pp.215-228.
Leibenstein, H., 1966, "Allocative Efficiency Vs 'X-Efficiency'", *American Economic Review*, vol. 56, June, pp. 392-415.
Leibfritz, W., Thornton, J., and Bibbee, A., 1997, *Taxation and Economic Performance*, Economics Department Working Papers No. 176. Paris: OECD.
Leontief, W., 1971, "Theoretical Assumptions and Nonobservable Facts", *American Economic Review*, vol. 61, March, pp. 1-7.
Lindbeck, A., 1986, "Limits to the Welfare State", *Challenge*, January-February, pp. 31-36.
Lindbeck, A., 1995, "Hazardous Welfare-State Dynamics", *AES Papers and Proceedings*, v. 85, no. 2. pp. 9-15.
Lindsey, L.B., 1990, The Growth Experiment: How the New Tax Policy is Transforming the U.S. Economy, New York: Basic Books
Lipsey, R.G., and Lancaster, K., 1956, "The General Theory of Second Best", *Review of Economic Studies*, vol. 24, pp. 11-32.
Little, I.M.D. 1957, *A Critique of Welfare Economics*, Oxford: Clarendon Press.
Little, I.M.D. 1993, *Macroeconomic Analysis and the Developing Countries: 1970-1990*, San Francisco: Institute for Contemporary Studies Press.
Lovell, C.A.K., 1993, "Production Frontiers and Productive Efficiency", in Fried, H.O., Lovell, C.A.K., Schmidt, S.S., (eds) 1993, *The Measurement of Productive Efficiency: Techniques and Applications*, New York: Oxford University Press.
Marschak, J., and Andrews Jr. Wm. H., 1944, "Random Simultaneous Equations and the Theory of Production", *Econometrica*, vol. 12, nos. 3 & 4, July-October.
Marshall, A., 1890, 1961, *The Principles of Economics*, 9th (variorium) edition, with annotation by C.W. Guillebaud, London: Macmillan.
Marshall, A. 1907, *Elements of Economics of Industry*, fourth edition, London: Macmillan.
Martins, J.O., and Scarpetta, S. and Pilat, D., 1996, "Mark-up Ratios in Manufacturing Industries: Estimates for 14 OECD Countries", Economics Department Working Papers No. 162 (OECD/GD (96) 61 Paris: OECD.
Maasoumi, E., 1986, "Reduced Form Estimation and Prediction from Uncertain Structural Models," *Journal of Econometrics*, vol. 31, February, pp. 3-29.
Mayer, T., 1993, *Truth Versus Precision in Economics*, Aldershot, England: Edward Elgar.
McCann, E., Small, J., and Caragata, P.J., 1995, *An Endogenous Effective Tax Rates Model*, Working Paper No,. 10, Working Papers on Monitoring the Health of the Tax System, Wellington N.Z.: Inland Revenue, December
Matthews, K., 1992, Could the U.S. Really Raise $45 Billion From Foreign Firms?, *Tax Notes*, vol.2, November, pp-577-579;
McIntyre, R.S., and Spinner, J., 1986, *130 Reasons Why We Need Tax Reform*, Washington, D.C: Citizens for Tax Justice.
McIvor, G., 1996, "Sweden Likely to get Nod on Alcohol Curb", *Financial Times of London*, December 3, p. 3.
McKenzie, K., Mintz, J., and Scharf, K., 1993, "Differential Taxation of Canadian and US Passenger Transportation", Chapter 21 in *Report of the Royal Commission on National Passenger Transportation* vol. 4, Ottawa: Supply of Services, Canada.
Melton, A.W., 1936. "The End-spurt in Memorization Curves as an Artifact of the Averaging of Individual Curves", *Psychological Monographs*, vol. 47, pp. 119-134.
Mintz, J., 1988, "An Empirical Estimate of Corporate Tax Refundability and Effective Tax Rates", *Quarterly Journal of Economics*, vol. 103, pp. 225-32.
Mintz, J., 1995, "The Corporation Tax: A Survey", *Fiscal Studies*, vol. 16, no. 4, pp. 23-68.
Mitchell, W.C., 1937, "The Social Sciences and National Planning", in Mackenzie, E. (ed) *Planned Society: Yesterday, Today and Tomorrow*, New York: Prentice Hall.
Morrison, C.J., and Schwartz, E., 1996, "State Infrastructure and Productive Performance", *American Economic Review*, vol. 85, no. 5, pp. 1095-1111.
Musgrave, R.A., 1959, *The Theory of Public Finance*, New York: McGraw-Hill.
Nelson, R., R., 1991, "Why Do Firms Differ, and How Does it Matter?", *Strategic Management Journal*, vol. 12, pp. 61-74.
Nelson, R.R., 1995, "Recent Evolutionary Theorizing About Economic Change", *Journal of Economic Literature*, vol. XXXIII, March, pp. 48-90.

Nelson, R.R., and Winter, S.G., 1982, *An Evolutionary Theory of Economic Change*, Cambridge: Harvard University Press.
Niskanen, W.A., 1971, *Bureaucracy and Representative Government*, Chicago: Aldine-Atherton.
NZPC, 1980, *Public Expenditure and Its Financing: 1950-1979*, Wellington: New Zealand Planning Council.
OECD, 1991, *Taxing Profits in a Global Economy*, Paris: Organisation for Economic Cooperation and Development.
OECD, 1993, Economic Surveys: New Zealand, Paris.
OECD, 1996, *Competition, Regulation and Performance*, Directorate for Financial, Fiscal and Enterprise Affairs, Committee on Competition Law and Policy, DAFFE/CLP (95) 37.
Olson, M., 1996, Distinguished Lecture on Economics in Government, "Big Bills Left on the Sidewalk: Why Some Nations are Rich, and Others Poor", *Journal of Economic Perspectives*, vol. 10, no. 2, Spring, pp. 3-24.
Pack, H., 1994, "Endogenous Growth Theory: Intellectual Appeal and Empirical Shortcomings", *Journal of Economic Perspectives*, vol. 8, no. 1, Winter, pp.55-72.
Park, T., 1979, *Reconciliation Between Personal Income and Taxable Income, 1947-1977*, Washington D.C.: Bureau of Economic Analysis (mimeo).
Peden, E.A. and Bradley, M.D., 1989, "Government Size, Productivity, and Economic Growth: the Post-War Experience. *Public Choice*, vol. 61, pp. 229-245.
Peden, E.A., 1991, "Productivity in the United States and its Relationship to Government Activity: An Analysis of 57 Years, 1929-1986." *Public Choice*, vol. 69, pp. 153-173.
Peters, W., 1997, *The Budget Economic & Fiscal Update,1997*, Wellington: The Treasury, 26 June.
Phelps, E.S., 1994, *Structural Slumps: The Modern Equilibrium Theory of Unemployment, Interest, and Assets.* Cambridge, MA: Harvard University Press.
Porcano, T. 1986. "Progressive, Proportional or Regressive." *The Journal of the American Taxation Association,"* Spring, pp. 17-31.
Porter, P.K., and Scully, G.W., 1995, "Institutional Technology and Economic Growth", *Public Choice*, vol. 82, pp. 17-36.
Rae, DE., 1996, "Let's Go Shopping, but with tax cuts or government spending?", *Business Outlook*, The National Bank of New Zealand, December, p.5-6.
Rahman, A., 1992, "The Informal Financial Sector in Bangladesh: An Appraisal of its Role in Development", *Development and Change*, vol. 23, pp. 147-168.
Reder, M.W., 1943, "An Alternative Interpretation of the Cobb-Douglas Function", *Econometrica*, vol. 11, pp. 259-64.
Reder, M.W., 1947, *Studies in the Theory of Welfare Economics*, New York: Columbia U. Press.
Reder, M.W., 1947a, "A Reconsideration of the Marginal Productivity Theory", *Journal of Political Economy*, vol. 55, no. 5, pp.450-458.
Redman, D.A., 1994, "Karl Popper's Theory of Science and Econometrics: The Rise and Decline of Social Engineering", *Journal of Economic Issues*, Vol. XXVIII, No. 1, March.
Revenue Canada, 1996, *Managing Compliance*, Note by the Delegate From Canada, Special Sessions on Consumption Taxes, Directorate for Financial, Fiscal and Enterprise Affairs, Committee on Fiscal Affairs, DAFFE/CFA/CT (96) 14, Paris: OECD.
Richardson Report, 1994, *Organisational Review of the Inland Revenue Department*, Report to the Minister of Revenue (and on tax policy, also to the Minister of Finance) from the Organisational Review Committee, Wellington, NZ, April.
Rice, E.M., 1992, "The Corporate Tax Gap: Evidence on Tax Compliance by Small Corporations", in Slemrod, J., (ed) 1992. Op. Cit.
Rogers, A., and Caragata, P.J., 1995, *Effective Tax Rates: Zero Tax Payments and the Migration of Firms Across Tax Bands,*, Working Paper No. 15, December, Working Papers on Monitoring the Health of the Tax System, Wellington, New Zealand: Inland Revenue.
Rodik, D., "Why Do More Open Economies Have Bigger Governments?", NBER Working Paper Series Working Paper 5537, December, Cambridge, MA: National Bureau of Economic Research.
Rogerson, R., 1997, "Theory Ahead of Language in the Economics of Unemployment", *Journal of Economic Perspectives*, vol. 11, no. 1, Winter, pp. 73-92.
Rose, R., 1985, "Maximising Tax Revenue While Minimising Political Costs", *Journal of Public Policy, vol. 5, no 3, pp289-320.*
Roubini, N., and Milesi-Ferretti, G.M., 1994, *Taxation and Endogenous Growth in Open Economies*, Working Paper No. 4881, Cambridge, MA: National Bureau of Economic Research.
Rustow, H.J., 1926, *Accumulation and Crises: A Contribution Toward the Theory of the Business Cycle* doctoral dissertation at the University of Heidelberg.
Rustow, H.J., 1967, "The Development of the Shares of Wages and Profits in an Industrial Society", *The German Economic Review*, vol. 5, no. 2, pp 7-115. Wissenschaftliche Verlagsgesellschaft M.B.H Stuttgart.
Rustow, H.J., 1978 "The Economic Crisis of the Weimar Republic and How It Was Overcome - A Comparison with the Present Recession", *Cambridge Journal of Economics*, vol. 2, pp. 409-421.

Rustow, H.J., 1991, Paths to Full Employment: The Failure of Orthodox Economic Theory, London: Macmillan (originally published in Germany in 1984 as "Neue WegeVollbeschaftigung" by Duncker and Hobblot Gmb H.)
Salter, W.E.G., 1960, *Productivity and Technical Change*, London: Cambridge University Press.
Sato, K., 1967, "Taxation and Neo-classical Growth", *Public Finance*, vol. 22, no. 3, pp. 346-70.
Saxton, C.C., 1942, *The Economics of Price Determination*, London: Oxford University Press.
Schneider, F., and Pommerehne, W.W., 1985, *The Decline of Productivity Growth and the Rise of the Shadow Economy in the U.S.*, Denmark: University of Arhus (mimeo)
Scholes, M.S. and Wolfson, M.A., 1992, *Taxes and Business Strategy: A Planning Approach*, Englewood Cliffs, New Jersey: Prentice Hall.
Scully, G.W., 1988, "The Institutional Framework and Economic Development", *Journal of Political Economy*, vol. 96, no. 3, pp. 652-662.
Scully, G.W., 1991, Tax Rates, Tax Revenues and Economic Growth, Policy Report No. 98, National Centre for Policy Analysis, Dallas.
Scully, G.W., 1992, *Constitutional Environments and Economic Growth*, Princeton, New Jersey: Princeton University Press.
Scully, G.W., 1995, "The 'Growth Tax' in the United States", *Public Choice, vol. 85, pp.71-80.*
Scully, G.W., 1996, *Taxation and Economic Growth in New Zealand*, Working Paper No. 14, Working Papers on Monitoring the Health of the Tax System, Wellington, NZ: Inland Revenue, March.
Scully, G.W. 1996a, *The Growth-Maximising Tax Mix in New Zealand*, Working Paper No. 20, Working Papers on Monitoring the Health of the Tax System, Wellington, NZ: Inland Revenue, August.
Scully, G.W. 1996b, *Taxation and Employment in New Zealand*, Working Paper No. 23, Working Papers on Monitoring the Health of the Tax System, Wellington, NZ: Inland Revenue, August.
Scully, G.W., 1996c *Taxation and Employment in the United States*, Dallas, Texas: National Center for Policy Analysis, Policy Report, in draft.
Scully, G.W., 1996d, "Rule and Policy Spaces and Economic Progress: Lessons for Third World Countries," *Public Choice*, in press.
Scully, G.W., 1996e, "Taxation and Economic Growth in New Zealand", *Pacific Economic Review, vol. 1, no. 2pp. 169-77.*
Scully, G.W., 1997, *Reply to Formal Review by E. Seiper.*
Scully, G.W, 1997a, *Reply to Jackson Critique of Scully Paper*, (mimeo), University of Texas at Dallas, August.
Scully, G.W., and Stroombergen, A.., 1997, *The Equity-Efficiency Trade-Off in New Zealand: A Preliminary Analysis*, Working Paper No. 33, Working Papers on Monitoring the Health of the Tax System, Wellington, NZ: Inland Revenue, August.
Secrist, H., 1924, *Expense Levels in Retailing: A Study of the 'Representative Firm' and of 'Bulk-Line Costs in the Distribution of Clothing*, Chicago: The Bureau of Business Research, Northwestern University School of Commerce.
Seiper, E., 1997, Formal Review by E. Seiper of G.W. Scully, Taxation and Economic Growth in New Zealand, Revised IRD Working Paper No. 14, 28 March 1996, Canberra: Australian National University (Produced for the New Zealand Treasury).
Senior, N. 1862, *Report of Inspectors of Factories*, October 31, as cited in Clark (1923:6)
Simon, H. A., and Bonini, C.P., 1958, "The Size Distributions of Business Firms", *American Economic Review*, vol. 48, pp.607-17.
Sims, C.A.,1980, "Macroeconomics and Reality," *Econometrica*, vol. 48, January, pp. 1-40.
Slemrod, J., 1992, "Why Do People Pay Taxes: Introduction", in Slemrod, J., (ed) *Why People Pay Taxes: Tax Compliance and Enforcement*, Ann Arbour: University of Michigan Press.
Slemrod, J., (ed) 1992a, *Why People Pay Taxes: Tax Compliance and Enforcement*, Ann Arbour: University of Michigan Press.
Slemrod, J., 1991, "Comment", on Usher (1991) op. cit., in Bird (1991) op. cit.
Slemrod, J., 1990, "Optimal Taxation and Optimal Tax Systems", *Journal of Economic Perspectives*, Vol. 4, pp. 157-178.
Slemrod, J., 1985, "An Empirical Test for Tax Evasion", *Review of Economics and Statistics*, vol. LXVII, no. 2, May, pp. 232-238.
Small, J., 1995, The Marginal Costs of Taxation in New Zealand: A Sensitivity Analysis of the Diewert and Lawrence Model, Working Paper No. 16, Working Papers on Monitoring the Health of the Tax System, Inland Revenue, December.
Smith, A., 1786, *An Inquiry into the Nature and Causes of the Wealth of Nations*, Fourth Edition, vol. I, II, III, London: A. Strahan and T. Cadell in the Strand.
Spiro, P.S., 1996, "The Impact of Income Taxes on Job Creation", *Canadian Tax Journal*, v. 44, no. 3, pp. 1-27.
Steindl, J., 1965, *Random Processes and the Growth of Firms*, New York: Hafner Publishing Co.
Stiglitz, J.E., 1978, "Notes on Estate Taxes, Redistribution, and the Concept of Balanced Growth Path Incidence", *Journal of Political Economy*, vol. 86, no. 2, pt. 2, April, pp. S137- S150.
Stern, N., 1992, "From the Static to the Dynamic: Some Problems in the Theory of Taxation", *Journal of Public Economics*, vol. 47, pp. 273-297.
Summers R. and Heston A., 1991, "The Penn World Table (Mark 5): An Expanded Set of International Comparisons 1950-88", *Quarterly Journal of Economics,* May, pp. 327-368.

Tanzi, V.,1980, "The Underground Economy in the United States: Estimates and Implications", *Banca Nazionale del Lavoro*, vol. 135, pp. 427-453.
Tanzi, V., 1992, "Theory and Policy: A Comment on Dixit and on Current Tax Theory", *IMF Staff Papers*, vol. 39, no. 4, December, pp. 957-966 (followed by Dixit's reply).
Tanzi, V., 1996, Globalization, Tax Competition and the Future of Tax Systems, Fiscal Affairs Department, Washington DC: International Monetary Fund.
Tanzi, V, and Schuknecht, L., 1997, "Reconsidering the Fiscal Role of Government: The International Perspective", *AEA Papers and Proceedings*, v. 87. No. 2, pp.164-168.
Tanzi, V, and Schuknecht, L., 1995, "The Growth of Government and the reform of the State in Industrial Countries", IMF Working Paper 95/130, Washington DC: Fiscal Affairs Department, International Monetary Fund.
Taussig, F.W., 1919, "Price-Fixing as Seen by the Price-Fixer", *Quarterly Journal of Economics*, vol. 33, February, pp. 205-241.
Taussig, W., 1925, *Principles of Economics*, New York: The Macmillan Co. (original edition 1911).
Thomas, J.J., 1992, *Informal Economic Activity*, LSE Handbooks in Economics, New York: Harvester/Wheatsheaf.
Thomas, W., Convery, E., Cox, D., and Ho, C.C., 1996, *Federal Tax Compliance Research: Individual Income Tax gap Estimates for 1985 1988, and 1992*, Publication 1415 (Rev. 4-96), Washington D.C.: Internal Revenue Service.
The Treasury, 1996, *Historical Fiscal Updates*, Wellington New Zealand.
Todd, J., 1997, *1997 Retirement Income Report: A Review of the Current Framework*, Interim Report, Periodic Report Group, Wellington: The Treasury.
Tullock, G., 1967, "The Welfare Cost of Tariffs, Monopolies and Theft", *Western Economic Journal*, vol. 5, June, pp 227-234.
Usher, D., 1991, "The Hidden Costs of Public Expenditure" in Bird, R. M., (ed) *More Taxing Than Taxes: The Taxlike Effects of Nontax Policies in LDCs*, San Francisco: Institute for Contemporary Studies.
Vickrey, Wm, 1993, "Today's Tasks for Economists", *American Economic Review*, v. 83, no. 1, March, (1-10.
Vincent, S.B., 1912, "The Function of the Vibrissae in the Behaviour of the White Rat", *Behavioural Monographs*, 5.
Viner, J., 1931, "Cost Curves and Supply Curves", reprinted in American Economic Association, 1953, *Readings in Price Theory*, London: George Allen and Unwin.
Watkins, G.P., 1915, "A Third Factor in the Variation of Productivity: Load Factor", *American Economic Review*, vol.5, pp.753-786.
Wearing, A., and Headey, B., 1997, "The Would Be Tax Evader: A Profile", *Australian Tax Forum*, v. 13 (3-17).
Wiles, P.J.D., 1956, *Price, Cost and Output*, Oxford: Basil Blackwell.
Wilkes, C., 1993, "The State as an Historical Subject: A Periodization of State Formation in New Zealand", in Roper, B., and Rudd, C., 1993, *State and Economy in New Zealand*, Auckland: Oxford University Press.
Woodall, P. 1995, "The World Economy", *The Economist*, 7 October, Survey, pp. 5-44.
World Bank, 1997, *World Development Report: The State in a Changing World*, New York: Oxford University Press.
Wright, P.G., 1917, "Value Theories Applied to the Sugar Industry", *Quarterly Journal of Economics*, November, pp.101-121.
Wright, T.P. 1936, "Factors Affecting the Cost of Airplanes," *Journal of Aeronautical Engineering Sciences*, vol. 3, pp. 122-128.
Zee, H.H., 1997, Taxation and Unemployment, *Tax Notes International*, Jan. 20, pp. 225-51.
Zeeman, E.C. 1979, "Foreword", in Thompson, M., *Rubbish Theory*, Oxford: Oxford University Press.
Zellner, A., 1970, "Estimation of Regression Relationships Containing Unobservable Variables", *International Economic Review*, vol. 11, pp. 441-454.

GPSR Compliance

The European Union's (EU) General Product Safety Regulation (GPSR) is a set of rules that requires consumer products to be safe and our obligations to ensure this.

If you have any concerns about our products, you can contact us on ProductSafety@springernature.com

In case Publisher is established outside the EU, the EU authorized representative is:

Springer Nature Customer Service Center GmbH
Europaplatz 3
69115 Heidelberg, Germany

Batch number: 10704039

Printed by Printforce, the Netherlands